CHALLENGING AUTHORITARIANISM IN MEXICO

Between 1964 and 1985, Argentina, Chile, Mexico, Brazil, Paraguay, and Uruguay experienced a period of state-sponsored terrorism commonly referred to as the "Dirty Wars." Thousands of leftists, students, intellectuals, workers, peasants, labor leaders, and innocent civilians were harassed, arrested, tortured, raped, murdered, or "disappeared."

Many studies have been done about this phenomenon in the other areas of Latin America but, strangely, Mexico's Dirty War has been excluded from this particular scholarship. Here, for the first time, is a sustained look at this period of Mexican history and a consideration of the many facets that make up the nearly two decades of the Mexican Dirty War. The case studies in the book present narratives of particular armed revolutionary movements as well as thematic essays on gender, human rights, culture, student radicalism, the Cold War, and the international impact of this state-sponsored terrorism.

With contributions by: Alexander Aviña, Fernando Herrera Calderón, Elaine Carey, Adela Cedillo, Héctor Guillermo Robles Garnica, Alan Eladio Gómez, Jorge Luis Sierra Guzmán, Elizabeth Henson, Lucía Rayas, Romain Robinet, and Verónica Oikión Solano.

Fernando Herrera Calderón is Visiting Assistant Professor at Beloit College.

Adela Cedillo is a graduate student in Latin American Studies at the National Autonomous University of Mexico. She's the author of *El fuego y el silencio: Historia de las Fuerzas de Liberación Nacional de México (1969–1974)*, the first comprehensive history on the organization that gave birth to the Zapatista National Liberation Army (EZLN).

CHALLENGING AUTHORITARIANISM IN MEXICO

Revolutionary Struggles and the Dirty War, 1964–1982

Edited by Fernando Herrera Calderón and Adela Cedillo

Routledge
Taylor & Francis Group

NEW YORK AND LONDON

First published 2012
by Routledge
711 Third Avenue, New York, NY 10017

Simultaneously published in the UK
by Routledge
2 Park Square, Milton Park, Abingdon, Oxon OX14 4RN

Routledge is an imprint of the Taylor & Francis Group, an informa business

© 2012 Taylor & Francis

The right of the editors to be identified as the authors of the editorial material, and of the authors for their individual chapters, has been asserted in accordance with sections 77 and 78 of the Copyright, Designs and Patents Act 1988.

All rights reserved. No part of this book may be reprinted or reproduced or utilised in any form or by any electronic, mechanical, or other means, now known or hereafter invented, including photocopying and recording, or in any information storage or retrieval system, without permission in writing from the publishers.

Trademark notice: Product or corporate names may be trademarks or registered trademarks, and are used only for identification and explanation without intent to infringe.

Library of Congress Cataloging in Publication Data
Challenging authoritarianism in Mexico : revolutionary struggles and the dirty war, 1964-1982 / edited by Fernando Calderón and Adela Cedillo.
   p. cm.
  "Simultaneously published in the UK"—T.p. verso.
  Includes bibliographical references and index.
  1. Mexico—Politics and government—1946-1970. 2. Mexico—Politics and government—1970-1988. 3. Social movements—Mexico—History—20th century. 4. Revolutionaries—Mexico—History—20th century. 5. Guerrillas—Mexico—History—20th century. 6. Student movements—Mexico—History—20th century. 7. Peasant uprisings—Mexico—History—20th century. 8. Political violence—Mexico—History—20th century. 9. State-sponsored terrorism—Mexico—History—20th century. 10. Partido Revolucionario Institucional—History—20th century. I. Cedillo, Adela. II. Calderón, Fernando (Fernando Herrera)
  F1236.C47 2012
  972.08´2—dc23

ISBN: 978-0-415-88903-2 (hbk)
ISBN: 978-0-415-88904-9 (pbk)
ISBN: 978-0-203-13322-4 (ebk)

Typeset in Bembo
by HWA Text and Data Management

Printed and bound in the United States of America on acid-free paper by Edwards Brothers, Inc.

CONTENTS

Acknowledgments vii
Acronyms and Glossary ix
Preface xv
Héctor Guillermo Robles Garnica

Introduction: The Unknown Mexican Dirty War 1
Fernando Herrera Calderón and Adela Cedillo

1 Madera 1965: Primeros Vientos 19
 Elizabeth Henson

2 Seizing Hold of Memories in Moments of Danger:
 Guerrillas and Revolution in Guerrero, Mexico 40
 Alexander Aviña

3 In the Vanguard of the Revolution: The Revolutionary Action
 Movement and the Armed Struggle 60
 Verónica Oikión Solano

4 "Por la reunificación de los Pueblos Libres de América en su Lucha
 por el Socialismo": The Chicana/o Movement, the PPUA and the
 Dirty War in Mexico in the 1970s 81
 Alan Eladio Gómez

5 From Books to Bullets: Youth Radicalism and Urban Guerrillas in
 Guadalajara 105
 Fernando Herrera Calderón

6	A Revolutionary Group Fighting Against a Revolutionary State: The September 23rd Communist League Against the PRI-State (1973–1975) *Romain Robinet*	129
7	Armed Struggle Without Revolution: The Organizing Process of the National Liberation Forces (FLN) and the Genesis of Neo-Zapatism (1969–1983) *Adela Cedillo*	148
8	Subjugating the Nation: Women and the Guerrilla Experience *Lucía Rayas*	167
9	Armed Forces and Counterinsurgency: Origins of the Dirty War (1965–1982) *Jorge Luis Sierra Guzmán*	182
10	Transcending Violence: A Crisis of Memory and Documentation *Elaine Carey*	198

Contributors	211
Bibliography	215
Index	228

ACKNOWLEDGMENTS

Since the idea of this book first came to mind we have contracted a number of debts. The authors of this volume would like to express our sincere gratitude to friends, colleagues, and supporters of this project. We are tremendously grateful for all the support and confidence that was given to us after taking on this endeavor. Our greatest debt is to Kimberly Guinta and Rebecca Novack at Routledge. From the very moment this process began they were always available to answer questions, offer their suggestions, and facilitate the completion of this volume. Words cannot express how grateful we are for all their help. Also, we would like to thank the anonymous reviewers for their detailed evaluation of the content in this book. Their suggestions and constructive critiques were helpful in polishing the content and ideas herein.

This volume also came to fruition with the help of Elaine Carey, who read the book proposal and offered her thoughts and suggestions from an early point in the process. We appreciate her letting us "pick her brain" and learn from her. We would also like to express our thanks to Alex Aviña, Beth Henson, and Jecca Namakkal, who read different parts of this volume and used their own expertise in making comments and suggestions for revisions. Colleagues and friends also provided support throughout this process. We would like to thank Jennifer Boles, Shane Dillingham, Steve Allen, Melanie Huska, Alex Wisnoski, Alan Fujishin, and Christopher Gunderson.

Writing about this period in Mexican history has also brought us in contact with people that lived during and survived the Dirty War. Only some of their stories can be found in this book, but we would like to thank all of them. We want to express our sincere gratitude to ex-militants and family members of the "disappeared" from the states of Chihuahua, Sinaloa, Jalisco, Nuevo

León, Guerrero, Tabasco, and Chiapas for allowing us to use their voices in reconstructing this history. Without their testimonies this volume would be incomplete.

Last but not least, we would like to express our appreciation to the contributors of this volume for writing these essays and entrusting us with their valuable work. Thank you for your patience throughout the entire process. We hope this is only the beginning of a long conversation, and that we will continue to work together in reconstructing this dark period in history.

ACRONYMS AND GLOSSARY

ACG	Asociación Cívica Guerrerense or Guerrerense Civic Association
ACNR	Asociación Cívica Nacional Revolucionaria or National Revolutionary Civic Association
AGN	Archivo General de la Nación or National Archive
AIAC	Asociación Indígena de Autodefensa Campesina or Indigenous Association of Farmers Self-Defense
AIT	Alianza Internacional Terrorista or International Terrorist Alliance
AJEF	Asociación de Jóvenes Esperanza de la Fraternidad or Association of Youth Hope of the Fraternity
ANOCE	Asociación Nacional Obrero Campesina Estudiantil or National Worker, Farmer, Student Association
Apertura democrática	Democratic opening
BCA	Brigada Campesina de Ajusticiamiento or Campesino Execution Brigade
BR	Brigada Roja or Red Brigade
BREZ	Brigada Revolucionaria Emiliano Zapata or Emiliano Zapata Revolutionary Brigade
Brigada Blanca	White Brigade
Cacique	Local political boss
Campesino	Peasant or farmer
CASA	Centro Acción Social Autónomo or Autonomous Social Action Center

CCI	Central Campesina Independiente or Independent Peasant's Union
CCRS	Centro Cultural Rubén Salazar or Rubén Salazar Cultural Center
CDR	Cuerpos de Defensa Rural or Rural Defense Corps
CER	Comité Estudiantil Revolucionario or Student Revolutionary Committee
CLETA	Centro Para la Libre Expresión Teatral y Artística or Center for the Freedom of Theatrical and Artistic Expression
CLR	Comité de Lucha Revolucionaria or Committee for Revolutionary Struggle
CNC	Confederación Nacional Campesina or National Campesino Confederation
CNDH	Comisión Nacional de Derechos Humanos or National Human Rights Commission
CNED	Central Nacional de Estudiantes Democráticos or National Center of Democratic Students
CNH	Consejo Nacional de Huelga or National Strike Committee
CNOP	Confederación Nacional de Organizaciones Populares or National Confederation of Popular Organizations
COCEI	Coalición Obrero Campesino Estudiante del Istmo or Student, Worker, Farmer Coalition of the Isthmus
CONASUPO	Compañía Nacional de Subsistencias Populares or National Company of Popular Subsistance
COP	Coalición de Organizaciones Populares or Coalition of Popular Organizations
CORA	Chicanos Organizados Revolucionarios de Aztlán or Organized Revolutionary Chicanos of Aztlán
CPMAG	Comité Político-Militar "Arturo Gámiz" or Arturo-Gámiz Politico-military Committee
CRJ	Colonia Rubén Jaramillo
CTM	Central de Trabajadores Mexicanos or Confederation of Mexican Workers
DAAC	Departamento de Asuntos Agrarios y Colonización or Office of Agrarian Affairs and Colonization
DFS	Dirección Federal de Seguridad or Federal Security Directorate
DGIPS	Dirección General de Investigaciones Políticas y Sociales or General Directorate of Political and Social Investigations
DIPD	División de Investigaciones para la Prevención de la Delincuencia or Research Division for the Prevention of Crime

DISEN	Dirección de Investigación y Seguridad Nacional or Directorate for Investigation and National Security
ECSCP	European Committee in Solidarity with the Chicano People
EIM	Ejército Insurgente Mexicano or Mexican Insurgent Army
Ejido	A form of corporative landholding in which the federal government remains the owner
EPLUA	Ejército Popular de Liberación Unido de América or Popular Army of Unified Liberation of America
EPR	Ejército Popular Revolucionario or Popular Revolutionary Army
Escuela Normales	Created to train high school graduates to be teachers
EYOL	Estudiantes y Obreros en Lucha or Students and Workers in Struggle
EZLN	Ejército Zapatista de Liberación Nacional or Zapatista Army of National Liberation
FALN	Fuerzas Armadas de Liberación Nacional (Puerto Rico) or Armed Forces of National Liberation
FANDA	Frente Amplio Nacional Democrático Anti-imperialista or Broad National Democratic Anti-Imperialist Front
FAP	Frente Armado del Pueblo or People's Armed Front
FAR	Frente Autentico Revolucionario or Authentic Revolutionary Front
FARO	Frente Artístico Organizado Revolucionario or Organized Revolutionary Artistic Front
FECSM	Federación de Estudiantes Campesinos Socialistas de México or Federation of Socialist Student Peasants
FEG	Federación Estudiantil de Guadalajara or Student Federation of Guadalajara
FEMOSPP	Fiscalía Especial para Movimientos Sociales y Políticos del Pasado or Special Prosecutor for Social and Political Movements of the Past
FEP	Frente Electoral del Pueblo or People's Electoral Front
FER	Frente Estudiantil Revolucionario or Student Revolutionary Front
FLN	Fuerzas de Liberación Nacional or National Liberation Forces
Foquismo	A guerrilla strategy theory created by the revolutionary Ernesto "Che" Guevara, which emphasizes the role of the military vanguard
FRAP	Fuerzas Revolucionarias Armadas del Pueblo or Revolutionary Armed Forces of the People

FSLN	Frente Sandinista de Liberación Nacional or Sandinista National Liberation Front
FUZ	Frente Urbano Zapatista or Zapatista Urban Front
GPG	Grupo Popular Guerrillero or Popular Guerrilla Group
Granaderos	Riot police
Hacienda	Large plantation
IMCRC	Instituto Mexicano-Cubano de Relaciones Culturales "José Martí" or "José Martí" Mexican-Cuban Institute for Cultural Relations
IPN	Instituto Politécnico Nacional or National Polytechnic Institute
IWW	Industrial Workers of the World
JCM	Juventud Comunista de México or Mexican Communist Youth
Latifundio	Large land estate
LCE	Liga Comunista Espartaco or Espartacus Communist League
LC23S	Liga Comunista 23 de Septiembre or September 23rd Communist League
LEAA	Law Enforcement Administration Assistance
LFOPPE	Ley Federal de Organizaciones Políticas y Procedimientos Electorales or Federal Law on Political Organizations and Electoral Processes
Los Enfermos	The Sick Ones, guerrilla group from Sinaloa
Los Guajiros	Guerrilla group with a presence in Chihuahua, Mexico City, Jalisco and Oaxaca
Los Halcones	The Hawks, a paramilitary group that orchestrated a massacre in 1971, dubbed the Halconazo
Los Lacandones	Guerrilla group from Mexico City which took the name of indigenous group from the Lacandon Jungle
Los Macías	Guerrilla group from Nuevo León
Los Mascarones	Theater group from Mexico City
Los Procesos	Guerrilla group from Nuevo León and Mexico City
LP	Línea Proletaria or Proletarian Line
LRUP	La Raza Unida Party
LULAC	League of United Latin American Citizens
MAR	Movimiento de Acción Revolucionaria or Revolutionary Action Movement
MEChA	Movimiento Estudiantil Chicano de Aztlán or Chicano Student Movement of Aztlán
MEP	Movimiento Estudiantil Profesional or Professional Student Movement

MLL	Movimiento Latinoamericano de Liberación or Latin American Liberation Movement
MLN	Movimiento de Liberación Nacional or National Liberation Movement
MMLM	Movimiento Marxista-Leninista de México or Marxist-Leninist Movement of Mexico
MRM	Movimiento Revolucionario del Magisterio or Revolutionary Teacher's Movement
MRP	Movimiento Revolucionario del Pueblo or People's Revolutionary Movement
M23S	Movimiento 23 de Septiembre or September 23rd Movement
NGEZ	Núcleo Guerrillero Emiliano Zapata or Emiliano Zapata Guerrilla Nucleus
OLAS	Organización Latinoamericana de Solidaridad or Latin American Solidarity Organization
Organización Partidaria	Partisan Organization, a coalition of Mexican armed revolutionary organizations
PAN	Partido Acción Nacional or National Action Party
PCM	Partido Comunista Mexicano or Mexican Communist Party
PDLP	Partido de los Pobres or Party of the Poor
PLM	Partido Liberal Mexicano or Mexican Liberal Party
PNR	Partido Nacional Revolucionario or National Revolutionary Party
PPS	Partido Popular Socialista or Popular Socialist Party
PPUA	Partido del Proletariado Unido de América or United Proletarian Party of America
PRD	Partido de la Revolución Democrática or Party of the Democratic Revolution
PRI	Partido Revolucionario Institucional or Institutional Revolutionary Party
PRM	Partido de la Revolución Mexicana or Mexican Revolution Party
PRPM	Partido Revolucionario del Proletariado de México or Revolutionary Party of the Proletariat of Mexico
Ranchería	Village
RCDC	Ramón Chacón Defense Committee
SEDENA	Secretaría de la Defensa Nacional or Department of National Defense
SEGOB	Secretaría de Gobernación or Department of State
SEP	Secretaría de Educación Pública or Department of Public Education

TENAZ	Teatro Nacional de Aztlán or National Theatre of Aztlán
UdG	Universidad de Guadalajara or University of Guadalajara
UDHR	Universal Declaration of Human Rights
UGOCM	Unión General de Obreros y Campesinos de México or General Union of Mexican Workers and Campesinos
UNAM	Universidad Nacional Autónoma de México or National Autonomous University of Mexico
UNS	Unión Nacional Sinarquista or National Synarchist Union
UP	Unión del Pueblo or People's Union
URS	Unión Revolucionaria Socialista or Socialist Revolutionary Union
VS	Vanguardia Socialista or Socialist Vanguard

PREFACE

Héctor Guillermo Robles Garnica

Challenging Authoritarianism in Mexico: Revolutionary Struggles and the Dirty War 1964–1982, arrives at a timely moment in Mexican history. The rise of new social movements and the ongoing revolutionary struggles in the states of Chiapas, Guerrero, and Oaxaca, as well as the precarious situation Mexican society is currently undergoing, have prompted a new interest in the violent decades of the 1960s and 70s. In the past six years journalists, students, scholars, novelists and poets, as well as former revolutionaries, have written an array of literature about the Dirty War. Mexico has always prided itself on its democratic traditions while military dictators ruled other countries in the Western Hemisphere. Yet, despite the growing literature, Mexican society continues to resist acknowledging that a Dirty War similar to those in the Southern Cone occurred in their own country. The 1970s remained a void in the historiography of revolutionary movements, until the year 2000, when declassified archives allowed scholars and researchers to evaluate a dark history from dusty and deteriorating boxes. With the revelation of new sources that document political violence and social inequality, a counter-history of the "politically stable" 1960s and 70s has begun to be reconstructed.

Political dissent is not new in Mexican history, in fact the track record of civic struggle, revolutionary movements, student radicalism, and peasant and worker militancy are deeply embedded in popular memory. To be more specific, the ongoing studies on the 1910 Revolution and post-revolutionary struggles help us understand how previous societies confronted political, social, and cultural authority and how their ideas informed future struggles. The armed struggles of the 1960s and 70s that challenged authoritarianism directly during the Cold War when state-sponsored repression pervaded Latin America, are now beginning to be used as a point of reference to fill a gap in Mexican history.

During the Dirty War the government accused dissidents of conspiring with foreign communists in an effort to destabilize the state, therefore legitimizing the use of excessive measures by security agencies to thwart armed struggles. Thousands of civilians were taken against their will and endured prolonged torture. Another outcome was the creation of political prisoners and "disappeared" in detention centers throughout the nation, especially in the Campo Militar No. 1 in Mexico City, and the Lecumberri Prison or the Black Palace, which today houses the National Archive. Human rights activists and survivors of state violence have incessantly demand the government investigate abuses against civilians; these exertions have produced only minor results, yet advocates for victims have not abandoned the fight for truth and justice.

The contributors to this volume are scholars of history and other disciplines who share a common interest in this period in Mexican history, and who have researched state and national archives and interviewed former revolutionaries. This book offers a broad perspective through case studies of particular armed movements and essays on gender, human rights, student radicalism, counterinsurgency and links with international revolutionary groups. More importantly, the essays include the voices of those who participated in the politico-military organizations. By incorporating their reflections and reasons for acting as they did, the reader obtains a more intimate look at these groups. The end product reflects the political reality of the day. For reasons detailed in this preface, this book will stimulate debate and further work on the Mexican 1960s and 70s. As one of the first English-language books on the Dirty War, it sets the stage for a re-evaluation of recent political and social history and will prove thought-provoking for students of insurgent movements and authoritarianism.

Héctor Guillermo Robles Garnica is a survivor of the Mexican Dirty War and a former member of two guerrilla movements: the Frente Estudiantil Revolucionario (Student Revolutionary Front, or FER), and subsequently the Fuerzas Revolucionarias Armadas del Pueblo (People's Revolutionary Armed Forces, or FRAP). He is the author of *Guadalajara: la guerrilla olvidada, presos en la isla de la libertad* (1996), and recently finished writing an update to his memoir.

INTRODUCTION

The Unknown Mexican Dirty War

Fernando Herrera Calderón and Adela Cedillo

At the height of the Cold War, a number of anti-communist authoritarian and military regimes took power in Latin America. Between 1964 and 1985, Argentina, Chile, Brazil, Paraguay, and Uruguay experienced periods of state-sponsored terrorism commonly referred to as Dirty Wars.[1] In each case, security forces harassed, arrested, tortured, raped, murdered, and/or disappeared thousands of leftists, students, intellectuals, workers, *campesinos*, and civilians. Yet, in the historiography of the Cold War in Latin America, Mexico has occupied a marginal place, particularly in regard to the political violence that characterized the country during the second half of the twentieth century.[2] The cycles of protests and repression between the 1950s and 1980s have been cited as instances of political conflict that did little to threaten the power of the *Partido Revolucionario Institucional* (Institutional Revolutionary Party, PRI), in power since the 1930s. Within the historiography of the Cold War in Mexico, the 1968 student movement in Mexico City has been the case most studied and continues to be an appealing topic among academics.[3] Nevertheless, a great deal of scholarship on the Dirty War remains undone.

The authors herein contribute to a new understanding of this period with original scholarship on the development of socialist-inspired armed revolutionary movements in the 1960s and 1970s that sought to overthrow the state, which, in their view, represented the interests of the national bourgeoisie and imperialism. While these movements failed in their objectives, the memory of guerrillas and repression has dimly survived in the social imaginary. The purpose of this volume is not merely to fill a lacuna in Mexican history overlooked by academics and society, but to add to the conversation about the long-lasting consequences and contributions of armed struggle to political culture and society. We propose that in order to understand contemporary social movements, insurgent politics, human rights, state hegemony, state terrorism, class struggle, and the strengthening of the drug cartels, it is crucial to take into account the magnitude of the Dirty War and the reasons for its exclusion from the historical narrative.

With regard to political violence, the literature on the Dirty War (which is largely in Spanish) is miniscule compared with the voluminous historiography of the 1910 Mexican Revolution. The fascination that this historical moment has generated can be ascribed to Mexico being the first Latin American country in the twentieth century to experience a revolution that led to the establishment of a one-party state with populist tendencies.[4] Although the Constitution of 1917 derived from this conflict declared that the government would be representative, federal, and democratic, instead a single party reigned uninterruptedly between 1929 and 2000.[5]

Scholars have shown that the political system under the PRI was authoritarian, patriarchal, politically and administratively centralized, and corporatist.[6] It attempted to unify society around revolutionary nationalism, yet closed political space to the opposition and systematically repressed social movements when it felt its authority questioned. Moreover, the political class or the self-labeled Revolutionary Family monopolized all public offices and preserved itself through the incorporation of regional *caciques* (political bosses), unremitting venality, and impunity.

The relative stability of this closed system also depended on welfare state policies.[7] The *priísta* governments promoted industrialization, carried out land distribution, advanced free and secular education, instituted social security, and expanded public services. Regardless, the governments also earmarked funds to modernize certain cities and regions considered important for economic growth, while other areas received less assistance, leading to regional imbalances and social inequalities.[8] While cities like Mexico City, Guadalajara, and Monterrey enjoyed tremendous economic expansion, in the countryside, large estates and *cacique*-style systems remained intact, causing poverty and the marginalization of indigenous communities. Thus, the state failed to meet its legal obligations to all its citizens.

Stabilizing development[9] brought about steady economic growth known as the Mexican Miracle, which also precipitated Mexico's transition from a rural to an urban country since the 1950s.[10] Economic prosperity lasted through the 1960s, leading the ruling class to dream of being on the path from the periphery to a fully modernized capitalist country. However, the miracle did not result in sustainable development, since the political economy fueled the production of intermediate goods and the protectionism of national industries and there was a dearth in technological investment or in capital goods.

Even before the beginning of the Cold War, the political spectrum was more or less defined: the right by the National Action Party (PAN) and the

National Synarchist Union (UNS), the left by the Mexican Communist Party (PCM), and in the middle stood the PRM-PRI that considers itself the center of gravity.[11] The relationship between the Lázaro Cárdenas administration (1936–1940) and the PCM was healthy, but began to crumble during the presidency of Manuel Ávila Camacho (1940–1946). Absorbed by Cold War rhetoric, the Miguel Alemán administration (1946–1952) aligned itself with the anti-communist bloc and outlawed the PCM.[12] The party's clout continued to erode within proletarian and peasant circles, especially when its cadres began to lead independent popular mobilizations that had nothing to do with the struggle for communism, which in turn further marginalized the PCM. Moreover, in the 1960s many leftist organizations began to adhere to a variety of Marxist tenets; Leninists, Trotskyists, Spartacists, Maoists, Guevaristas, as well as anarchists competed for dominance in universities, factories, and peasant communities.[13]

During the *sexenios* of Adolfo Ruiz Cortines (1952–1958) and Adolfo López Mateos (1958–1964), trade union protests surged throughout the nation. Factions of miners, railway workers, and teachers, upset by the *charrismo* of their union leaders, were the most active, and repressed.[14] Their struggles revolved around three main issues: labor (e.g. wage increases, better working conditions), union democracy, and autonomy from state control. In accordance with its authoritarian character and anti-communist stance, the PRI reacted violently against marches, strikes, and rallies they believed to be attached to international communists and subversives.[15] When railroad workers went on strike in 1958, led by Valentín Campa and Demetrio Vallejo, Secretary of State and future president (1964–1970) Gustavo Díaz Ordaz, spearheaded the suppression of the strike.[16] With the growth of working militancy the government sought new strategic measures, namely using the military rather than the police to crush dissent and guarantee civilian protection.

During the 1960s students emerged as major political actors.[17] Their movements proliferated in at least one-third of the nation, particularly in Sonora, Chihuahua, Nuevo León, Sinaloa, Jalisco, Michoacán, Guerrero, Puebla, Tabasco, and in Mexico City.[18] For the most part student demands pertained to their institutions. They fought for academic and institutional reform, broader access to higher education, improvements in infrastructure, intellectual freedom, and against unpopular administrators. Influenced by socialist ideology, some students began to incorporate social issues connected with labor and *campesino* movements. The changes in the dynamics of social protest led previously small and marginal movements to grow and demand the democratization of society. Even large groups of students participated in civic movements that brought down governors in Puebla, Guerrero, and Tabasco. While the government was more inclined to suppress workers and campesinos, students were not invulnerable to violence. On a number of occasions, university administrators called in security forces to quell student disturbances.

Even though for the most part the youth followed a nonviolent political line and were nonthreatening, the armed forces took brutal measures to thwart activism on campuses, violating university autonomy at will.[19]

While dozens of youth rebellions emerged in the 1960s throughout the country, the 1968 student protest in Mexico City was the largest counter-hegemonic movement in the postrevolutionary era. When a football game between two rival preparatory and vocational schools turned violent in late July 1968, authorities called in *granaderos* (riot police) to the melee who used excessive force against students and precipitated a vehement response, catalyzing the student movement and bringing different schools and universities across town together. Despite the movement's short existence, students organized thousands in rallies to denounce the lack of democracy, despotism, and state repression, as well as demanding that the PRI respect the rights of citizens enshrined in the 1917 Constitution.[20] Under the auspices of the *Consejo Nacional de Huelga* (CNH), the coordinating body of the movement, leaders and student representatives organized mass demonstrations. From the CNH a list of demands emerged that included first and foremost the abolition of the *granaderos*, the repeal of the social dissolution law, freedom for political prisoners, and respect for university autonomy. Early on, the government ignored students, even more so when they demanded a public dialogue with the authorities.

As the movement's political clout surged, Díaz Ordaz employed Cold War rhetoric to discredit students, arguing they were a part of an international communist conspiracy to create a political crisis in the advent of the Olympics. Political discontent mounted on the eve of the XIX Olympics in Mexico City and the government grew less tolerant and sought a "final solution" to student disturbances. On October 2, 1968 the movement culminated when the armed forces disrupted a mass rally in the Plaza de las Tres Culturas in Tlatelolco, an operation orchestrated by the Secretary of Interior, Luis Echeverría, Secretary of Defense, Marcelino García Barragán, and Presidential Chief of Staff, Luis Gutiérrez Oropeza. The massacre became a milestone in radical politics and political culture in general.[21] According to traditional historiography, the violent end of the movement pushed students into armed movements that attempted to overthrow the state. However, this premise overlooks the forerunners of the armed struggle prior to 1968 in the cities and the countryside.

The Revolutionary Obsession

The political class flaunted the 1910 Revolution as a source of legitimacy, even during the Cold War, when Western governments viewed revolutionary rhetoric with suspicion. The PRI claimed its revolutionary nationalism to be the ideal alternative to left- and right-wing authoritarianism and projected itself as progressive but not radical. For diplomatic reasons, no foreign government questioned the ruling party's successive electoral victories or denounced the way it settled internal conflicts, as in 1968. According to Lorenzo Meyer, "the United States and Western Europe resisted criticizing a government that remained stable within Latin America."[22] For the same reasons, Mexico became a formidable political force in the region, even opposing policies posited by the United States. For instance, Mexico opposed the expulsion of Cuba from the Organization of American States in 1962 and became the only country in the Western Hemisphere to maintain relations with the island.[23] Cuba became so close to the Mexican government that it denied support to Mexican guerillas in the 1970s.[24] The PRI government's skillful handling of diplomatic relations helped to strengthen their partisan interests.

During Luis Echeverría's tenure (1970–1976), one of his goals was to reinforce his government's international image. Following the tradition of political asylum carried out during the Cárdenas' years, Echeverría welcomed thousands of exiles from Latin America, namely Brazil, Chile, Argentina, Uruguay, Guatemala, Nicaragua, and El Salvador. However, welcoming political exiles reveals a number of contradictions within Mexico's foreign and domestic policies. By providing asylum, the PRI supported, for "humanitarian" reasons, guerrillas abroad while persecuting in the name of patriotism, anyone who questioned its revolutionary nationalism at home.[25]

Echeverría had played a key role in planning the massacre in Tlatelolco. On that account, when taking office he attempted to reconcile with the left by announcing an *apertura democrática* (democratic opening), a measure meant to co-opt student leaders by offering them public positions.[26] Despite his peacemaking rhetoric, Echeverría did not tolerate what he deemed provocations from the left. When students in Mexico City organized a march to express their solidarity with the student movement at the Autonomous University of Nuevo León on June 10, 1971, a paramilitary group known as *Los halcones* (the Hawks) attacked demonstrators with clubs and semi-automatic weapons in San Cosme, killing and injuring an unknown number of people.[27] The incident deepened divisions within the urban left. The democrats or reformists maintained a channel of communication with government and demanded the incorporation of their parties into the electoral system, while independents neither went underground nor joined the system. In turn, the revolutionary left was drawn towards the armed struggle.[28]

While some people viewed the 1910 Revolution as a traumatic event that should not be repeated, the ultra-left believed its objectives remained unfulfilled, especially in regards to social justice. They concluded that only another revolution could build a legitimate political system and only under socialism would equality be achieved. What this faction failed to assess was the lack of appeal for the revolutionary dictatorship of the proletariat in a country that had already endured dictatorships and a revolution, and where the proletariat was far from counter-hegemonic. On the other hand, they also underestimated the PRI's power.

Against these odds, the ultra-left built its own revolutionary determinism. Activists in the 1960s and 1970s were politically formed in universities and schools, and radicalized by state repression and the influence of national liberation movements in China, Vietnam, Algeria, and above all Cuba.[29] Over the years students defied socially constructed ideas that identified them as apolitical, privileged, and individualistic by moving outside their sanctuary and participating in popular political mobilizations. Yet, for political reasons radical students never made a clear break from the university. Because the university was already a major epicenter of dissent against the state, the ultra-left hoped to use classrooms as revolutionary schools to build consciousness and forge a strong student vanguard.

Revolutionary War vs. Counterinsurgency War

During the 1960s and 70s there were two phases to the guerrilla movements: 1962 to 1968 and 1968 to 1982.[30] In 1962, the massacre of the agrarian leader Rubén Jaramillo and his family in Xochicalco, Morelos, was a watershed especially for the left, leading more people to begin to consider the possibility of armed resistance.[31] Between 1962 and 1968, small guerrilla groups of students and professionals were formed in the cities but were easily infiltrated by the Federal Security Directorate (DFS), and eliminated after performing their first armed actions.[32]

The catalyst for the armed struggle in Mexico was the *Grupo Popular Guerrillero* (Popular Guerrilla Group, GPG), which began operating in 1964 in the northern state of Chihuahua. The counterinsurgency campaign that followed the GPG's assault on the Madera army barracks on September 23, 1965 marks the beginning of the Dirty War. In the state of Guerrero, two rural guerrilla movements surfaced with a strong social base and survived well into the 1980s, despite persistent repression: the *Partido de los Pobres* (Party of the Poor, PDLP) and the *Asociación Cívica Nacional Revolucionaria* (National Revolutionary Civic Association, ACNR). During the second period (1968–1982), student radicals created large urban politico-military groups in different states, demonstrating the national extent of the conflict.[33] The end of this period coincides with the conclusion of José López Portillo's administration, when more than forty armed revolutionary organizations had been virtually eliminated from the political scene.

Guerrilla movements in Mexico shared the vanguardism, dogmatism, sectarianism, militarism, and volunteerism of the rest of the Latin American left. The assumption by urban guerrillas that workers would automatically join a revolutionary struggle once they realized the vanguard had their interests at heart, led to disappointment. Not only did workers not join the armed movement, but the independent labor movement rejected the guerrillas' political line.[34] Similarly, while peasant responses varied, most of them continued to work in official or independent campesino organizations. Therefore, the guerrillas were alienated from every social movement and from every semi-legal organization, but this does not mean all armed revolutionary movements were unrepresentative fringe groups, given that some were able to draw on popular support, though not enough to succeed.

Several characteristics set the Mexicans apart from other armed guerrilla organizations in Latin America: they could not count on support from Cuba, or any other socialist country, nor were they supported by armed struggles abroad.[35] They also tended to go through a number of splits, until more than forty organizations emerged. Each had its own platform, principles, strategies and tactics, and adhered to an assortment of ideologies. Finally, even though the Mexican government received military support from the USA, the armed movement was not completely destroyed. After a prolonged reconstruction, new organizations ascended with organic links to the armed struggles of the 1970s. In the 1990s, organizations that survived the Dirty War surfaced under new names: the Zapatista Army of National Liberation (EZLN) and the Popular Revolutionary Army (EPR).[36]

The administrations of Díaz Ordaz, Echeverría, and López Portillo aligned themselves with the rigid national security doctrine promoted by the United States. From within the Secretariat of Interior and Defense, high-ranking officials and officers engineered an anti-subversive policy. To believe that the guerrilla movements of this period, even at their peak, genuinely menaced the security of the nation was far-fetched, given that divisions between social movements and the moderate and armed left prohibited a coordinated overthrow of the government.[37] Nevertheless, the government's goal was to exterminate nascent outbreaks in order to prevent further dissent, but this proved counterproductive since state-sponsored violence only increased recruitment for armed organizations.

Initially authorities dismissed the presence of guerrilla groups, but when it was forced to recognize their existence, they worked with the media to dehumanize revolutionaries and portray their actions as criminal.[38] Both the PRI and the media also engaged in psychological warfare, using terms like delinquents, savages, mentally ill, and terrorists to spread fear throughout society. The government institutionalized arbitrary arrests, torture, extrajudicial executions, forced disappearances, and irregular trials as weapons of war, but they never legally sanctioned or formally declared a state of siege. Further, the Attorney General's Office, which was in charge of public safety not only failed to fulfill its duties, but also upheld the systematic violation of the rule of law, as did the Supreme Court of Justice. With these practices, the government performed unprecedented human rights abuses against revolutionaries, and also their family members, friends, neighbors, and other innocent civilians. In the mountains of Sonora, Chihuahua, Guerrero, Oaxaca, and Chiapas, peasant communities were terrorized and ravaged during the counterinsurgency campaigns.[39] The armed forces used low-level bombing, scorched-earth tactics, and starvation to weed out sympathizers and guerrillas.

Since the government gave repressive forces free reign to eradicate guerrilla movements, their imaginations took flight as they came up with sadistic methods of torture to use during interrogations. They used electric shocks, water boarding, mock executions, and sexual violence, and the most barbarous methods involved torturing the militants' babies.[40] Testimonies by former prisoners reveal that detainees lived under inhumane and degrading conditions in secret prisons that resembled concentration camps.[41] Although there has never been an official investigation regarding their fate, testimonies by both repressors and the victims reveal horrific stories. According to their claims, prisoners were either executed, buried in mass graves, or cremated, while others were taken on the so-called "death flights" where they were shot, put onto military planes and dumped in the Pacific Ocean. There has been no initiative until now to create a comprehensive census of victims of the Dirty War, but it is estimated that more than 3,000 people disappeared and were executed, 3,000 were political prisoners, and 7,000 were victims of torture.[42] One soldier who carried out "death flights" said that 1,500 "disappeared" were thrown out of planes into the ocean.[43] This is a telling figure given that in Chile, according to the Rettig Report, there were little more than 2,000 "disappeared" during the dictatorship of Augusto Pinochet.[44] In other words, although the repression in Chile was massive, the number of missing persons in both countries is similar.

Those who argue, as did the renowned Mexican journalist Julio Scherer, that both the military and guerrillas participated in a Dirty War (echoing the Argentinian "two devils" thesis), overlook the fact that state violence was overwhelming disproportionate to revolutionary violence.[45] The casualties caused by guerrillas against security forces were smaller compared with the executions carried out by the counterinsurgency units. The state also acted "to remove the water from the fish," by terrorizing communities to discourage people from aligning with revolutionaries.

Faced with the first economic crisis in twenty years, 1976 also marked a political crisis given that for the first time in its history, the PRI ran uncontested in that year's presidential race. Echeverría's plan for development and democratic opening faded in the distance. Newly elected López Portillo decreed an electoral reform to facilitate the inclusion of the opposition in congress, giving the system its first taste of democracy in decades.[46] The reform was sanctioned in 1977 and one year later the Amnesty Act was enacted, benefiting 1,539 political prisoners and fifty-seven exiles and fugitives, although it left the cases of more than 1,000 disappeared in limbo.[47]

Whether guerrilla movements contributed to political reform has been an ongoing topic of discussion. The emergence of both social movements and the armed struggle during the 1970s was instrumental in bringing about reforms, but political violence had greater weight in precipitating these changes. The government sought a political solution to the high economic and social costs of the Dirty War and the partial failure of the counterinsurgency campaign to prevent the subversive actions. The radical wing effect occurred, as the presence of extremists increased support for moderate demands.[48] Thus, the negotiations did not benefit the guerrillas but the democrats, though the amnesty made it possible for those who wished to return to legality to become politically active again.

In addition to political reform, López Portillo also boosted economic reform. In 1978 the international context was favorable for Mexico to become a major exporter of crude oil. GDP rose to 8 percent, unemployment declined, and public spending expanded. However, oil surpluses were poorly managed and by 1981 a worldwide oversupply of oil erupted. López Portillo's term ended in 1982 with an unprecedented economic crisis, a huge external debt, and the nationalization of banks in an effort to curb capital flight, making his administration emblematic of the ruling party's breakdown.[49]

When Miguel de la Madrid assumed the presidency in December 1982, the fight against subversion was over, not in the government's discourse but in its actions. In 1983, de la Madrid ordered the Research Division for the Prevention of Crime (DIPD) to be dissolved and promoted the restructuring and purging of the federal police.[50] Just two years later he ordered the discontinuation of the DFS and replaced it with the Directorate for Investigation and National Security (DISEN).

The men of the military and police who conducted the counterinsurgency used their power to engage with drug cartels.[51] In fact, Aravá planes used in the "death flights" were simultaneously employed to transport marijuana to Nuevo Laredo.[52] Impunity from the past left the door open for the present drug war.

Historiography of the Mexican Revolutionary Struggles

Today the Dirty War has yet to capture the public's interest or become a topic of discussion within academic circles. There are a variety of explanations why this is the case. First, the myth of the *pax priísta* aims to minimize moments of upheaval.[53] Studies of this period tend to focus on populism, election frauds, the failure of land reform, moderate economic prosperity, the rise of the middle-class, peaceful social movements, counterculture, and international relations.[54] None of these works take into account the gravity of the Dirty War or how this period offers a window onto socio-political and cultural issues after 1968.

In civil society, the Dirty War is only a vague memory not incorporated into the historical narrative. The PRI was able to impose a distorted memory of the past and a culture of silence on civil society, which made little effort to prevent the memory of this period from being buried, fearing government repression. It was not until the EZLN uprising in 1994 that the topic of armed struggle was brought to the center of the debate. Some survivors of the Dirty War began writing memoirs reflecting on their actions and gave interviews to the media.[55] While most former revolutionaries have remained silent, committees have been formed by victims' family members in Chihuahua, Sinaloa, Nuevo León, Jalisco, Michoacán, Guerrero, and Mexico City since the late 1970s, kindling a movement for justice for the disappeared.

With the end of the ruling party's seventy-year perfect dictatorship in 2000, human rights organizations pressured the government to create the *Fiscalía Especial para Movimientos Sociales y Políticos del Pasado* (Special Prosecutor for Social and Political Movements of the Past, FEMOSPP) in 2001.[56] The creation of this office coincided with the opening of the archives of the *Secretaría de Gobernación* (Department of State, SEGOB) and the *Secretaría de la Defensa Nacional* (Department of National Defense, SEDENA), the main institutions responsible for counterinsurgency, which controlled the documents housed in the *Archivo General de la Nación* (National Archive, AGN).

While the documents made available by the military are limited; the SEGOB-DFS archive has information on a wide range of political, social, religious, and cultural organizations, as well as intelligence reports on three to four million people.[57] A part of this archive is devoted to armed revolutionary groups and people who suffered persecution, imprisonment, torture, exile, execution, and forced disappearance. In contrast to other archives of terror in Latin America, DFS files contain an assortment of documents, including magazines, press releases, propaganda seized from "terrorists" at the time of their arrest, judicial statements, records, reports on confrontations with guerrillas, photographs, and maps. However, the documentation was not gathered in accordance with professional standards, given that the agency's objective was not a judicial reconstruction of the facts, but data that would lead to the guerrillas. Thus, the military and police versions of the counterinsurgency campaign are questionable.

Despite the bureaucratic hurdles placed to view these files, since 2002, a number of journalists, former guerrillas, relatives of missing persons, and academics have visited the AGN, and within the first few years since their declassification various articles, theses, and books on the Dirty War began to appear in bookstores.[58] The FEMOSPP research team gathered its findings into a "Historical Report to Mexican Society." In more than 800 pages, the report provided a comprehensive overview of the period, specifically focused on war crimes and crimes against humanity.[59] Looking at the Dirty War from a different perspective, Kate Doyle, director of the Mexico Project of the National Security

Archive, and her team have released declassified reports from the US State Department detailing the United State's role during this period.[60]

Contributions

The authors gathered in this volume come from a wide range of US, Mexican, and European universities, and are scholars on the topic of the Dirty War. In the last decade they have produced original research and made this period a topic of discussion and inquiry. However, writing these histories has not been an easy task. These authors faced difficulties accessing primary sources in archives, particularly the secret police records detailing the counterinsurgency campaign. While Mexico's "archive of terror" was declassified during the Fox administration, censorship continues at the AGN. Apart from issues of accessibility, locating former guerrillas to interview has been challenging, given that many fear political repression and are trying to cope with the trauma of the past.

The essays presented here deal with the various regional experiences of urban and rural movements, as well as the transformation of campesinos, students, indigenous people, women, and Chicanos into revolutionary subjects. Although the authors' interpretations regarding the emergence of armed revolutionary organizations differ, every work addresses the issue of state terrorism, how armed struggles materialized, and the ideologies they followed.

Elizabeth Henson offers a comprehensive look at the *Grupo Popular Guerrillo* (Popular Guerrilla Group, GPG), the first modern socialist guerrilla movement, which began its struggle in the mountains of Chihuahua. Henson traces the history of mestizo armed resistance in the highlands and the way it was reactivated by the guerrillas in the 1960s. Through a historical survey, the author elaborates on the emergence of powerful agrarian and student movements suppressed by the state government. This essay also analyzes how the myth of the guerrilla *foco* prompted revolutionaries to mistakenly believe that once the vanguard took the first step, the campesinos would join the armed struggle. In keeping with the theme of rural guerrilla movements, Alexander Aviña questions the dominant historiographical interpretation that guerrilla movements tried to impose alien projects onto the communities they emerged from, precipitating state terrorism. Instead, he examines the structural causes of endemic political violence in the state of Guerrero and the legacies of rebellion that shaped the utopias of the *Asociación Cívica Nacional Revolucionaria* (National Revolutionary Civic Association, ACNR) and the *Partido de los Pobres* (Party of the Poor, PDLP). He also shows how these experiences emerged from civic movements that ended in state-sponsored massacres and took up arms in self-defense, explaining the development of the counterinsurgent state of exception that reduced the citizens of Guerrero to mere objects of state power.

Verónica Oikión Solano offers an approach to the history of the *Movimiento de Acción Revolucionaria* (Revolutionary Action Movement, MAR), the only Mexican armed struggle supported by a foreign government, North Korea. The author evaluates the group from the inside and discusses the difficulties of building a clandestine armed vanguard and how infighting and the inability to resolve disagreements impeded the development of revolutionary praxis. Oikión also addresses the factors that led to the group's internal decay: the failure to comprehend national reality, subjectivism, and improvisation, all elements that made revolutionaries easy targets for counterinsurgency units. Looking at the Dirty War from an international perspective, Alan Eladio Gómez highlights the connections between the Chicano internationalist movement and movements in Mexico, namely the *Partido Proletario Unido de América* (PPUA), and explores the imagination of a greater revolutionary Mexico. The author focuses on Chicano activists who suffered torture and imprisonment in Mexico and the United States as a result of their revolutionary solidarity. He reveals how not only ideologies and utopian visions, but also experiences with state violence, were shared across borders. The author notes that although the Chicano movement as a whole did not support armed struggles in Mexico in the 1970s, there was significant political-cultural exchange among transnational movements that later influenced other struggles.

The role of students in armed revolutionary organizations manifested itself in different parts of the country. In major universities, students entertained the idea of going underground. Fernando Herrera Calderón's essay looks at student radicalism post-1968 and how urban revolutionary groups organized around a student-proletarian identity. Through his assessment of the *Frente Estudiantil Revolucionario* (Student Revolutionary Front, FER) of Guadalajara, Calderón demonstrates how students renegotiated their positionality as "privileged" individuals in order to authenticate their role as revolutionaries. At a time when student-led urban guerrilla movements were going underground without considering the barriers between them and the proletariat, the FER was one of the first movements to address this issue and sought ways to unite youth, workers, and students across class boundaries. In 1973, after working independently, the FER and other armed groups joined forces and created a single revolutionary organization. Romain Robinet presents a historical overview of that organization, the *Liga Comunista 23 de Septiembre* (September 23rd Communist League, LC23S), which became Mexico's largest urban guerrilla movement of the 1970s as well as the most violent. He depicts the group's social composition, structure, ideology, propaganda, military strategies, achievements, failures, and ultimate extermination. Robinet characterizes the conflict between the PRI and the *Liga* as a micro civil war in which both sides competed for the title of revolutionaries. Robinet shows that the *Liga*, despite being rejected by mainstream society, still managed to establish a social base with more than 1,000 supporters.

Besides evaluating the regional and national contexts in which these organizations emerged, one of the objectives of this volume is to understand the connections between the armed struggles of the 1970s and current revolutionary movements in Mexico.[61] Adela Cedillo analyzes the formation of the *Fuerzas de Liberación Nacional* (National Liberation Forces, FLN) from Monterrey, Nuevo León, and inquires why the FLN spent 24 years preparing for a socialist revolution that never took place, and why, despite being a political-military organization, it never directly confronted the state. To explain this anomaly, the author employs collective action theories to visualize the mediation between structures and agents. Cedillo also studies the processes that shaped the ethnic political subject and how the alliance between the FLN and radicalized *campesinos* in Chiapas later gave birth to the *Ejército Zapatista de Liberación Nacional* (Zapatista Army of National Liberation, EZLN), one of the most unique armed revolutionary organizations of the post-Cold War era.

Looking beyond armed struggle, Lucía Rayas and Jorge Luis Sierra Guzmán address the Dirty War from a gender and counterinsurgency angle. The experience of female revolutionaries differed from those of men. Rayas's essay shows how women, despite being social transgressors, reproduced traditional gender roles within the armed organizations, whose leaders argued that the struggle for women's rights was a matter of bourgeois democracy. The author also examines the symbolic meaning of torture for women and its impact on their subjectivity. Jorge Luis Sierra Guzmán looks at the counterinsurgency strategy of containment and suppression that the government used to combat the guerrillas, along with efforts to discredit them through psychological warfare in the media. The author also evaluates how the rise of subversive organizations prompted the government to comprehensively overhaul its national security doctrine, armed forces, and paramilitarize urban security units, namely the *Halcones* and the *Brigada Blanca*.

Elaine Carey's essay concludes by asking a simple question: "Why was Mexico's violent past able to reside in the shadows for so long?" The author's contribution addresses a litany of reasons why the Dirty War has not become a national debate despite its relevance to contemporary Mexico, and describes the origins of the human rights movement as a response to the atrocities committed by the PRI regime.

Despite the fact that the Dirty War lasted more than 15 years and had a greater national impact than has been admitted, producing a record number of cases of torture, disappearance, and murder along with bolstering the growth of the human rights movement, it continues to be neglected. While Mexico's Dirty War has been considered "light" compared with other repressive regimes in Latin America, today this argument must be reconsidered. The authors of this volume hope this work will inspire new debates about this period, leading to a new understanding of the Cold War in Mexico.

Notes

1. Over the years the term "dirty war" has been associated with a litany of countries that experienced long periods of state-sponsored repression. One will find the term being used in scholarship on Peru, Bolivia, and the civil wars of Central America.
2. While recently published scholarship on the Cold War in Latin America has produced valuable contributions to our understanding of this period, the Mexican Dirty War continues to be overlooked as a case study. See for example: Daniela Spenser, ed., *Espejos de la guerra fría: México, América Central y el Caribe* (México, DF: CIESAS/Porrúa, 2004); Gilbert M. Joseph and Daniela Spenser, eds., *In front the Cold. Latin America's New Encounter with the Cold War* (Durham: Duke University Press, 2008); Greg Grandin and Gilbert Joseph, eds., *A Century of Revolution: Insurgent and Counterinsurgent Violence during Latin America's Long Cold War* (Durham: Duke University Press, 2010); Hal Brands, *Latin America's Cold War* (Cambridge: Harvard University Press, 2010) and Enrique Desmond Arias and Daniel M. Goldstein, ed., *Violent Democracies in Latin America* (Durham: Duke University Press, 2010).
3. See Elaine Carey, *Plaza of Sacrifices: Gender, Power, and Terror in 1968 Mexico* (Albuquerque: University of New Mexico Press, 2005) and Eric Zolov, *Refried Elvis: The Rise of the Mexican Counterculture Movement* (Berkeley: University of California Press, 1999).
4. For further information on the debate regarding Mexican populism see Jorge Basurto, "Populism in Mexico: From Cárdenas to Cuauhtémoc," in *Populism in Latin America*, ed., Michael L. Conniff (Tuscaloosa: University of Alabama Press, 1999); César Cansino and Israel Covarrubias, *Sobre el populismo. En el nombre del pueblo. Muerte y resurrección del populismo en México* (Ciudad Juárez: Universidad Autónoma de Ciudad Juárez y Centro de Estudios de Política comparada, Xalapa, 2006) and Amelia M. Kiddle and María L.O. Muñoz, eds., *Populism in 20th Century Mexico: The Presidencies of Lázaro Cárdenas and Luis Echeverría* (Tucson: University of Arizona Press, 2010).
5. The party had various names: Partido Nacional Revolucionario (National Revolutionary Party, PNR, 1929–1938), Partido de la Revolución Mexicana (Mexican Revolution Party, PRM, 1938–1946), and finally the PRI. While other political parties were allowed to hold insignificant amounts of power, within electoral laws their mobility was limited in order to assure they were unable to threaten the ruling party's hegemony. Through this form of rule, the PRI was able to control the population and establish its political dominance. Lorenzo Meyer, "El presidencialismo: Del populismo al neoliberalismo," *Revista Mexicana de Sociología*, 55, 2 (April–June 1993), 60. This does not mean the PRI was an all-powerful entity, exerting a monolithic control over the country. Depending on regional context, the PRI has had to negotiate their power with *caciques* and popular groups. See also Jeffrey W. Rubin, *Decentering the Regime: Ethnicity, Radicalism, and Democracy in Juchitán, Mexico* (Durham: Duke University Press, 1997).
6. A number of state-run organizations were formed to function as mediators between the government and workers and peasants. These included: the *Workers Confederation of Mexico* (CTM), the *National Campesino Confederation* (CNC) and the *National Confederation of Popular Organizations* (CNOP), which intended to unite all trade unions and social organizations in the country. See Luis Javier Garrido, "El partido de la revolución institucionalizada." *La formación del nuevo estado en México (1928–1945)*, (México, DF: Siglo XXI Editores, 1982).
7. See Roderic Ai Camp, *Politics in Mexico: The Decline of Politics* (Oxford: Oxford University Press, 1996) and Jonathan Schlefer, *Palace Politics: How the Ruling Party Brought Crisis to Mexico* (Austin: University of Texas Press, 2008).

8 For example, between 1950 and 1963, 10% of the population monopolized half of the national income, while the remaining 90% received the other half. Luis Medina, *Hacia el nuevo Estado: México, 1920–1994* (México, FCE, 1995), 170.
9 Medina, *Hacia el nuevo Estado*, 170 and Edward Buffie and Allen Sangines Krause, "Mexico 1958–86: From Stabilizing Development to the Debt Crisis," in *Developing Country Debt and the World Economy*, ed., Jeffrey D. Sachs (Chicago: University of Chicago Press, 1989), 141–168.
10 John W. Sherman, "The 'Mexican Miracle' and Its Collapse," in *The Oxford History of Mexico*, ed., Michael C. Meyer and William H. Beezley (Oxford: Oxford University Press, 2000), 575–607.
11 In 1948, the renowned left-wing ideologue, Vicente Lombardo Toledano, founded the Partido Popular Socialista (PPS), which was more moderate than the PCM, and over the years became an ally of the PRI.
12 Barry Carr, *Marxism and Communism in Twentieth Century Mexico* (Lincoln: University of Nebraska Press, 1992); Arnoldo Martínez Verdugo, ed., *Historia del comunismo en México* (Mexico DF: Grijalbo, 1985); Carlso Illades, *Las otras ideas: El primer socialismo en México, 1850–1935* (México, DF: Era, 2008).
13 José Revueltas dubbed fragmentation on the left as "left-wing groupuscule." José Revueltas, *Ensayo sobre un proletariado sin cabeza* (México, DF: Era, 1980).
14 A *charro* leader is a government-appointed union boss.
15 Political movements were often suppressed under the social dissolution law (art. 145 and 145 bis of the Federal Penal Code), which criminalized acts of sabotage, rebellion, sedition, or mutiny, but in fact was used to stifle civil and political liberties. The government also used unlawful methods such as espionage, infiltration, and physical force against movements, parties, and organizations. Sergio Aguayo, *La charola. Una historia de los servicios de inteligencia en México* (México, DF: Grijalbo, 2001).
16 Valentin Campa, *Mi testimonio: Memorias de un comunista mexicano* (México, DF: Ediciones de Cultura Popular, 1978).
17 The US Embassy in Mexico reported 53 student rebellions between 1963 and 1968. Aguayo, *La charola*, 119.
18 Lucio Rangel Hernández, *La Universidad de Michoacana y el movimiento estudiantil, 1966–1989* (Morelia: Instituto de Investigaciones Históricas, Colegio Primitivo y Nacional de San Nicolás de Hidalgo, 2009); José René Rivas Ontiveros, *La izquierda estudiantil en la UNAM: Organizaciones, movilizaciones y liderazgos (1958–1972)* (México, DF: Porrúa, 2007); Salvador Martínez Della Rocca, *Estado y universidad en México, 1920–1968: Historia de los movimientos estudiantiles en la UNAM* (México: J. Boldó i Climent, 1986); Manuel Lara y Parra, *La lucha universitaria en Puebla, 1923–1965* (Puebla: Benemérita Universidad Autónoma de Puebla, 2002); Donald Mabry, *The Mexican University and the State: Student Conflicts, 1910–1971* (College Station: Texas A&M University Press, 1982).
19 See Imanol Ordorika, "The Limits of University Autonomy: Power and Politics at the Universidad Autónoma de México," *Higher Education* 46, 3 (October 2003): 361–388; Daniel Levy, "University Autonomy in Mexico: Implications for Regime Authoritarianism," *Latin American Research Review* 14, 3 (1979): 129–152.
20 See Fernando Solana and Mariángeles Comesaña, ed., *Evocación del 68* (México, DF: Siglo XXI, 2008); Salvador Martínez Della Rocca, ed., *Voces y ecos del 68* (México: Porrúa, 2009); Gilberto Guevara Niebla, *La Libertad nunca se olvida* (México, DF: Cal y Arena, 2004); Ramón Ramírez, *El movimineto estudiantil de Mexico*, vol. 1–2 (México, DF: Era, 2008).
21 It is believed that between 100 and 400 victims perished during the massacre. Kate Doyle, "The dead of Tlatelolco," http://www.gwu.edu/~nsarchiv/NSAEBB/NSAEBB201/index.htm (accessed January 8, 2011).

22 Lorenzo Meyer, "La visión general," in Ilán Bizberg y Lorenzo Meyer coords. *Una historia contemporánea de México: transformaciones y permanencias* (México, Océano, 2003), 17.
23 See Jürgen Burchenau, "A Warmer Cold War: Mexico on Revolutionary Change and the US Reaction in Guatemala and Cuba," in *In Front the Cold*, 119–149. Philip Agee, an ex-CIA agent said that the CIA itself asked the government of Adolfo López Mateos to maintain relations with revolutionary Cuba to have a platform to facilitate operations against the island. Philip Agee, *Diario de la CIA* (Barcelona: Laia, 1978), 430.
24 Jorge Castañeda, who had access to first class information for being the son of a Mexican diplomat and his personal closeness to the island during his youth, confirms this point. Jorge Castañeda, *Utopia Unarmed: The Latin American Left after the Cold War* (New York: Vintage Books, 1994), 105.
25 Pablo Yankelevich, ed., *México, país refugio. La experiencia de los exilios en el siglo XX* (México, Plaza y Valdés/CONACULTA, 2002).
26 For information on how the PRI reconciled with students and intellectuals after 1968, see Roderic A. Camp, *Intellectuals and the State in Twentieth Century Mexico* (Austin: University of Texas Press, 1985).
27 Jacinto R. Munguía, "El Ejército supo del Halconazo," *La Revista 26*, 26 July & 1 August 2004, 16, 17–18; Heberto Castillo, "El Halconazo," *Proceso*, 14 July 2002, 38; Rogelio Cárdenas Estandía, *Luis Echeverría Álvarez: Entre lo personal y lo político* (México: Editorial Planeta, 2008), 98–99, 102; and Orlando Ortiz, *Jueves de Corpus* (México, DF: Editorial Diogenes, 1972).
28 Adela Cedillo and Ricardo Gamboa, "Interpretaciones sobre los espacios de participación política después del 10 de junio de 1971 en México," in *Violencia y sociedad. Un hito en la historia de las izquierdas en América Latina,* Verónica Oikión and Miguel Ángel Urrego, eds. (Morelia: COLMICH/Universidad Michoacana, 210), 97.
29 Throughout this work the authors discuss the meaning and significance of *foquismo*. See also John Foran, *Taking Power: On the Origins of Third World Revolutions* (Cambridge: Cambridge University Press, 2005); Michael Gonzalez, "The Culture of the Heroic Guerrilla: The Impact of the Cuba on the 1960s," *Bulletin of Latin American Research*, 3, 2 (1984): 65–75; Thomas C. Wright, *Latin American in the Era of the Cuban Revolution* (Santa Barbara: Praeger, 2000); Diana Sorensen, *A Turbulent Decade Remembered: Scenes from the Latin American 1960s* (Stanford: Stanford University Press, 2007).
30 In 1960 a group of Latin American activists founded the Movimiento Latinoamericano de Liberación (Latin American Liberation Movement, MLL) in Mexico City, with the help of Lorenzo Cárdenas Barajas, a retired captain in the Mexican army. The MLL was one of the first groups to embrace the idea of liberating the continent from imperialism through a coordinated armed struggle. Although it established guerrilla training camps in Mexico, the MML is not considered the beginning of revolutionary struggles in Mexico because it never performed armed actions. AGN, DFS, [Statement of Lorenzo Cárdenas Barajas], Exp 28-82-69, L-1, H-8-19.
31 Rubén Jaramillo was an heir to the Zapatista movement, who combined public struggle with armed resistance throughout his career. Soldiers killed him along with his pregnant wife and three sons on May 23, 1962 in Xochicalco, Morelos, despite his having received an official pardon. According to Tanalís Padilla, "the audacity of this act left the 'Xochicalco massacre' etched in public memory for decades to come." Padilla, *Rural Resistance in the Land of Zapata: The Jaramillista Movement and the Myth of the Pax-Priísta, 1940–1962* (Durham: Duke University Press, 2008).
32 See Laura Castellanos, *México armado (1943–1981)*, (México, DF: Era, 2007), Fritz Glockner, *Memoria Roja* (México, DF: Ediciones B, 2007) and Enrique Condés Lara, *Represión y rebelión en México* (1959–1985), vol. I–III (México, DF: Porrúa, 2007–2009).

33 It is important to note that the guerrilla organizations were present in almost every state, contrary to the prevailing view that only Guerrero experienced major armed conflicts.
34 The Democratic Tendency of the Electrical Union Workers of Mexico was the main protagonist of the so-called worker insurgency of the 1970s. They considered the guerrillas irresponsible and inexperienced in the realm of mass undertakings. *Insurgencia obrera y nacionalismo revolucionario* (México, DF: Ediciones "El Caballito," 1973), 117.
35 The military training the government of North Korea provided to the founders of the Revolutionary Action Movement, between 1969 and 1970, is an exceptional case. See Fernando Pineda Ochoa. *En las profundidades del MAR (el oro no llegó de Moscú)*, (México, DF: Plaza y Valdés Editores, 2003). There is also a case of a small group, the Marxist-Leninist Movement in Mexico, who received military training in China; nothing has been written about this organization, whose members were arrested between 1967 and 1972.
36 Carlos Montemayor, *La guerrilla recurrente* (México, DF: Debate, 2007).
37 Jorge Luis Sierra Guzmán, *El enemigo interno: Contrainsurgencia y fuerzas armadas en México* (México, DF: Plaza y Valdes, 2003) and Carlos Montemayor, *Violencia de estado en México: Antes y después de 1968* (México, DF: Grijalbo, 2010).
38 See Jorge Mendoza García, "La guerrilla socialista contemporánea en México; Los medios de información y el trato a la guerrilla," in *Movimientos armados en México, siglo XX*, vol. 1 (Zamora: CIESAS and Colegio de Michoácan, 2006).
39 "Guerrero: Terror y crimen," *Excélsior*, 23 April 1973.
40 "Testimonio de Bertha López de Zazueta," in David Cilia Olmos and Enrique González Ruíz eds, *Testimonios de la guerra sucia* (México DF: Editorial Tierra Roja, 2006), 29, 31.
41 Sierra Guzmán, *El enemigo interno*, 8, and also reported by Fiscalía Especial para Movimientos Sociales y Políticos del Pasado and José Sotelo Marbán et al., *Informe ¡Que No Vuelva a Suceder!* (Mexico City: February 2006), http://www.gwu.edu/~nsarchiv/NSAEBB/NSAEBB180/index2.htm (accessed January 20, 2011).
42 We developed this estimate by cross-referencing archival research, the FEMOSPP report, and figures from human rights organizations.
43 Gustavo Castillo García, "Acosta y Quirós ordenaron asesinar a más de mil 500, dice testigo protegido," http://www.cesarsalgado.net/200211/021118b.htm (accessed February 15, 2011).
44 "Informe de la Comisión Nacional de Verdad y Reconciliación (Informe Rettig)," http://www.ddhh.gov.cl/ddhh_rettig.html (accessed Fabruary 15, 2011).
45 Julio Scherer y Carlos Monsiváis, *Los patriotas: de Tlatelolco a la guerra sucia* (México: Aguilar, 2004).
46 The Federal Law on Political Organizations and Electoral Processes (LFOPPE) was enacted in late 1977.
47 Not everyone granted amnesty belonged to armed groups. Hundreds were farmers arrested for drug cultivation, though it is clear the government wanted to bulk up the number for propaganda purposes. The number of missing persons has been investigated by an array of human rights organizations. "Desaparecidos en México": http://www.desaparecidos.org/mex/des/ (accessed March 3, 2011).
48 Doug McAdam, John D. McCarthy, and Mayer N. Zald eds, *Comparative Perspectives on Social Movements: Political Opportunities, Mobilizing Structures, and Cultural Framings*, (Cambridge: Cambridge University Press, 1996), 38.
49 Medina, 194.
50 The DIPD made up the nucleus of the White Brigade, a counterinsurgent organization established by López Portillo to wipe out urban guerrillas.

51 See Luis Astorga, *El siglo de las drogas. El narcotráfico, del Porfiriato al nuevo milenio* (México, Plaza y Janés, 2005).
52 Pascal Beltrán del Río, "El Arava, el avión de la muerte," *Proceso*, 1356, October 27, 2002, 15.
53 Padilla, op. cit.
54 Gabriel Careaga, *Mitos y fantasias de la clase media en México* (México, DF: Cal y Arena, 2005); Christopher White, *Creating a Third World: Mexico, Cuba, and the United States during the Castro Era* (Albuquerque: University of New Mexico Press, 2007).
55 Gustavo Hirales, Salvador Castañeda, and Saúl López de la Torre, among others. It should be noted the first works on the Dirty War were novels, poems, and short stories. Novels like *La guerra de Galio* by Héctor Aguilar and *Guerra en el paraíso* by Carlos Montemayor, are examples. See also Alberto Ulloa Bornemann, *Sendero en tinieblas* (México, DF: Cal y Arena, 2004).
56 The creation of the FEMOSPP was prompted by a recommendation of the National Human Rights Commission (CNDH), which in 2001 conducted the first serious attempt to investigate the disappearances carried out during the Dirty War, issuing the "Special Report on Complaints of Forced Disappearances in the 70's and early 80's," as well as "The Investigative Report Into Alleged Disappearances in the State of Guerrero during 1971 to 1974" which is available on its website: http://www.cndh.org.mx/lacndh/informes/espec/desap70s/.
57 Sergio Aguayo, "Oculta CNDH datos sobre desaparecidos" http://www.sergioaguayo.org/biblioteca/Alicia%20de%20los%20Rios%204.pdf, accessed January 10, 2011. Within the State Department's archive is also the General Directorate of Political and Social Research (DGIPS), the office responsible for the systematization of information. This collection contains more than 3000 boxes but the documentation was deliberately looted and disorganized.
58 It would be impossible to enumerate all the works that have appeared on the Dirty War. The first academic works include Verónica Oikión Solano and Marta Eugenia García Ugarte, eds., *Movimientos armados en México en el siglo XX*. 3 v. (Morelia, CIESAS/COLMICH, 2006); Sierra Guzmán, *El enemigo interno*; as well as Glockner's *Memoria Roja*, Castellanos,' *México Armado* and Condés,' *Represión y rebelión*.
59 The team that prepared this report lacked proper institutional support. In fact, the version researchers produced was not accepted as "official" and was censured. To this day, there is nowhere to consult the original report.
60 A draft of the FEMOSPP report was filtered to the National Security Archive: http://www.gwu.edu/~nsarchiv/NSAEBB/NSAEBB180/index2.htm.
61 Although the importance of these organizations is not studied in this volume, the Zapatista rebellion of 1994, for example, had a crucial impact on the political culture of contemporary Mexico.

1

MADERA 1965

Primeros Vientos[1]

Elizabeth Henson

Introduction

Madera, Sierra of Chihuahua, Mexico. Just before dawn on September 23, 1965, a squad of 13 poorly armed young men who called themselves the *Grupo Popular Guerrillero de la Sierra* (GPG) attacked an army base on the edge of this town of 12,000 inhabitants, expecting to find some 70 soldiers asleep in the barracks. Minutes later, soldiers who had camped on the outskirts fell on them from behind and cut off their retreat; they killed eight guerrillas but five escaped with the help of townspeople into the surrounding mountains. Four soldiers were killed and a fifth died of wounds; soldiers killed a deaf milkman when he disobeyed an order to halt. The governor of the state, former revolutionary war general Práxedis Giner Durán, refused efforts of family members to remove the bodies and ordered them to be thrown into a common grave without shrouds. "They wanted land? Give it to them until they're full!"[2]

Weeks after the attack, President Gustavo Díaz Ordaz ordered 5,000 hectares of land to be distributed to the Ejido Belizario Domínguez[3] and Giner signed an agreement giving 39,000 hectares to form the Ejido Huizopa, both in the municipality of Madera.[4] In 1971, President Luis Echeverría distributed 256,000 hectares of Bosques de Chihuahua (Chihuahua's Forests), the local logging company and the guerrilla's principal antagonist, to form the largest ejido in the republic, that of El Largo, whose members continued to supply lumber to the company.[5]

The attack on the base developed from a popular movement that had organized demonstrations, land invasions, and armed self-defense by campesinos[6] and students throughout the state during the previous six years. Mid-century industrial growth—the so-called Miracle—had long put increasing pressure on campesinos, both landless workers whose demands for ejidos had languished for decades and serrano smallholders confronting encroaching timber barons. In November 1959, caciques had assassinated a Madera schoolteacher who had been advising campesinos in conflict with Bosques de Chihuahua, setting off a cycle of recurring protests. Students at the normal schools (teachers' training schools, called *normalistas*) joined petitioners for ejidos in land invasions, many of them in the fertile valley of the Río Conchos, dominated by vast agribusiness. Protesters occupied the downtown plaza in front of the Office of Agrarian Affairs (DAAC) for months at a time on two separate occasions. Students from the preparatory schools (high schools), the state university, and the normal schools raised both their own demands and those of the campesinos. In the sierra, smallholders and ejidatarios battled caciques allied with Bosques de Chihuahua as they sought to open new tracts to large-scale timbering. These various currents of resistance united in the General Union of Mexican Workers and Campesinos (UGOCM), under the auspices of Vicente Lombardo Toledano's Popular Socialist Party (PPS), whose General Secretary in Chihuahua was the young normalista and later schoolteacher Arturo Gámiz, a member of the PPS youth section who had attended secondary school at the Instituto Politécnico Nacional (IPN) in Mexico City and taken part in the wave of strikes which ended with an army occupation of the dormitories.[7] The strength of the movement was such that two presidents of the republic were compelled to meet with its leaders.

The armed component of Mexico's first guevarist group came from the sierra, from people whose propensity for armed self-defense easily loaned itself to *foquista* revolutionary theories then gaining currency within the broader movement. Unlike many later armed movements undertaken by students frustrated by their inability to bring about social change through other means—this was not the case in Guerrero—the roots of the original *Grupo Popular Guerrillero* (GPG) were endemic. I would argue for the importance of the popular movement that produced the GPG and against its teleological collapse into fascination with the guerrilla, a figure that tends to eclipse all others. As in the revolution of 1910, Chihuahua fielded an army whose social origins were various.

The attack represented the confluence of two traditions of armed struggle, one being *foquismo* inspired by the Cuban revolution of 1959 and the other dating back to the eighteenth- and nineteenth-century Apache Wars, when mestizo settlers were given land in return for defending the frontier. These serrano ranchers, who have been described by Alonso, Fuentes Mares, Jordán, Katz, Knight, Nugent, and Orozco[8] in similar terms, now fought to defend semi-autonomous rural communities in isolated hinterlands threatened by the expansion of logging. The Revolution of 1910 began in the sierra and they had been a major component of Pancho Villa's Army of the North.

In the early 1960s, the UGOCM led hundreds of land invasions and demonstrations receiving broad support; federal agrarian officials had ordered the state authorities to satisfy some of the protesters' demands, but the state remained adamant in opposition. Giner's recalcitrance resulted in the radicalization of protests. In early 1964, the GPG, led by Gámiz and Salomón Gaytán, whose father had fought for the expropriation of a local hacienda and whose land had been taken by the caciques, emerged in the sierra and withstood repeated attempts by rural police and federal troops to dislodge them, expropriated a large cache of automatic weapons, and enjoyed the protection of local campesinos.

The Cuban Revolution of 1959 mounted a challenge to the traditional communist parties, the PPS and the *Partido Comunista Mexicano* (PCM), who took their leadership from Moscow. The orthodox parties had long given up on revolution and advocated the negotiation of successive stages, based on the notion that Latin America's mode of production was semi-feudal and must evolve into capitalism to create the conditions for socialism. This strategy tied the masses and their vanguard to an alliance with sectors of the elite, while emphasizing the importance of the urban working class over rural workers and subsistence farmers.

The Cuban Revolution would not have happened without the handful of guerrilla fighters based in the rugged mountains who acted in defiance of the traditional communist party, which only offered support when faced with a *fait accompli*. It also would not have happened without the workers and students in the cities and canefields, whose contribution has been downplayed in the official myth.[9] But it was the *barbudos* from the sierra and not the party leaders who took power and whose achievement opened the way for a new formulation of revolutionary strategy.

With *foquismo*, Latin America became a source of ideas; other exports have been Liberation Theology, *la nueva canción*, and dependency theory. *Foquismo* held that a small band of dedicated revolutionaries could demonstrate elite vulnerability and grow into a magnetic center, a *foco*, capable of attracting campesinos, students, workers, and foreign journalists, eventually maturing into a people's army. The initial conditions were unimportant, what mattered was the revolutionary will. This theory received its definitive explication in *Revolution in the Revolution?*[10] written by the French philosopher and journalist, Régis Debray. First published in French in 1967, it would not have been available to the militants of the UGOCM but the ideas were already in wide circulation.

Foquismo implied a dramatic break with existing practices and beliefs. By insisting that the revolutionaries could themselves bring about the necessary conditions for the mobilization of forces sufficient to bring down US-backed dictatorial regimes, the *foquistas* challenged the orthodox doctrine, which required the maturing of objective and subjective conditions. They also posed an explicit challenge to the traditional party, by insisting the vanguard would emerge in the course of struggle. The image of triumphant *barbudos* entering Havana on tanks proved irresistible to tens of thousands of young people. Their attempts to apply the Cuban model to a variety of circumstances resulted in disaster.

The guerrilla movement led by Arturo Gámiz was among those failures. Gámiz seems to have believed the Cuban myth, which he had studied in Che Guevara's *Guerra de Guerrillas*, and he and his companions took the leap between being convinced of the necessity for armed struggle to believing the same masses who mobilized for land invasions were only waiting for the signal to rise up in arms. The consequences were tragic and resulted in repression that drove the remnants of the movement underground. It later emerged in two distinct currents: as successor guerrilla organizations, the GPG–Arturo Gámiz and the Movimiento 23 de Septiembre (September 23rd Movement), and in the legal and aboveground Committees for Popular Defense, who fought for urban land in Chihuahua City.

Cuba's support for all Latin American movements except Mexico became more pronounced as the US blockade tightened and Cuba had less to lose. Mexico had been the one Latin American government that defied the USA in refusing to join the Organization of American States' boycott of Cuba.[11] The Cuban refusal to support Mexican revolutionary movements contributed to the blanket of silence which muffled the Mexican experience for many years. While members of solidarity movements in the USA publicized atrocities committed by regimes in Brazil and the Southern Cone, they ignored similar activities in Mexico, where they occurred under a civilian regime.

Agrarian Struggles

The struggle for land has animated generations of revolutionaries but the small farming unit, whether cooperative or not, rarely provides a dignified living. The failure of the ejido system was obvious long before the dissolution of Article 27 of the Constitution, which promised land to the landless, in the early 1990s and cannot be blamed only on greed and corruption. The ejidos assumed an impossible burden: to provide social justice and a livelihood to their members, to feed the growing cities and their march to industrialization, and to provide the state with a mechanism for the political incorporation of campesinos. Their creation did not take into account demographic pressure on lands that were frequently marginal to begin with. Economic conditions in the country as a whole and beyond its borders favor large agricultural extensions geared to foreign markets; the corn and beans subsistence farm in the long run produces only migrant workers. The small plot at best is part of a mixed strategy for family survival: illegally rented out or marginally farmed and combined with wage labor, migration, handicrafts, and small-scale retail sales, it provides an additional source of income or food.

The miseries of wage labor must have been a powerful incentive to demand increased land. Working conditions in the expanding lumber industry were grim; accident rates were high in both the *monte* and the sawmills. In the *monte*, the workers camped out for weeks, in danger from animals, falling trees, and other injuries. In town the work was more secure, although poorly paid and dangerous as well.[12] Conditions in mining were even more perilous, tightly controlled, and isolated.[13] The majority of migrant workers remained caught in a cycle of seasonal migration, with low wages, family separation, and periodic deportation, unable to get ahead.

The destruction of *latifundio* laid the basis for modern Mexico as it freed capital to flow into industry. But changes in land ownership have not brought substantial improvement in the lives of campesinos. The ejidos and smallholders have been isolated as large-scale entrepreneurial agriculture has expanded and captured more of the market. The largest ejido in the Republic, El Largo, in the Madera district, derives little benefit from its forests; profits go to the companies, which control its processing and distribution.[14]

Chihuahua

> To annoy a Chihuahuan serrano is not only injust but dangerous, and it is pointless to try to make him recognize any authority.
> —José Fuentes Mares

The Sierra Madre Occidental is a heavily forested chain of mountains and canyons running north and south between Chihuahua and Sonora. There the indigenous people revolted five times during the seventeenth century against Jesuit attempts to concentrate them in villages. Abandoned with the Jesuit expulsion in 1767, they fled to the sierra and took up nomadic herding, preferring their isolated rancherías until the mid-twentieth century.

The first mestizos arrived in search of gold and silver in the 1630s. Nearby ranches supplied beef and tallow and developed into haciendas. Other settlers arrived in the eighteenth century to populate a string of military settlements established to withstand attacks by nomadic Commanche and Apache warriors. Their settlers were given land grants and tax exemption as inducements to remain in inhospitable territory.[15] After Independence, these pioneers battled US incursions, the French Intervention, and the Wars of Reform with no help from a distant federal government, while the California Gold Rush increased pressure on US tribes to move south across the border.

In 1886, soldiers defeated Victorio and the Apache wars came to an end. The truce between smallholders and *hacendados* likewise ended as the haciendas sought to expand, now free from the threat of invasion, and rancheros defended their independence. The completion of the railroad linking Juárez with Mexico City led to an export cattle boom and rise in land prices, harming local communities.[16] The pueblos resented the railroad for expropriating land, cutting down trees, carrying out minerals, and moving in troops. The railway brought benefits as well and the railway workers bore the germs of socialism, bringing migrant workers into contact with international labor insurgency and contributing to the Revolution of 1910.[17]

In 1884, the federal government began to survey the enormous tracts of land which smallholders had used as a commons. The surveyors were granted as much as one-third of the land in payment; the rest was sold to investors, many of them foreign. The elite enclosed the commons, depriving smallholders of firewood and pasture; landowners also sought expansion into the military colonies. A political assault combined with the economic threat: in line with Porfirian centralizing policies, local elected political leaders were replaced by appointed *jefes políticos*, often local caciques or outsiders; attacks on the *municipio libre* were among the principal causes of a number of rural rebellions, including the one at Tomóchic.[18]

During the Indian wars, the people of the serrano frontier had been constructed as the embodiment of civilization in contrast to savage Indians. Once the savages who defined the serranos as *gente de razón* were gone, the serranos themselves, in their recalcitrant resistance to authority, were constructed as obstacles to progress.[19] Now the elite no longer needed them to fight and coveted their land. In the words of Friedrich Katz, the frontier was becoming a border. The serranos were poor and egalitarian and their frontier democracy depended on a weak state. The culture of armed resistance forged over decades of warfare continued to animate them while the consolidating Porfirian state attempted to impose a monopoly on violence.[20]

Madera

In 1899, Arizona rancher William C. Greene purchased the copper mine at Cananea, Sonora; he went on to buy dozens of mines and several million acres of timberland in Chihuahua. He also purchased the railway from El Paso to Terrazas, north of Madera, hoping to extend it to provide timber to the Cananea mine.[21] He constructed the sawmill town of Madera in a valley and formed the Sierra Madre Land and Lumber Company. Madera began as a company town, with 100 US-style wooden houses, still known as the American barrio, for foreign managers, and another neighborhood, without running water or electricity, for the Mexican workers.[22]

In 1906, Mexican workers at the Cananea mine went on strike, demanding equal pay with US workers and an eight-hour day. The strike turned into a riot, rebellious miners burned company installations, and several people were killed. In response, Greene called on a mob of US vigilantes led by Arizona Rangers and subdued the strikers. The strike exposed the shaky underpinnings of Greene's incipient empire; he went bankrupt in the recession of 1907. In Madera, 2,000 workers were laid off after working months without pay. Greene's property in the Sierra passed into the hands of the state of Chihuahua, who sold some of it to US investors.[23] These vast holdings, together with the immense landholdings of the family of the newspaper magnate, William Randolph Hearst, the Hacienda Babícora, were fought over for decades by local campesinos, many of them smallholders dispossessed by expanding haciendas and railroad construction in the 1880s. In the years preceding the 1910 Revolution, the Guerrero District—which Fernando Jordán called the Longitude of War[24]—rebelled again and again.

In 1938, following decades of protest, President Lázaro Cárdenas granted a portion of the Babícora to the *Unión de Veteranos de la Revolución*; gunmen kept the community from taking possession. The following year, they invaded the land and their leader, Socorro Rivera, was assassinated.[25]

Between 1946 and 1952, business interests centered around the *Banco Comercial Mexicano* bought sawmills, railways, and obtained forestry concessions for hundreds of thousands of hectares and formed the company *Bosques de Chihuahua*, headquartered in Madera City. The founders of *Bosques* included Miguel Alemán Valdez, former president of the republic; Eloy Vallina, a Spanish empresario who founded the Mercantile Bank; General Antonio Guerrero; banker Carlos Trouyet; two former governors, Teófilo Borunda and Tomás Valle; and members of the powerful Terrazas and Almeida families. The concession included nearly 260,000 hectares in addition to lumber obtained from private and ejidal owners. The group went on to found Comermex, one of the most powerful financial institutions in the Republic. They constructed several factories in nearby Colonia Anáhuac to produce plywood and cellulose, the latter to fill orders for wood pulp resulting from changes in the paper manufacturing process.[26] The Chihuahua group also sold lots to cattlemen, although the land was not theirs to sell; Tomás Vega Portillo, José Ibarra Ronquillo, and the Hermanos Prieto formed the company, Cuatro Amigos (the Four Friends), with 250,000 hectares and attempted to dislodge local smallholders who had attempted to regularize land titles based on possession in vain.[27]

With the aggressive push to extract timber from the forests of the sierra, industrialists backed by state authorities used local caciques, mostly notably the Cuatro Amigos, to appropriate land through intimidation and violence.[28] The land hunger shown by protesters reflected the precarious condition of hundreds of rancheros throughout the area, many living for generations on lands now claimed by *Bosques de Chihuahua*. Mining areas such as Batopilas and Dolores, near the Sonora border, had long polluted the surrounding countryside and consumed its forests for timbers and fuel. But the impact of mining was local compared with that of timbering, whose production was now being exponentially increased to supply the needs of a growing market. The increase in unsustainable lumbering also threatened the survival of indigenous people by eroding the material basis of their culture.

From the UGOCM to the Grupo Popular Guerrillero

Governor Práxedis Giner Durán, who ruled Chihuahua from 1962 to 1966, failed to understand a significant tenet of the regime's success: they governed through negotiation and reforms from above, using them to defuse and deflect struggles from below and only resorting to violence when all else failed. During a time of mass social effervescence when the movement offered ample opportunities for compromise and concession, Giner met protest with repression. Nor did the local caciques mediate between the state and the campesinos; instead they devolved into sheer brutality: rape, torture, kidnappings, the torching of homes, assassination, and the expropriation of land and livestock. It was the affront to the dignity of the campesinos, as much as the demand for land, that fed the revolt that eventually turned into an assault on the state itself. The serranos had long been willing to endure poverty and isolation in return for autonomy; now industrialization was encroaching, behind the guns of the same small-time caciques they had been battling for decades.

Francisco Luján Adame, a Madera schoolteacher and member of the UGOCM, had spent years helping the local campesinos with their petitions for ejidos, including that of Cebadilla de Dolores, where he had been the registered agent since 1949.[29] On November 26, 1959, Luján was stabbed to death at his home in Madera.[30] The UGOCM organized a caravan protesting his murder; 600 people joined it on the way to Chihuahua City, some 175 kilometers away. Sympathy strikes broke out in the nearby processing plants where workers were also negotiating for changes in their contracts; normalistas took to the streets in support of striking workers and campesinos.[31] The murder of Professor Luján began a cycle of protest and repression. Shortly afterwards, Alvaro Ríos Ramírez arrived from Mexico City as the state delegate to the UGOCM to continue Luján's work. It was Ríos who introduced direct action tactics of long-distance marches between cities, land invasions, and occupations of public spaces; he organized the mass meeting in Madera where he, Arturo Gámiz, and the Gómez brothers spoke together for the first time.[32]

Arturo Gámiz García, who became the General Secretary of the state chapter of the UGOCM and later leader of the *Grupo Popular Guerrillero*, was born in Suchil, northern Durango, in 1940. Little is known of his early life beyond his participation in the PPS youth group and the strike movement at the IPN.

He arrived in Chihuahua in 1957 and taught elementary school in La Junta, a sawmill town on the edge of the sierra, until 1959 when he entered the State Normal School in Chihuahua City where he came into contact with activists of the UGOCM.[33]

Pablo and Raúl Gómez Ramírez were also members of the PPS and leaders of the UGOCM in Delicias, the irrigated agricultural district along the Río Conchos. Both were teachers in the rural normal schools; Pablo was also a medical doctor. Both ran for local offices on the PPS ticket in the state elections of 1965.

On December 11, 1962, Arturo Gámiz arrived at Mineral de Dolores to give classes to 85 children. Dolores was close to the Sonora border, virtually inaccessible due to lack of adequate roads and bridges, a former mining town dating from colonial times. Gámiz had met the Gaytán brothers, UGOCM activists from the area, in Chihuahua City, where they suggested the assignment to Dolores, which had been without a teacher for some 28 years. Gámiz initially gave classes in the plaza, while the community constructed a new building.[34]

The Gaytán family were smallholders who had been dispossessed. The father, Rosendo, had fought with Socorro Rivera for the Babícora. His sons Juan Antonio, Salvador, and Salomón were active in the UGOCM.[35] Salomón and Juan Antonio Gaytán lost their lives in the armed movement; a third brother, Salvador, participated in both the GPG and in the September 23rd Movement, fought in Guerrero with Lucio Cabañas, and only returned to Chihuahua in 1992.

The nucleus of the nearby[36] ejido Cebadilla was formed in 1948, as the community sought to regain land which had been taken by Francisco Portillo to form the Hacienda Sírupa, granted a 25-year certificate of inaffectability by Alemán.[37] The community pressed for additional land, winning parcels of various sizes over the years. They are now engaged in small-scale logging. Cebadilla had long been a center of operations for the Ibarra family who manufactured illicit *sotol* there.[38] The Ibarras had constructed a barbed wire fence through the town center to keep the townsfolk from watering their animals at a spring-fed pond; activists later tore down that fence.

On December 7, 1962, Salvador Gaytán won election as sectional president in Dolores as a candidate of the PPS against the local boss who had held that office for decades and invited Gámiz to the area. The community wrested control of its reservoir and communal orchard from the caciques; they built basketball and volleyball courts and initiated vaccination campaigns. They built a bridge over the Sírupa River. They renewed the petition for amplification of the Ejido Cebadilla, which had languished for a number of years in the hands of the agrarian bureaucracy.[39]

In January 1963, interim governor Raúl González Herrera sent UGOCM leaders, including Alvario Ríos, to meet with President Adolfo López Mateos and Roberto Barrios, director of the federal DAAC.[40] They returned to lead land invasions throughout the state. Although police and army forces dislodged most of them, 310 campesinos succeeded in founding the Community Professor Francisco Luján Adame in Gómez Farías.[41] In May, Gámiz published a series of articles in *La Voz de Chihuahua*, a small radical newspaper, detailing the misery of rural communities subjected to forced expropriations, human rights violations, and the accelerating exploitation of their forests.[42] The state government replied with violence and repression.

In September 1963, the UGOCM and 300 campesinos, students, and teachers occupied the central plaza in downtown Chihuahua City in front of the *Departamento de Asuntos Agrarios y Colonización* (Department of Agrarian Affairs and Colonization, DAAC), again receiving massive popular support. Among their demands were the retention of Pablo and Raúl Gómez in their current teaching positions, the release of political prisoners, and an end to logging.[43] Concerns about excessive logging and its impact on the watershed were not paramount but were present. In the morning they mounted mute protests on the patio of the nearby statehouse and in the early evening they paraded about downtown with banners. One of their banners read: "A cow gets 30 hectares, and us—how many? and when?"[44] They had a number of inconclusive meetings with the governor, Eduardo Juarez Santoscoy, state director of the DAAC, and Francisco Javier Alvarez, director of the State Department of Education.[45] These meetings indicated both the pressure exerted on the state by the continuous protests and the state's attempts to pacify the movement through promised concessions. One wonders how much time Gámiz and the other teachers spent in the classroom.

On September 23, Gámiz met with Vicente Arreola, representing Bosques de Chihuahua, in the office of the state prosecutor, Hipólito Villa Rentería; Arreola promised to put an end to the harassment of campesinos.[46] On September 25, 1963, outgoing President López Mateos granted a meeting to five leaders of the UGOCM, among them Ríos, Gámiz, and Pablo Gómez. A few days later Arturo Gámiz was arrested by the state judicial police; massive demonstrations led to his prompt release.[47] Gunmen continued to intimidate the campesinos in the sierra with impunity, protected by the police and soldiers. As the violence practiced by the state and its surrogates increased, so did the militancy of the campesinos and students.

In October 1963, the UGOCM organized the semi-clandestine First Encounter of the Sierra Heraclio Bernal[48] in Cebadilla de Dolores. Two hundred delegates, among them PPS militants from six states, attended the event. Influenced by Cuba's turn to socialism, participants debated the use of armed struggle to achieve global revolution but finally voted against it.[49] Nevertheless, the First Encounter signaled the beginning of a break on the part of the more radicalized sectors of the PPS, its youth group, and the UGOCM.[50] After the meeting, students destroyed the Ibarra's barbed wire fences and the army arrested five students.[51]

In December 1963, police and soldiers closed the rural normal schools and arrested Arturo Gámiz along with other leaders of the UGOCM and dozens of students. When informed that the students were demanding the reopening of their dormitories, Giner remarked, in a meeting with the state Secretary of Internal Affairs, "I would rather turn those schools into pigpens. But in Mexico City they do not understand."[52] In response to the petition of women students, Giner replied, "Why do they want dormitories, since they like to sleep with the campesinos in the fields?"[53]

The army assisted landlords in taking back invaded lands and mercenaries assaulted campesinos in the sierra; several civilians were wounded by gunfire. Seven campesinos of Dolores were hung from trees in an attempt at interrogation, among them José de la Luz Gaytán, age eleven.[54] When gunmen employed by the Ibarra clan fired on UGOCM members in Huizopa, State Attorney General José Melgar de la Peña denounced them in an article published in the newspaper, *Norte*. However, no arrests were made in that case.[55]

Gámiz went face-to-face with the governor a number of times, once arguing with him publicly in the patio of the state house.[56] General Antonio Gómez Velasco arrived in Chihuahua in December 1963 as chief of the military zone and forced José Ibarra to leave Madera.[57] The campesinos continued to insist on their demands.

In January and February 1964, the UGOCM organized yet more land invasions, with the participation of vast numbers of campesinos, students, and *normalistas*. Some of the occupied properties belonged to the Hacendados of the Revolution, among them the families of Antonio Guerrero, Pedro Almada, Rogelio Quevedo, and prominent politicians, Hilario Gabilondo and Ignacio Siquieros; others belonged to Anderson Clayton Company, US cotton growers.[58] The governor responded by closing the normal schools yet again and sending soldiers and rural police to clear the land, arresting protesters, and accusing their leaders of federal crimes. The opposition intensified.

The Second Occupation of the DAAC

The coming presidential elections added tension to an already explosive situation. Vicente Lombardo Toledano announced the PPS's support for PRI candidate Gustavo Díaz Ordaz and the state section of the UGOCM came under increasing pressure to contain the mass movement. A split in the UGOCM became inevitable, between Gámiz with his advocacy of armed self-defense and national and state leaders, Jacinto López and Alvaro Ríos. Meanwhile, Judith Reyes, protest singer, editor of the radical newspaper, *Acción*, and the only woman in the leadership of the local UGOCM, ran for the federal senate under the banner of the People's Electoral Front (FEP).[59]

In 1964, the United States ended the Bracero Program, which had provided agricultural work to tens of thousands of Mexican campesinos since the beginning of World War II. Thousands of workers returned to Mexico, many settling in the border states, exacerbating the demand for land and work. The rural normal school of Saucillo, recently moved from Flores Magón, with 300 female students between the ages of twelve and eighteen, and Salaices, with 300 males, were under continual surveillance by police and soldiers who held the students under an ineffective but menacing state of siege; nevertheless, the students continued to participate in land invasions.[60]

On February, campesinos and students once again occupied the offices of the DAAC; the police dislodged them with tear gas and arrested 30 students. Protesters returned and began a sit-in at the Plaza Hidalgo where they stayed until June, while students sent them rations and supporters baked tortillas on the patios of downtown apartment buildings.[61] While exhausting and disruptive to family life, these occupations and invasions provided a forum for new ways of collective living; they should be examined in their own right and not only in terms of their results.

In March, Pablo Gómez announced his candidacy as substitute deputy in Delicias for the PPS, while his brother Raúl Gómez ran for federal deputy in Guerrero; Arturo Gámiz, now in hiding, announced his support.[62]

Federal officials, less beholden to the local interests of cattlemen, timber interests, and other large landowners and hoping to prevent another Cuba, attempted to diffuse the growing climate of violence, sending federal officials to negotiate with the state; their efforts were unsuccessful.[63]

When presidential candidate Gustavo Díaz Ordaz attempted to speak in the capital, Chihuahua, in April, a student climbed the reviewing stand and attempted to take the microphone and the crowd began yelling slogans against the local authorities, the PRI, and the candidate himself. Security forces escorted Díaz Ordaz from the platform; the crowd then burned the reviewing stand, scorching the façade of City Hall.[64]

Meanwhile, in Delicias, a number of agrarian leaders, among them Raúl and Pablo Gómez, were arrested; Díaz Ordaz secured their release and met with them briefly, promising to find a solution to the agrarian question.[65] On April 12, the state released a number of political prisoners; others, among them Judith Reyes, were arrested for burning the reviewing stand.[66]

In April, Pablo Gómez chased down a bus carrying two students from Saucillo, young women who had decided to take up arms and join the guerrillas in the sierra; Gómez convinced them to return to school.[67] On June 7, 300 campesinos, exhausted by months of struggle, abandoned the occupation of the plaza, accepted the governor's promise of support, and returned home in buses sent by the state.[68]

When Gámiz was released from jail following the occupation of the DAAC, he took up arms, along with a handful of comrades, and never went back to teaching. The mountains and canyons of northwestern Chihuahua offered an ideal terrain and a population accustomed to armed self-defense. They named the new organization the *Grupo Popular Guerrillero de la Sierra* (GPG).

With the support of local serranos, the GPG carried out a series of attacks on detachments of both the army and state police, confiscating weapons and ammunition and rescuing prisoners. According to the report published by former president Vicente Fox's Office of the Special Prosecutor, agents of the Federal Security Directorate (DFS) were able to infiltrate the circles of students and campesinos in and around the UGOCM, but were never able to penetrate the GPG itself, at least in Chihuahua.[69] While both state and national security forces regarded the GPG, UGOCM, and their supporters as "communists" and "subversives," publicly they called them common delinquents and horse thieves. According to the report, the federal agents assigned to the case lacked sufficient training to analyze the politics of the group or the causes, which led them to take up arms.[70]

What seems clear is that the state underestimated their capacity for action and support among serrano communities and that the surveillance was insufficient. No one in the leadership of the GPG's clandestine group was ever arrested;[71] Gámiz was detained in connection with urban protests but quickly released. The state was helpless to prevent the development of these guerrillas, which contributed to the confidence that led them to assault the barracks.

The first public action of the GPG took place in Madera in February 1964, when they burned a bridge and then a house and captured a radio station in Mineral de Dolores.[72] In May 1964, Salomón Gaytán shot Florentino Ibarra, José Ibarra's brother, in revenge for the assassination of Carlos Ríos, a Pima activist with the UGOCM, and went into hiding.[73] The Secretary of National Defense sent a company of soldiers after the guerrillas, who hired guides among the serranos who led them about in circles; the troops resorted to torturing civilians, hanging them in trees, and dangling them from helicopters flying close to the rocks.[74] In July, the GPG attacked the Ibarra home in Cebadilla where the judical police were staying, burned the house, and set its residents free in their underwear.[75]

The state attorney general's office created a group of spies within the student movement and paid them to inform; they temporarily achieved a split in what had been a united front of campesinos and students. Schoolteachers were beaten and fired from their jobs.[76]

In May 1965, Salvador Gaytán took up arms and left office. He penned a declaration, which ended with his promise to lay down arms whenever the authorities brought the caciques to justice.[77] Several successful attacks on soldiers followed, adding to the guerrillas' cache of automatic weapons.

The Second Encounter of the Sierra Heraclio Bernal and Its Resolutions

In the city, students from the normal schools founded support groups and some of them attempted to join the forces in the sierra but soon returned to town, overwhelmed by the harsh physical conditions. At this point the GPG realized the need for training to incorporate townsfolk.[78]

In January 1965, while Gámiz was in the sierra, the state UGOCM split. Supporters of Lombardo wanted to turn towards electoral campaigns, putting a brake on the mass actions. The supporters of Gámiz proposed participation in the elections while continuing the mass protests and building a parallel, clandestine organization for armed campesino self-defense. This tripartite strategy, of mass protests, electoral participation, and armed self-defense, seemed a refusal to choose among alternatives. In fact, the group's goal was to unite the leaders emerging from the mass movement into a political–military *foco* headquartered in the sierra with its own urban support network that would eventually form links throughout the country.[79] This position recognized that the limits of armed self-defense in the sierra had been reached and proposed a national strategy.

In January 1965, the Second Encounter of the Sierra Heraclio Bernal was held in northern Durango. Five Resolutions were presented to clarify the GPG's objectives, facilitate their national diffusion, and encourage the leadership to coalesce; they ended with a call for immediate armed struggle. These documents, along with Gámiz's pamphlet, "Student Participation in the Revolutionary Movement," were widely disseminated.[80]

The Resolutions are the only written indication of the ideology that motivated the GPG, although I would argue that they did not adequately reflect the group's ability to maneuver on the ground. The text exhibited a curious mixture of teleological orthodox Marxism and *foquismo*; much of the analysis appears to be borrowed wholesale from Marxist–Leninist analyses then in vogue. They are remarkable for their lack of a specific analysis of Chihuahuan history or recent events in Mexico, such as the wave of strikes which had rolled through Mexico City a few years before which Gámiz had participated in. They portray no understanding of the corporative nature of the Mexican state or its ability to co-opt autonomous movements through rewards and preemptive reform. In the Resolutions—as in Giner's Chihuahua—the state offered only *palos* and no *pan*. They contained scathing attacks on the PCM and the PPS and advocated the creation of armed guerrilla groups throughout the countryside. I would suggest that the Resolutions' failure to account for the state's propensity to negotiate may have stemmed from the authors' having taken much of the analysis wholesale from a source which did not take Mexico into account.

The GPG in Mexico City and Beyond

In early 1965, members of the GPG established a headquarters in Mexico City and engaged in military training, contacted other revolutionary groups, such as the *Movimiento Revolucionario del Pueblo*, and attempted unsuccessfully to raise money for further actions in the sierra.[81] The person they trusted for military training was a former captain of the Mexican army, Lorenzo Cárdenas Barajas, who claimed to have trained Fidel Castro's companions during their years in Mexico. Cárdenas Barajas may have been acting on behalf of the National Defense Department.[82]

In spring, the National Education Ministry announced that certain teachers, among them Pablo Gómez, would be reassigned to schools far from their zone of influence to separate them from the movements they led.[83] Raúl had already been assigned to the small town of Ojinaga on the US border.

GPG members formulated a plan to assault the army barracks in Madera while still in Mexico City. It was a curious target for a group that had repeatedly announced their battle was with the state and not federal government. This insistence, however, did not accord with the revolutionary aspirations outlined in the Resolutions, which aimed at broader targets. The barracks themselves were provisional and consisted of buildings owned by Bosques de Chihuahua; they housed detachments sent to Madera in pursuit of the GPG itself.

The original plan was to assault the barracks, occupy downtown, take over the bank and the radio station, and broadcast an appeal to local campesinos to rise up in arms. The group counted on acting with some 30 to 40 combatants armed with the automatic weapons expropriated earlier. The GPG had been emboldened by previous success and judged that an action of so spectacular a character could lead the campesinos to join them in a popular guerrilla war.[84] Not everyone was comfortable with the plan, particularly Pablo Gómez who hesitated until the last minute.

Two weeks before the attack, Arturo Gámiz and Salomón Gaytan published a letter accusing Giner of cowardice and reiterated that once their goals were met and the local caciques removed and the land returned, they would lay down their arms.[85]

In early September, they left for Chihuahua City, where they met to make final plans. They typed up stencils of the Resolutions of the Sierra and printed them on a borrowed mimeograph machine, calling themselves "Ediciones Línea Revolucionaria" and joking that their ink-stained fingerprints covered the documents.[86] Some of them sequestered a taxi from Torreón to Chihuahua; they held the driver for several days then paid him a considerable sum of money and released him. Afterwards, the driver remarked, "They seemed like good kids."[87]

On the way to Madera, they encountered a number of mishaps. Salvador and Juan Antonio Gaytán travelled for a week through the sierra on foot, without provisions, carrying some 60 pounds each of automatic weaponry, which had been expropriated and stashed in various locations. They were delayed by late summer rains and neither they nor the weapons made it to the assault.

The university students sent to Madera to reconnoiter had attracted police attention, failed to find the meeting place, and gone back to the capital. Among the information they failed to relay was the fact that there were some 125 troops, not 70 soldiers, in the barracks.[88]

The group that met on the eve of the assault consisted of 14 people with a pitiful assortment of firearms, including two muskets, a single-loading shotgun, two .22s, molotov cocktails, some dynamite, and homemade grenades that failed to detonate. The plans had counted on 31 people with high-powered weapons. They decided to go ahead, planning to assault the barracks and retreat to the nearby sierra. Gámiz met arguments for waiting for arms and information with accusations of cowardice.[89]

Just before dawn, they formed a semicircle around the barracks and Ramón Mendoza shot out the light bulb above the main door. "Surrender! There's no hope!"[90] Surprise gave the guerrillas an initial advantage. Then they hesitated instead of retreating; troops fell on them from behind and cut off the retreat. The firefight lasted approximately one and a half hours. Army troops killed eight, including Gámiz, Gómez, and Salomón Gaytán. The other dead were eventually identified as Miguel Quiñonez Pedroza, director of the rural school at Ariseáchic in the Sierra Tarahumara; Rafael Martínez Valdivia, a law student at the university; Oscar Sandoval Salinas, a student at the state normal school; Antonio Escóbel Gaytán, campesino and nephew of Salomón Gaytán; and Emilio Gámiz García, state normal school student and Arturo Gámiz's younger brother. Of the thirteen, only Pablo Gómez, 39 years old and father of five children, was older than 25.

Five guerrillas escaped: Ramón Mendoza into the sierra with the help of a railway worker who shielded him behind the locomotive; Florencio Lugo, with a bullet wound in his leg; Guadalupe Escóbel Gaytán; Francisco Ornelas; and Matías Fernández.[91] Five soldiers were killed and ten were injured.[92] Some townspeople claimed that many more soldiers were killed and secretly buried; the story indicates the respect in which the guerrillas were held.[93]

The bodies of the dead guerrillas were heaved onto the back of a lumber truck and paraded around town in the rain, then dumped on the plaza and left overnight. All were mutilated, sown with machine gun fire, and Gámiz's head was shattered.

General Tiburcio Garza Zamora, Commander of the Fifth Military Zone, arrived with Giner from Chihuahua that day, where the governor had given a press conference stating, "Nothing happened here, absolutely nothing."[94] Family members arrived to claim the bodies; Giner ordered them into a common grave.[95]

Immediately after the action, the Fifth Military Zone took charge, preventing state and other federal authorities access, forbidding the autopsies required by law, and only cooperating with the federal security agency.[96] Meanwhile, the army unleashed a ferocious wave of repression, mobilizing troops and sending planes against the five survivors. Hundreds of townsfolk were arrested, stripped, and held overnight at the Madera airport, bound hand and foot. Colonel, later General, José Hernández Toledo, who presided over the attack on students in Hermosillo in 1967 and the massacre at Tlatelolco a year later, joined the search party.[97] On September 25, the state congress called on the federal government for aid, enumerating the guerrilla actions of the year before.[98]

On September 30, journalist Victor Rico Galán and photographer Rodrigo Moya travelled to Madera and Cebadilla de Dolores; their sympathetic account was published in the national magazine, *Sucesos para todos*,[99] two weeks later, receiving national attention. The UGOCM, PPS, and PCM condemned the action performed by the guerrillas.[100]

On October 31, 1965, defying military orders, Pablo Gómez's wife and niece cleaned the grave and left flowers; 500 people arrived at the cemetery two days later.[101]

Aftermath

The breakthrough in the discussion of revolutionary movements of the 1960s and 70s came with the opening of the archives of the National Security apparatus by President Vicente Fox in 2001, which allowed researchers access to long-hidden information. The opening had been intended to discredit the PRI; in fact, the documents demonstrated a depth of corruption and brutality from which the PAN itself could not claim immunity.

On September 23, 2003, Carlos Montemayor presented his novel, *Las armas del alba: Una novela*,[102] a thoroughly researched but fictional recreation of the events, in the Municipal Theatre of the City of Chihuahua, to an overflowing crowd including relatives of Lucio Cabañas and Genero Vásquez. The four surviving attackers shared the platform. Born in Parral, Chihuahua, Montemayor had left the state to attend the UNAM as a young man. He had been acquainted with members of the GPG in Chihuahua City where he had collaborated with the radical newspaper, *Acción*, and he experienced the government's attempt to portray them as criminals as a moment that changed his life.[103] His novel broke the silence that had muffled these events for decades. Montemayor later published *La fuga*,[104] about Ramón Mendoza's escape from prison, and a posthumous novel, *Las mujeres del alba*.[105] These works opened the floodgates of public memory, allowing the public discussion of matters that had been shrouded in secrecy for decades.

The Chihuahuan guerrilla movement was a turning point between old methods of struggle harkening back to the Revolution of 1910 and earlier battles on the frontier and forms derived from the New Left and its repudiation of orthodox communist movements; it opened the door to a series of armed movements whose demands went far beyond the fulfillment of the agrarian provisions of the Constitution of 1917. In the midst of the so-called Miracle—economic growth, urbanization, and the rise of a middle class—it revealed the depth of discontent, both among campesinos destined to pay the price and among students supposed to be its beneficiaries. Events in Chihuahua and throughout the Republic in the 1960s and 70s shattered whatever remained of the ruling regime's claims to a revolutionary heritage and led the way to autonomous social movements which proliferated in the following decades. Los Primeros Vientos—the first winds—swept out the old and made room for the new.

Notes

1 A version of parts of this article was published in *Chihuahua Hoy 2009*, the Interdisciplinary Annual Journal of the Universidad Autónoma de Ciudad Juárez, Chihuahua.
2 Victor Rico Galán, "De la desesperación a la muerte," *Sucesos para todos*, 13.
3 *El Heraldo de Chihuahua*, 1 October 1965, 1.
4 Francisco Ornelas Gómez, *Sueños de libertad* (Chihuahua: no publisher, 2005), 195.
5 Luis Aboites, *Breve historia de Chihuahua* (México, DF: El Colegio de México, 1994), 166.
6 The term campesino refers to smallholders of rural property, ejidatarios, and landless agricultural workers. See Christopher R. Boyer, *Becoming Campesinos* (Stanford: Stanford University Press, 2003).
7 Jesús Vargas Valdez, "Los Olvidados," *La Fragua de los Tiempos*, March 18, 2001, http://www.madera1965.com.mx/buscadocs.html (accessed April 10, 2011).
8 Ana M. Alonso, *Thread of Blood: Colonialism, Revolution, and Gender on Mexico's Northern Frontier* (Tucson: University of Arizona Press, 1995); José Fuentes Mares, *...Y México se refugió en el desierto: Luis Terrazas, historia y destino* (México: Editorial Jus, 1954); Fernando Jordán, *Crónicas de un país bárbaro* (México: Asociación Mexicana de Periodistas, 1956); Friedrich Katz, *The Life and Times of Pancho Villa* (Stanford: Stanford University Press, 1998); Alan Knight, *The Mexican Revolution* (Cambridge: Cambridge University Press, 1986); Daniel Nugent, *Spent Cartridges of Revolution: An Anthropological History of Namiquipa, Chihuahua* (Chicago: University of Chicago Press, 1993); Victor Orozco Orozco, *Diez ensayos sobre Chihuahua* (Chihuahua: Doble Hélice, 2003).
9 Julia Sweig, *Inside the Cuban Revolution* (Cambridge: Harvard University Press, 2002), 2.
10 Régis Debray, *Revolution in the Revolution? Armed Struggle and Political Struggle in Latin America* (New York: Grove Press, 1967).
11 Mexico played a double game with Cuba and the USA, relaying information to the US State Department on occasion. See Kate Doyle, "Mexico's Foreign Policy Toward Cuba," National Security Archive website, March 2, 2003, http://www.gwu.edu/%7Ensarchiv/NSAEBB/NSAEBB83/index.htm (accessed May 15, 2011).

12 María Guadalupe del Socorro López Álvarez, "Poder, desarrollo y medio ambiente en el ejido forestal 'El Largo' y sus anexos: Chihuahua (1971–1994)," MA Thesis, Universidad Autónoma Metropolitana, Unidad Xochimilco, 1996, 21–36.
13 John M. Hart, in *The Silver of the Sierra Madre* (Tucson: University of Arizona Press, 2008) discusses the working conditions in the Batopilas mine, just south of the Guerrero District.
14 See François Lartigue, *Indios y bosques: Políticas forestales y comunales en la Sierra Tarahumara* (México, DF: CIESAS, 1983); López Alvarez, op. cit., 38.
15 Katz, 12.
16 Mark Wasserman, *Capitalists, Caciques, and Revolution: The Native Elite and Foreign Enterprise in Chihuahua, Mexico, 1854–1911* (Chapel Hill: University of North Carolina Press, 1984), 104.
17 Ibid., 76.
18 See Heriberto Frías, *Tomóchic* (Chihuahua: Instituto Chihuahuense de la Cultura, 2006).
19 Alonso, op. cit.
20 Ibid., 46.
21 Samuel Truett, *Fugitive Landscapes: The Forgotten History of the U.S.–Mexico Borderlands* (New Haven: Yale, 2006), 99.
22 Miguel Angel Parra Orozco, *Oro Verde: Madera, Vida de una Región Chihuahuense* (Chihuahua: no publisher, 1998), 42–44.
23 Parra Orozco, 51; Francisco R. Almada, *El Ferrocarril de Chihuahua al Pacífico* (México: Editorial Libros de México, 1971), 158.
24 Jordán, op. cit.
25 Noé G. Palomares Peña, *Propietarios Norteamericanos y Reforma Agraria en Chihuahua, 1917–1942* (Juárez: Universidad Autónoma de Ciudad Juárez, 1991), 129–131.
26 Aboites, 160.
27 Parra Orozco, 99.
28 Aboites, 160–161.
29 Registro Agrario Nacional, Chihuahua City, 1160/23.
30 *El Heraldo de Chihuahua*, November 28, 1959, 3.
31 Fiscalía Especial para Movimientos Sociales y Políticos del Pasado, *Informe Histórico a la Sociedad Mexicana*, "Inicios de la guerrilla moderna en México," [draft version] National Security Archives, http://www.criterios.com/Documentos/050_El_inicio_de_la Guerrilla_Moderna_en_ Mexico.pdf (accessed March 15, 2006), 16.
32 Vargas Valdez, op. cit.
33 Ibid.
34 José Santos Valdés, *Madera: Razón de un Martirologio* (México, DF: no publisher, 1968), 83, 87.
35 Parra Orozco, 99.
36 There has been confusion in the secondary sources about the Mineral de Dolores and Cebadilla de Dolores. The former is a colonial mining town and the latter a community dating from the early twentieth century. Nearby is a relative term; there is no road connecting the two and they are divided by a deep arroyo.
37 RAN, Chihuahua City, 1160/23. These certificates could be granted to livestock owners to allow them to hold more land than the constitution allowed.
38 "Inicios…," 12.
39 Santos Valdés, 71.
40 AGN, DFS, Exp. 100-5-2, L-1, H-102-103.
41 Santos Valdés, 73.
42 *La Voz de Chihuahua*, May 12, 1963.
43 AGN, Exp.100-5-3, L-1, H-115 & 148.

44 Photo, http://www.madera1965.com.mx (accessed July 24, 2008).
45 AGN, DFS, Exp. 100-5-2, L1, H-135.
46 AGN, DFS, Exp. 100-5-3, L-1, H-202.
47 "Inicios…," 11.
48 Heraclio Bernal was a revolutionary bandit who fought against the Porfiriato in northern Durango.
49 Fiscalía Especial para Movimientos Sociales y Políticos del Pasado, *Informe Histórico a la Sociedad Mexicana*, "Orígenes de la guerrilla moderna en México," National Security Archives, http: www.gwu.edu/~nsarchiv/NSAEBB/NSAEBB180/index.htm (accessed November 30, 2006), 250.
50 "Inicios," 11.
51 "Madera '65: Cronología: ¿Cómo se fue Fraguando el Ataque?," *El Heraldo de Chihuahua*, September 23, 1995.
52 Carlos Montemayor, *Las armas del alba: Novela* (México, DF: Joaquín Mortiz, 2003), 165.
53 Santos Valdés, 107.
54 Laura Castellanos, *México Armado: 1943–1981* (México, DF: Ediciones Era, 2007), 74.
55 "Inicios," 12.
56 Santos Valdés, 127–129.
57 Ibid., 129.
58 "Inicios," 13.
59 Fritz Glockner, *Memoria Roja: Historia de la guerrilla en México (1943–1968)*, (México, DF: Ediciones B, 2007), 132.
60 Santo Valdés, 148.
61 Ornelas Gómez, 152.
62 "Inicios," 14.
63 Montemayor, *Las armas*, 145–146.
64 *El Correo de Chihuahua*, April 7, 1964.
65 "Madera '65," 3.
66 Ibid.
67 Ornelas Gómez, 260.
68 Glockner, 145.
69 Inicios, 10.
70 Ibid., 9.
71 Ibid., 10.
72 Ibid., 18.
73 Santos Valdés, 87.
74 "Inicios," 19.
75 Ibid., 20.
76 Ibid., 14.
77 Santos Valdés, 81–84.
78 Inicios, 18–19.
79 Marco Bellingeri, *Del agrarismo armado a la guerra de los pobres: Ensayos de guerrilla rural en el México contemporáneo, 1940–74* (México, DF: Ed. Casa Juan Pablos, 2003), 86.
80 Copies are available online on the website dedicated to the group: www.madera1965.com.mx.
81 Glockner, 180.
82 "Orígenes…," 261; also see Adela Cedillo Cedillo, "El fuego y el silencio. Historia de las Fuerzas de Liberación Nacional Mexicanas (1969–1974)," BA Thesis, UNAM, 2008, 112–113 for counter-argument.
83 Santos Valdés, 134.

84 Montemayor, *Las armas*, 128–133.
85 Castellanos, 65.
86 Orozco Orozco, 254.
87 Ibid., 251–253.
88 Montemayor, *Las armas*, 133–139.
89 Ibid, 203.
90 Glockner, 194.
91 Both Lugo and Ornelas have published *testimonies*: Florencio Lugo, *23 de septiembre de 1965: El asalto al cuartel de Madera* (México, DF: Yaxkin AC, 2007); Ornelas Gómez, op. cit.
92 *El Heraldo de Chihuahua*, September 24, 1.
93 Ornelas Gómez, 204.
94 Rico Galán, op. cit.
95 Montemayor, *Las armas*, 72.
96 "Inicios," 24.
97 Orígenes, 265.
98 Santos Valdés, 123–124.
99 Rico Galán, op. cit.
100 Glockner, 207.
101 Orígenes, 267.
102 Montemayor, *Las armas*, op. cit.
103 Mónica Mateos-Vega, "Existe otro México clandestino más peligroso que la guerrilla: Entrevista con Carlos Montemayor," *La Jornada*, February 28, 2007, online (accessed May 29, 2008).
104 Carlos Montemayor, *La fuga* (México, DF: Fondo de Cultura Economica, 2007).
105 Carlos Montemayor, *Las mujeres del alba* (México, DF: Grijalbo, 2010).

2

SEIZING HOLD OF MEMORIES IN MOMENTS OF DANGER

Guerrillas and Revolution in Guerrero, Mexico

Alexander Aviña

> Articulating the past historically does not mean recognizing it "the way it really was." It means appropriating a memory as it flashes up in a moment of danger …
> —Walter Benjamin, *On the Concept of History*

Cadmus in Guerrero

In Greek mythology, Cadmus founded the city of Thebes after a long journey that initially saw him fruitlessly search for a sister who had been abducted by Zeus. At the famous oracle of Delphi, Cadmus was told to abandon the search and instead follow a sacred cow. This cow, the oracle enjoined, would lead him to a site where he was to found a city. Having reached the future site of Thebes, a number of Cadmus' companions, sent to fetch water at a nearby spring, met an untimely end, killed by a ferocious dragon. Cadmus vanquished the dragon and, following Athena's advice, sowed its teeth in the ground. A group of fierce warriors called Spartoí instantly sprang from the ground and fought one another after Cadmus cast a stone amongst them. Five surviving Spartoí, along with Cadmus, went on to build the Citadel of Thebes and found the city.

A figure akin to Cadmus haunts the (until recently) unchallenged and hegemonic historiography on the Latin American Lefts that emerged in the immediate aftermath of World War II and continued into the not-so Cold War years. Mimicking earlier narratives that emanated from national security and counterinsurgent-minded regional elites (Ranajit Guha warned us of this long ago), scholars like Jorge Castañeda, David Stoll, and Hal Brands explained the emergence of a Latin American armed guerrilla left during the 1960s by positing a guerrilla Cadmus figure complete with beret, unkempt beard, and utopian dreams of a Castroist Cuba.[1] Largely middle-class, urban, and innately radical, these guerrilla Cadmuses traveled into the rural hinterlands and urban slums of Latin America after 1959, sowed dragon teeth into the ground, and led hapless locals into suicidal, violent adventures. In the process, the guerrilla Cadmuses provoked Latin American militaries to unleash terror, dirty wars, and, in most cases, violent dictatorships. Utopian, vanguardist and ultra-left violence begat state terroristic violence. The guerrilla devil unleashed the military devil and civilian populations suffered equivalent terror from both sides.[2]

Lucio Cabañas provides the historically-grounded counterpoint from the southwestern Mexican state of Guerrero. In May 1973, six years after he escaped an assassination attempt at the hands of state police forces and fled to the mountains that tower above Guerrero's Pacific coastline, the rural schoolteacher-turned-guerrilla leader provided a history lesson to the gathered rural and urban guerrillas. He detailed a much longer history, one that began not with a group of innately radical Cadmuses dreaming of revolution, but with a series of constitutionally-based civic social movements that began in late-1950s Guerrero and ended in state-sponsored massacres. In didactic schoolteacher fashion, Cabañas outlined a historical process of gradual popular radicalization that began with the massacres of campesinos, students, and workers in 1960–1962 who peacefully marched demanding the fulfillment of constitutional rights; continued with the everyday assassinations of social dissidents and protestors in 1963–1967; and, culminated with a series of military counterinsurgency campaigns that violently targeted all civilians in 1967–1973. We took to the mountains, Cabañas explained, "because the government came to assassinate, to burn, to kill, to execute,"

> ... first the government arrived killing, persecuting, jailing, beating, raping ... with its wealthy gunmen, its white guards, its state police forces, killing the people and attacking communities ... but we fought back, we [the guerillas] arrived and fired back.[3]

All this occurred, he concluded, before he and Genaro Vázquez—another schoolteacher-turned-guerrilla leader—organized separate armed movements in Guerrero. "And those who work hard [peasants and workers] know this."[4]

Until recently, and with important watershed exceptions, few historical works challenged what I dub as the Cadmus interpretations of the Cold War Latin American guerrilla left.[5] The Cadmus narrative, like the modern counterinsurgency theories it bears a striking resemblance to, treat popular "organic" insurgencies as an impossibility, an "unthinkable event"[6] that presupposes an inherent inability on the part of the popular masses to self-organize, resist, and make revolutions. Hence, the need to posit outside radicalized agitators ("terrorists" or "accidental guerrillas" in current parlance),[7] in Cuban and/or Soviet garb, as the guerrilla apostle instigators of armed movements doomed to defeat. The masses can only react in some uncontrollable Pavlovian animalistic fashion—a reaction readily susceptible to outside manipulation, direction, and interests. This conceptualization of popular political culture and praxis (or lack thereof) itself is based on the following presupposition: popular violence and revolutionary terror spring from ideological sources imbued with utopian zeal. Timeless, metaphysical utopian ideas that always lead to terror take the place of historical context and process.

In contrast, Cabañas' talk cited earlier reveals a different history. His analysis grounds the causes of processual popular radicalization within a broader social field in which violence structured social relations. He holds local-regional political and economic elites responsible for violently repressing reformist popular civic movements that simply demanded the application of guaranteed constitutional rights. As popular mobilizations based on the 1917 Constitution and ideals of the Mexican Revolution continued and again experienced state terror, guerrerenses like Cabañas experienced an instance of the Hegelian "negation of the negation."[8] They moved from viewing the ruling Institutional Revolutionary Party (PRI) as illegitimate to conceptualizing PRI state power itself as illegitimate, as usurpation and betrayal; hence, the need to wage revolution.[9] Cabañas and hundreds of guerrerense smallholding and middling peasants, students, and schoolteachers—supported by dozens of communities—took to the mountains as both a political response to a decade-long campaign of state terror, and as a revolutionary attempt to create a form of political organization of power ruled by the "poor." From elsewhere in Guerrero, Vázquez, the leader of those early popular civic movements, experienced a similar process of radicalization as he embarked on a revolutionary guerrilla campaign of national liberation.

This chapter explores how the peasant guerrilla organizations led by Cabañas and Vázquez, the Party of the Poor (PDLP) and the National Revolutionary Civic Association (ACNR) respectively, historically emerged as the cumulative armed phase of a protracted social struggle—a social struggle in which state and elite terror committed against reformist movements radicalized broad sectors of Guerrero's largely rural population who chose to actively support two revolutionary guerrilla movements by the late 1960s. To understand the ACNR and PDLP guerrilla movements, this chapter employs what historian Steve J. Stern termed "multiple time scales;" that is, an approach that contextualizes the insurgencies within a longer history of peasant politics and mobilizations and the more immediate "moments of fluidity and rupture" represented by the 1960s.[10] Such an approach reveals both guerrilla insurgencies as complex and historical processes with deep and profound roots and speaks to the chronic irresolution of rural problems in Mexico. Indeed, it represents an urgent and pressing form of historical interpretation considering that guerrillas presently continue to (re)emerge in rural Guerrero.

A Burning Patience: 1910–1960

> In the dawn, armed with a burning patience shall we enter the Splendid Cities.
> —Arthur Rimbaud, *A Season in Hell*

In twentieth-century Guerrero, history implacably fails to stay in its place as dictated by the "empty, homogenous"[11] construct of capitalist-modernity time: that place is a far-removed, disconnected past. Memories saturate the cultural topography of the state's heterogeneous regions. Execution sites, like the Pozo Meléndez outside of Iguala or the trees of the "Trozadura" near Atoyac, stand in as reminders of unresolved social conflicts and the deadly costs of defying the powerful and the wealthy. Last names like Zapata, Cabañas, Escudero, and Figueroa situate entire families' places within such social conflict: on the side of the rebellious poor or with the reactionary forces. As Lucio Cabañas reminded an audience of PDLP campesino supporters, combatants, and visiting urban guerrillas in 1973 when discussing the likely incoming state governor, Rubén Figueroa: "... that relative and descendant of the Figueroa family that betrayed the struggle of [Emiliano] Zapata [during the 1910s] ... you know ... the family from Guerrero that allowed itself to be used against Zapata."[12] Zapata's struggle, as part of the Mexican Revolution some 60 years removed from the PDLP guerrilla movement, remained alive in rural Guerrero—as did its regional political-military defeat at the hands of the rancher Figueroa family.[13] Yet, defeat failed to dislodge powerful ideas unleashed by the Zapatista movement in Guerrero; namely, the conviction that the masses govern their country under the banner of local (patriarchal) democracy and economic justice (agrarian reform).

Yet, it took some time for those radical Zapatista ideals to gain a foothold in the region and amalgamate with longer held, local "hidden transcripts" of municipal democracy and democratic-patriarchal land tenure. For despite Guerrero's standing as the only other state beside Morelos to claim an official Zapatista governorship in 1914–1915, its coastal regions remained hesitant until the early 1920s. When local Zapatista officers Pablo, Pedro, and Tiburcio Cabañas returned to their Costa Grande homes, intending to implement the radical political and economic precepts of the 1917 Constitution, they helped to locally redefine Zapatismo "as a broad struggle of all the poor."[14] Carmen Téllez, a campesina from the coastal municipality of Atoyac, recalled, "[General] Pablo Cabañas did not mess with Madero, Carranza or Obregón ... he only wanted the lands of the sierra not belong to the rich and wealthy of Atoyac."[15] Elaborating an emotionally-laden and radical class discourse that pitted the "poor" against the "wealthy" (campesinos versus caciques) aided the Cabañas' as they organized and struggled throughout the 1920s to make manifest hard-fought constitutional rights in the everyday lives of peasants and workers. The arena for such struggles, at least initially, was a constitutional one. Intractable regional power-holders and their privately financed paramilitary guards—not to mention the continued civil strife at the national level—ensured that the arena became violent. Campesino responses subsequently combined legal, constitutionally-based political activity with self-defense guerrilla activity and military actions.[16] "Taking up arms" and fleeing to the mountains took its place alongside lawsuits, the organizing of leftist political parties and rural unions, and sending appeals for presidential help.

Popular attempts to democratize regional politics and economic production, continually attacked with a violent ferocity by regional oligarchs, failed to win many national political allies. At least, not until 1934, according to popular campesino memories. "No [politician] remembered the agrarian law, no one could enforce respect for the Constitution," a Costa Grande campesino recalled, "until the arrival of Cárdenas, who with such facility distributed land ... and fulfilled his campaign promises to change the living conditions of the campesino class of Atoyac."[17] The arrival of Lázaro Cárdenas, military veteran of the Revolution and former governor of the state of Michoacán, to the presidential office in 1934 seemed to indicate the beginnings of the "redemption"[18] of a Mexican Revolution gone astray during the 1920s; or, at least his political discourse indicated so during a months-long presidential campaign that took him all over Mexico. As president, Cárdenas institutionalized and legitimized some of the demands articulated by Guerrero's campesinos during the 1920s and early 1930s: agrarian reform, redistribution of arable lands, credit, irrigation systems, and rural infrastructural development. In doing so, in implementing economic and political reforms enshrined in the 1917 Constitution, the president seemingly evinced that the post-revolutionary state could fulfill revolutionary promises.[19]

Cárdenas and Cardenismo thus became key cultural referents in regional campesino political cultures of coastal Guerrero. Many campesinos embraced agrarian reform based on the ejido (collective landholding) model and organized to obtain those other promises articulated by Cárdenas: agricultural technology, credit, schools, roads, and hospitals.[20] Coffee-producing campesinos in the municipality of Atoyac like Rosendo Radilla[21] believed such promises indicated that, as Cárdenas declared in 1934, "progress would be socialized [and] campesinos would constitute the principal beneficiaries of economic development."[22] The populist president's ruling tenure was subsequently remembered as a time when the post-revolutionary state embodied the driving utopias and promises unleashed by the 1910 Revolution because it collaborated with campesinos in their favor. Ensuing presidential administrations would face popular evaluations and criticisms fundamentally based on comparisons with the constantly re-imagined Cardenista "utopia"[23]—a utopia challenged at every instance during and after the *michoacano* president's tenure. *Cacicazgos* became resilient Hydras in the Mexican countryside.[24]

After 1940, economic power assumed new and different last names in coastal Guerrero. Jacinto, Bautista, Blanco Téllez, Becerra Luna, and García[25] all pointed to the existence of transparent social relations between elites and campesinos—made all the more transparent by the willingness of these elites to wield violence—in contrast to a fetishism of commodities "abound in metaphysical subtleties and theological niceties."[26] White Guard guns and assassinations of non-conformist campesinos assumed the place of such subtleties and niceties. Caciques and cacicazgos, long a basic form of the organization of political and economic power in the state, weathered popular revolutions and social democratic legislation—new times brought new caciques. Campesino smallholders engaged in coffee and copra production on Guerrero's Pacific coastline during the 1940s knew which cacique families monopolized and controlled access to processing machinery, transportation networks, and markets. They knew who cornered the markets, undersold smallholder producers, provided credit at exorbitant debt-peonage rates, and ordered murders. Despite losing land and political clout during the Cárdenas years, Guerrero's agrarian bourgeoisie—first linked to Spanish merchants houses prior to the 1930s, followed by transnational corporations beginning in the late 1940s—refigured itself as a commercial bourgeoisie able to slowly and forcefully co-opt political power.[27]

Yet, campesino challengers to the post-1940 economic and political system of domination possessed potentially powerful weapons in their arsenal: popular interpretations of the Mexican Constitution and 1910 revolutionary legacies; and, a subaltern political palimpsest that combined long-held demands for local democracy and land with a Cardenista populist vision of economic development that emphasized the laboring masses over national and foreign capital. As it embarked on a path of capitalist modernization based on industrialization and large-scale agrobusiness, and centralized political rule, the PRI regimes after 1940 nonetheless felt compelled (and constrained) to heed revolutionary histories that marked out different national paths to the future. The PRI, indeed, proved quite adept at co-opting popular interpretations of the 1910 revolution and radical heroes.

The post-1940 PRI regime, though, played a dangerous game in its attempt to garner and possess revolutionary and moral legitimacy—particularly when its articulated revolutionary-nationalist discourse failed to match a program of inequitable capitalist development and one-party political rule. Popular movements that emerged during the 1940s and 50s to protest PRI policies tactically exposed the gap between revolutionary discourse and reactionary policies to reveal the rollback of key social reform policies carried out by presidents Manuel Ávila Camacho and Miguel Alemán Valdés (1940–1952). They challenged modifications to agrarian reform law that practically ended the institutional redistribution of land and changes to the labor codes that severely restricted workers' rights in the name of "national unity." Movements in Morelos, Mexico City, and the northern states resisted President Alemán's elevation of rapid industrialization into what historian Barry Carr characterized as a "state religion"—a policy that repositioned the countryside as subsidizer of capitalist modernization.[28] And they did so using the Constitution while decrying a PRI betrayal of the revolution.

Popular mobilizations in Guerrero during the 1950s shared the tactics and discourse utilized by these movements. They worked within the legal arena and based their diverse demands on the Constitution: land, schools, labor rights, agricultural credit, infrastructural development geared toward small and middling rural producers, and municipal autonomy. For they sensed a regional and national betrayal of their constitutional rights. Independent rural unions, in particular, highlighted the exclusionary aspects of an exploitative modernization. Organized copra and coffee-producing campesinos in the 1950s, motivated by a vision of economy democracy sustained by the Constitution, challenged and sought to undermine a rural system of domination that fused political and economic power in the hands of regional caciques willing to use terror as a means of social control. That rural vision of economic democracy, essentially involving a collective campesino takeover of the production and exchange processes, suggested the continued existence of unredeemed revolutionary promises and constitutional rights.[29] Subsequent PRI regime responses in the form of hesitant piecemeal reforms, the co-optation of movement leaders, and (increasingly) violence only bolstered the case that something was rotten in Guerrero and throughout rural Mexico.

1960

1960 marked the beginnings of a new framework of political communication between the governing PRI and the campesinos, workers, and middle classes of Guerrero. Political theorists like Giorgio Agamben would describe the framework as a (counterinsurgent) "state of exception" in which the Mexican state reduced the citizens of Guerrero to a "bare life," as mere objects of state power (not political subject-citizens) whose biological existence depended on the behest of the Mexican state.[30] This counterinsurgent state of exception gradually developed throughout the 1960s in response to a series of state-wide popular movements that demanded, generally, the redemption of their civic rights as Mexican citizens. State violence and terror became instruments of rule to confront and destroy new political democratic forms developed by a populace in Guerrero that demanded the end of boss politics and a more equitable form of economic development based on constitutional precepts. By the late 1960s recurrent state terror, in the form of massacres and everyday violence, committed against peaceful and reformist popular movements, radicalized and convinced many guerrerenses of the necessity of armed resistance and rebellion.

The subsequent "dirty war"—a less theoretical name for state of exception—unleashed by the Mexican military convinced even more. A "new" revolution, they concluded, was needed.

Yet, in the late 1950s, such revolutionary thoughts proved practically non-existent in Guerrero. Still poor, overwhelmingly rural and agricultural, and on the peripheries of the "Mexican Miracle," guerrerenses who participated in large-scale political movements remained squarely within a civic and constitutional framework. They, like contemporary electoral movements in San Luis Potosí, land invasions in Chihuahua, and national labor strikes, expected the governing PRI to live up to its constitutional responsibilities and its self-fashioned historical legacy as the "institutionalized revolution" or the "revolution turned into government." In the midst of a Cold War and a few hundred miles from a Cuban Revolution that functioned as a sort of judgmental-comparative mirror, the regime essentially faced a governance test put forth by a series of national and regional popular movements. Guerrero provided one such test in 1959.

Only three state governors had served out their entire gubernatorial terms in the history of Guerrero. By 1959, General Raúl Caballero Aburto faced an unprecedented state-wide and multi-class social movement that threatened to prevent him from becoming the fourth governor. A long-time military man originally from Guerrero yet lacking regional cacique or popular bases of support, the general ruled the state as his own personal barracks beginning in 1957. He packed the state government with family members who demonstrated a penchant for corruption, embezzlement of public funds, and violence. Disregarding the constitutionally enshrined popular demand for local democracy, the general imposed his candidates for municipal presidencies throughout the state—in general, bad political choices according to embedded agents working for the *Dirección Federal de Seguridad* (DFS, Federal Security Directorate).[31] Imposed municipal presidents, for example, in Coyuca de Benítez and Tlacotepec possessed personal histories of criminality that included accusations of murder. The implementation of new taxes and fees that largely targeted the state's lower and middling classes also contributed to the governor's unpopularity. His public safety "depistolization" programs, as a later DFS report posited, ultimately provoked state-wide popular mobilizations seeking his removal.[32]

For the general, using five police bodies under his direct control, transformed the depistolization program into a campaign of repression, extrajudicial killings, and the criminalization of public protest. By January 1959, a telegram sent by a courageous newspaper director from Acapulco to future president Gustavo Díaz Ordaz, described the murders of at least 1,000 guerrerenses at the hands of state police forces that contained criminal gunmen loyal to the general.[33] The terror served a purpose: the use of violent criminals-turned-police-officers enabled and ensured the nepotism, extortion, and illicit enrichment that characterized the Caballero governorship.[34]

Guerrerenses responded in 1959 with the creation of a state-wide, multi-class, and democratic social movement that began with one demand: the removal of General Caballero as governor. Urban middle-class professionals, small businesspersons, teachers, and low-ranking state bureaucrats joined campesinos, urban labor unions, students, disaffected PRI militants and local politicians to create a hegemonic bloc that acted upon President Adolfo López Mateos suggestion that "caciques remain in power as long as the community tolerates them."[35] Spearheaded by the Guerrerense Civic Association (ACG) and its young leader Genaro Vázquez—working within a broader umbrella organization dubbed the Coalition of Popular Forces (COP)—the social movement that initially demanded "death to bad government" developed into something more powerful. In the course of two years of social struggle characterized by civil disobedience, marches, protests, sit-ins, strikes, and violent responses from Caballero, the *cívicos* (as ACG members were known) and their allies forged a democratic definition of citizenship based on active mobilization in defense and application of constitutional rights. Or, in the words of one participant, "what took place some fifty years ago is happening today in Guerrero ... back then the people saved itself through the use of arms while today that struggle is conducted with the weapons of law."[36]

Genaro Vázquez and Lucio Cabañas emerged as key social activists and leaders during the two-year struggle waged against Caballero. Their participation represented the convergence of two different (though not exclusive) political trajectories of social activists. Older and educated in Mexico City during the 1950s at the National Teacher Training School, Vázquez possessed a history of activism and organizing by the time he helped found the ACG in 1959. He participated in the 1958 teachers strike and take over of the Secretariat of Public Education building led by Othón Salazar and the Revolutionary Teacher's Movement (MRM). In addition to his work as an urban schoolteacher, Vázquez worked with guerrerense campesino organizations as their official representative before the Agrarian Department in Mexico City—a relationship that later enabled him to recruit independent labor unions to the ACG movement. Politically and ideologically "anti-party" and non-sectarian, Vázquez thus developed as an activist in Mexico City (while never losing contact with Guerrero as he told an interviewer during his later guerrilla days) prominently engaged in independent union struggles and strikes—fully embracing the revolutionary-nationalist legacies of 1910 and 1917.[37]

Cabañas, in contrast, emerged from a rural network of provincial teacher training schools expanded during the 1930s by Cárdenas. Noted for their radicalism, one that combined Cardenista, liberal, and socialist influences, these schools trained the sons and daughters of campesinos to become rural schoolteachers. In practice, they produced what Gramsci coined as organic intellectuals that assisted local communities in matters beyond classroom walls: from hygiene and agricultural methods to organizing campesinos into unions and cooperatives.[38] An entire generation of rural schoolteachers served as the articulators of local grievances against the state.[39] Additionally, Cabañas came from a family that produced famous Zapatista officers who waged guerrilla rebellions during the 1920s and participated in the Cardenista agrarian reform of the 1930s. During the ACG movement against Caballero, Cabañas studied at the Rural Teacher Training School of Ayotzinapa, cradle of Guerrero communism, where he later obtained his rural schoolteacher title and joined the Mexican Communist Party (PCM). Years later as a guerrilla leader, Cabañas would utilize both networks, the *normales rurales* and the PCM, to help sustain and develop the PDLP guerrilla insurgency.[40]

By the end of 1960, General Caballero ruled the state in name only. The broad, widespread social movement he provoked spread throughout the state, resulting in daily protests, general strikes, and the peaceful takeover of some municipal governments. As ACG and COP leaders gathered evidence to indict the general before the federal congress, rank and file cívicos organized sit-ins in the capital city of Chilpancingo—resulting in their constant attack by state police forces and newly arrived army troops in November 1960. That same month, to commemorate the fiftieth anniversary of the Mexican Revolution, 20,000 guerrerenses silently marched in the streets of Chilpancingo. They carried signs that demanded General Caballero's resignation, proclaimed the death of the Revolution, and pledged loyalty to President López Mateos. At the end of the march collective singing of the national anthem broke the silence, as did a number of speakers who reaffirmed "our struggle was framed within state and federal laws, especially within that marked by the state constitution of Guerrero."[41] The state's response proved different. A massacre perpetrated by army troops erupted on December 30, 1960 in Chilpancingo when soldiers shot an electrician who attempted to hang a banner on a light-post that read "Death to Bad Government." The subsequent military attack against civilian protestors left at least 23 dead, 40 wounded, and 55 tortured in a series of clandestine, makeshift prisons.[42] Days later, the Senate voted to remove the general from his post.

The 1960 Chilpancingo massacre failed to demobilize the social movement that emerged to confront General Caballero or change its strategy of demanding political and socioeconomic reforms via constitutional pathways. Yet something changed. For the social movement produced new political democratic forms, independent and acting from without PRI party parameters, that forced the ruling party to face a populace in Guerrero that demanded the end of boss politics. How would the PRI respond to a social movement that forced it to match revolutionary-nationalist discourse with practice?

In retrospect, the Chilpancingo massacre seemingly provided the answer. Pragmatism and negotiation, as predominant methods of rule, gave way to terror and massacres. Historian Sergio Aguayo suggests that the Chilpancingo massacre (among other contemporary regional instances of state violence) offered a model for the later PRI planners of the 1968 Tlatelolco student massacre.[43] In Guerrero, beginning in 1961, it offered an immediate model for more massacres committed against guerrerenses who continued to press for profound political and socioeconomic reform. When the ACG transformed itself into an opposition political party for the 1962 state elections it faced daily harassment, the illegal detention of party leaders (including Vázquez), and election fraud. Using a more explicit class discourse, the ACG formed into a political party, as it announced to poor campesinos from Iguala in September 1962, to struggle for "a true democracy that highlights and resolves the economic problems of the humble people and the implementation of social justice."[44] "With the Mexican Constitution in hand [working] within the Law," the ACG suffered another massacre in Iguala on December 30, 1962.[45] In the aftermath of the Iguala massacre, ACG and other dissidents lived a "Terror in Guerrero" that included extrajudicial executions, torture, and the razing of entire communities throughout 1963 and 1964.[46] By the end of 1963 such terror had convinced Vázquez—and many more guerrerenses—that "the electoral path does not resolve problems and the secret and universal vote is a bourgeois trick."[47]

"Two projects of the same political phenomenon:"[48] The ACNR and PDLP

If the 1960s began with promises of democracy and revolutionary redemption, the decade waned amidst a climate of violence and the criminalization of dissidence. Popular demands for socio-economic justice and political reform, based on constitutional rights, ended in bloodbaths and the quotidian persecution of popular protest. The intransigence of the PRI and its use of terror stimulated a gradual and uneven process of popular radicalization. For schoolteachers and social activists like Vázquez and Cabañas, this process entailed political travels and experiences within a fractured old Mexican Left largely represented by Marxist political parties and labor unions; and a critical engagement with Marxism "as a theory of how to understand and act in the world."[49] This process of critical engagement, amidst a context characterized by political persecution and flight from government agents, offered new political routes in the aftermath of violently shutdown constitutional channels of redress.

As he studied with "heretical" communists expelled from the PCM in Mexico City during the mid-1960s, Vázquez continued his work of organizing popular protests and independent peasant unions in Guerrero that sought an economic and political democracy fundamentally based on popular interpretations of the 1910 revolution. He participated in the Cardenista revival of revolutionary nationalism tinged with anti-imperialist sentiments fired by the Cuban Revolution represented by the Movement of National Liberation (MLN) in 1961–1962. Collaboration with PCM experiments in creating a national peasant union and a popular electoral front during the mid-1960s only led Vázquez to the "round universe of Stalinist reformism" and internal sectarian fights.[50] Cabañas, in contrast, engaged the Marxism of the PCM through the lens of a rural schoolteacher immersed in the local forestry and land struggles of peasant communities in which he worked in 1963–1964.[51] While he participated in the same leftist political movements at the national level as Vázquez, though often in opposition to his ACG comrade as a PCM militant, Cabañas remained committed to local community struggles that protected ejidal lands and natural resources from encroaching caciques and multi-national corporations.

Such political experiences and travels (at the national, regional, and local levels) grounded the developing Marxist ideologies of Vázquez and Cabañas in the everyday experiences of poor and middling guerrerenses. Social praxis shaped and fashioned the heterodox revolutionary Marxisms that both men employed in their gradual transition from Old Left social activists to New Left guerrilla leaders. In the course of violently suppressed social struggles throughout the 1960s, Vázquez and Cabañas intimately learned that the accumulation of past injustices (e.g. massacres) along with the unfulfilled promises of 1910 could—and later did—mobilize a widespread radicalized base of popular support for rebellion. They learned, to quote Walter Benjamin, that revolution entailed a "tiger's leap into the past" nourished by "the picture of enslaved forebears, not the ideal of emancipated heirs."[52] Popular struggles, in sum, contoured the development of heterodox and "parochialized"[53] Marxisms grounded in local-regional histories of rebellion; informed by international revolutions and guerrilla redefinitions of Marxism; nourished by sentiments of redemptive vengeance; and, fueled by the redeemed promise of a nation ruled by the laboring masses. In other words, to paraphrase George Orwell, justice and liberty formed the pillars of the ideologically "unsound" Marxisms of Vázquez and Cabañas.[54]

If state terror ultimately stimulated popular radicalization and the emergence of guerrilla insurgency as a political option, the political persecution of Vázquez and Cabañas provided the igniting spark. The de facto suspension of constitutional rights in Guerrero, legally codified by a 1965 state law that criminalized dissent, forced Vázquez to assume a semi-clandestine life avoiding state agents and arrest warrants. Cabañas had already been expelled from the state in 1965, transferred by education authorities to the northern state of Durango for his participation in successful community movements against local cacique interests. Authorities in Durango returned the schoolteacher in 1966 after Cabañas organized a women's union in his school's community and participated in a multi-class civic movement that demanded the creation of a local steel industry.[55] Later that year, Guerrero state police forces unlawfully detained Vázquez in front of the MLN office in Mexico City and took him to the state prison in Iguala. "The most dangerous agitator of the state,"[56] as DFS analysts characterized the ACG leader, would languish in that prison for nearly two years, avoiding assassination attempts. From his prison cell, Vázquez called for "the development and consolidation of the Vanguard Proletarian Party [for] the Armed Political Combat of the Masses." In other words, he exhorted national liberation to overthrow "an oligarchic pro-imperialist and neocolonial" PRI regime.[57]

As Vázquez remained in jail plotting his escape, Cabañas became embroiled in another community movement—this time in Atoyac where he joined a group of poor families who demanded the ousting of an unpopular school rector generally perceived as corrupt and arbitrary. By April 1967, local schoolteachers, activists, and campesinos joined the movement that radicalized in the face of obdurate municipal and state governments. They soon demanded the liberation of political prisoners, including Vázquez, and the removal of the state governor who, according to numerous popular organizations, led "a government of Bad caciques."[58] After the movement's participants took over Atoyac's main plaza with a sit-in, local oligarchs and caciques began to issue violent threats. On May 18, 1967 as Cabañas began his speech to the protestors, state police forces fired into the crowd, killing seven and wounding dozens. The massacre only stopped when soldiers stationed in Atoyac intervened.[59] With the help of the local populace, and a network of rural schoolteachers, Cabañas escaped into the neighboring Sierra del Sur mountain range. Months later in August another massacre rocked coastal Guerrero. Rank and file copra workers who attempted to democratically retake their union in Acapulco were ambushed by state police officers, paramilitary guards, and paid gunmen. They killed, depending on the source, 23 to 40 copra workers and wounded hundreds more.[60] Popular rage spread throughout the region. For the people could endure bad government, corrupt officials and poverty, Cabañas observed, "but not massacres, that cannot be endured."[61]

State terror, as a ruling tactic used by a PRI regime unwilling to implement political and socio-economic reforms, thus produced guerrillas. The continued massacres of civilians, by the end of 1967, created a popular political climate amenable to insurgency as a form of exacting peasant vengeance. Campesino leader Hilario Mesino recalled that time when "we [campesinos] were angry."[62] Cabañas too recalled that campesinos from the mountain communities surrounding Atoyac wanted to descend on the city with machetes in hand to attack the "rich merchants" they blamed for the May 1967 massacre. Red and black graffiti slogans began to appear on walls in Atoyac while sustained whispers of killing the "rich" frightened local caciques and businesspersons.[63]

The transformation of cities like Atoyac into "fortresses" controlled by army battalions after the 1967 massacres only raised the ire of campesinos that complained of intrusive searches conducted by soldiers.[64] This populace, composed largely of poor and middling campesinos and *ejidatarios*, wanted vengeance. They wanted a *Vehmgericht* "to take vengeance for the misdeeds of the ruling class."[65]

By the end of 1968, such political sentiments of vengeance materialized into widespread popular support for the separate guerrilla organizations led by Vázquez and Cabañas—a support noted in recently declassified intelligence documents.[66] Following his dramatic prison escape in April of that year, Vázquez transformed the ACG into the guerrilla ACNR in the mountains near Atoyac. In the course of four years, using a state-wide support network forged initially during the 1960 social movement against General Caballero and linked to urban cells in Mexico City, the ACNR attempted to create a revolutionary antechamber for national liberation in Guerrero. In a 1971 interview, Vázquez provided the necessary steps for the revolutionary process: first, the establishment of popular bases of support to sustain the ACNR; second, the projection of armed actions on the national level in collaboration with other organizations; and, subsequently, coordinating continental movements throughout Latin America to defeat US imperialism.[67]

Yet the successful transition from a multi-class civic social movement to revolutionary peasant guerrilla group proved practically impossible. Vázquez and an ACNR combat group that rarely numbered more than 30, never fully completed the first step described above. The (in)famous public status of Vázquez, along with his highly publicized prison escape, led state authorities to concentrate their military counterinsurgency campaigns on the ACNR and its support network—unconstitutional campaigns that committed rape, torture, and murder against suspected ACNR collaborators and their communities.[68] The use of high-profile kidnappings to obtain ransom money and liberate imprisoned guerrillas, too, kept regime attention focused on the ACNR as it constantly harassed and attacked the group in the coastal mountains of Guerrero from 1969 to 1972. By early 1972, Vázquez and a small number of guerrillas sought sanctuary in Cuernavaca and Mexico City. After leaving Mexico City for the state of Michoacán on February 2, 1972, their car crashed near the city of Morelia. The official government version stated that Vázquez died as a result of the accident. The guerrilla version, sustained by his widow Consuelo Solís and second-in-command José Bracho, contends that soldiers killed the guerrilla leader by striking him in the head with a rifle.[69]

In contrast to Vázquez (and aided by the government's focus on the ACNR), Cabañas managed to organize a mass revolutionary organization that began as a kind of campesino tribunal (*Vehmgericht*) targeting local caciques in late 1967 and later became a peasant guerrilla force of at least 240 combatants that ambushed

Mexican military detachments in 1972–1974—and managed to organize short-lived guerrilla cells in at least three other states.[70] From 1967 to 1974, the PDLP and its military wing, the Campesino Brigade of Executions (BCA)—note the connotation of class terror—waged a popularly-supported "revolution of the poor" in order to overthrow the PRI ("the government of the rich") and create a national political community "in which the poor govern everything."[71] Bringing to mind Robespierre's famous quote about popular justice and thunderbolts, the PDLP announced in May 1969 after making its first public appearance that "when we begin to kill, tyrants will die, the same tyrants that ordered the executions of campesinos and students … it's our generation's turn to exact demands from the Priísta government that betrayed the [1910] revolution."[72] In essence, the PDLP waged a revolution both fueled by a contemporary campesino socialist understanding of class war as the rich versus the poor and enriched by memories of a betrayed past revolution. This revolution of the poor displayed subversive utopian imaginings of worlds not yet born but rooted in visions of an unredeemed past refracted through the present—a present characterized by state terror, massacres, and authoritarianism.

Conclusion

> … the prophetic gaze that catches fire from the summits of the past.
> —Walter Benjamin[73]

Like the ACNR's struggle for national liberation, the PDLP's revolution of the poor ultimately failed militarily. For the PRI regime and its security apparatuses knew that popular support constituted the key to the PDLP's military successes in 1972–1973. Thus the regime ordered a vast military counterinsurgency campaign that brutally attacked the familial, neighborhood, syndical, community and municipal networks that nourished the PDLP—and, importantly, those networks and communities that attempted to remain neutral in the struggle. Counterinsurgency campaigns operated on the premise that all campesinos concealed an inner guerrilla sensibility. Rape, torture, disappearances, death flights, strategic hamlets, the rationing of food and medicine, and the razing of villages turned coastal Guerrero into a theater of war. Conservative estimates list 500 to 1,000 guerrerenses that remain "disappeared" to this day.[74]

The scope and furious intensity of the military counter-guerrilla operations implied the success Cabañas and the PDLP enjoyed in recruiting support from dozens of Costa Grande communities—and the political threat they represented to the ruling regime. With a revolutionary Marxism grounded in local-regional traditions of rebellion, rural understandings of class warfare,[75] and sentiments of redemptive vengeance, the PDLP achieved high levels of peasant support noted by internal military documents. Yet, terror eventually succeeded in physically isolating the guerrilla movements from broader nonviolent social movements, a resurgent national labor mobilization, and from their peasant support base. Counterinsurgency operations effectively and brutally corralled the guerrillas in coastal Guerrero; in turn, contouring an increasing ACNR and PDLP militarism—to the detriment of political organizing and cultivating popular support—that sought to disrupt the military's siege of the state. State terror thus secured a short-term military victory for the PRI regime but failed to defeat the political ideas and utopias unearthed and re-imagined by the ACNR and PDLP.

Thus it seems that Cadmus is nowhere to be found in Cold War Guerrero. In place of sown dragon teeth and spontaneous Spartoí guerrillas, this chapter briefly highlighted a sustained and gradual process of popular political radicalization—propelled by state terror—in which revolutionary violence emerged as a political modality. Unpacking this historical process in Guerrero revealed disparate yet interconnected stories of popular movements moved by chronic injustice and social democratic ideals furiously crushed by elite and state terror. A look at historical context highlighted a rural Mexican region located on the economic peripheries of a national capitalist modernization program (the postwar "Mexican Miracle") thoroughly dependent upon the repression of protest, diminution of social reforms, and authoritarian rule. Heeding historical contingency we saw the organizing of the ACNR and PLDP and their decision for violent insurrection, like Salvadoran communists of the 1930s, made "in clear-eye agony" after repeated instances of state terror[76]—and not part of a communist plot planned and arranged in Havana. A different story thus emerges when historical process, context, and contingency constitute the principal analytical lens—not ideologically-inflicted metaphysical ruminations on a "spontaneous" armed left conceptualized as pathologically violent.

Notes

1 Jorge Castañeda, *Utopia Unarmed: The Latin American Left after the Cold War* (New York: Vintage Books, 1994); David Stoll, *Between Two Armies in the Ixil Towns of Guatemala* (New York: Columbia University Press, 1993); David Stoll, *Rigoberta Menchú and the Story of all Poor Guatemalans* (Boulder: Westview Press, 2008, 2nd edn); Hal Brands, *Latin America's Cold War* (Harvard: Harvard University Press, 2010). See also Paul Lewis, *Generals and Guerrillas: The Dirty War in Argentina* (Westport, CT: Praeger, 2002); John W. Sherman, "Comparing Failed Revolutions: Recent Studies on Colombia, El Salvador, and Chiapas," *Latin American Research Review* 41:2 (2006), 260–268.

2 Castañeda's *Utopia Unarmed* represents the most widely read articulation of this argument. For Castañeda, Cuba, in particular the 1959 revolution and the ensuing intelligence apparatus led by Manuel "Red Beard" Piñeiro, constitutes the primary source of political radicalization for the Latin American guerrilla left—not the violent rollback of short-lived social democratic gains exercised by dictatorial and authoritarian regimes during the 1950s and 60s. State terror and the erasure of legal

channels for political redress are not treated as radicalizing triggers. The complex, simultaneously local and transnational histories of the Latin American guerrilla left are thus reduced to Castroist imitations, Cuban exports of revolution, and the conspiratorial machinations of "Red Beard" and his G-2 intelligence apparatus. Castañeda does look at the guerrilla groups covered in this chapter as examples of insurgencies that did not receive Cuban aid—only to deprive them of historical contingency and significance: "the movement led by [Lucio] Cabañas was weak, localized, and doomed to defeat." See Castañeda, *Utopia Unarmed*, 87. For his broader argument on Cuba see Chapter 2, 51–89.
3 *Un hombre llamado Lucio: Comandante: Lucio Cabañas Barrientos, Vol. I–II* (Discos Pueblo Rebelde). These compact discs contain a number of Cabañas' recorded talks and speeches (which fell into military hands during a raid of a guerrilla camp in late 1973 or early 1974). The transcribed talk cited here can also be found in Luis Suárez, *Lucio Cabañas, el guerrillero sin esperanza* (México: Grijalbo, 1985), 198–199.
4 Ibid.
5 For instance, see Greg Grandin, *The Last Colonial Massacre: Latin America in the Cold War* (Chicago: University of Chicago Press, 2004); Daniela Spenser, ed., *Espejos de la guerra fría: México, América Central y el Caribe* (México, DF: CIESAS/Porrúa, 2004); Verónica Oikión Solano and Marta Eugenia García Ugarte, eds., *Movimientos armados en México: Siglo XX* (Zamora, MI: CIESAS/El Colegio de Michoacán, 2006).
6 Michel-Rolph Trouillot, *Silencing the Past: Power and the Production of History* (Boston: Beacon Press, 1995), 70–107.
7 For currently influential examples, see David Kilcullen, *The Accidental Guerrilla: Fighting Small Wars in the Midst of a Big One* (Oxford: Oxford University Press, 2009); David Kilcullen, *Counterinsurgency* (Oxford: Oxford University Press, 2010).
8 G.W.F. Hegel, *Science of Logic* (Cambridge: Cambridge University Press, 2010 edn), 97–120; Frederick Engels, *Anti-Dühring* (Progress Publishers, 1947), chapter VIII at http://marxists.org/archive/marx/works/1877/anti-duhring/index.htm. My reading of the "negation of the negation" is also greatly influenced by the work of Slavoj Zizek. See Slavoj Zizek, *In Defense of Lost Causes* (London: Verso, 2008), 337–380 & 381–419.
9 Ibid., 416–417.
10 Steve J. Stern, "New Approaches to the Study of Peasant Rebellion and Consciousness: Implications of the Andean Experience," in *Resistance, Rebellion, and Consciousness in the Andean Peasant World: 18th to 20th Centuries*, ed., Steve J. Stern (Madison: University of Wisconsin Press, 1987), 12–13.
11 Walter Benjamin, "On the Concept of History," in *Selected Writings: Volume 4, 1938–1940*, eds., Howard Eiland and Michael W. Jennings (Cambridge, MA: The Belknap Press of Harvard University Press, 2003), 395.
12 *Un hombre llamado Lucio*; and, Suárez, *Lucio Cabañas*, 199.
13 For an account of this historical episode see, Ian Jacobs, *Ranchero Revolt: The Mexican Revolution in Guerrero* (Austin: University of Texas Press, 1983).
14 Andrea Radilla Martínez, *Poderes, saberes y sabores: una historia de resistencia de los cafeticultores: Atoyac, 1940–1970* (Chilpancingo: Imprenta Candy, 1998), 104.
15 Carmen Téllez, interviewed by Andrea Radilla Martínez, September 1988, in Radilla Martínez, *Poderes, saberes y sabores*, 104.
16 For an account of these struggles of the 1920s see Armando Bartra, *Guerrero bronco: campesinos, ciudadanos y guerrilleros en la Costa Grande* (México, DF: Era, 2000), 43–56.
17 José Téllez Sánchez, interviewed in Radilla Martínez, *Poderes, saberes y sabores*, 132.
18 *Marjorie Becker, Setting the Virgin on Fire: Lázaro Cárdenas, Michoacán Peasants and the Redemption of the Mexican Revolution* (Berkeley: University of California Press, 1995), 155–162. The radical "populist" rupture marked by Cárdenas' presidency has been questioned by historians. See Arnaldo Córdova, *La revolución en crisis: la aventura*

del maximato (México: Era, 1974); Jürgen Buchenau, "Plutarco Elías Calles and Revolutionary-Era Populism in Mexico," in *Populism in 20th Century Mexico: The Presidencies of Lázaro Cárdenas and Luis Echeverría*, eds., Amelia M. Kiddle and María L.O. Muñoz (Tucson: University of Arizona Press, 2010), 38–57.
19 Bartra, *Guerrero bronco*, 57–73.
20 Tanalís Padilla, *Rural Resistance in the Land of Zapata: The Jaramillista Movement and the Myth of the Pax-Priísta, 1940–1962* (Durham: Duke University Press, 2008), 5–7; Radilla Martínez, *Poderes, saberes y sabores*, 110–113.
21 Tita Radilla, interview with the author, Atoyac de Alvarez, 16 May 2007.
22 Lázaro Cárdenas, quoted in Radilla Martínez, *Poderes, saberes y sabores*, 110.
23 Ibid., 115–116. As Radilla Martínez argues, "hope and the desire to fight or resist [after 1940] largely emanated from [peasant] experiences with Cardenismo."
24 As a regional form of "boss" political rule and organization, *caciquismo* did not always form a complimentary pair with corporatist state rule. See Alan Knight, "Caciquismo in Twentieth-Century Mexico," in *Caciquismo in Twentieth-Century Mexico*, eds., Alan Knight and Wil Pansters (London: Institute for the Study of the Americas, 2005), 7. For a series of excellent case studies see Roger Bartra, ed., *Caciquismo y poder político en el México rural* (México: Siglo XXI, 1975).
25 Bartra, *Guerrero bronco*, 122–126. See also AGN, DGIPS box 550, file 1; DGIPS box 673, file 2; DGIPS box 1195B, file 4, 235–236 & 264–266; AGN, SDN box 94, file 281, 227; AGN, DFS Exp. 100-10-16-4, L-4, H-396 & 404; DFS Exp.100-10-16-4, L-5, H-30-32, 37-38, 41 & 46-49; and DFS Exp. 100-10-16-2, L-2, H-148.
26 Karl Marx, *Capital: A Critique of Political Economy, Volume 1* (New York: Penguin Classics, 1990 edn), 163.
27 Bartra, *Guerrero bronco*, 77, 84; Lorena Paz Paredes and Rosario Cabo, "Café caliente," in *Crónicas del sur: Utopías campesinas en Guerrero*, ed., Armando Bartra (México: Era, 2000), 131. See also Armando Bartra, *Los herederos de Zapata: movimientos campesinos posrevolucionarios en México, 1920–1980* (México: Era, 1985), 79–89; Marco Bellingeri, *Del agrarismo armado a la guerra de los pobres: Ensayos de la guerrilla rural en el México contemporáneo, 1940–1974* (México: Casa Juan Pablos, 2003), 111–115.
28 Barry Carr, *Marxism and Communism in Twentieth-Century Mexico* (Lincoln: University of Nebraska, 1992), 143.
29 Francisco Gomézjara, "La experiencia cooperativa coprera de Costa Grande, Guerrero," *Revista del México Agrario* 9:4 (1976), 133–137; Florencio Ursúa Encarnacíon, *Las luchas de los copreros guerrerenses* (México: Editora y Distribuidora Nacional de Publicaciones, 1976), 69–75; Bartra, *Guerrero Bronco*, 76–79; Radilla Martínez, *Poderes, saberes y sabores*, 185–190.
30 Giorgio Agamben, *Homo Sacer: Sovereign Power and Bare Life* (Stanford: Stanford University Press, 1995), 5–12, 17–20, 181–182. Gerry Kearns' use of the concept in relation to Britain and Ireland proved particularly insightful. See Kearns, "Bare Life, Political Violence, and the Territorial Structure of Britain and Ireland," in *Violent Geographies: Fear, Terror, and Political Violence*, eds., Derek Gregory and Allan Pred (London: Routledge, 2007), 7–36.
31 AGN, DFS, Exp. 100-10-1, L-7, H-90, 93-94; and, DFS Exp. 48-54-60, L-1, H-122.
32 AGN, DFS, Exp. 48-54-60, L-1, H-1-3 & 17; and, DFS Exp. 100-10-1, L-7, H-94.
33 Ignacio de la Hoya, director of *La Verdad*, cited in Salvador Román Román, *Revuelta cívica en Guerrero (1957–1960): la democracia imposible* (México City: INEHRM, 2003), 181.
34 AGN, DFS, Exp. 100-10-1, L-7, H-94.
35 *Así*, 19 March 1960, cited in Román Román, *Revuelta cívica*, 136.
36 Pablo Sandoval Cruz, *El movimiento social de 1960* (Chilpancingo: Universidad Autónoma de Guerrero, 1999), 56–57.

37 Consuelo Solís (Vázquez's widow), interview with the author, 30 May 2007; José Bracho, interview with the author, 9 March 2007; and, Francisco Gómezjara, "El proceso político de Jenaro Vázquez Rojas hacia la guerrilla campesina," *Revista Mexicana de Ciencias Políticas y Sociales* 88 (April–June 1977), 88–89.
38 Maria Lorena Cook, *Organizing Dissent: Unions, the State and the Democratic Teachers' Movement in Mexico* (University Park: Pennsylvania State University Press, 1996), 108.
39 Padilla, *Rural Resistance*, 100.
40 Suárez, *Lucio Cabañas*, 53; Bartra, *Guerrero bronco*, 72.
41 COP leader Pablo Sandoval Cruz, quoted in Alba Teresa Estrada Castañón, *El movimiento anticaballerista: Guerrero 1960, Crónica de un Conflicto* (Chilpancingo: Universidad Autónoma de Guerrero, 2001), 85; Sandoval Cruz, *El movimiento social de 1960*, 52–56.
42 Differing numbers of casualties exist depending on the source. Román Román's study of the 1960 social movement, the most exhaustive to date, lists 23 dead (including two soldiers) and 40 wounded. Government sources at the time listed a lower number and blamed the victims for having provoked the massacre. AGN, DFS, Exp. 100-10-1, L-7, H-102-104; Sandoval Cruz, *El movimiento social de 1960*, 64–70; Román Román, *Revuelta cívica*, 555–569.
43 Sergio Aguayo, *La charola: Una historia de los servicios de inteligencia en México* (México: Grijalbo, 2001), 135–136.
44 AGN, DFS, Exp. 100-10-16-2-62, L-1, H-144-145.
45 AGN, DFS, Exp. 100-10-1-16-2, L-10, H-215; DFS, Exp. 100-10-16-2-62, L-1, 279, 281-290; US Embassy in Mexico, Confidential Airgram to the Department of State, 3 January 1963, National Archives-National Security Archives, RG 59, 1960–63, Box 1511, Folder 712.00/12-362. Document obtained from Kate Doyle, ed., "After the Revolution: Lázaro Cárdenas and the Movimiento Nacional de Liberación," National Security Archive Electronic Briefing Book No. 124, posted 31 May 2004.
46 "Terror en Guerrero," *Política*, 15 May 1963, 28, quoted in Bartra, *Guerrero bronco*, 99–100.
47 Bartra, *Guerrero bronco*, 91.
48 José Bracho, interview with the author, Acapulco, Guerrero, 9 March 2007.
49 Grandin, *The Last Colonial Massacre*, 182.
50 Gomézjara, *Bonapartismo y lucha campesina*, 292.
51 Bartra, *Guerrero bronco*, 105.
52 Benjamin, "On the Concept of History," 394–395.
53 Barry Carr, "The Fate of the Vanguard under a Revolutionary State: Marxism's Contribution to the Construction of the Great Arch," in *Everyday Forms of State Formation: Revolution and the Negotiation of Rule in Modern Mexico*, eds., Joseph and Nugent, 326–354.
54 George Orwell, *The Road to Wigan Pier* (London: 1937), 173–178.
55 AGN, DGIPS, box 447, 190–199. For the local steel industry demands and popular movement see Paul Lawrence Haber, *Power from Experience: Urban Popular Movements in Late Twentieth-Century Mexico* (University Park: Penn State University Press, 2006), 129–130.
56 AGN, DFS, Exp. 100-10-3-4-66, L-1, H-136; and, AGN, DGIPS box 500, file 5, 283-284, 294, 309.
57 "Lineamientos Programáticos de la A.C.G.," 22 August 1967, in Aranda, *Los cívicos guerrerenses*, 107–122.
58 AGN, DFS, Exp. 100-10-1-67, L-24, H-67-69; AGN, DGIPS box 549, file 3; and, AGN, DFS, Exp. 100-10-1-67, L-24, H-175.
59 Tita Radilla, interview with the author, Atoyac de Alvarez, Guerrero, 15 May 2007; AGN, DFS, Exp. 100-10-1-67, L-24, H-99-101; AGN, DFS, Exp. 100-10-3-67, L-1,

H-202; AGN, DGIPS box 462, file 1, 3–4, 265–267, 535–536, 688. See also Bartra, *Guerrero Bronco*, 109; Hipólito Simón, *Guerrero, amnistía y represión* (México: Grijalbo, 1982); and, Bellingeri, *Del agrarismo armado*, 178. Subsequent intelligence reports placed the entire blame on the activists: AGN, DFS, Exp. 100-10-1, L-24, H-99-101.
60 AGN, DGIPS box 1488A, file 3, 57–67; "Guerra Sucia en Guerrero," in Fiscalía Especial para Movimientos Sociales y Políticos del Pasado and José Sotelo Marbán et al., *Informe ¡Que No Vuelva a Suceder!* (México: February 2006), 26; Bellingeri, *Del agrarismo armado*, 133–134.
61 Suárez, *Lucio Cabañas*, 55.
62 Hilario Mesino, interviewed in Gerardo Tort, director, *The Guerrilla and the Hope: Lucio Cabañas* (2005); Hilario Mesino, interview with the author, Atoyac de Alvarez, Guerrero, 17 May 2007.
63 Suárez, *Lucio Cabañas*, 58; AGN, DGIPS, box 462, folder 2, 16; DGIPS box 463, folder 1, 836; AGN, DFS, Exp. 100-10-1-67, L-26, H-31; and, DFS, Exp. 100-10-1-67, L-29, H-10-11.
64 AGN, DGIPS, box 530, folder 3, 218–219.
65 Karl Marx (1856), "Speech at the anniversary of the *People's Paper*," in *Marx and Engels Selected Works, Volume 1* (Moscow: Progress Publishers, 1969), 500; found at http://www.marxists.org/archive/marx/works/1856/04/14.htm. Marx described the Vehmgericht as a secret tribunal that existed in Germany during the Middle Ages that punished overbearing or criminal members of the ruling class.
66 For instance, see: AGN, DGIPS box 530, folder 3, 242; DGIPS box 2946A, 1–8; and, AGN, DFS, Exp. 100-10-16-4-72, L-5, H-94-106.
67 Ortíz, *Genaro Vázquez*, 67–83. The interviews were conducted by a leftist Mexico City newspaper, *¿Por qué?* during the summer of 1971.
68 For a description of these campaigns, see Alexander Aviña, "'We have returned to Porfirian Times: Neopopulism, Counterinsurgency, and the Dirty War in Guerrero, Mexico, 1969–1976," in *Populism in 20th Century Mexico: The Presidencies of Lázaro Cárdenas and Luis Echeverría*, eds., Amelia M. Kiddle and María L.O. Muñoz (Tucson: University of Arizona Press, 2010), 106–121.
69 Consuelo Solís, interview with the author, Mexico City, 30 May 2007; José Bracho, interviews with the author, Acapulco, Guerrero, 9 March & 15 May 2007.
70 Rafael Aréstegui Ruiz, "Campesinado y lucha política en la Costa Grande de Guerrero," (Thesis) Universidad Autónoma de Guerrero, 1984, cited in Bartra, *Guerrero bronco*, 171. A DFS report dated 25 August 1972 estimated at least 400 fulltime guerrillas. AGN, DFS 100-10-16-4, L-5, 313-318.
71 AGN, DFS, Exp. 80-21-72, L-1, H-105-106.
72 AGN, DGIPS, box 549, file 3; and, AGN, DFS, Exp. 100-10-1-69, L-33, H-371-372.
73 Walter Benjamin, "On the Theory of Knowledge, Theory of Progress," in *The Arcades Project*, trans. Howard Eiland and Kevin McLaughlin (Harvard: Harvard University Press, 1999), 473.
74 For an account of the Dirty War in Guerrero see, "Guerra Sucia en Guerrero," *FEMOSSP Filtrado*.
75 In late 1974, Cabañas provided a succinct definition of rural class struggle in the Costa Grande: "as long as two divided classes exist, the poor on one side and the rich on the other side, there will be fights, there will be struggle. And that is the fight called class struggle because it involves the rich and poor classes." Suárez, *Lucio Cabañas*, 327–328.
76 Greg Grandin, "Living in Revolutionary Time: Coming to Terms with the Violence of Latin America's Long Cold War," in *A Century of Revolution: Insurgent and Counterinsurgent Violence during Latin America's Long Cold War*, eds. Greg Grandin and Gilbert Joseph (Durham: Duke University Press, 2010), 20.

3

IN THE VANGUARD OF THE REVOLUTION

The Revolutionary Action Movement and the Armed Struggle

Verónica Oikión Solano

Introduction

My first work on the history of the *Movimiento de Acción Revolucionaria* (Revolutionary Action Movement, or MAR) was published some years ago,[1] but several questions remained unexplored which I would like to elucidate here. My intention is to reconsider the group's activities in the context of the Cold War and thus gain a deeper understanding of the group's emergence during a period of increasing political closure within Mexico's authoritarian system. Also examined is the influence of international political movements, especially in the late 1960s, and the radical shift on the issue of militancy in the Latin American left following the Cuban Revolution.[2]

Utilizing two analytical axes, my aim is to clarify some of the most significant aspects of the group's revolutionary praxis. The first axis analyzes the organization's vision of the armed struggle from its condition as a clandestine group in the vanguard of the revolution, a perspective that led me to reassess the group's proposals in order to reach a better understanding of the objectives it pursued in assuming that role, and the meaning that its military-political praxis took on in those clandestine conditions. Up to now, the true dimensions and scope of the group's goals have neither always been recognized nor examined with the rigor that its activities merit. Moreover, it is clear that no single, unified conceptualization of the group's clandestine operations existed within the movement itself, as different militants held distinct views on this issue.[3]

Secondly, I examine this guerrilla group's internecine conflicts and internal polarization, which contributed to the failings and errors that characterized the movement and directly affected those entrusted with carrying out its objectives.

The group's internal struggles, which I argue are crucial to understanding the atmosphere in which it operated, began during its military training in North Korea and later surfaced in a faction that came to oppose the actions of Fabricio Gómez Souza, the group's self-appointed maximum leader, and his closest allies. Despite a formal agreement that leadership was to be collective, Gómez Souza faced accusations of arrogance, paternalistic attitudes, abuse of authority, and a lack of tact when it came to problem-solving. But unconformities also arose directly from the group's theoretical-conceptual zigzags as to the kind of revolution it wished to undertake and how to carry it out. This leads me to suggest that the group's action plan lacked congruence and resulted in a partial, misguided analysis of Mexican reality in the 1960s, 70s, and 80s. For example, due to its underestimation of the strength of the State, subjectivism and improvisation characterized its revolutionary conscience and attempts to confront that entity, and thus derailed its revolutionary project. Another factor that weakened the movement was the limited and ineffective diffusion of its goals among the general population. The consequent lack of broad social acceptance or approval thwarted any chance it might have had to construct a firm base of popular support and legitimize the armed struggle.

This approach to the history of the MAR stresses the period from its founding in 1966 to the mid-1970s, when most of its guerrilla actions occurred. During that period, it experienced profound changes in leadership, structure and political orientation, while dealing with dire situations that imperiled its very existence. Internal divisions and mergers with other groups precipitated many of those adjustments. Finally, the last section summarizes the group's transformation from the late 1970s through the 80s, particularly in light of the new political context that emerged after Mexico's 1977 Political Reforms.

The Olympus of the Revolution

According to testimonies,[4] the MAR was founded at the Peoples' Friendship University, Patrice Lumumba, in Moscow by Mexican students[5] on scholarship from the *Instituto de Intercambio Cultural México-URSS*, who organized study groups[6] to discuss readings, debate, and evaluate the social and political problems in Mexico and Latin America.[7] Those talks and their analysis of Marxism–Leninism led them to conclude that the time was ripe for a new revolution in Mexico. But such a proposal went against the revisionist Soviet line that postulated a non-violent transition to socialism, despite lauding the Bolshevik Revolution.[8]

Convinced that a social insurrection was imminent, the initial group— Gómez Souza, Alejandro López Murillo, Camilo Estrada Luviano, Salvador Castañeda, José Luis Guerrero, J. Candelario Pacheco and Leonardo Mendoza— discontinued their university studies and underwent a transformation from students to guerrillas. "Their ... personal and political affinities ... caused a profound change in the dynamics of their discussions, which went from informal talks to serious debates and exchanges ..."[9] Those changes altered their mindset so drastically that they came to believe that they were preordained to spark a revolution in Mexico based on a guerrilla-style armed struggle. Also, they simply assumed that the masses would automatically join their cause, under the guiding light of Guevarism and Vietnamese Marxism, a model that the group readily appropriated since its members had denounced Soviet revisionism.[10]

Still in Moscow, this small group of Mexicans decided to call their new organization the Revolutionary Action Movement, and to solidify its structure, "as we understood that it was to be political in content but militaristic in form, and that its propaganda would profess revolutionary action ..."[11] In its "Declaration of Principles,"[12] the MAR outlined a political program which held that conditions in Mexico, both objective and subjective, were propitious for an armed struggle[13] that would set off a socialist revolution and ultimately seize power.[14] While militants surmised that revolutionary change would come about under the leadership of workers,[15] this premise proved incorrect once the struggle against the government began given, much to their dismay, support from the proletariat never occurred. Truthfully, the group's revolutionary discourse failed to attract that sector of the population. According to Castañeda, "we drafted a declaration of principles, a task that took much time [...] We knew (military) training was necessary, but couldn't stay in Moscow ... so we spent about a year looking for a place."[16] Though the group stated, contradictorily, that it did not pretend to lead the revolutionary process and that "[it] was not going to make the revolution," one of its militants revealed the group's willingness to join with other movements and "subordinate ourselves to them," as they had no intention of fighting to attain "revolutionary hegemony ..."[17]

Such ambivalent positions affected other constitutive elements of the organization, especially when the founding nucleus returned to Mexico in 1968, and determined that the leadership would be joint, or collective, based on a seven-member board; a measure that was soon abandoned when Gómez Souza forcefully consolidated his power. A second problem concerned the absence of any effective screening process for evaluating potential recruits.[18] These two elements reflect the inadequacy of the group's earlier analyses "of the operative situation, a lack of minimal preparation [and] a rampant subjectivity that gave raise to indiscretions, premature incorporations and desertions."[19] It should be noted that many individuals who rushed to join the group were attracted by its aura of mysticism and social romanticism, but were sorely lacking in theoretical and political preparation. Clearly, others were influenced by Mexico's bloody repression of the student movement in 1968–1971, and the tight restrictions on access to political activity in the country's institutional framework. Still others were intent upon confronting the government through direct action. Motivated by feelings of desperation born out of the events of the summer of 1968, when students at many universities, including a large group from the state of Michoacán scarred by their experience of the *nicolaita* student movement,[20] broke away from the *Central Nacional de Estudiantes Democráticos*[21] (CNED, "National Center of Democratic Students," dominated by the Mexican Communist Party) to join the ranks of the clandestine MAR, under the motto, "We don't want the Olympics, we want revolution."

Despite these fissures in its structure and political line, the MAR precipitously sought out military training, but finding a country willing to provide instruction proved too arduous. Several potential partners adduced excuses to refuse their services, but eventually North Korea accepted.[22] We can assume that the government's justification for agreeing to train militants was their certainty that armed struggles would eventually take power and extend the network of intercontinental support for socialism. Yet even though the North Koreans were aware that the conditions for an armed insurrection in Mexico did not exist, they still went ahead to support their cause.[23] But from early 1969 to mid-1970, a total of 53 Mexican "revolutionaries" traveled in three groups to train at North Korean camps.[24] In addition to their military training they received lessons on Marxist-Leninist theory from a North Korean perspective,[25] a factor that undoubtedly engendered theoretical differences with respect to the "nature" of the revolution.

While in Asia, Gómez Souza's intimate circle re-evaluated its concept of revolution and, influenced by the North Korean, Vietnamese and Chinese models, adopted the form called "popular democratic revolution," arguing that "in order to achieve socialism it must be a popular democratic revolution." In contrast, a sector that followed Castañeda, Pacheco and López Murillo leaned towards defining the revolution in strictly socialist terms.[26] Due to these growing internal tensions, the first rivalries surfaced even before the militants ended their training in North Korea. Most of the initial schisms were caused by the leadership's authoritarian approach, its tendency to delegate important tasks to just a few trusted members, and its marginalization of low-ranking militants.[27] Apart from these discrepancies, members were at odds over the concept of revolution itself, likely due to the group's excessive militarism and lack of alliances with civil society and other social movements.[28] Indeed, confusion was so great that some members stated that "the party's political option and the army's military option seemed pretty much the same."[29] This accumulation of errors and disagreements impeded the smooth functioning of the organization. The self-critical attitude of Castañeda and Pacheco led them to characterize the group's status upon the return of members to Mexico as follows: "despite all that has been said, the group's two branches—one urban, called *2 de Octubre*, the other rural, the *Ejército Popular*—were nothing more than projects, illusions far from crystallization […] the 'powerful' urban apparatus was in reality a small group of comrades plagued by interpersonal frictions, serious organizational deficiencies, limited material resources and political differences."[30]

At the conclusion of training in North Korea in September 1970, leaders of the MAR promised to resolve all the problems and correct the organizational errors committed as soon as it began clandestine activities in Mexico. But this never happened, so subjectivism re-emerged, impositions increasingly replaced decisions, and personal conflicts and resentments intensified. Conditions became so difficult that "Only the strong desire to participate in the revolution among most members [prevented] a crisis."[31] The group's return to Mexico fostered an urge to quickly outline plans, but they were haphazard and reflected little programmatic planning along guerrilla lines. In that context, one sector of the MAR metaphorically argued for the need to "strike while the iron is hot," and "take the armed struggle to the mountains." That faction argued that as soon as their comrades arrived to Mexico City, they should be "loaded onto trucks and hauled off to the mountains."[32] In the cities, meanwhile, operations continued with two main objectives in mind: first, to conduct what they called "expropriations"—usually assaults on banking institutions—to obtain economic resources,[33] a practice that continued throughout the organization's existence, though often with unfavorable results; and, second, a proposal for armed revolutionary groups to carry out political kidnappings, a tactic that was never actually implemented because of a lack of the congruent planning required to sustain such an operational strategy. It should be stressed, however, that some former militants confirmed that this was indeed one of the group's political lines.[34]

Castañeda criticized those accelerated, vertiginous approaches in a document written in July 1970 that recommended a series of measures to improve the group's functioning and the performance of its revolutionary actions. For example, he suggested dividing the group into two sections, one of which would be entrusted exclusively with issues of security. He wrote that "these comrades would have the great responsibility of assuring that the organization's activity would never cease, but [would] advance and develop, always leading by example." The other was to assign weaker, less experienced militants to groups of no more than three under the direction of a political-military supervisor, who would be responsible for raising their "political and military level …" Two more important recommendations included, first, to establish a presence in certain urban and rural areas, chosen for their political, economic and military importance; and, second, to permanently conceal the group's guerrilla actions. Under this scheme, militants would normally be deployed in groups of no more than five, but when necessary could split into smaller units or coalesce to "strike the enemy where it hurts the most, and recruit new members for the struggle." In both urban zones and the countryside, groups would set up "commandos" capable of acting in unison according to their respective areas of specializations and tasks assigned, which could include distributing propaganda, organizing new commandos and training schools, or assuring that the MAR was well financed and never ran short of supplies. The goal was for "each group to have a director and assemble one or more commandos to orchestrate actions when deemed necessary." The commandos, in turn, would be sub-divided into a series of forces, including "political prisoner liberation units," "sabotage units," "terrorism commandos" (to fight the "bourgeois terrorism that subjugates the people"), and "expropriation units." The rationale was that all these measures would lead to a well-coordinated clandestine network that stretched[35] "from the countryside to city," and would supply food, medicines, military material, logistical information and security.

Using the knowledge acquired in North Korea, Castañeda delineated the conditions and criteria for establishing military training schools for recruits and revolutionaries. He held that "creating schools must occur in due time, not just yet [as] to do so now would be tantamount to underestimating the enemy and overestimating our own capacity."[36] He also stressed the importance of camouflaging those centers and moving them frequently to keep them hidden from the authorities. But his guidelines were largely ignored by the leaders and were not reflected in the group's organizational structure and activities. In fact, in January 1971 there were still large gaps in the group's clandestine cover and, in some cases, these had worsened due to the its accelerated growth, given it had recruited almost 100 militants.[37] In the second half of 1971, several improvised military training schools were hastily set up at various sites in Mexico,[38] despite fears that this meant "going beyond the organization's real possibilities." The main role of those schools was to teach the "concept of struggle."[39]

The members of the *Comisión Coordinadora de Reclutamiento* (Recruitment Committee) argued that the MAR was developing "in denial of the existence of a true revolutionary vanguard," which should have been the central foundational expression of its concept of a revolutionary, insurrectionary nucleus,[40] though it did perceive—somewhat messianically—that this was "its *raison d'être* ...;" that is, "[The MAR] was born to fill that void, to undertake that historical task" under a halo of predestination. Though the MAR had not yet carried out the tasks "that the historical moment demands," members argued that it had "a revolutionary theory that had not fallen from the sky, but was the product of intense study and enormous effort. We would never deny our organization's achievements, but nor do we obfuscate them to the point of denying the existence of grave errors that may shatter [them] and all they could signify."

Based on this statement, the Commission went on to list, from its viewpoint, the most serious problems that plagued the group. First, the recruitment and selection of new members was not being conducted under strict security measures, nor was care taken to ensure that the incorporation of new militants was "voluntary and conscious." Second, the list readdresses concerns over the group's training process, specifically the need to improve its "ideological and disciplinary" training, because the actions of various militants who confused "discipline with blind obedience to orders and keeping silent about mistakes made by their superiors" were causing chaos. Also cited was the judgment that excessive criticism of errors by leaders had blossomed into a "frankly counterrevolutionary attitude." An additional problem was that the group lacked mechanisms through which the bases could communicate their criticisms to leadership, a situation that bred "rumors and gossip." Finally, the leaders' overestimation of the level of consciousness among the rank-and-file was manifested in its imposition of an ironclad discipline that punished those who rejected it and resulted in disparate criticism of members, as some were labeled "exemplary" while others were deemed "low and despicable." It is easy to see how this situation often engendered frustrations and quarrels.

In its analysis, the Commission made it clear that as long as the MAR failed to recognize its failings through assessments and self-critiques, it would be unable to "effectively take its place at the vanguard of the revolutionary process," a goal that the Commission deemed a priority, despite the group's original posture that welcomed the possibility of merging with other groups. Moreover, the Commission recognized the group's undeniable "ideological backwardness and lack of [internal] cohesion." While elucidating all these shortcomings, the Commission was careful to explain that they were not the fault of any one person, but that resolving them would require a collective commitment that the organization "has not yet been able to achieve." The opposing view, held by those closest to Gómez and expressed in testimony by Pineda, argued that the group did indeed carry out regular "assessments, in which *everyone* had the right to express their opinion …," though he does mention isolated cases of insubordination, desertions, and "conscious sabotage."[41]

Based on its diagnosis, the Commission presented a series of proposals designed to correct these anomalies, the first of which was a commitment to hold a "broad meeting to discuss and analyze current problems," re-evaluate conditions in Mexico, appraise the state of revolutionary movements worldwide, and "update or ratify certain aspects of our organization's revolutionary theory." This latter point was most significant, as it implied the assumption that the concept of the revolution that they pretended should be subject to wide scrutiny and, eventually, to modifications under a more inclusive scheme. The Commission stipulated that all opinions and criticisms be presented in writing, and invited each faction within the MAR to foster discussion and propose measures designed to resolve the pending issues; a restructuring that would allow "less active militants to participate directly in talks and take part in finding the best solutions."

The second aspect that received a comprehensive overhaul was the theoretical component, as greater emphasis was placed on analytically discussing the group's political orientation, the objective and subjective conditions propitious for launching the socialist revolution in the world—especially Mexico—and the transition period from capitalism to a the socialist state.[42] Other points mentioned included the nature of the revolution, including the forces and relations of production, and goals for adjusting the structures and correlations between those forces in the international context; the struggles that the organization should undertake in the economic, ideological and political spheres according to its Leninist perspective; the principal of democratic centralism in relation to the group's conditions and needs; and, finally, the nature of its leadership, which would entail questioning the performance of the current leadership of Gómez. The second part of this theoretical section focused on a "discussion and analysis of the military position" based on four sub-divisions proposed to analyze how to facilitate the group's "transition from a clandestine existence to open engagements with the enemy in the countryside and city." Additionally, talks were held to assess the feasibility of launching the armed struggle in rural areas and urban centers simultaneously.

A third point referred to organizational measures, once again touching upon the sensitive topic of leadership. A proposal was presented to "ratify or restructure leadership and the coordinating commissions of the different working groups." In other words, the question was whether the faculties assigned to the leaders should be modified so as to restrict the existing attributions and thus improve relations between them and the commissions in order to achieve a more efficient delegation of responsibilities. In addition to these matters, militants also questioned the organization's internal regulations and discipline, and proposed "a short-and-long term work plan" that would include new working groups assigned to specific tasks.

The Commission concluded its report with two final proposals: first, that the comrades López, Castañeda, Felipe Peñaloza García, Elia Hernández, and Maldonado be obliged to attend the meeting; and, second, that the assembly be of a "constitutive [character to form a group] called 'Manuel Arreola Téllez.'"[43] Despite these preparations, however, the constitutional congress never took place,[44] so all the theoretical baggage and revolutionary praxis remained up in the air and the opportunity to build the framework of a "politically and organizationally capable"[45] armed nucleus was lost. To further complicate matters, leaders made a fateful decision: threaten internal dissenters with execution. Castañeda and Pacheco stated that "instead of seeking satisfactory solutions […] they turned to threats and took concrete steps to physically eliminate some comrades. How paradoxical! We had yet to fire a shot against our adversaries, but were on the verge of becoming the first casualties!"[46]

A Labyrinth of Chaos

Perhaps, as Castañeda implies,[47] had that meeting been held in 1970 it would have modified the future course of the MAR. Haplessly, that never occurred and, in February 1971, disaster struck, as 19 members of the MAR were captured[48] in a blow that proved to be a breaking point that radically altered the group's evolution,[49] "transformed its immediate objectives, and modified its trajectory."[50] The surprise arrest of those 19 comrades galvanized support among students in Michoacán and Nuevo León, a reaction that reflected the support the group enjoyed among radical, politicized students. In fact, the massive detention triggered a response that, against all expectations, favored the MAR, as several students soon opted to join the armed struggle, swelling the group's ranks and ensuring that it would live to fight another day.[51]

But even with the incorporation of those new recruits, the group's situation was still precarious, for the imprisonment of key leaders and militants threatened to critically handicap the entire movement. Bearing the stark reality of life behind prison walls proved too much for some members, who were unable to adapt to their new surroundings. One revolutionary described those circumstances in the following terms:

> ... mutual mistrust, enormous insincerity and demoralization that approached desertion in some cases [and] exacerbated ideological divisions, the many personal frictions, total disorganization, clear manifestations of defeatism in some, including the supposedly "brilliant leader" [Gómez], and clear signs of a loss of perspective, all as a result of this head-on collision with reality.[52]

As if this were not enough, just three months after their fall, those political prisoners tried to disseminate a document entitled *Algunas verdades sobre el MAR* ("Some Truths about the MAR") from inside the infamous Lecumberri Prison. Their text set forth a series of clarifications about the group and, more importantly, details of detainees' brutal experience with torture as the authorities strove to pry information out of them. Unfortunately for them, their action proved fruitless because the media firmly, under the government's thumb, accused them of being revolutionaries and terrorists; an image that was disseminated to coincide with a virulent anti-communist campaign that the government implemented to stigmatize the organization.[53]

Amidst this bleak, conflict-ridden situation, personal antagonisms among the prisoners worsened when a small group that included Cardona, Peñaloza and Pineda set out to form a new nucleus and selected certain prisoners to join in. A second factor that contributed to the group's deterioration was Gómez's proposal to divide the imprisoned militants into two sections, assuming that each "current" would perform better by working independently, since at that juncture any kind of cooperative initiative was simply unfeasible. The split resulted in the creation of two groups: the "Manuel Arreola Téllez" band led by Gómez, and the "Pablo Alvarado Barrera" faction that included the prisoners who recognized the leadership of Castañeda and Pacheco. The latter group accepted the split, not with an eye to forming a "pressure group," but because "some sincerely believed that it was the best way to prevent the situation from becoming even more problematic; though most considered it an incorrect way to resolve, [and] put an end to, their differences."[54] In fact, the formation of the two commands did backfire, as it only intensified tensions between the sectors and exacerbated the pre-existing factionalism. A proposal that Castañeda and Pacheco presented to their fellow prisoners was designed "to seek ways to achieve true unity among the group's political prisoners, and linkages with imprisoned militants from other revolutionary organizations so as to increasingly solidify collective life in every way."[55] But their suggestion never materialized into concrete action, rather lost in the limbo of incarceration.[56]

Immersed in this dire situation, and forced to operate in secret, the group's reconfigured leadership (including Octavio Márquez, Horacio Arroyo, Martha Maldonado, Paulino Peña, Guillermo Moreno, José Luis Martínez and José González),[57] finally held the organization's long-programmed assessment session, but it did little more than ratify its ideological foundations and political-military posture, and recognize that its mistakes had affected all members, especially those who were in prison. In a tone surprisingly removed from reality, that meeting was described as a "success," as it rectified "the errors and deformations suffered in North Korea."[58] This prefigured a new stage that involved rebuilding the armed group with the militants who had not been arrested and a new batch of recruits.[59] In this way, the MAR managed to subsist in secret, still clinging to the ineluctable principal of its eventual revolutionary triumph.

Another result of this transformation was the controversial fusion with the *Grupo 23 de Septiembre*,[60] led by Manuel Gámez, aka *Julio* and Rodolfo Gómez, aka *El Viejito*, which surfaced in Chihuahua as heir of the *Grupo Popular Guerrillero*. In the first semester of 1972, this merger led to the formation of a new organization: the *Movimiento de Acción Revolucionaria-23* (MAR-23),[61] one of two groups (the other was the *Organización Partidaria*, fueled by *Los Procesos*)[62] that gained particular notoriety in Mexico in that year. The new organization was characterized by more coherent planning[63] that led to the establishment of new training schools. Also, a new round of "expropriations" in several states, including Chihuahua, Coahuila, Sonora, Jalisco, Michoacán, Aguascalientes, and Guanajuato, all confirmed the group's determination to continue the insurgence[64] through the use of urban guerrilla war tactics. Inevitably, informants[65] and infiltrations[66] led to the arrest of many militants who were caught in acts of violence in 1972–1973. In fact, the group's security systems were still so weak and lacking in rigor that MAR-23 became easy prey for the tenacious repression exercised by the apparatus of State control.[67]

When the opportunity arose to form a "bilateral coordination" with Lucio Cabañas' *Partido de los Pobres* (Party of the Poor) in 1972,[68] the problems that the organization had been grappling with since its transformation into MAR-23 resurfaced, this time with such severity that they set off an organic crisis in the national directorship and exposed the group's weak internal structure and contradictions in its revolutionary actions. At the same time, internal postures regarding the leadership that should govern the armed group became polarized: "upon fusing with the *Grupo 23 de Septiembre*, the MAR came to understand that the movement's evolution would be directed by members of *Grupo 23*, as they had more experience and, in reality, were the ones teaching guerrilla tactics to new recruits."[69]

Due to these inter-group divisions, plus the founding of the *Liga Comunista 23 de Septiembre* (LC23S) in March 1973, some units of MAR-23[70] broke away, shifting their revolutionary spirit, experience and technical-military capacity to the seat of that new organization. This caused even more instability and disequilibrium in the MAR, though several of its original militants did not defect. For example, its nucleus—now mostly young students from the *Universidad Michoacana* and rural normal schools—continued to operate in Michoacán, independently of both MAR-23 and the LC23S,[71] because they perceived that the leaders of those groups, "sought to act as ideologues and *caudillistas* [sic]."[72] However, throughout 1974, the group's activities in Michoacán, including expropriations, recruitment and military training, were frustrated by the frequent arrests of its militants.[73]

Also in mid-1974, members of MAR-23—Octavio Márquez and Armando and Javier Gaytán—attempted to establish a guerrilla base in the mountains of Chihuahua[74] by availing itself of links with members of the *Liga Comunista Espartaco* (LCE), whose leaders, Alberto Ulloa and Vicente Estrada, had a close, formal relationship with Cabañas' *Partido de los Pobres*.[75] They jointly proposed a meeting of the leaders of the LCE and the MAR, "to explore the possibility of forming one sole organization, acting under the acronym MAR," but the State's intelligence services detected them before the proposed union could be consummated and the project was abandoned.[76]

In the same period, revelations by an imprisoned militant named José Antonio Castillo led to the elimination of the guerilla base that members of the MAR and the *Partido de los Pobres* had established in the *Huasteca Hidalguense*; a military action that left several militants dead or missing.[77] The events of 1974–1976 reveal additional ruptures in the MAR that definitively marked its decline, marked by guerrilla actions that became more and more sporadic and disconnected. Underlying this were the group's intrinsic contradictions, internal fatigue, infiltrations, confessions and betrayals, all of which further debilitated it. Moreover, the lack of contact and/or permanent alliances with civil and social movements and, especially, other armed organizations, resulted in dispersals, theoretical confrontations and never-ending mutual suspicions that impeded its covert activities (due to inadequate coordination and a total absence of confidentiality), and intensified the dogmatic bias of its political-military posture.[78]

In 1977, the José López Portillo government introduced its program of Political Reform and an Amnesty Law that accompanied it, developments that would weaken the MAR even more, given the amnesty granted to imprisoned militants and to members of other movements their freedom,[79] under the condition that they would opt for a legal, public alternative: that is, they would have to lay down their arms and join opposition political parties.[80]

From another angle, although the implementation of the Political Reform was not directed primarily at the armed movement,[81] it was certainly spurred in part by the pressure brought on by the military-political praxis of those groups. Hence, it could be argued that the guerrilla movement was "a catalyst for the Political Reform ... an indirect and unintended achievement of its actions."[82] The government may have felt forced to draft the Political Reform as a means of linking the development of democracy to the elimination of the causes that had led to the emergence of armed groups in the first place. Moreover, the ten years of insurrectionary violence (1965–1977) had accelerated the erosion of Mexico's existing political system and obliged the state to cede some ground and institute reforms. At least indirectly, guerrilla movements played a role in "the transformation of the Mexican political culture."[83]

Sectarianism, a Prolonged Popular War, Self-criticism and the Bitter End

The demise of the MAR can be attributed to several factors. First, as an alternative to the appeal of participating in an armed uprising, potential militants were also being recruited by opposition political parties and social movements active during this period. Not surprisingly, militants who abandoned the armed revolutionary movement were harshly criticized and vilified as "revolutionary charlatans, Marxist–Leninist revisionists, opportunists, reformists" and "traitors to the proletariat."[84] But those criticisms stood in stark contrast to an emerging strategic posture based on new theoretical elements that sought to keep alive the group's clandestine activities; a development that seems to indicate that the individuals who continued to militate in the MAR had finally come to recognize. All of this after their terrible experience in prison, the torture and execution of their comrades, which led them to recognize that one of the armed group's greatest failures was, in their words: "that those who do not put rigorous security measures into practice erroneously believe that the triumph of the socialist revolution is just around the corner, only a question of time, etc.; however, we now believe that *we must prepare ourselves for a prolonged war against the bourgeoisie* and, therefore, are obliged to remain alive and free."[85]

These modifications of the group's revolutionary strategy and tactics were proposed in 1976 by the leaders José Luis Martínez and Elín Santiago,[86] who included in their analysis the need to attract the masses to the MAR and its goals in order to strengthen the organization's claim to represent the vanguard of the revolution. They argued that as "the revolutionary struggle advances, this broad organization of the masses will progressively be transformed into a grassroots revolutionary organization that will unite the people, not only to resolve their concrete, immediate problems, but also, and fundamentally, [to prepare them] for the political struggle to seize power." The goal was to consolidate a popular front that would combine large-scale, mass struggles with the armed uprising as aspects of "the revolutionary process."[87] This new conception of the character of the revolution presupposed a more realistic assessment of the conditions that existed in Mexico, a self-critique of the armed movement, its lack of significant political relationships "with the people," excessive factionalism, its lack of vision regarding the masses and the construction of a popular front, and its opportunistic postures.[88] This repositioning process enabled the MAR to establish contact, alliances, and collaborations with several legally-established, public, social and political organizations without, however, having to abandon its links to, and interchanges with other armed organizations.[89] These factors also help explain why the MAR was able to survive for so long[90] (1966 to early 1990s), compared with other groups whose existence on the national scene was more ephemeral.

Three years later, however, those bridges of communication suffered a calamitous reversal: both Martínez and Santiago were killed, and many militants were captured in an operation that took place in April 1979 in Torreón, Coahuila.[91] That severe blow left no alternative but to try to rebuild the group's leadership once again. In the winter of 1983, the group ratified a decision to maintain its clandestine character and commitment to "forge a national front of the masses, mobilized through revolutionary tactics."[92]

At an Internal National Conference organized in February 1987, the MAR decided to change its name to *MAR 9 de Abril*, to commemorate its fallen leaders, but the truth is that the group was on the verge of disappearing because of continual police harassment.[93] Might this late change of name suggest that the organization was attempting to distance itself from its original project, especially in light of the fact that political and social conditions in Mexico in the 1980s were significantly different from those that had reigned in the previous two decades? Perhaps, but clearly by conserving part of its original name, the recently founded *MAR 9 de Abril* showed its intention to keep the legacy of the original MAR alive in its renewed political imaginary.

However, plagued by a whole series of internal organizational problems and criticisms from its few remaining militants, the *MAR 9 de Abril* slowly began to ebb away in the late 1980s and early 90s. Soon, it was totally isolated, and before long had disappeared completely. Paradoxically, its core leaders then opted to abandon the armed struggle and become politically active in a recently formed, social-democratic opposition political organization called the *Partido de la Revolución Democrática* (Party of the Democratic Revolution, known by its initials, PRD). With that, they definitively turned their back on the group's original proposal to become the very vanguard of the revolution.

Conclusion

The cost of the state-sponsored repression of these armed groups was extremely high in terms of human lives and there is no doubt that its response was out of all proportion to the real threat that the armed organizations represented. For those who spent years behind bars the consequences were devastating, as they saw political goals crushed both on the personal and collective levels, especially when they realized that they had failed to preserve the group's unity. It is clear that right from the group's formative period, its ideological and political-military divisions had polarized militants until, with time, two irreconcilable camps emerged. Finally, the group's inability to garner popular support helps explain its weakness in the face of state hegemony. Reflecting on his time spent in the MAR, Castañeda later recognized that:

> The state's onslaught destroyed several groups, [people] were killed, disappeared, [were taken] prisoner [or] were persecuted and exiled. This was the cost they inevitably had to pay for their precocity, misreading of reality, inability to assimilate experiences [and] lack of pragmatism. Forced to follow the path they had blazed and led into an ambush, they inevitably collided with the vanguard conception from which they had always fled.[94]

Like all the other armed revolutionary organizations, the MAR also failed to achieve its fundamental goal of establishing a socialist state in Mexico. Despite its later efforts to remake itself and forge bonds with other groups, the endeavor was unsuccessful, doomed to fail because of internal contradictions, inherent limitations and its frail organization. In the end, the spirit of rebellion that galvanized those armed groups was fueled by a utopian dream. But in the twenty-first century those chimeras from the past have been transfigured into a new paradigm that seeks a rupture from Mexico's authoritarian past and manifests in myriad ways just how urgently state and society in Mexico require a profound transformation.

Acknowledgments

I would like to thank Paul Kersey for his help with the translation and research assistant Alfredo Herrera López.

Notes

1. Verónica Oikión, "El Movimiento de Acción Revolucionaria. Una historia de radicalización política," *Movimientos armados en México, siglo XX*, vol. 2, eds., Verónica Oikión and Marta Eugenia García (Zamora: El Colegio de Michoacán/CIESAS, 2006), 417–460.
2. Consuelo Sánchez, "El significado actual de la rebelión estudiantil de 1968. Más allá del liberalismo y la izquierda liberal," *Memoria*, no. 247, CEMOS, October 2010, 62.
3. See a longer version of José Luis González Carrillo's testimony in an interview in Enrique Condés Lara's *Represión y rebelión en México (1959–1985)*, vol. 3 (México: Editorial Miguel Ángel Porrúa, 2009), 61. Salvador Castañeda, one of the group's founders explained that secrecy meant not only isolating militants from the population, but also a more complex strategic process of constructing a clandestine network to provide guerrilla cells with a subsistence base.
4. See Fernando Pineda, *En las profundidades del MAR (El oro no llegó de Moscú)*, (México: Plaza y Valdés, 2003); Salvador Castañeda, *La negación del número (La guerrilla en México, 1965–1996: una aproximación crítica)*, (México: Ediciones Sin Nombre, 2006); also, statements by MAR members obtained under torture, in *Fondos Documentales, Dirección Federal de Seguridad*, and *Dirección de Investigaciones Políticas y Sociales, Archivo General de la Nación*.
5. Most militants had prior political experience in the *Juventud Comunista* (JC) and at the *Universidad de Sonora, Universidad Michoacana de San Nicolás de Hidalgo*, and rural schools; see Alejandro Peñaloza, "La Lucha de la Esperanza: Historia del MAR (1965–1971)," BA Thesis, ENAH, 2004, 121–122.
6. Recruits were required to read Ho Chi Min, Vo Nguyen Giap, Maoist texts, Fanon's *The Wretched of the Earth*, speeches by Fidel Castro, and Che Guevara's writings on guerrilla warfare; see Condés Lara, 37 and Salvador Castañeda, *La patria celestial* (México: Ediciones Cal y Arena, 1992), 61.
7. We must also consider the legacy of *cardenismo* and students appropriated of that tradition. José Francisco Paredes Ruiz said, "… when very little […] I began to listen to my father speak about the Mexican and Cuban Revolutions …" That was how he developed an interest in Marxist themes; AGN, DIPS, box 2417, "Movimiento de Acción Revolucionaria," 11 March 1971.
8. After the Soviet Union Communist Party's 20th Congress (February 1956), a new Soviet line postulated a non-violent transition to socialism and peaceful coexistence, a policy largely justified as an attempt to prevent a nuclear war. Under this new plan, the USSR suspended its support of armed struggles in Latin America.
9. Letter by Salvador Castañeda and J. Candelario Pacheco G., "Pablo Alvarado Barrera command of prisioners politics, a Nuestras compañeras de Santa Marta [Acatitla]," n.d., Mandeville Special Collections Library, University of California, San Diego, Armed Revolutionary Organizations of Mexico, Documents and Publications MSS 0523, series 17 *Movimiento de Acción Revolucionaria*, reel 8, folder 3.
10. Ibid.
11. Alejandro Peñaloza interview with Fabricio Gómez in *La Lucha de la Esperanza*, 70. Gómez said they planned to build their revolutionary army by forming "small guerrilla cells, a classic guerrilla struggle, with small detachments capable of uniting and separating quickly, attacking troops, and dispersing rapidly…." Ibid., 85.

12 See letter by Castañeda and Pacheco, "Declaración de principios del MAR," and "Algunas verdades sobre el M.A.R. (Movimiento de Acción Revolucionaria)," a document by "Los Presos Políticos del Movimiento de Acción Revolucionaria," Lecumberri, México, May 1971, reproduced by "Grupo 'Arturo Gámiz,'" AGN, FDFS, Exp. 11-207-71 H-257-259 L-5.
13 The MAR wrote its own manual on guerrilla warfare, *Estrategia y Táctica Guerrillera*, and circulated it among militants. See statements by Rafael Chávez and Doroteo Santiago, AGN, FDIPS, box 2714.
14 Pineda, 43–44; the MAR applied a revolutionary strategy drafted by Vladimir Lenin to the Mexican situation; see Castañeda and González Mancilla's conversation on revolutionary subjectivity, AGN, FDIPS, vol. 2539, 29 July 1972.
15 Peñaloza interview with Gómez, *La Lucha de la Esperanza*, 71, 86. Gómez added that the group intended to recruit "workers, people with political training and, especially, a proletarian mindset ..."
16 Peñaloza interview with Castañeda, *La Lucha de la Esperanza*, 68. At that time, there were only 10 militants.
17 Ibid., 67–69; see the MAR's "*Declaración de Principios*" and statement by *Pancho* in "Cuaderno Manuscrito número ocho," AGN, FDIPS, vol. 1913-A, exp. 2.
18 Militants said they were urged to informally invite brothers, relatives, friends, acquaintances and schoolmates to join up.
19 Letter by Castañeda and Pacheco.
20 Verónica Oikión, "El movimiento universitario de 1966 en Michoacán: una historia de confrontación política," in *154 años de movimientos estudiantiles en Iberoamérica*, eds., Silvia González and Ana María Sánchez (México: Instituto de Investigaciones Bibliográficas, UNAM, 2011), 387–402. The legacy of student movements and political activism in Michoacán induced students to join the MAR. At a rally at the *Colegio de San Nicolás* (Morelia) in 1972, "Felipe Hincapié Alvarado took the stage to give a historical overview of the 1963 and 1966 student movements, explaining that many jailed MAR members were veterans of those rebellions. He urged everyone there to support and sympathize with the struggle the MAR had begun"; see "Estado de Michoacán," AGN, *FDFS*, exp. 100-14-1-72 L-22 H-104-105.
21 Verónica Oikión, "Juventud y revolución. La central nacional de estudiantes democráticos," panel presentation, *XIII Reunión de Historiadores de México, E.U. y Canadá*, Querétaro, 26–30 October, 2010.
22 According to testimony by Alejandro López and Martha Maldonado, the Cubans refused to finance or train MAR militants for fear it would jeopardize relations with Mexico's government. After failing to gain Cuba's support, López asked the Vice-Minister of the Cuban FAR, Sergio del Valle, if his government would recommend them to the North Koreans. After several talks, the North Koreans agreed to train them, Condés Lara, 33–34.
23 Adela Cedillo, *El fuego y el silencio. Historia de las Fuerzas de Liberación Nacional* (México: Edición del Comité del 68, 2008), 110; Condés Lara, 34–35.
24 Statements by jailed militants explain that widespread bureaucratic corruption allowed them to obtain the documents required to leave Mexico.
25 Oikión, "El Movimiento de Acción Revolucionaria," 433–436. Militants arrived at the training camp in three sets; see AGN, FDIPS, box 2750, exp. 2. While in North Korea, militants learned about that nation's revolution, karate and judo, how to handle explosives, shoot 38-caliber pistols and AK-10 rifles, and use bazookas and grenades. Training included simulated attacks, sabotage, ambushes, blockades and counterattacks; AGN, FDIPS, box 1144-B.
26 Oikión, "El Movimiento de Acción Revolucionaria," 437, and interview with Rogelio Raya in Peñaloza, *La Lucha de la Esperanza*, 133. Castañeda observed

that the MAR was not pro-Soviet because, "In a period of profound divergences between the Soviets and North Korean, especially on the issue of armed struggle, it was impossible to be pro-Soviet and receive military training in North Korea," Castañeda, *La negación del número*, 49.
27 Letter by Castañeda and Pacheco.
28 Raymundo Ibarra mentions that the MAR "is a movement totally isolated from the population." Peñaloza, *La Lucha de la Esperanza*, 105–106.
29 Peñaloza, *La Lucha de la Esperanza*, 97. Gómez also admitted that the MAR was "isolated from the population. It had a very militarist vision […]. I don't know if the time wasn't right, recruitment was poor, or [we] lacked a concrete strategy [to] communicate with the masses …," ibid., 100.
30 Castañeda, *La negación del número*, 51.
31 Ibid.
32 Ibid., 51–52.
33 From the outset, the MAR recognized the importance of expropriations: "The revolution is expensive and the people cannot sustain it since they are deprived [of resources] … the money hoarders (bankers) will be robbed to defray the costs of revolution," "Algunas verdades sobre el M.A.R."
34 Condés Lara, 54–55.
35 According to Raya, the group tried to build an urban network, but failed miserably. Peñaloza, *La Lucha de la Esperanza*, 86.
36 AGN, *FDFS*, Exp. 11-207-71 H-57-75 L-2.
37 Gómez estimated that there were between 90 and 120 militants; Peñaloza, *La Lucha de la Esperanza*, 102. In November 1970, Ana María Parra and Armando González held meetings in Mexico City to encourage young people to join; see "Liga Comunista 23 de Septiembre. Brigada Roja," 19 June 1975, AGN, FDIPS, box 2779.
38 According to Gómez, "the function of these schools was to educate new recruits," and "help them understand the cultural, political, and economic reasons why we're fighting."
39 Training centers were established in the state of México and Querétaro, and in cities like Guadalajara, Jalapa, Salamanca, San Miguel de Allende, Oaxaca, Puebla, Pachuca, Acapulco, Morelia, Pátzcuaro, La Piedad, Zamora, around Lake Chapala, and in the *Meseta Purépecha* in Michoacán, but some recently arrived North Korean militants criticized them. Castañeda said, "We were against establishing these schools because the group was still very weak, short of militants, lacked adequate military training, organization, and a security system to guarantee they'd be protected." Peñaloza, *La Lucha de la Esperanza*, 94; see also *Comisión Coordinadora de Reclutamiento*.
40 Gómez defended this theoretical concept, saying "the MAR was part of the revolutionary vanguard," Peñaloza, *La Lucha de la Esperanza*, 102.
41 Pineda, 51–54. Gómez claimed there were no serious internal divisions: "There were some differences, one or two comrades disagreed with the work methods, maybe they were right, maybe not, it was impossible for us to hold collective meetings to vote on things … [but] it was agreed that decisions would be taken by the leadership …," Peñaloza, *La Lucha de la Esperanza*, 137.
42 The *Frente Amplio* never materialized, surely due to a lack of affinity with other social movements.
43 AGN, FDFS, Exp. 11-207-71 H-57-75 L-2, "A los compañeros de la Dirección" by the *Comisión Coordinadora de Reclutamiento*, 7 January 1971. The proposal was for the group's plenary to be named after Manuel Arreola Téllez, killed in a fatal firearms accident during military instruction.
44 Castañeda's faction repeatedly called for an internal assessment, but this caused tensions. He said, "finally, after some time, they said yes [*sic*], but so-and-so can't

attend; I mean we couldn't be there [...] we were discussing that when the group suffered its first blow," Peñaloza, *La Lucha de la Esperanza*, 136–137.
45 Ibid., 85.
46 Letter by Castañeda and Pacheco. It is difficult to ascertain if internal executions took place, as no documents or testimonies mention this practice explicitly; see Castañeda, *La negación del número*, 55. Perhaps paranoia caused divisions and distrust among militants under constant police harassment.
47 Castañeda, *La negación del número*, 55, "... it all began after the secret police detected one of the training schools ... then, during a visit by the leadership the entire school fell."
48 "Algunas verdades sobre el M.A.R.," "Arrests began on February 16 of that year. Up to then, the judicial police weren't sure what they were dealing with, as they had little information on the MAR. DFS documents on the ambush say that they 'arrived' in search of bank robbers but found guerrillas," AGN, FDFS, Exp. 11-207-71 H-257-259 L-5.
49 Letter by Castañeda and Pacheco, "In summary, we're inclined to think that we ended up in prison because of our own errors, ineffective security measures, police brutality, and some astuteness on their part."
50 "*Boletín de Prensa*" signed by the *Procuraduría General de la República*, Mexico City, 15 March 1971; Press Conference by the *Procurador*, David Franco Rodríguez, AGN, FDIPS, box 1144-A; Oikión, "El Movimiento de Acción Revolucionaria," 445. Condés Lara argues that the raid "nipped" the group's revolutionary project "in the bud," but I disagree, because the MAR survived for a long time despite the array of conditions aligned against it. Clearly the February raid was devastating, but it did not eliminate the MAR; Condés Lara, 52.
51 AGN, FDFS, Exp. 100-17-3-71 H-11 L-8. In Monterrey, "Approximately 200, mostly high-school, students held various impromptu meetings to protest the jailing of MAR members," in Morelia, the *Comité Pro-Presos Políticos Nicolaitas* formed to support their peers detained in Mexico City, AGN, FDFS, Exp. 100-14-1-71 H-246 L-20.
52 Letter by Castañeda and Pacheco.
53 For examples of the campaign against the radical ultra-left, see José G. Cruz, *Traición a la Patria*, a libel that circulated widely, distorted information, and described recently arrested members of the MAR as criminals and traitors, while hinting at an "international red threat." Security agents reported that in Aguascalientes, at least, the government conducted "investigations" to "report inhabitants' reactions to the repressive measures that the government implemented to thwart attempts to provoke instability that could harm the people and the nation." Reports affirm that public opinion approved the measures and supported "expelling Soviet Embassy officials, because in that office [sic] movements designed to damage Mexico are born, coached and guided." Thus, it was necessary to "focus all energies on punishing those who, while serving foreign interests, forget that the *Patria* and the wellbeing of the Mexican people must be placed above all else," "Informe del Estado de Aguascalientes," 19 March 1971, AGN, FDIPS, vol. 612, exp. 1.
54 Letter by Castañeda and Pacheco.
55 Ibid.
56 Pineda recognized that discussions and debates ended up "disuniting us." See Alberto Ulloa, *Sendero en tinieblas* (México: Ediciones Cal y Arena, 2004), 211–212.
57 Pacheco joined the leadership quite early, but a few months later was arrested in Puerto Vallarta. When arrested, Andres González declared that Gómez "gives instructions from the *Cárcel Preventiva* [prison]"; "Movimiento de Acción Revolucionaria," 29 July 1972, AGN, FDIPS, vol. 2539.
58 Letter by Castañeda and Pacheco.

59 Alma Gómez, a MAR leader, offered to recruit militants for the guerrilla in rural normal schools in Oaxaca, Sonora, Sinaloa and Nayarit.
60 See "Estatutos y Reglamento," AGN, FDIPS, vol. 2953; "Plan Estatal de Organización del Movimiento Revolucionario 23 de Septiembre," AGN, FDIPS, box 2955; "Cuadernos Manuscritos," AGN, FDIPS, vol. 1913-A, exp. 2. Contact with the *Grupo 23 de Septiembre* involved Javier Gaytán, a MAR member who introduced Gómez to Salvador Gaytán, a *23 de Septiembre* militant, in August 1970; Pineda, 135–136.
61 Report entitled "Estado de Sonora. Información de Hermosillo," with statements by Estanislao Hernández that confirm the first meeting of the MAR and the *Grupo 23 de Septiembre* when the former returned from training in North Korea. It occurred when Gómez sent Hernández to Parral, Chihuahua, to "make contact with workers and peasants and provoke agitation," 26 March 1974, AGN, FDIPS, box 1920; "Liga Comunista 23 de Septiembre," 28 March 1974, AGN, FDIPS, vol. 2689; Pineda, 135–136. In his statements, Edilberto Castellanos said that he and other militants were sent to Parral in October 1970 to find "a suitable place to install a rural guerrilla" in the Sierra of Chihuahua. See 14 February 1972, AGN, FDIPS, box 2750, exp. 2.
62 For additional information, see Pineda, 183.
63 According to Pineda, after "the fusion with the *Grupo 23 de* Septiembre" the MAR "divided the country into three large sectors and began to form clandestine cells throughout the nation." According to testimony by Humberto Coronado, the booty from the group's "expropriations" was used to purchase guns and hand grenades from an American, which were then distributed to the cells. See Pineda, 164 and "Estado de Chihuahua. Información de Chihuahua." The attack on the armored truck was by MAR members, two of whom were held by the state police, 28 July 1972, AGN, FDIPS, vol. 943, exp. 1.
64 See "Cuaderno Manuscrito número doce," AGN, FDIPS, vol. 1913-A, exp. 2.
65 "Algunas verdades sobre el MAR," section 2 "Aclaraciones"; Condés Lara, 57–58.
66 We have more precise information on the issue of infiltrations: according to testimonies gathered by Condés Lara, the police sent an officer to the women's prison who eventually befriended a prisoner named Ana María Parra and obtained information on the group. Luis Alvarado also mentions that a former militant assured him that "the MAR might have been infiltrated by spies, because while in jail and after their release various comrades received benefits and special treatment." Others, however, "doubt that federal forces infiltrated the movement"; see Luis Antonio Alvarado, "El Movimiento de Acción Revolucionaria y su influencia en la Reforma Política mexicana en 1977," BA Thesis, Universidad Nacional Autónoma de México, 2008, 73.
67 "Movimiento de Acción Revolucionaria," México, 10 February 1972, AGN, FDIPS, vol. 2494; "Estado de Michoacán," México, 29 September 1972, AGN, FDFS, exp. 100-14-1-72 H-104-105 L-22; 25 October 1973, AGN, FDIPS, vol. 2654; 25 November 1973, AGN, FDIPS, vol. 2654; Declarations by Hernández, 28 March 1974, AGN, FDIPS, vol. 2689; Pineda, 164.
68 Simón Hipólito, *Guerrero, amnistía y represión* (México: Editorial Grijalbo, 1982); Pineda, 161–165. The contact between the *Partido de los Pobres* and the MAR was Wenceslao José; see 31 May 1975, AGN, FDIPS, box 2778. He had links to Vicente Estrada of the *Liga Comunista Espartaco* and was close to Lucio Cabañas; see "Liga Comunista Espartaco," 10 November 1974, AGN, FDIPS, box 2738. For more information on how Cabañas was contacted, see DFS, 28 March 1974.
69 See testimony by Hernández in "Informe del Director del DFS," México, 28 March 1974, AGN, FDIPS, vol. 2689, one exp.; Pineda, 168–169.
70 See confession by Roberto Gallangos, 30 June 1975, AGN, FDIPS, box 2753. Wenceslao José was the MAR's representative in meetings on the group's merger with

the *Liga*. Estanislao Hernández, Marisol Orozco *'Verónica,'* Arnulfo Ariza *'Ricardo,'* Paulino Peña *'Pancho'* and Wenceslao José, among others, joined the LC23S. Those who stayed in MAR-23 differed with the *Liga*'s position that the former should function only as "the operative armed branch of the new organization"; Condés Lara, 64.

71 Through contact with Félix Edmundo Mendieta *'Fidel,'* young people from Michoacán joined the MAR. See 24 November 1974, AGN, FDIPS, vol. 2741.
72 AGN, FDIPS, box 2714; Amafer Guzmán denied that the MAR would join the *Liga*, because the two group's political and ideological positions were not on a par; see Julio Pimentel and Abdallán Guzmán Cruz, "Sobre la guerra sucia en Michoacán," *Cambio de Michoacán*, 25 June 2005; Pável Guzmán, "Guerrilleros michoacanos," *Cuarto Poder de Michoacán*, 10 January 2011.
73 AGN, FDIPS, box 271; AGN/FDFS, 11-207-74/H-219/L-11, and 25 November 1974, AGN, FDIPS, vol. 2741, confirm that the arrests of young militants set off mobilizations organized by the *Casa del Estudiante Nicolaita*.
74 See declarations by Javier Gaytán, who with *Abel,* his brother Armando, and Octavio Márquez, agreed "to create a reconnaissance team in the Sierra of Chihuahua for the purpose of establishing a guerrilla unit there." Márquez commissioned Javier to contact Alberto Ulloa, "to discuss the possibility of setting up a meeting with leaders of the *Liga Comunista Espartaco* and the MAR." See "Estado de Morelos," 5 September 1974, and "Movimiento de Acción Revolucionaria," 7 October 1974, AGN, FDIPS, box 2724.
75 See "Liga Comunista Espartaco," 7 September 1974, AGN, FDIPS, box 2724, and "Liga Comunista Espartaco," 10 September 1974, AGN, FDIPS, box 2738, 121–125.
76 "Movimiento de Acción Revolucionaria," statements by Javier Gaytán, 7 September 1974, AGN, FDIPS, box 2724, one exp.
77 Pineda, 200–209.
78 In mid-August 1975, some members of the MAR tried to join the LC23S, but the latter group resisted, fearful that they might try to seize control of the movement because of its supposedly "bourgeois tendencies"; see "Informe General," México, 13 August 1975, AGN/FDFS, exp. 11-235-75/H-221-224/L-32.
79 "Movimiento de Acción Revolucionaria," 13 January 1975, AGN, FDIPS, vol. 2785, one exp., 10 August 1977. Thanks to the Reform, seven more members of the MAR were freed; AGN/FDFS, exp. 11-207-77/H-66-67/L-13.
80 Verónica Oikión, "El impacto de la oposición armada en la Reforma Política del Estado. Las decisiones de 1977," in *Formas de gobierno en México. Poder político y actores sociales a través del tiempo*, ed.,Víctor Gayol (Zamora: El Colegio de Michoacán, 2011). The Reform diluted any possibility of revolutionary transformations.
81 I disagree somewhat with Cedillo's view that the Political Reform was directed primarily towards the underground armed left and not the democrat left. See Cedillo, *El fuego y el silencio*, 340–341.
82 Alvarado, 21.
83 Ibid., 128.
84 "Manual de medidas de seguridad," n.d., Mandeville Special Collections Library. University of California, San Diego, Armed Revolutionary Organizations of Mexico, Documents and Publications MSS 0523, series 17 Movimiento de Acción Revolucionaria, reel 8, folder 11.
85 Ibid.
86 Alberto López, "Semblanza de José Luis Martínez Pérez," 5 April 2007, http://investigacionesrubenjaramillomenez.blogspot.com/2009/04/homenaje-al-movimiento-de-accion.html

87 "Puntos estratégicos" and "Puntos tácticos"; the "Presentación a los trabajos de estrategia y táctica" contains new slogans like "*¡Con el pueblo a la lucha!*" ("To the struggle with the people!") and "*¡Con el pueblo a la victoria!*" ("To victory with the people!"), Mandeville Special Collections Library, University of California, San Diego, Armed Revolutionary Organizations of Mexico, Documents and Publications MSS 0523, series 17, Movimiento de Acción Revolucionaria, reel 8, folder 12.
88 Ibid.
89 Pineda, 217–218; Condés Lara, 69–70. Alliances were forged with social movements in Chihuahua, Sonora, la Comarca Lagunera, the Valley of Mexico, Morelos, Puebla, Veracruz, Guerrero and Michoacán. See, "Semblanza de José Luis Martínez Pérez," 5 April 2007. Also, the MAR joined the so-called "unity process" with the *Asociación Cívica Nacional Revolucionaria*, the *Partido de los Pobres* and the *Unión del Pueblo* through what was called the "*Cuadrilátera,*" or simply "*Cuadri*"; that is, a "national guerrilla coordination." See López's document, "A los que no conocimos por su nombre," 12 April 2004, and "Línea Política," Mandeville Special Collections Library, University of California, San Diego, Armed Revolutionary Organizations of Mexico, MSS 0523, series 17, Movimiento de Acción Revolucionaria, reel 8, folder 5.
90 Clearly, the armed group's long survival was also a function of ongoing recruitment by new militants, especially students, who sought to form new units. In fact, the recruitment process may be a key to understanding how the MAR managed to repeatedly renew its nucleus despite the severe setbacks it suffered (Salvador Castañeda, pers. comm., 5 February 2011).
91 Pineda, 211–218; Condés Lara, 70–71; López, "Semblanza de José Luis Martínez Pérez," 5 April 2007.
92 "Planteamientos básicos," winter 1983, Mandeville Special Collections Library, University of California, San Diego, Armed Revolutionary Organizations of Mexico, Documents and Publications MSS 0523, series 17, Movimiento de Acción Revolucionaria, reel 8, folder 13.
93 Alberto López, "A los que no conocimos por su nombre," 12 April 2004.
94 Castañeda, *La negación del número*, 83.

4

"POR LA REUNIFICACIÓN DE LOS PUEBLOS LIBRES DE AMÉRICA EN SU LUCHA POR EL SOCIALISMO"

The Chicana/o Movement, the PPUA and the Dirty War in Mexico in the 1970s

Alan Eladio Gómez

On Thursday October 2, 1975, at a military checkpoint in Vallecillo, just south of Monterrey, the state capital of Nuevo León, Mexico, approximately two and a half hours south of the Texas–Mexico Border, Mexican Federal Police agents arrested Ramón Raúl Chacón of Mercedes, Texas, Andrés Pablo de la O Castarena of México, and Elsy Morales from Colombia, accusing them of traveling in a vehicle with a false compartment of weapons.[1] Chacón, who was a prisoner's rights activist with the Puerto Rican *Independentistas* (freedom fighters), Black radicals and other Chicanos, while incarcerated at Leavenworth Penitentiary in the late 1960s, was working as a teacher at El Colegio Jacinto Treviño (CJT), an Antioch affiliated Chicano College in South Texas. All three were taken to the Monterrey office of the *Dirección Federal de Seguridad* (Federal Security Directorate), or DFS, the primary intelligence gathering and political police institution in Mexico at the time. Chacón and de la O were accused of transporting arms with the intention to incite rebellion, as well as being members of the *Partido Proletario Unido de América* (United Proletariat Party of América) or PPUA, a transnational Maoist inspired guerrilla organization founded in 1975 in central Mexico in the wake of the military excursion into the *Colonia Rubén Jaramillo*, a squatters camp in Cuernavaca, Mexico established in 1973.

Mexican print media and DFS officials claimed that Chicano activists in San Antonio—specifically Mario Cantú—were founding members of the PPUA; and that the PPUA was part of a larger "global terror network" called the *Alianza Internacional de Terroristas* (International Terrorist Alliance, AIT). Reports from *El Norte* compared the PPUA with the Symbonese Liberation Army (the group responsible for the kidnapping of newspaper heiress Patty Hearst in 1974). They also alleged that de la O was connected with the Black Panthers, had traveled throughout the southwestern USA to raise funds and purchase munitions, and was part of the Mexican Communist Youth (*Juventud Comunista Mexicana*) transporting guns for Pablo Gómez Alvarado, secretary general of the communist party in Mexico.[2] Chacón and de la O were tortured into signing confessions. During a transfer from one holding cell to another, and for some reason un-cuffed, de la O escaped shirtless and barefooted in a daring dash from the Federal Security Building through the streets of Monterrey. During the chase, a DFS officer shot at and missed de la O, instead killing a young boy. Chacón was imprisoned for 18 months.[3]

Ramón Chacón was not the only Chicana/o (and US citizen) to be tortured outside of the USA during the Dirty Wars of the 1970s in Latin America. Rubén Solis, member and candidate for state treasurer candidate for the Chicano third political party, *La Raza Unida Party* (LRUP) from Texas, was arrested and tortured in Mexico by the DFS in 1973. Olga Talamante, an organizer from California who had established political connections throughout Mexico, specifically with *Los Mascarones*, a theater group from Mexico City (a key connection between Chicanas/os and Mexican social and cultural movements), and a cadre of the Fuerzas de Liberación Nacional (FLN) in Chiapas, as well as with Central and South America, was arrested and tortured in Argentina in 1974.[4] All three were involved in connecting elements of the Chicana/o Movements with struggles in Mexico and Latin America, while bringing the influence of Third World struggles to the political terrain of the United States. The particular state violences they endured were exemplary of broader counter-insurgency wars against social movements throughout North, Central and South America during this period. Between the FBI, CIA, and Defense Intelligence counter-insurgency programs in the United States, to the Dirty Wars in Latin America, revolutionaries who engaged in international struggles were the targets of state terror for multiple nations.[5]

This story of how Chacón gets from Leavenworth to South Texas to a prison in Mexico, and the movement organizations that he was part of, gives insight into the radical politics in Central/South Texas in the early 1970s, particularly in San Antonio, Texas. It weaves Chicana/o and Mexican social history by uncovering connections between ex-*pintos*,[6] a landless people's movement, and rural guerrilla peoples' army in central and southern Mexico.[7] Uncovering and highlighting contours of international trajectories within the Chicana/o Movement that inspired solidarity—and for some direct engagement—with social movements in other parts of the world, contributes to a growing literature on Chicana/o radicalism, transnational social movements, and the political cultures of a US Third World Left during the 1970s.[8] The histories of connections between the Chicana/o Movement and revolutionary movements in Mexico specifically, and international revolutionary solidarity in general, have been narrated in different contexts. I offer a few "lines of flight" tracing elements of Chicana/o radicalism in the 1970s that looked to revolutionary movements internationally for inspiration, and for some, to join with in struggle.

The goal of this chapter is simple: outline connections between Chicana/o Movement participants and organizations in Texas and radical and revolutionary social movement organizations in Mexico within the context of state repression in *both* the USA and Mexico, and US–Mexican geopolitical relations during the 1970s; specifically, the connections with the *Partido Proletario Unido de América* (United Proletariat Party of América) or PPUA. Recognizing the multiple crosscurrents of radical histories between *Aztlán* and Mexico not represented in this research, my goal is to sketch the contours of a "counter-topography" of Chicana/o radicalism during the 1970s that negotiates a radical trajectory not fully contained by but that finds an articulation within the Chicana/o Movement: armed struggle in Mexico.[9] That said, above and underground political work demanded secrecy and small groups.[10]

"The Long 1960s/Mexican New Left"

During the late 1960s and early 70s, the United States experienced a series of political and economic crises precipitated by social movement activity at all levels across the country—from the grassroots to the war theater, from the college campuses to the agricultural fields and shop floors, in barrios, ghettos and middle class neighborhoods across the USA, folks were revolting against the confining logics of the social relations predicated on capitalism, white supremacy, heterpatriarchy and nationalism. The state terror of the FBI's COINTELPRO operations devastated social movements, including Chicana/o organizing efforts. The expansion of the criminal justice apparatuses and militarization of the police, both funded by the Law Enforcement Administration Assistance (LEAA), created the conditions for the incarceration of massive numbers of poor people and people of color. Economic attrition as ideology and the abandonment of the social-welfare state and the social wage happened just at the moment when historically marginalized communities had finally gained (limited) civil, social and economic rights. A nascent color-blind racism characterized the transition from "the conservative 1960s" to the even more repressive neoliberal 1970s and 80s as economic, political and cultural shifts characterized the social terrain, and the left and right battled for traction and influence in policy matters.[11]

The momentum of the 1960s civil rights and the anti-war movement was indeed shifting between 1968 and 1973 as the state increased repressive measures and movements realigned. While not in full retreat during the 1970s, elements of social movements who had not staked all—or any—expectations on the state, continued a process of political recomposition.[12] As historian Dan Berger explains about the 1970s, people were

> learning new languages. Their politics merged from widespread efforts, capitalizing on newly available political space and rejecting what they saw as failed directions of the recent past, to experiment with alternative praxes. Radicals attempted to redefine political affinity in ways frequently messier and often smaller than the beloved community of the previous decade. These alternative political communities were led by people whose voices of perspective had often been unheard a few years earlier: women, indigenous peoples, gays, lesbians, bisexuals and transgender people, Puerto Ricans, environmentalists, people with disabilities, and others [Chicanas/os for the purpose of this essay].[13]

The struggle for economic, social and political equality intensified in the 1970s, as did the concentration of revolutionary oriented movements, as people made connections between structures of domination, domestic and foreign policy, as well as spaces for possible intersectional resistance. Some of these formations included but were not limited to the Black Liberation Army, the different Puerto Rican Independence groups, the George Jackson Brigade, the Chicano Liberation Front, Weather Underground, and in the late 1970s, the League of Revolutionary Struggle and the *Movimiento de Liberación Nacional,* both comprised of Chicana/o and Puerto Rican militants.[14]

1968 was a year of global rebellion and global repression; in the 1970s these trajectories of revolution and state violence continued.[15] For example, in Mexico the massacre at Tlatelolco on October 2, 1968, and subsequent violence on June 10, 1971 at the hands of the paramilitary group *Los Halcones* which had received training in the USA, revealed the depth of a state in crisis.[16] It is important to locate the assassination of the agrarian leader and Zapatista Rubén Jaramillo and his family in 1962, as well as the repression against the railroad workers and teachers in the 1950s, as a precursor to the cycle of violence that catalyzed in Mexico during the 1970s. Chicana/o activists followed these events closely, as they would come to figure prominently in the Chicana/o narrative about politics in Mexico. The power and meaning of 1968 in Mexico crossed borders.

These repressive events in Mexico signaled a profound political crisis in the Mexican corporatist state that mirrored a larger crisis across Latin America.[17] The Mexican state, through the "Echeverría doctrine," engaged with social actors on two fronts: state sponsored terror that devastated social movements and stifled political organizing; and political rhetoric, specifically Echeverría's *la apertura democrática* (democratic opening) which was ostensibly aimed at reincorporating the left and expanding the corporatist Mexican state. Promises of land distribution, the appointment of former opposition leaders to university and government posts, the promotion of a "nationalistic" economic policy, and the use of a pro-Third World language characterized the rhetoric of the Democratic Opening.[18] Echeverría's political program was contradictory depending on the audience. While publicly claiming a democratic opening, hundreds, perhaps thousands of Mexicans, were disappeared, tortured, and assassinated during his presidency.[19] At the same time that the state was acting against civilians and the media was escalating fears of social unrest, subversion, communist infiltrations and chaos, right wing organizations in Latin America as well as in the United States and Mexico gained prominence.[20]

After the Tlatelolco and Jueves de Corpus Christi massacres, many young people re-invented themselves and their organizations. Some chose to go underground and join the urban and rural guerrilla formations emerging at this time. Eric Zolov characterizes the overlap of counterculture and radical politics as a "New Left."[21] For example, in the aftermath of the violence of 1968 and 1971 respectively, artists, musicians and activists established the *Frente Artístico Organizado Revolucionario* (Organized Revolutionary Artistic Front) or FARO, in Mexico City in late 1968; and CLETA (Centro para la Libre Expresión Teatral y Artística) in 1973. Both organizations used culture as a vehicle to critique the authoritarianism of the Mexican state and organized a social movement as artists as a means to challenge the structures of the cultural status quo.[22]

In 1974 CLETA, in close collaboration with the Chicana/o theater umbrella organization TENAZ (Teatro Nacional de Aztlán), organized the *Quinto Festival de Teatro Chicano/Primer Encuentro Latinoamericano de Teatro* in Mexico City. For two weeks theater groups from across the continent shared their art, talked politics and established connections that would strengthen throughout the decade. After the gathering a number of Chicanas and Chicanos stayed in Mexico and with Mexican teatristas inspired by the Chicano Movement, created a chapter of the student organization MEChA (Movimiento Estudiantil Chicano/a de Aztlán) at the *Universidad Nacional Autónomo de México* (National Autonomous University of Mexico) or UNAM.[23] In addition to FARO and CLETA, political and cultural organizations, labor unions, student groups and farmers' delegations reached out to Chicanas and Chicanos as they travelled throughout the USA, bringing news and updates from movements south of the border. Chicanas and Chicanos also traveled to Mexico, as part of delegations, or as individuals, establishing a variety of political and cultural connections.

"Seeing like a (hemispheric) State":[24] Chicanas/os and the Echeverría Doctrine

From the perspective of the Mexican state, specifically during the regime of Luis Echeverría, but also later with José Lopez Portillo (1976–1982), Chicanas/os were politically expedient. Echeverría's politics toward the "Chicanomexicana" community were two-fold: establish a stable working relationship with key (male) Chicano leaders; and attend to the bi-national issues like migration, water rights and immigration, that were more relevant than ever because of growing Mexican communities in the USA.[25] The former led to division among Chicana/o organizations, particularly with regards to Echeverría's role in both the violence of 1968 and the emerging Dirty War. In addition, Echeverría had his own agenda as a self-stylized "progressive" left-leaning leader in Latin America, as a result foreign policy issues, particularly relations with the United States, were approached by way of specific goals. As we will see below, Chicanas/os, particularly in San Antonio, would play an important role in Echeverría's foreign policy strategy with Richard Nixon.

The different relationships between organizations in the Chicana/o Movement, the Mexican government and Mexican social movements must be understood in relation to Cold War politics. During the Cold War, in particular the 1960s and 70s, Mexico played a crucial role for the United States by maintaining intelligence assets throughout Latin America, especially in Cuba. As Kate Doyle points out, "… the tolerance that the United States had for the intransigence of Mexico was based on a secret pact between the leaders of the Mexican state and their counterparts in the United States."[26] In addition to this direct link to intelligence on Cuba, there was special interest in social movements and organizations that were making links across borders, most evidenced by the least known of the FBI COINTELPRO operations, the Border Coverage Program (BOCOV). One of six COINTELPRO initiatives, the Border Coverage Program, in operation from 1960 to 1971, focused on the political links between organizations in the US–Mexico Borderlands and in Mexico. Of all the COINTELPRO initiatives, the least is known about BOCOV.[27] What we do know is that agents "developed sources for infiltrating radical and criminal groups," and specifically targeted the communist party and labor organizations, as well as creating front organizations for possible long-term intelligence gathering. For example, a memorandum from the San Antonio FBI office to Director Hoover, from April 24, 1970, under the subject headline, "COUNTERINTELLIGENCE and SPECIAL OPERATIONS," indicates, "In the near future, San Antonio will submit recommendations regarding a cover intelligence organization and is considering dovetailing its recommendation with the SECOMEX program." In response, Hoover directs the San Antonio office, "Although Latin American or Mexican–American projection was not indicated in prior communications regarding the establishment of a cover intelligence operation, these [sic] areas of racial or political orientation would definitely be considered."[28]

President Echeverría also had concerns about the connections between political activists on both sides of the border working together. According to former director Philip Agee, Luis Echeverría was a CIA asset, codenamed

LITEMPO.[29] This close relationship between US intelligence agencies and high-level Mexican officials during a time of heightened security issues with Cuba and Chile proved central to the USA's ability to maintain its hegemonic position in hemispheric politics. Echeverría, as president of Mexico or as a CIA asset, promoted himself to the United States, and used radical activists in the USA as a foil for his own political motives.

In a conversation with Nixon in 1972 in Washington DC, Echeverría repeatedly mentioned examples of how coalitions between activists like Mario Cantú from San Antonio, Puerto Rican activists, and Angela Davis as a threat to US security. Echeverría presented himself to Nixon as the new Latin American man, putting forth what he called the "Echeverría Doctrine," his "principals of the Third World vis-á-vis the great powers of the world."[30] These principles included preferred markets for US investments, "a progressive attitude within a framework of freedom and of friendship with the United States," and a shared concerned for security. Essentially, at the same time that Echeverría had a public left-leaning foreign policy, particularly toward Cuba and Chile, Echeverría played up the threat of communism to the USA particularly from Cuba and Chile, a threat also present in the connections between people of color in the USA and movements in Latin America. Nixon's response surely elated Echeverría: "let the voice of Echeverría rather than the voice of Castro be the voice of Latin America."[31] Echeverría played on the historical anti-communist sentiment of the US government, providing examples on how the US and Mexican governments could justify its covert dirty wars against social movements.

The Chicana/o Movement in San Antonio

In 1971, an unprecedented, if unexpected, unity among Mexican American and Chicana/o organizations occurred during the week of September 11th, at "an extraordinary but little noticed political event" when groups from across the political spectrum came together for "La Semana de la Raza" (Week of the People).[32] Sponsored by Mario's Restaurant, the League of United Latin American Citizens (LULAC), the GI Forum (Mexican American veterans organization), and Murguía Printers, La Semana de la Raza featured cultural events, rock bands, educational presentations, and political speeches from a who's who of the Chicana/o Movement from across the state and country. Members from the local chapter of the community defense organization the Brown Berets, the student organization MEChA, United Farm Workers, La Raza Unida Party, and the Mexican American Youth Organization, came together with cultural workers from Mexico, to participate in commemorations of the massacre of Tlatelolco and the murder of the Chicano journalist Rubén Salazar in 1971.[33] Mario Cantú was chair of the celebration and the imprint of his radical politics is evident in the programming.[34] The FBI also took note of the gathering, particularly the presence of *Los Mascarones* from Mexico City, identifying them as "a group of students that are socialist oriented."[35]

San Antonio has historically been situated at a crossroad of radical imaginaries. Since the late nineteenth and early twentieth century, radical socialists, the Industrial Workers of the World (Wobblies), the anarchist *Partido Liberal Mexicano* (Liberal Mexican Party), and other transnational labor and political formations characterized the city's political terrain. The Flores Magón brothers (Ricardo and Enrique) and the *Partido Liberal Mexicano*, had a major influence on the Mexican Revolution, but also on the political culture of San Antonio, Texas, the southwest Borderlands, and I would argue the entire spectrum of the US left at the turn of the twentieth century.[36] In 1913 for example, Charles Cline of the IWW (Industrial Workers of the World) and Magonista supporter Jesus Mari Rangel were imprisoned in Carrizo Springs, Texas, while on their way to join Emiliano Zapata's army. They were later tried in San Antonio.[37] Activists and journalists like Sara Estela Ramírez and the Idar family of Laredo, as well as Emma Tenayuca, a labor organizer, one-time member of the Communist Party and self-declared anarchist, from San Antonio, Texas, were inspired by radical labor and revolutionary movements in Mexico, while actively organizing for the rights of workers, women and others in the southwest.[38] As a result, the US and Mexican governments targeted many of these organizations for surveillance, infiltration and elimination. As the Chicano historian Manuel Callahan explains, "as part of the radical labor movement of the early twentieth century and the 1910 Mexican Revolution that spilled over the border into the US Southwest, [there was] severe repression against labor organizations, anarchists, and the Mexican population of the Southwest by local, state, and federal authorities." Continuing, Callahan emphasizes, "Assisting local law enforcement were the US Bureau of Investigation and the Mexican Secret Service, as well as private detective agencies such as Pinkerton, Furlong, and Theil."[39] A significance precedent for surveillance of trans-border political organizing throughout the century, even early on in the century, punishment and death—in the political and everyday—attached itself to transnational surveillance.

Decades later, during the Chicano Movement, San Antonio reflected a wide spectrum of political influences and organizations that echoed the radical diversity of the earlier years. In addition to the above-mentioned organizations, the *Universidad de los Barrios, Colegio de los Batos: School of Freedom*, a community-based education outreach center, brought university students, Brown Berets, gang members and other youth together. The Centro Acción Social Autónomo (CASA), later renamed TU-CASA, organized for labor and migrant rights; and the Texas Farmworkers had a strong base of support in San Antonio. As in other cities in the Southwest and Midwest, people organized civic engagement projects, community organizing and labor rights campaigns, and protests against racial segregation in housing and education, police brutality, and lack of drainage infrastructure.

Prisons and Revolution

Chacón, born in Delany, deep in South Texas, on January 5, 1942, was "raised among the poor and suffered the consequences: racism, exploitation and oppression ..."[40] After graduating from high school, he worked at various local jobs and in 1967 was arrested and sentenced to 66 months for trafficking a controlled substance.[41] Chacón identified as a Magonista, an anarchist, and was considered a radical political theorist in Leavenworth. This is significant on at least two levels: Magon inspired Chacón's political theories, his ideas for social change, his project for revolution. In a larger sense, Magon inspired many prisoners to keep his revolutionary spirit alive in the cells of Leavenworth. Magon died in Leavenworth on November 21, 1922 (many accuse the prison of neglecting his diabetes), so his presence, his hauntings, accompanied folks at night; and later, accompanied their dreams outside the walls.[42]

While in Leavenworth, and inspired by Magon and other revolutionary theorists like George Jackson and Franz Fanon, Chacón and fellow Chicanos *pintos* Raúl Salinas, Mario Cantú, Alberto Mares, Victor Bono, Beto Gudino and others, organized with Puerto Rican *Independentistas*, Black Muslims and Black Liberation Army members, Native Americans and radical whites as part of the prison rebellions taking place across the country in the early 1970s.[43] Organizing cultural history classes, publishing a newspaper, and establishing the political organization *Chicanos Organizados Revolucionarios de Aztlán* (CORA), they brought in a number of outside representatives from Chicana/o political and cultural groups, and developed a political analysis of society from the perspective of a "backyard-form of colonialism" that emphasized Third World solidarity.[44] According to Salinas, "that's how we got to ... *Wretched of the Earth* by Franz Fanon. Where Chácon got it from, I don't know. Who his peers or his mentors were, in there or out, before he appeared into our midst ... I guess we never bothered to ask. And so, you know from Fanon to Amilcar Cabral—the struggle in Guinea Bissau; seriously looking at Mao and what was going on down there; Vietnam ..."[45] These were the experiences and inspirations that Chacón brought with him upon release to Texas.

After a seven-year stint on a drug conviction, Mario Cantú was released from Leavenworth in 1969 and returned to San Antonio to run his family's restaurant. Cantú continued to support his comrades at Leavenworth, ensuring there was a steady supply of newspapers, audio recordings, and visitors that brought information about social movements across the USA and Latin America. In fact, Cantú introduced *Los Mascarones* and news about guerrilla movements in Mexico and Guinea Bissau to comrades like Chacón and Salinas. Later, after their release, Cantú provided the means to engage in revolutionary work. It was Salinas that connected Chacón and Cantú: "Another brother who is about to get out soon has gone to the 'hospi' in Ft. Worth. His name is Ramón Chacón and

I would like for you to send him a few lines. He knows of your correspondence with us, heard the records, read the materials, etc. He is one of the brothers who taught us the most about politics and progressive thought."[46]

Cantú identified as a Chicano Marxist.[47] Politicized in prison in a similar manner to Chacón, and particularly through his contact with radical thinkers and revolutionaries like the Puerto Rican *Independentistas*, Cantú located his experiences growing up in the Mexican *barrio* as important to understanding police violence, racism, and injustice. After his release, Cantú immersed himself in local, national and international politics. Access to resources allowed Cantú freedom and power, this in turn he used to support movements on both sides of the border.

Mario's Restaurant was a center of political action in San Antonio, "a hotbed of political intrigue," everyone from mainstream politicians and community organizers to government agents and gunrunners gathered at Cantú's place. In 1969, Cantú established the Centro Cultural Rubén Salazar (CCRS) that served as a cultural center, meeting space and training area; it was also an international destination for the radical left traveling between the USA, Latin America, and Indian Country. Cantú traced his family ancestry to Lucio Blanco, a revolutionary leader from Tamaulipas. Lucio Blanco would eventually become Cantú's *nom de Guerra* during his time with the PPUA.[48] Both Cantú and Chacón took the ideas they were exposed to behind bars and adapted them to their context in Texas and later Mexico. Though Chacón would work out of deep south Texas, the connections were strong in San Antonio, particularly through the CCRS and the Colegio Jacinto Treviño.[49]

Cantú was not squeamish about making public his position on the Mexican government, nor his critique of US imperialism in Latin America. Cantú protested Echeverría's visit to San Antonio in 1972 (and again in 1976), publicly demanding justice for political prisoners and targets in the Dirty War, as well as a reinstatement of freedom of speech. Cantú represented the politics of the Mexican and Latin American left, exposing the paramilitary violence organized by the Mexican government against students, farmers and workers, and emphasizing the urgency of supporting Mexican social movements rather than the Mexican government.[50]

La Colonia Ruben Jaramillo

La Liga 23 de Septiembre was established in Guadalajara, on March 30, 1973, at 7pm, in response to the critical need for land and shelter, six families occupied abandoned development lots that belonged to the governor's son in the La Villa de las Flores area, in Temixco, México, south of the capital, Cuernavaca, in the central state of Morelos. The seven hundred families planned the takeover of an assembly of the Asociación Nacional Obrero Campesina Estudiantil—ANOCE

(National Worker, Farmer, Student Association) the previous week did not show up. Frustrated, and despite police patrols in the area, Florencio "El Güero" Medrano Mederos, one of the organizers, rode his motorcycle around the area encouraging families to come and mark off their piece of land. Slowly, more and more people came, and the land was quickly occupied and marked off, each claim measuring 400 square meters. By the end of the week there were some 50 families, and by August 1973, there were some 10,000.[51]

The immediate response by federal and state officials was repression; but folks held steady during the first week. Soon thousands of people joined the occupation. In the first general assembly, held on April 2, 1973, the new *colonos* agreed on the name of Colonia Rubén Jaramillo (CRJ) for their new community, in honor of the agrarian leader killed by the government in 1962.[52] The *Comité de Lucha* (Struggle Committee) would eventually engage in multi-level negotiations with regional, state and federal officials over land titles and social services.[53]

Land occupations are a basic strategy of poor people's movements. It is important to make a distinction between land struggles by campesinos in rural areas, and campesinos that move to urban areas in search of a livelihood and living space to settle. At the time, Temixco was a semi-urban, largely uninhabited area south of the state capital Cuernavaca. After the end of the Mexican Revolution, President Lázaro Cardenas (1934–1940) made some 20 million hectares of land available to *campesinos* so that by 1940 more than 50 percent of Mexico's agricultural production came from communal ejidal lands.[54] After World War II, private interests began a process of re-enclosure that by the 1960s had largely transformed Mexican agriculture into private commercial agriculture.[55] But the bottom line was that need for land outpaced the PRI's political will to redistribute lands. So people took things into their own hands.

But who was Florencio "Güero" Medrano Mederos? Medrano was born in Tlatlaya, in the state of Mexico, to a poor campesino family.[56] Early experiences with the power of rural landowners and their *pistoleros* marked Medrano's life:

> The light-skinned one did not learn to read and write until later on and his vocation as a guerrillero can be traced to his experiences as a young boy when he was in a ditch holding his first magnum under his body and he heard how the soldiers took his uncle Martín Medrano who had led an uprising and as a result the army had almost finished off all the Medranos in Palma Grande.[57]

Unlike Genaro Vázquez and Lucio Cabañas who were formally trained teachers, Medrano grew up working odd jobs, first in Guerrero, then in Mexico City, and later in Cuernavaca. Medrano was part of Danzós Palominos' Independent Peasant's Union (CCI) and worked with Genaro Vázquez in the

Asociación Cívica Guerrerense (ACG). From 1964 to 1966, Medrano was a militant in the *Movimiento Marxista-Leninista de México*, that at the beginning of the 1970s he converted to the *Partido Revolucionario del Proletariado de México*.[58] It was during this time that he spent a month in jail in 1966 for a land invasion in his hometown. Through the PRP he traveled to China from June to December of 1969 as part of a delegation where he received ideological and tactical training.[59] In addition to spending time in Mexico City and China, Güero traveled to Ciudad Juárez, Los Angeles (where he was jailed for reasons not yet known), Eagle Pass, San Antonio and the CJT.[60]

In addition to collective work brigades to build houses and the infrastructure of CRJ, the inhabitants established their own internal community security, "La Guardia Roja" (the Red Guard). Medrano, drawing directly from his experiences in China, set out to establish the first "popular commune in the Mexican Republic" in order to demonstrate that "a group of people can oppose the government but also convert itself into a political force."[61] Unique to *La Colonia Rubén Jaramillo* was Medrano's goal of establishing a land base from which to launch and sustain a Maoist-inspired people's war that emerged from a particular set of conditions in the Mexican countryside, and a history of land-based movements going back to the Revolution, of which both the encampment and its namesake were a direct descendent.

With the goal of circulating the struggle nationally and internationally, representatives from *La Jaramillo* traveled to various parts of the state of Morelos and across the country, particularly Guerrero, Oaxaca and Mexico City, to share the news of the land takeover and garner support, speaking to students, unions, neighborhood committees, and other political groups.[62] Students from the National Autonomous University of Mexico (UNAM), the National Polytechnic Institute (IPN), and a host of other schools, joined cultural workers, *campesino* and labor organizers in the collective labor organized by the Brigadas de Cansancio (Exhaustion Brigades) and Domingo Rojos (Red Sundays).[63] In addition, groups like CLETA and Los Mascarones performed and distributed literature about socialism and struggles in other parts of the world.[64]

According to an interview with Cantú in 1978, the connections between Chicanos in Texas and the CRJ were established "Four years ago, thru [sic] activities in progress, [when] we had contact with el 'Güero' when he was working openly in the Colonia Rubén Jaramillo."[65] Whereas Marxist–Leninist ideas had influenced the direction of Los Angeles and National CASA during this same time, it was a Maoist political formation that attracted Cantú and others to support armed peasants south of the border.[66] It was also during the summer of 1973 that Cantú, Salinas and Chacón met again for the first time outside of prison. After a poetry reading at the University of Texas at Austin, where Salinas also led a discussion about Chicanos in prison, he then traveled to San Antonio where he met up with a group of Brown Berets, Cantú, and

Chacón at the CCRS. From San Antonio, Chacón took Salinas to Mercedes and the *Colegio Jacinto Treviño*, and then on to Mexico.[67]

During the summer of 1973, solidarity events, work days, and negotiations with the government continued, as did infiltration of *La Jaramillo* by police agents and repression by the military. On September 24th, a delegation from the CRJ that had traveled to Tepecuicuilco, Guerrero to meet with representatives of the *Partido de Los Pobres*, was ambushed by the military; Primo Medrano, El Güeros's cousin, was killed, Rafael Urióstegui and Carlos Rosales were gravely wounded, and five other were detained—including an unnamed woman who was pregnant.[68] Four days later, on September 28, 1973, almost six months since the initial arrival of the first families, elements of the Army, State and Federal Judicial police forces, led by Brigadier General Francisco Andrade Sánchez, invaded the CRJ and arrested 14 people, including members of the Struggle Committee. Medrano escaped with other members of the Red Guard. The army did not leave until 1981. Though government agents had already infiltrated the CRJ, the confrontation gave the government added reason to pursue Medrano and his supporters as an armed group. Pedro, one of Medrano's brothers, went into exile to California. Dick Reavis explained that "Pedro Medrano tells me [Reavis] that when the squatter camp fell Güero told him 'somebody from our family has got to survive, so I want you to go to California.'"[69]

"Por la reunificación de los Pueblos Libres de América en su Lucha el Socialismo"

Though an initial gathering of some 40 representative of various revolutionary formations was convened on September 28, 1974 in the city of Puebla, Mexico, to discuss the formation of a political party and a peoples' army, it wasn't until January 10, 1975 that the PPUA held its founding congress.[70] As stated in the founding documents of the party, the guiding principle of the PPUA was to take power through armed struggle: "The rich use violence to exploit the people. The people will use violence to liberate the people." A statement entitled, ¿Quiénes Somos? (Who We Are), explained:

> Our party is made up of workers, farmers, and a few revolutionary intellectuals. As part of the poor people of Mexico and the world, we have not taken up arms because of a love for war, but we have seen that it is the only way that the rich will leave us in peace.[71]

The document situated the PPUA within a longer trajectory of Mexican revolutionary movements, noting the differences between guerrillas isolated in the mountains without support from the people and an army of the people:

"… In our struggle, not only will young men and young women participate, but also the elders and children … If they [capitalist countries] are united to exploit us, we must also realize only by uniting and coordinating our struggle with the struggle of all the peoples of America and the world, we will be able to defeat our powerful enemies … For the Reunification of the Free Peoples of America in their Struggle for Socialism!"[72]

The General Program identified three main goals: 1) organize and develop a clandestine Party across the country; 2) organize and train a clandestine "Peoples Army" (*Ejército Popular de Liberación Unido de América*) or EPLUA in rural areas; and 3) strengthen mass organizations at a national level by developing the *Frente Amplio Nacional Democrático Anti-imperialista* (FANDA), so that in the event of an armed invasion by imperialists Mexico would be ready to unite all social classes under the direction of the PPUA.

The ideology of the PPUA can be understood through their actions, while their first publication, *La Lucha Del Pueblo: Órgano Oficial del Partido Proletario Unido de América*, gives insight into their particular beliefs. First, the layout: in the upper right-hand corner of the cover, and covering the entire back page, features two male figures shaking hands while kneeling: then on the left (facing right) holding a scythe and wearing a wide-brimmed hat is a farmer; the figure on the right (facing left) holding a hammer with a derby-style hat is a factory worker. Behind them are three images: a M-16 rifle with the barrel pointing toward the sky, flanked by two corn stalks. Across the bottom are the letters PPUA.

In addition to the editorial mentioned above, there are four short articles (on Vietnam, the role of intellectuals in a revolutionary movement, women's liberation and class struggle, and an explanation of capitalism), a message from the Central Committee (CC) to the First Congress, and a call for contributions to the newspapers. The "Message from the Central Committee" clearly stated that the goal of the party is to take political power through armed struggle, and offered suggestions and guidance on revolutionary discipline among the ranks, democratic centralism for decision making, and a united front against imperialism.[73] The CC emphasized that revolutionary struggle and action will be taken by a revolutionary formation of *campesinos,* the working class, and progressive intellectuals working (this theme is amplified in an article specifically directed to the intellectual class) together to combat imperialist ideology, organize land struggles, and educate the Mexican people about socialism. The "message" ended with the call (in all capitals) for "the destruction of borders and the reunification of the Free Peoples of America in their struggle for socialism." As Rothwell argues, "Of all the political forces that took a large part of their inspiration and ideological orientation from the experience of the Chinese Revolution, Medrano and his guerrillas were the only ones to make sustained efforts at creating base areas for a protracted people's war according to the Maoist model."[74]

Like other revolutionary formations, the PPUA took part in the kidnapping of wealthy "capitalists," politicians, and revolutionary expropriations (targeting banks and other financial institutions). On November 13, 1974, the commando group "Miguel Enríquez" of the *Ejército Popular de Liberación Unido de América*— EPLUA—kidnapped Sara Martinez de Davis, the wife of a wealthy American investor, Thomas Davis. The group was comprised of Andres Pablo de la O Castorena, Pedro Vargas, Maricela de la O Castoreña (alias Lorena Guevara) and Pedro Moreno.[75] In exchange for the safe return of Mrs Davis, the EPLUA demanded cash and tax-exempt land titles. Mrs Davis was released soon after payment. Bishop Sergio Arceo Mendez, "the red bishop," was the intermediary.[76] Regrouping near the "Casa de los Conejos" in the Iztapalapa District in Mexico City where the operation had been planned, the commando unit met up with other PPUA members, as well as three Chicanos. "In front of everyone, el Güero opened [the packages] and started to count them [money]. When the final count was $40k he explained that half was for the Chicanos organizing the PPUA in the North of the country."[77]

Torture of a US Citizen

Seven days after his arrest, Ramón told his side of the story. On October 9th, Ernesto Chacón, the brother of Ramón and a LRUP leader in Wisconsin, visited him in prison, accompanied by an official from the US Consulate.[78] According to Ramón, after his arrest, he was held incommunicado for three days, during which he was stripped naked, beaten and tortured. He was interrogated by a person with an American accent who was not interested in the charges of gun-running but in Chacón's activities in the USA.[79] One of the techniques used was "the water technique": "[Chacón's] hands and feet were tied, [he was] knocked down, mouth gagged, [and a] water hose down his nostrils."[80] Ernesto reported that he saw the bruises on Ramón's stomach: "My brother looked tired, weak and worried. He [Ramón] said he had signed some kind of statement under pressure."[81] From the time of his initial arrest to his meeting with his brother, the charges of inciting rebellion had been added to the charges of transporting guns.[82] Ramón Chacón insisted on his innocence, insisting he had simply accepted a ride with a friend. He argued that the arrest was a set up; and that the Mexican authorities waiting at the checkpoint knew his name and had an extensive file on his activities.[83]

In the days after Chacón was taken into custody, the DFS—in conjunction with the police in the city of Nuevo Laredo, Mexico—arrested Salvador Abundis Guzmán at a local hospital (he suffered from hepatitis), along with his wife Silvia Fuentes, accusing them of forming part of the AIT.[84] Cantú went on the defensive. In the days following the arrests he made a number of public statements denying the existence of, or any affiliation with, the PPUA. He highlighted the US government's role in the dirty wars in Mexico and across Latin America, and called for an immediate investigate into torture of Chacón, insisting that alleged links between gun-running and drug trafficking were red herrings.[85] Three months later, at a press conference on January 3, 1976, Cantú changed the story. He presented the program of the PPUA in order to "To correctly inform the public and clear up whatever misunderstanding that might exist as a result of what the press in Mexico and the USA has published."[86] Cantú addressed the position of the party in relation to the Chicano Movement accepting "full responsibility for the importation of the people's weapons confiscated."[87]

The press conference touched on the majority of the topics that would dominate US–Mexico policy for the next 30 years: drugs, immigration, capitalism, corruption and the power of social movements. Cantú's statements also caused concern within the Chicana/o community in San Antonio. George Velásquez, from *La Universidad del Barrio* commented, "his public statements on behalf of his one-man organization spread confusion. He undercut us [the other movimiento organizations]."[88] Chacón was still imprisoned and had not yet been sentenced. In an undated letter (circa Dec 1975 / Jan 1976) from Medrano to Cantú, there is no mention of Chacón's case, but Medrano does communicate that as a result of Cantú's declarations of support, "many organizations have taken it [support] as a done deal and not as a project, which is how we interpret it, as a result said organizations are coming to us looking for resources, which puts us in a tight position ..."[89] It is not clear from the letter what organizations Medrano is referring to.

In early 1976, to mobilize support for Ramon's freedom, Chacón's brother Ernesto, Concepción Chacón—Ramón's wife, Narciso Alemán, one of the co-founders of the Colegio Jacinto Treviño, and Rubén Solis, who had been tortured in Mexico the previous year, organized the Ramón Chacón Defense Committee (RCDC) and began a national campaign.[90] A year later, after little headway by the committee, on April 3, 1977, Ramón Raúl Chacón González and Salvador Abundis Guzmán were sentenced to 20 years in prison for being members of a terrorist organization and conspiring to incite rebellion.[91] Three days later an arrest warrant was issued for Mario Cantú under the same charges.[92] Then, surprisingly, shortly over a month later, on May 17, 1977, Chacón was released from the Monterrey prison where he had spent 19 months. The intelligence report that documents his release stated that for a "lack of documentation to legally be in the Mexican Republic he was deported."[93] Upon release, Chacón re-integrated himself into the movement in Texas.[94]

As the RCDC caravan traveled throughout the southwest, the PPUA held its Second Congress in January of 1976 in the state of Puebla.[95] Shortly thereafter, on February 6, 1976, four months after Chacón's arrest, the Dirección Federal de Seguridad (DFS) produced the first full-length report on the PPUA. Seven pages, the report included copies of the "Programa General" and copies of the official newspaper of the PPUA, "La Lucha del Pueblo."[96] According to the *Informe Histórico,* on December 11, 1975, arrest orders were given for Medrano and seven other PPUA militants. The DFS claims that the PPUA had established connections with the Frente Armado del Pueblo (FAP) and that Medrano had formed the *Comando 9 de la Brigada de Ajusticiamiento del Partido de los Pobres* (PDLP). In addition, there was a rapprochement between the PDLP, the Organización Clandestina Union del Pueblo (UP), the Frente Auténtico Revolucionario (FAR), the Movimiento Armado Revolucionario (MAR), the Organización Independiente de Pueblos de la Huasteca, and the PPUA.[97]

It is not until two years later that Medrano reappears. On October 7, 1978, a little over five years since the army invaded *La Jaramillo,* some 600 *campesinos* organized as the *Asociación Indígena de Autodefensa Campesina*—AIAC (Indigenous Association of Farmer Self-Defense)[98] and armed with shotguns and machetes, invaded some 1,800 hectares of land near Tuxtepec, Oaxaca. Leopoldo Degives, Daniel López Nelio and Florencio Medrano were the named leaders involved, while the organizations present were the Unión General de Obreros y Campesinos de México—UGOCM (General Workers and Farmers Union of Mexico), and the Coalición Obrero Campesino Estudiante del Istmo—COCEI (Student, Worker, Farmer Coalition of the Isthmus).[99]

A news crew from NBC filmed the occupation and freelance reporter Dick Reavis covered it for *Texas Monthly.* Cantú was representing the group "US Solidarity with the People of Mexico—Liga Ricardo Flores Magón."[100] In an interview shortly after the land invasion, Cantú explained his role, "let's say I am the link between the revolutionary movement and the press here in the US ... This is very important because it was the first time that something like this had been done between the Chicano Movement and the Revolutionary Movement in Mexico."[101] Cantú finished the interview in his provocative style, "If they [PPUA] need money or guns and if I can I will give it to them. My participation is to arm the people of Mexico, protect them, and defend the sovereignty of Mexico."[102]

Travel to Oaxaca violated the terms of Cantú's probation for the charges stemming from a 1976 INS raid on his restaurant and his arrest for "shielding" undocumented workers. He returned to Texas briefly in November, but instead of staying in San Antonio he went into self-exile to France in late December.[103] For the next year Cantú traveled across Europe meeting contacts set up by Judith Reyes, working closely with Isaías Rojas, a writer for the magazine *Por Qué?*, a popular and controversial political publication that the DFS forced to shut down in 1974.[104] Isaías had been kidnapped by the Brigada Blanca and forced into exile in Rome in 1976. There, Cantú, Rojas and others founded the Comité en Solidaridad con el Pueblo Mexicano (Committee in Solidarity with the People of Mexico).[105] This group of exiled activists also organized the

European Committee in Solidarity with the Chicano People (ECSCP) that had affiliated groups in Spain, France, England, Italy and Germany.[106] With the support of Amnesty International, Daniel Jacoby of the International Federation for the Defense of the Rights of Man, and US allies like Angela Davis, who traveled to the Basque Country to support the ECSCP, they attempted to take the issue of human rights violations of Mexican immigrants, political prisoners in Mexico, and police brutality against Chicanas/os to the arena of international Human Rights.[107]

While self-exiled in France, Cantú learned of the death of Medrano. Yet there are differing versions as to how he died. What is certainly true is that after Medrano gave an interview to Francisco Salinas Ríos of the magazine *Revistas de Revistas*, in October 1978, the military circle began to close on him and his unit. Operating in the area of Tuxtepec, Oaxaca, according to Poniatowska, Medrano was killed on March 26, 1979 by the military.[108] The DFS documents, as well as the *Informe Histórico* indicated that Medrano was shot during a confrontation with the military and died two days later from the wound.[109] The *Austin American Statesman* reported that Medrano was fatally wounded in a "shootout with private security guards protecting a large plantation near the village of San Ysidro Progreso, north of Oaxaca."[110] A document published in Madrid, Spain on April 20, 1979 by the *Comité Europeo de Solidaridad con El Pueblo Chicano* combined the two versions, highlighting that Medrano's death was the result of the "military, preventative police and the DFS, reinforced by bands of para-military police forces of the *caciques* in the zone."[111]

In order to provide a unique understanding of nationalism and internationalism at the intersection of US and Mexican Cold War politics, this chapter emphasized connections between people and organizations in the USA and Mexico, a transnational perspective that cuts across ethnic and area studies approaches by focusing on state violence and geopolitics on the one hand, and ideological influences, social movements, and processes of political radicalization on the other. It has taken us from the federal prison cells in Leavenworth, Kansas to the torture room of the DFS in Monterrey, Mexico; from the urban streets of San Antonio, Texas to the rural landscapes of Cuernavaca, Mexico; from Magonista inspired Chicano revolutionaries in South Texas to a Maoist inspired Mexican People's Army spread across southern Mexico.

Though this chapter introduced organizations and movements, events and connections. Cantú, Chacón and Medrano are at the center of *this* story, but they are not *the* story. In re-covering their lives, the intention is to highlight the movements that they were part of for further research; and to emphasize that the 1970s were a fertile time for social movements, that people continued to organize, resist domination and create community. Given the national and international networks of the Chicana/o Movement at the time, specifically solidarity between the Chicana/o Movement, the Black underground, the

American Indian Movement and the Puerto Rican Independence movement, the connections with radical and revolutionary social movements in Mexico, Latin America and other continents are broader and more extensive than represented here.

Notes

1 Bill Towery, "Tortured in Mexico," *San Antonio Light*, 17 October 1975; "Press Release," Ramón Chacón Defense Committee, n.d., Raúl Salinas Personal Archives (hereafter RSPA).
2 "Descubren el Laredo Madriguera de la AIT," *El Norte*, 5 October 1975.
3 "Estado de Nuevo León," DFS, 2 Oct 1975, 11–249, Exp. 2 Fs. 1, AGN; untitled, Investigaciones Políticas y Sociales (IPS), n.d. 11-249-75, Exp. 1, Fs 19, AGN; "Chicano Activist Arrested," *The Rag* vol. 10 no. 4 (24 November 1975), 7. The record is silent concerning the possible torture of Morales.
4 "Declaraciones de Rubén Solis García y Joaquin Vite Patiño, Presuntos Reponsables en el Contrabando de Armas," DFS, 2 Julio 1974, 2710, 1–13, AGN; Alicia Muñoz Cortes, "The Struggle of the Mujeres to Liberate Olga Talamante, A Political Prisoner." MA Thesis, San José State University, 1999; "Feminism, Torture, and the Politics of Chicana/Third World Solidarity: An Interview with Olga Talamante," *Radical History Review* 101 (Spring 2008): 160–178.
5 Ward Churchill and Jim Vanderwall, *The COINTELPRO Papers: Documents from the FBI's Secret Wars Against Dissent in the United States* (Boston: South End Press, 2001); and Joy James, ed., *Imprisoned Intellectuals: America's Political Prisoners Write on Life, Liberation and Rebellion* (Lanham, MD: Rowman and Littlefield, 2003).
6 As Ben Olguín explains, *la pinta* is the Chicana/o vernacular [caló] Spanish term for prison—a truncated alliterative abbreviation of *penitencia*, the Spanish word for "penitentiary." Pinto is the masculine caló noun identifying a male prisoner. See *La Pinta: Chican/o Prisoner Literature, Culture, and Politics*, (Austin: University of Texas Press, 2010), 23–32; quote is from 23.
7 I use Chicana/o Movement instead of Chicano Movement because it is commonly accepted in the field and it is more inclusive of the historical reality. I also use Chicano(s) and Chicana(s) to refer to individuals or groups. I do use Chicano or Chicano organization when that was either in the evidence or the way that organizations self-defined.
8 Cynthia Young, *Soul Power: Culture, Radicalism, and the Making of a U.S. Third World Left*, (Durham: Duke University Press, 2006); Maylei Blackwell, *¡Chicana Power!: Contested Histories of Feminism in the Chicano Movement* (Austin: University of Texas Press, 2011); Laura Pulido, *Brown, Black, Yellow and Left: The Making of the Third World Left in Los Angeles, 1968–1974* (Berkeley: University of California Press, 2006); Elizabeth Martinez, "A View from Nuevo Mexico: Recollections of the *Movimiento* Left," *Monthly Review* vol. 54 no. 3 (July–August 2002), 79–86; Jorge Mariscal, *Brown-Eyed Children of the Sun: Lessons from the Chicano Movement, 1965–1975*, (Alburquerque: University of New Mexico Press, 2005); Dan Berger, ed., *The Hidden 1970s: Histories of Radicalism*, (New Jersey: Rutgers Press, 2010).
9 Cindy Katz, "On the Grounds of Globalization: A Topography for Feminist Political Engagement," *Signs*, Vol. 26, No. 4, (Summer, 2001), 1229.
10 The radical left in Mexico and the USA has historically come under direct attack by the various government entities, thus increasing the difficulty of organizing, growing, connecting with other movements, or creating counter-hegemony. That

is not to say that the left has not been influential, nor to conflate the two historical genealogies, but simply to emphasize the larger context of organized and targeted state violence.
11 Peter Farber and Jeff Roche, *The Conservative 1960s*, (New York: Peter Lang Publishing 2003); Michael Flamm, *Law and Order: Street Crime, Civil Unrest, and the Crisis of Liberalism in the 1960s*, (Columbia University Press, 2007); Berger, op. cit.
12 Harry Cleaver, "The Inversion of Class Perspective in Marxian Theory: From Valorization to Self-Valorization," in *Open Marxism: Theory and Practice* Vol. II, eds. Werner Bonefeld, Richard Gunn and Kosmas Psychopedis, (London: Pluto Press, 1992), 106–144.
13 Dan Berger, *The Hidden 1970s*, 5.
14 Jalil Muntaqim, "On the Black Liberation Army," in *We are Our Own Liberators: Selected Prison Writings*, (Montreal: Abraham Guillen Press, 2003): 29–42; Daniel Burton-Rose, *Guerrilla USA: The George Jackson Brigade and the Anticapitalist Underground of the 1970s*, (Berkeley and Los Angeles: University of California Press, 2010); Oscar López Rivera, "A Century of Colonialism: One Hundred years of Puerto Rican Resistance," in *Warfare in the American Homeland: Policing and Prison in a Penal Democracy*, ed., Joy James, (Durham: Duke University Press, 2007): 161–196; Dan Berger, *Outlaws of America: The Weather Underground and the Politics of Solidarity* (Oakland: AK Press, 2006); Jeremy Varon, *Bringing the War Home: The Weather Underground, the Red Army Faction, and Revolutionary Violence in the 1960s and 1970s* (Berkeley: University of California Press, 2004).
15 On 1968 as a global phenomenon, see George Katsiaficas, *The Imagination of the New Left: A Global Analysis of 1968* (Boston: South End Press, 1987).
16 Kate Doyle, "'Los Halcones': Made in the USA" *Proceso* 1388, 8 June 2003, 36–42; Raúl Álvarez Garín, *La Estela de Tlatelolco: Una Reconstrucción histórica del Movimiento estudiantil del 68* (México: ITACA, 2002); Raúl Jardón, *El Espionaje contra el Movimiento Estudiantil: Los documentos de la Dirección Federal de Seguridad y las agencies de inteligencia estadounidense en 1968* (México: Editorial ITACA, 2003).
17 Greg Grandin, *The Last Colonial Massacre: Latin America and the Cold War* (Chicago: University of Chicago Press, 2004).
18 Carlos Tello, *La Política Económica en México, 1970–1976* (México: Siglo XXI, 1979).
19 Jorge Luis Sierra Guzmán, *El Enemigo Interno: Contrainsurgencia y Fuerzas Armadas en México* (México: Plaza y Janes, 2003), 19.
20 Alvaro Delgado, *El Ejército de Dios: Nuevas revelaciones sobre la extrema derecha en México* (México: Plaza y Janes, 2004).
21 Eric Zolov, "Expanding our Conceptual Horizons: The Shift from an Old to a New Left in Latin America," *A Contracorriente: A Journal of Social History and Literature in Latin America*, Vol. 5, No. 2, Winter 2008, 47–73.
22 FARO brought together different organizations; its slogan was "No hay arte sin ideología" (There is no art without ideology). See "Los Artistas Revolucionarios de México de Solidarizan con los Obreros en Huelga de Rivertex," Letter of Solidarity published in ¿Porque?, no. 219, 7 September 1972.
23 Ernesto Reyes, interview by author, tape recording, Mexico City, 27 July 1999; Alma Martinez, "Un Continente, Una Cultura?: The Political Dialectic for a United Chicana/o and Pan American Popular Political Theater Front, Mexico City, 1974," PhD Dissertation, Stanford University, 2006.
24 James C. Scott, *Seeing like a State*, (New Haven: Yale University Press, 2007).
25 Arturo Santamaria Gómez, *La Política entre México y Aztlán: Relaciónes Chicano Mexicanas del 68 a Chiapas 94* (Universidad Autonóma de Sinaloa and California State University, Los Angeles: 1994), 95; 57.
26 Kate Doyle, "Archivos Abiertos," *Proceso*, 1374, 2 March 2003, 39. My translation.

"Por la reunificación de los Pueblos Libres de América en su Lucha por el Socialismo"   101

27 On BOCOV, see Brian Glick, *Covert Action Against U.S. Activists and what we can do About It*. Boston: South End Press, 1989, p. 12; on Phoenix office, see http://phoenix.fbi.gov/history.htm.
28 SAC, San Antonio to Director of FBI, April 24, 1970; Director of FBI to SAC, San Antonio, April 21, 1970. Both available online at http://www.icdc.com/~paulwolf/cointelpro/specialops.htm. On COINTELPRO and the Chicana/o Movement, see Ernesto B. Vigil. *The Crusade for Justice: Chicano Militancy and the Governments War on Dissent* (Madison: University of Wisconsin Press, 1999); Pulido, 2006; Oropeza, 2005.
29 Philip Agee, *Inside the Company: CIA Diary* (New York: Bantam, 1984).
30 June 15, 1972, 10:31 am—12:10 pm, Conversation No. 735-1, Cassette Nos. 2246–2248, Oval Office, National Archives and Records Administration, Washington, DC. The audio of this and other conversations have been archived at http://www.gwu.edu/~nsarchiv/NSAEBB/NSAEBB95/
31 Ibid.
32 David Montejano, *Quixote's Soldiers: A Local History of the Chicano Movement, 1966–1981*, (Austin: University of Texas Press, 2010), 145.
33 A Los Angeles County sheriff's deputy shot and killed Salazar, a well-known Chicano journalist, during the Chicano anti-war moratorium of August 29, 1970.
34 Montejano, 145–148.
35 Memorandum on "Los Mascarones," US Department if Justice, FBI, San Antonio, Texas, September 24, 1971. MCP, BLAC, Box 1, Folder 5.
36 Juan Gómez Quiñones, *Sembradores: Ricardo Flores Magon y El Partido Liberal Mexicano: A Eulogy and Critique*, Monograph No.5 (Chicano Studies Center Publications: University of California, Los Angeles, 1973).
37 Thanks to Manolo Callahan for pointing out this case.
38 Emilio Zamora, *The World of the Mexican Worker in Texas* (College Station: Texas A&M University, 1993); Raquel Rosas, "(De)Sexing Prostitution: Race, Reform, and Sex Work in Texas, 1889–1920," forthcoming PhD dissertation, University of Texas at Austin.
39 Manuel Callahan, "This Is No War of Bandits: *Los Mártires de Tejas, 1913*," n.d., 2–3, unpublished manuscript in author's possession.
40 Mario Cantú, "Confidencia de Prensa," 1976, San Antonio, Tx., 3, and Box 2, Folder 13 MCP, BLAC.
41 Security Report, "Estado de Nuevo León," Folder 19-36, L-3, DFS, Archivo General de la Nación.
42 Alan Eladio Gómez, "'Nuestras vidas corren casi paralelas': Chicanos, Puerto Rican *Independentistas*, and the Prison Rebellion Years at Leavenworth, 1969–1972," in *Behind Bars: Latino/as and Prisons in the United States*. ed. Suzanne Oboler, (Palgrave-MacMillan, November, 2009).
43 Liz Samuels, "Improvising on Reality: The Roots of Prison Abolition," in Dan Berger, ed., *The Hidden 1970s: Histories of Radicalism*, (Rutgers University Press, 2010), 21–38.
44 Louis Mendoza, ed., *Raúl Salinas and the Jail Machine: My Weapon Is My Pen*, (Austin: University of Texas Press, 2006).
45 Raúl Salinas, interview by author, audio recording, Austin, TX, 16 June 2004.
46 "Letter to Mario Cantú Jr." February 29, 1972, reprinted in *My Pen is My Weapon*. Translation by Ben Olguín.
47 Interview with Mario Cantú by Linda Fregoso, audio recording, 5 March 1980, Longhorn Radio Network Mexican American Programs, Special Collections, BLAC.
48 Letter from the Central Comité of the PPUA to Lucio Blanco, Puebla, Mexico, 8 February 1976, Box 3, Folder 1, MCP, BLAC.

49 Colegio Jacinto Treviño was the first Chicano college in the United States. The CJT was not only a radical pedagogical alternative to traditional higher education, it was also a political project and community space targeted by the FBI for surveillance.
50 "Liberation through Struggle," *Semana de la Raza Program,* September 1973, 4. Box 3, Folder 12, MCP, BLAC.
51 Mathew Rothwell, "Transpacific Revolutionaries: The Creation of Latin American Maoism," in *New World Coming: The 1960s and the Shaping of Global Consciousness,* ed., Karen Dubinsky, et al., (Canada: Between the Lines, 2009), 106–114; Elena Poniatowska, *Fuerte es el Silencio* (Era: México, 1980), 206–207.
52 Rubén Jaramillo, a combatant in the Mexican Revolution and political leader from Morelos, who throughout the first half the 20th century was a central figure in political movements in Mexico particularly around land struggles. See Marco Belligeri, *Del agrarismo armado a la guerra de los pobres* (México: Casa. Juan Pablos, 2003); Tanalís Padilla, *Rural Resistance in the Land of Zapata: The Jaramillista Movement and the Myth of the Pax-Priísta, 1940–1962* (Durham: Duke University Press, 2008).
53 Poniatowska, 226–228.
54 Gustavo Esteva, *La Batalla en el México Rural* (México: Siglo XXI, 1980), 17.
55 Ibid. Midnight Notes Collective, "New Enclosures," in *Midnight Oil: Work, Energy, War, 1973–1992* (Brooklyn: Autonomedia, 1992) 317–333.
56 DFS security documents identify his birthplace as Tlatlaya; Poniatowska (251) and Castellanos (238) both identify Guerrero as his birthplace. See Laura Castellanos, *México armado: 1943–1981* (México, DF: Era, 2007).
57 Poniatowska, 197. My translation.
58 Castellanos, 239.
59 Israel González, Aquileo Medrano Mederos, Rafael Equihua, ingeniero Francisco Javier Fuentes Popoca, Israel González and Antonio García de León also went to China. DFS 100-15-1-73 L-397 H-12, quoted in *Informe Histórico a la Sociedad Mexicana,* vol. 7, 439.
60 Poniatowska, 249; Dick Reavis "My Recollections of Guero," May 12, 2002, Box 1, Folder 4, DRP-BLAC.
61 Poniatowska, 237. My translation.
62 "Estado de Morelos," DFS, 6 Junio 1973, 100-15-1, Exp. 13 Fs. 54, AGN.
63 Poniatowska, ibid. 243; "Estado de Morelos," DFS, 17 Aug. 1973, 100-15-1, Exp. 13 Fs. 335, AGN.
64 "Colonia 'Rubén Jaramillo' de Cuernavaca, Mor." DFS, 17 Aug. 1973, 100-15-1, Exp. 13 Fs. 335, AGN.
65 Alfredo de la Torre, interview with Mario Cantú, *Caracol* vol. 5 no. 4 (Dec. 78), 11.
66 Pulido, 2006; Ernesto Chavez, *"¡Mi Raza Primero!" (My People First!): Nationalism, Identity, and Insurgency in the Chicano Movement in Los Angeles, 1966–1978,* (Berkeley: University of California Press, 2002).
67 Raúl Salinas, interview by author, audio recording, Austin, TX, 16 June 2004. Salinas is not specific about where in Mexico they went, only that he received "basic training."
68 Castellanos, 239; Poniatowska, 266.
69 "My Recollections of Guero," May 12, 2002, Box 1, Folder 4, DRP-BLAC.
70 PPUA, "Programa General del Partido Proletario Unido de América," n.d., copy in author's possession.
71 PPUA Central Committee, "¿Quiénes Somos?," *La Lucha del Pueblo: Órgano Oficial del Partido Proletario Unido de América,* vol. 1 no. 1 (July 1975), 1–2, RSPA. This document was printed in mass in San Antonio, Texas. Letter from Florencio "El Tío" Medrano to Mario Cantú, San Antonio, TX (circa early 1976), Box 3, Folder 3, MCP, BLAC.
72 Ibid., 1–2

73 Signed by Florencio Medrano Mederos, president of the Central Committee of the Party and the First commander of the People's Army of United Liberation of America (Ejército Popular de Liberación Unido de América); Julio Roldán, VP of the CC and Commissioner of Communications; and Fortino Estrada, VP of the CC and Military Commissioner of the Army. The "call for submissions" is signed by the Commission on Education and Culture (Leticia Estrada).
74 Rothwell, 207–208.
75 Organigram de PPUA," DFS, 6 Oct. 1978, 11–249, H-50 L-1, AGN. Miguel Enriquez Espinosa was a leader of the *Movimiento de Izquierda Revolucionaria* (MIR), part of the Chilean resistance movement against the Pinochet dictatorship and was killed on October 5, 1974.
76 Alfonso Ibarra, "'Se Cumplierón las Exigencias,' Dice la Familia de la Señora Martínez Davis," *Excelsior* 11 December 1874; and "Partido Proletario Unido de América," DFS, 6 Feb. 1976, 11–249, L 2, 92, AGN; Carlos Fazio, *La Cruz y el Martillo,* (México: Planeta, 1987).
77 Quote is from Poniatowska, 274; Dick Reavis writes that the kidnapping was "disastrous," no ransom was paid and the lands were not worth much. "My Recollections of Guero," May 12, 2002, Box 1, Folder 4, (DRP-BLAC).
78 Bill Towery, "Tortured in Mexico," *San Antonio Light,* 17 October 1975; "Smuggling of U.S. Guns into Mexico Said Rising," *The Monitor* 26 October 1975.
79 Ibid., "Press Release," Ramón Chacón Defense Committee, n.d., RSPA.
80 "Ramón Raúl Chacón Political Prisoner in Mexico," Ramón Chacón Defense Committee newsletter, n.d., RSPA.
81 Bill Towery, ibid.
82 "Dos de AIT quedan bien presos," *El Norte,* 15 October 1975.
83 Ramón Chacón Defense Committee, "Libertad for Ramón Raúl Chacón," n.d.
84 "Abundiz y su Esposa Trasladados a Monterrey, N.L.," *El Diario de Nuevo Laredo,* 7 October 1975; "Monterrey, N.L.," DFS, 3 Oct. 1973, 11–249, Exp. 1 Fs. 18–22, AGN; "Estado de Nuevo León," DFS, 3 Oct. 1973, 11–249, Exp. 1 Fs. 1–3, AGN.
85 "Mexican Torture Probe Pushed," *San Antonio Light,* 17 December 1975; "Mario Cantú niega y apela a LEA y HK," *El Norte,* 15 October 1975; "CIA, FBI are linked to Torture of 2 Men," *San Antonio Light,* 17 October 1975. Box 3, Folder 3, MCP, BLAC.
86 "Activista chicano hablará hoy del tráfico de armas," *San Antonio Light* 3 January 1976.
87 Mario Cantú, "Confidencia [sic] de Prensa," 1976, San Antonio, TX, 3, and Box 2, Folder 13 MCP, BLAC; "PPUA Calls Press Conference in the U.S.," English reprint of press release, *Bracero: Órgano de la Liga Flores Magon,* vol.1, no.1 (1976), 3, Box 4, Folder 1, MCP, BLAC.
88 Quoted in Montejano, 196.
89 "Querido Compañero Mario," undated letter to from Florencio Medrano to Mario Cantú, Box 2, Folder 2, MCP, BLAC.
90 RCDC, "Press Release," n.d., RSPA.
91 "Imponen 20 años a dos agents del PPUA aquí," *El Norte,* April 3, 1977.
92 "Ordenan apresar a Mario Cantú," *El Norte,* April 6, 1977.
93 "Estado de Nuevo León," DFS, 5 Mayo 1977, 100-17-1, Exp. 3 Fs. 231, AGN.
94 "Reunión del Pueble/People's Gathering," flyer, TU-CASA, Rubén Salazar Cultural Center, 26 June 1977, Box 3, Folder 1, MCP, BLAC. At this gathering Chacón shared the stage with Bert Corona, William Kunstler, Jose Molina (CLETA), Margie Ratner (Center for Constitutional Rights), Nicasio Dimas, and Mario Cantú.
95 Castellanos, 259.
96 "Partido Proletario Unido de América," DFS, 6 Feb. 1976, 11–249, L 2, Fs. 91–97, AGN.

97 *Informe Histórico*, vol. 7, 490, indicates that some of the groups came together at the Congress; Castellanos, 290.
98 Formerly the Frente Campesino Independiente (FCI).
99 José Coronado Pérez, "Armados con Machetes y Escopetas 600 Campesinos Toman 1,800 Hectáres," *Excélsior* 8 October 1978.
100 De la Torre interview; "Mario Cantú Backs Revolt," *San Antonio Light* 10 October 1978; Press Release, United States Committee in Solidarity with the People of Mexico—Liga Ricardo Flores Magon, 5 June 1978, Box 3, Folder 5, MCP, BLAC; Reavis, "Unreliable Witness," *Texas Monthly* July 25, 1980, 10.
101 De la Torre interview, 16.
102 De la Torre interview, 16. In an undated letter to Cantú, Medrano admonishes Cantú for his statements as "many organizations are asking us for help and we can't even solve our own problems," Letter from "El Tío" [Güero] to Mario Cantú, Box 13, Folder 3, DRP, BLAC.
103 "Statement by Mario Cantú," dated December 4, 1978, Paris, France. Reprinted in *Caracol*, May 1979, 4.
104 For a brief discussion of the political history of *Por Qué?*, and its enigmatic and controversial editor Mario Menéndez, see Jacinto Rodríguez Munguía, *La otra guerra secreta: Los archivos prohibidos de la prensa y el poder,* (México: Debate, 2007), 207–219.
105 Letter from Mario Cantú to Corky Gonzalez, 20 May 1980, Box 2, Folder 6, MCP, BLAC.
106 "El Movimiento Chicano Denuncia: CARTER NO RESPETA LOS DERECHOS HUMANOS," Comité Europeo de Solidaridad con El Pueblo Chicano, n.d. Box 3, Folder 5, MCP, BLAC.
107 "El régimen mejicano, culpable de la tragedia de los emigrantes a Estados Unidos," *Egin*, 12 Matatzak 1979, Box 3, Folder 5, MCP, BLAC.
108 Poniatowska, 275–276; "Asesinan en México al Dirigente Guerrillero Florencio Medrano (Güero)," Comité Europeo de Solidaridad con el Pueblo Chicano, 20 Abril 1979, Madrid, España, Box 2, Folder 1, DRP, BLAC.
109 *Informe Histórico,* 490.
110 Larry Jolidon, "Revolutionary dies, Mexican rebel leader killed, leaves void among followers," *Austin American-Statesman*, April 14,1979.
111 "ASESINAN EN MEXICO AL DIRIGENTE GUERRILLERO FLORENCIO MERANO (GÜERO), *Comité Europeo de Solidaridad con El Pueblo Chicano*, April 20, 1979, 1, Box 2, Folder 1, DRP-BLAC.

5

FROM BOOKS TO BULLETS

Youth Radicalism and Urban Guerrillas in Guadalajara

Fernando Herrera Calderón

> The people at all times have the inalienable right to alter or modify their form of government.
> —1917 Mexican Constitution, Article 39

Luis Echeverría, the newly elected President of Mexico, took office in 1970 in the midst of a brewing crisis. His election was controversial, yet a part of Mexican society were optimistic about his political program, of *apertura democrática* (democratic opening), and the president's willingness to reconcile with students in the wake of the 1968 student massacre.[1] For the most part the *Partido Revolucionario Institucional* (Institutional Revolutionary Party, PRI) failed to cajole the majority of society into believing Mexico was entering a new phase of true democratic opening. In the early 1970s, a revolutionary volunteerism imbued youth circles across the nation and prompted thousands to reject mainstream politics and the empty promises of Echeverría and the PRI, by opting instead for armed resistance as a means to topple the ruling party and implement a revolutionary government. Undertaking an endeavor of this magnitude came across as utterly quixotic, absurd, and even pointless, to a majority of Mexican society.[2] Without popular support and lacking comprehensive training in guerrilla warfare, urban guerrilla movements appeared destined for a tragic end. Yet, despite unfavorable conditions, a faction of the student population were determined to propagate a new revolution and demonstrate that despite their privileged positionality as students they would not be deterred from spearheading the struggle. While urban guerrillas fought counterinsurgency forces on city streets, the university also remained a place of contention.

At the University of Guadalajara in the early 1970s, hundreds of students were involved in violent clashes to regain control of the university from the mafia-style student group loyal to the PRI, the *Federación Estudiantil de Guadalajara* (Student Federation of Guadalajara, FEG), whose members were known as *fegistas*.[3] University administrators, local politicians, and the police portrayed the provocations against the FEG as acts orchestrated by rebels simply looking to create havoc, until five armed students kidnapped Javier Macías Chávez, President of the student body and loyal to the FEG, at the Number 4 Preparatory School in 1971.[4] Weeks later the kidnappers were apprehended and Macías Chávez was freed unharmed. The detainees were summarily interrogated, tortured, and temporarily "disappeared"[5] by secret service agents ahead of being showcased to the public as trophies, to be humiliated, thus portraying the PRI as a pillar of democracy. Official interrogation reports identified the culprits as militants belonging to the *Frente Estudiantil Revolucionario* (Student Revolutionary Front, FER)—whose members were known as *feroces* (the ferocious)—a student organization turned urban guerrilla movement founded by radical-leftists and barrio youth at the University of Guadalajara in 1970.

Besides describing the transition of the FER from a student group to an armed revolutionary organization, this chapter focuses on a number of key elements that shaped the FER and transformed it into one of the most celebrated guerrilla movements of the 1970s. While most people believe that the armed struggles of the 1970s were comprised of student groups disconnected from mainstream society, I argue that the rise of the FER offers a counter-story. This case study demonstrates that the FER sought to democratize the university before going underground. Also, the group's strong proletarian background allowed it to connect with politically and socially marginalized students. By attempting to reclaim the university from the FEG they pushed for educational reform and fought the ruling party's official propaganda, using intellectual weapons and revolutionary rhetoric, from within the ivory tower. Despite their peaceful intentions, within a year members were forcefully pushed underground by repeated violence. Because political violence had become so prevalent at the University of Guadalajara, and it had become increasingly clear that the government was funding the FEG, the more radical faction of the group, spearheaded by the Campaña brothers, entertained the possibility of joining the growing number of armed struggles proliferating throughout the country.[6] Yet the FER lacked a number of essential components, namely ideological uniformity, a strong membership of militants, and training in urban guerrilla warfare.

Why did Guadalajara transform into a seedbed for revolutionaries and why does the FER hold a special place in the social imaginary of the Mexican Dirty War? This has largely to do with the *feroces'* invaluable contributions to insurgent politics and the ethos of student-revolutionary militancy. First, the organization sought new ways to organize the masses by building on the methods of previous popular political mobilizations and armed struggles. Student-revolutionaries believed universities had been transformed into "factories" to produce agents for the state and promote the ruling party's propaganda. At a time when radical students were precipitously going underground and assuming they were prepared to organize the masses, *feroces* initially resisted taking such an accelerated leap and instead envisioned building a revolutionary movement in universities and high schools from the bottom up.[7] While students believed that class warfare was a vital component of revolutionary theory, *feroces* believed that an intellectual battle had to be won in the universities and high schools as well.

Second, being a student immediately created a social barrier between them and the social groups they sought to align with to overthrow the government. The relatively unfavorable historical track record of student–worker alliances in Mexico demonstrates the leeriness towards Mexican youth displayed by the proletariat and peasantry.[8] The FER worked to find schemes to facilitate the radicalization of workers and urban peasants, and prove that their struggles were historically interconnected. Against these odds the FER sought to ease the politicalization of popular groups by first recruiting proletariat youth in order to gain a foothold in working-class communities. This strategy would have a twofold outcome: it forged a student–proletariat identity among militants and garnered the attention of armed revolutionary organizations eager to put into practice the strategies hatched by the FER. These contributions to insurgent politics make the FER one of the most revered urban guerrilla movements amongst former revolutionaries and according to one ex-revolutionary, "a phenomenon."[9]

Milestones and Breakthroughs

In 1968 the student movement ended in a violent massacre at the Plaza of the Three Cultures in Mexico City, when the armed forces and secret service agents ambushed a peaceful demonstration, killing an uncertain number of students and bystanders, and arresting the movement's leadership. In response to the vicious onslaught there was talks amongst a small fraction of the student left that the only logical step open was an armed insurrection.[10] Taking such a radical leap sparked unfavorable reactions, especially from Gilberto Guevara Niebla, a well-known leader of the 1968 student movement. Niebla vehemently argued that "to go underground means doing nothing,"[11] and few actually accepted the calling. In fact, only the *Lacandones* from the National Polytechnic Institute in Mexico City were founded in direct response to the massacre.[12] Other groups participated in acts of revolutionary propaganda but it was not until 1971 that the proliferation of urban guerrilla movements occurred.

During the 1968 student movement, proponents of the armed struggle were present in demonstrations and discussions facilitated by the *Consejo Nacional de Huelga* (National Strike Committee), though their presence was substantially limited because of their direct action initiatives. Speaking about a rarely discussed undercurrent within the *Movimiento*, former leader of the student movement, Raúl Alvarez claimed, "hardliners were an ever present entity within the Movement, but their ideas contradicted the CNH's policy. They were very impatient, yet I respected their determination."[13] Openly allowing the advocacy for an armed struggle would have been detrimental to the student movements, contradicted its non-violent stance, and invited repression by the government who was desperately on the look out for any indications to bolster their own conspiracy theory that 68ers (members of the 1968 student movement in Mexico) were funded and controlled by foreign conspirators. Nevertheless, the PRI plotted conspiracy theories with unfounded evidence by routinely pinning spontaneous acts of violence on pseudo-revolutionaries working within the 1968 student movement.[14]

In the aftermath of the student movement the government executed an "offensive" against student militancy until the end of President Gustavo Díaz Ordaz's incumbency.[15] Despite the ebbing of student militancy in Mexico City, youth radicalism remained a leitmotiv in government discussions. Conspiracy theories attached students to a greater plot to destabilize Mexico and nourished a "South American syndrome" and represented the first signs of the Dirty War.[16] Fearing aftershocks of student antagonism in 1968, Congress voted to authorize the use of force to suppress activists, and less than a year after the massacre Mexico City's police force received substantial upgrades in their arsenal.[17] Díaz Ordaz exploited the politics of fear by sticking to his Cold War discourse. In his book, *1968: Los archivos de la violencia*, Sergio Aguayo Quezada juxtaposed the ambiance after 1968 to McCarthyism.[18] In his own words, Claudio Palacio Rivas, a student and member of the PCM, recalls that after 1968 security agencies launched a campaign "to arrest the entire world."[19] Even without having a concrete number of how many students were taken into custody during the sweeps, when the testimonies of students, political prisoners, and police records are compared they do indicate a sharp increase in detainees and the monitoring of students.[20] Still, even though the government was not discreet in discriminately picking up students, Secretary of Defense García Barragán denied prisoners were being tortured and held at Campo Militar No. 1.[21]

Given that the leadership of the 1968 student movement were imprisoned, there were few, if any, qualified activists to breathe new life into the movement. Student radicalism appeared to be in crisis, but the brewing political situations in other universities gave birth to a new crop of radicals with the same determination as their peers in 1968. Students' demands revolved around issues about education, as well as problems plaguing marginalized social groups in their area. For instance, at the Autonomous University of Sinaloa (UAS), college and high school students worked closely in conjunction with *campesino* communities by participating in rallies and demonstrations around issues like land reform and social reforms. Like their peers from Mexico City this new wave of student movements also experienced cyclical episodes of political violence on their campuses. The hostile political environment and the advocacy of direct action triggered students to put their political inclinations through a rigorous re-evaluation, and decide if shouting radical axioms, holding demonstrations, and remaining within their ivory tower sanctuary was producing serious results, not only for them but for society in general. Ultimately, a faction of the student movement at the UAS broke off and became the *Enfermos* (Sick Ones) guerrilla movement.[22] In other states similar situations transpired. Thousands felt that the nonviolent political line was antiquated and only produced meager outcomes. While hundreds believed it was necessary to transition to direct action, more believed the conditions were not in place. Politically charged debates on campuses bred a volatile environment that eventually catalyzed factions of student groups to go underground.[23]

Given the strong student composition of urban guerrilla movements, millions of hapless Mexican youth were harassed daily at the hands of police and secret agents during the Dirty War.[24] While students around the country condemned the massacre and expressed their solidarity for the dead and their imprisoned comrades, the armed struggle option was shared amongst just a few student radicals disconnected from each other, making the likelihood of an immediate collective response unfeasible.[25] Besides lacking committed militants, supporters of the armed struggle were also fighting the ongoing battle of convincing Mexican youth that history had placed onto them the responsibility of leading the masses against the state and the ruling class, which was protected by state government. Persuading students to embrace such a challenge in the wake of the massacre turned out to be an uphill battle, seemingly destined to fail. Post-1968, when advocates of the armed struggle spoke of revolution and overthrowing the state, society refused to hear such calls coming from individuals,[26] who despite demonstrating political awareness during the student movement lacked genuine experience in the workforce. Mexican society largely proceeded to base their hopes on a glorified image of worker militancy. Aligning the proletariat with students had been attempted in the past, and disastrously failed in previous student-orchestrated popular mobilizations.[27] Angered by the passivity of workers and the urban poor, the armed struggle option considerably dwindled between 1968 and 1970, yet it continued to be a possible road to take, especially within the *Juventud Comunista* (JC, Communist Youth).

Independent of divisions between radical and moderate factions in the student left, the passivity of workers, and low morale, tensions were mounting between the Mexican Communist Party (PCM) and the JC. After 1968, the PCM lost substantial clout, especially among its youth faction.[28] Militants voiced their anger at the JC's Third Congress in 1970, in which leaders arrived prepared to engage in an ideological battle with their older comrades.[29] A tense and uncomfortable atmosphere hovered over attendees as they waited for the conference to begin. Well-known student activist, Raúl Ramos Zavala, explained the fissures of the PCM's political agenda. Like dozens before him, Ramos Zavala vilified the PCM for being out of touch with the people, as well as their paternalistic treatment of the JC. He complained the PCM was inundated with reformists, complacent with the ruling party's political program and that under the thumb of the PCM the political autonomy of youth activists was highly restricted. No persons had ever officially called for the JCM to splinter off from the PCM for good, but on this occasion Ramos Zavala proposed the measure. Five months after the Third Congress the break was official, though not everyone relinquished their affiliation with the PCM. With the break, thousands of former PCM affiliates returned to their schools and colleges eager to begin a new era of political activism. However, this break also marked the starting point for new urban guerrilla movements, especially in Guadalajara.[30]

Student Activism in Guadalajara

The reasons for the rise of the FER can be traced back to the 1930s when student activism proliferated in the state of Jalisco. While the student movement in Guadalajara occurred in waves between 1963 and 1970, it never reached the same magnitude as the 1968 student uprising in Mexico City,[31] in the decades prior to the 1960s students at the University of Guadalajara and surrounding schools and colleges demonstrated that they were influential political actors. During the presidency of populist Lázaro Cárdenas (1934–1940), major changes to the educational system and curriculum were implemented under the auspices of socialist education. Inspired by Cárdenas' radical overhaul of education, student groups formed to protect popular education and increase the enrollment of students from underrepresented social groups. However, socialist education's radical pedagogy triggered an uproar from the bourgeoisie, political elites, and the Catholic Church. Together these factions spearheaded campaigns to overturn socialist education with the "pretext that foreign ideologies have no place in the University."[32] Eventually in the late 1940s socialist education was abandoned, but vestiges of its pedagogy remained intact in universities and schools. After 1950, Mexico's university system endured another stirring change to its curriculum, particularly in politically conservative regions. In Guadalajara, powerful families assisted in funding anti-radical student groups and used their political clout to infiltrate university politics. Eventually, students and groups with leftist leanings were marginalized, and spaces to express discontent and concerns about university matters were closed, resulting in the de-democratization of the university. Student groups mobilized against these changes in an attempt to hinder the institutionalization of curriculum which they deemed threatened intellectual freedom and promoted censorship. However, these mobilizations proved fruitless. Moreover, internal factionalism took a major toll on radical collective organizations.[33] Without a cohesive leftist student organization in place at the University of Guadalajara, the FEG was able to hold influential positions in student politics.

With the disintegration of leftist groups and the government's conservative turn, pro-government student groups surged, namely the FEG. Founded in 1949 by Carlos Ladewig Ramírez, the son of a distinguished politician from Jalisco, the FEG was connected to powerful political families. With an organic connection to influential people in politics the FEG functioned not only as a liaison between students and university administrators, but more importantly as a special interest group for Guadalajara's conservative elite and a springboard to political prominence.[34] Originally viewed as nationalists and avid anti-imperialists,[35] these labels changed once the Mexican government embraced anti-communist rherotic. *Fegistas* purported to sympathize with revolutionary movements, yet like the PRI they only did so with the conditions that they were not homegrown and would keep their hands away from Mexico. Also, the FEG "faithfully" aligned itself to the "revolutionary ideology of the bourgeois state."[36] With those ideas in mind the FEG marketed their political program with a progressive undertone—attracting students from heterogeneous backgrounds, giving the impression it represented all social groups within the university system. Soon after becoming the dominant voice at the University of Guadalajara in the early 1960s, the ruling party took notice of the FEG and began to immediately provide it with political support in order to assure it remained a power in student politics.

When the PRI began veering towards the right of the political spectrum, the FEG also began to change its political inclinations.[37] From an ideological perspective it became a champion of anti-communism and even pressured President Gustavo Díaz Ordaz (1964–1970) to be less lenient towards subversive groups. *Fegistas'* anti-leftist sentiments also transcended university boundaries. In an effort to mold students into champions of the ruling party's official propaganda, *fegistas* branched into high schools and preparatory schools throughout the city. From a young age students were exposed to political violence on their campuses and grew up either loathing the FEG or joining its ranks. Ramírez Ladewig regularly met with ruling party officials and local politicians to discuss the state of Jalisco's education system. In these meetings he embellished the predicaments facing the university and requested the state continue investing in the group and in exchange the FEG would see that student disturbances were contained or eliminated. His father responded favorably to Ramirez Ladewig's elaborated overview by funneling money into the group, supporting the ideological training of FEG militants, and inconspicuously infiltrating the university's administrative body by assigning positions of power to loyalists. From *Los Pinos,* Díaz Ordaz applauded the partnership forged by both sides and exalted their initiatives to create a "safe and comfortable space" for students to demonstrate their intellectual capacities.[38] Students who participated in the daily life of the university and remained complacent were made to believe they were in control of their education and actively participating in everyday policymaking. Those who explicitly complained about conditions were summarily repressed, accused of subversion, and excluded.

Political violence sponsored by the FEG manifested itself on a number of occasions throughout its reign, though it was not until the 1968 student movement when the group took violence to a new extreme. When the 1968 student movement began students at the University of Guadalajara were largely detached from what was going on in Mexico City.[39] Throughout the student movement political repression executed by the FEG mushroomed to unprecedented levels. *Fegistas* launched a violent offensive against supporters of the student movement at the university, as well as intercepting the flow of information between Mexico City and Guadalajara.[40] When the leaders of the student movement dispatched brigades on occasional trips to Guadalajara their liaisons were violently besieged by awaiting *fegistas*.[41] Likewise, students at the University of Guadalajara who manifested their solidarity with 68ers encountered similar consequences. The repression of 68ers and sympathizers spoke to the severity of the ongoing political, social, and cultural crisis at the University of Guadalajara. Censorship percolated into traditionally leftist departments judged to be safe spaces for radicals, and political violence reached its apogee when *fegistas* expanded to murdering students considered viable threats.[42] At the *Zone Militar* in Guadalajara, *fegistas* were allocated machine guns to crack down on student disobedience.[43] The group's effectiveness in impeding the opposition was complemented by its talent in persuading students to believe that communist tendencies were menacing their civil liberties and education.[44] To exemplify the FEG's reign beyond the University of Guadalajara, in September 1968 a prominent leader of the group published an article in Guadalajara's *El Sol* speaking *on behalf* of students from high schools, preparatory schools, and trade schools requesting the President to use force to eliminate the student rebellion.[45] When the student movement was finally crushed on October 2nd in the massacre at the Plaza of Tlatelolco, the FEG manifested their unconditional support for Diaz Ordaz and hailed the actions taken by the military.[46]

Power, Youth, Identity, and the FER

> It takes a long time to be young.
>
> —Pablo Picasso

The historical record before 1968 overlooks students' contributions to popular politics and much less to insurgent politics after the urban guerrilla experience. Because students enjoy certain privileges and amenities unavailable to marginalized groups, the agents of revolutionary change (peasants and workers) have found it difficult to take students' revolutionary commitment seriously.[47] When the Mexican student movement burst onto the scene in 1968, parts of society clearly exhibited their affinity towards students by marching alongside them in demonstrations, yet support for students was not ubiquitous.[48] Using the participation of a small percentage of workers, much less peasants, during the student movement, proponents of the armed struggle naively assumed these social groups would also join students and professionals in a revolutionary process. However, revolutionary groups like the FER tried to redress this issue in order to build a new revolutionary vanguard across social boundaries.

By the 1960s, leftist students were without a student organization at the University of Guadalajara that catered to their political objectives. Without a group in place to channel their demands to university administrators, much less challenge the FEG for the dominant voice on campus, leftist students' voices were outright ignored. The initiative to amalgamate independent student groups into a single bloc was tabled by activists from the School of Philosophy and Letters, the School of Economics, and the Law School at the University of Guadalajara. Creating a foundational base within these schools made sense given all three departments were major stronghold for the JCM and students sympathizers with different Marxists tenets.[49] Contrary to previous activists in Guadalajara this new wave of radicals was more ideologically attuned. Determined to have a voice within the university and to end the crisis of student militancy the FER was in created in 1970 by students from the University of Guadalajara and members of the JC. The founding nucleus was comprised of radicals with prior experience in student politics at the University of Guadalajara as well as others who initiated their political careers in the FER. The most politically "mature" militants arrived from the JC, though a large number who were unaligned with socialist or communist parties also exhibited political awareness.[50]

Secretly gathering on and off campus, militants addressed the crisis of student activism at the University of Guadalajara, the eroding of popular education, the lack of transparency and democratic opening, and devised plans to eliminate the FEG while exploring the prospects of fomenting a nationwide student movement. Apart from these discussions activists analyzed the oversights made by the 1968 student movement and sought to redress these mistakes, one being the 68ers' failure to mobilize proletarian youth.[51] The more revolutionary militants proposed defeating the *fegistas* with the same violent techniques they used to handicap adversaries.[52] However, carrying weapons was only justified for self-defense purposes, given the FER anticipated confrontations with *fegistas* once the group went public. However, before the FEG orchestrated attack on members of the FER, the local government was already in the process of fostering a bad image of the group. Because students from the University of Guadalajara with communist tendencies formed the group's backbone, the local government immediately presumed the FER was ideologically militaristic.[53]

As a student group, members of the FER sought to make a break from their privileged status by first appropriating the moniker of "student-proletariat." By adopting this singularity, revolutionaries anticipated that their political program for radical change would be taken seriously if they drew a clear linkage between the plights of workers and peasants, and those of students. Members of the FER lodged the argument that because politicians were not working-class or peasants, they were unsympathetic to issues plaguing proletarian and rural communities, yet they were making decisions affecting their daily lives.[54] However, before this cross-class alliance could materialize *feroces* had to authenticate their student–proletarian identity, therefore recruiting and indoctrinating proletarian youth became a prerequisite ahead of organizing workers. Leaders thus divided the FER into two branches. One was responsible for organizing in the university, the other was in charge of recruiting in proletarian neighborhoods.[55]

Like their peers in Sinaloa, the FER wanted to be more than a simple student group only out to improve their own group's political dilemmas. Student activism was limited and needed to expand its horizons by interlinking their demands with broader social issues. Leaders believed that barrio youth were genuine revolutionaries who merely required ideological orientation but would provide *feroces* with an "authentic" lens into proletarian life.[56] One of the barrios created as a result of the stream of migrants into Guadalajara in the 1940s and 50s in search of improving their economic circumstances, was San Andrés. Characterized by its working-class composition, San Andrés transformed into a decisive recruiting epicenter for the FER, and a space where its student–proletariat premise was tested and flourished. Barrio working-class youth grew up disadvantaged, lived within modest limits, and many were compelled to balance school as well as hold a part-time job in order to contribute to their family's income.[57]

Apart from the FER being made up of students from the University of Guadalajara, the second group that came to form a major part of the organization before and after it went underground were the *Vikingos* (Vikings), a barrio gang from the San Andrés neighborhood. In the early 1960s youth from the barrio began calling themselves Vikings to symbolize their loyalty to their respective barrio. Beyond its geographic connotation, youth who identified as Vikings appropriated the rebellious identity attached to the name. According to Aguayo Quezada, a close associate of the *Vikingos*, during the 1960s barrio youth were in the process of building a strong rebellious identity, which he based on economic shortcomings "but more likely a sense of irrelevance that characterized the decade."[58] Gangs were also spaces for building solidarity around a common identity. Antonio Orozco Michel, a former *feroz*, recalls that in gangs, youngsters quickly realized that one shared the same aspirations, shortcomings, and lack of alternatives as his or her peers.[59] Through these discussions barrio youth saw in each other more commonalities than differences, leaving little or no space for competition and bounded by all the idiosyncrasies that embodied barrio life. From language to dressing styles, these elements played a fundamental function in the construction of a counter-identity against the hegemonic social culture and the ruling party's idea of *Mexicandad*. While upper-class youth made every effort to distinguish their social milieu from *los lumpenes* (the lumpens), proletarian youth strived to maintain the barrio identity and refute the elitist lifestyle. Outside the barrio, local politicians and law enforcement categorized the group as a gang of delinquents, apolitical, and perpetuators of indiscriminate violence fueled by "class resentment."[60] Likewise, the Vikings' gangster-like behavior encouraged the criminalization of barrio youth. Law enforcement rarely entered San Andrés but outside its borders *Vikingos* faced daily discrimination. Police routinely victimized students on the streets, leading to a number of isolated skirmishes and prejudice-laden arrests. Incidents like these only strengthened prejudices against barrio communities,[61] and drew unaligned youth to join the Vikings.

Before establishing a presence in schools and the University of Guadalajara, the Vikings performed their own style of resistance against the local and federal government by protecting their communities, through acts of vandalism, petty crimes, and territorial protection. These actions were often counterproductive and served to keep out federal and local officials—further marginalizing disadvantaged communities. While Vikings were not apolitical, their socioeconomic background and reputation for being unruly impeded their political ambitions. In the absence of any political organizations willing to take the Vikings under their wing, militants sought to build a reputable name for themselves in the realm of student politics by establishing a presence in preparatory schools, high schools, and eventually the University of Guadalajara.[62] It was typical for *Vikingos* to attend preparatory schools affiliated to the University of Guadalajara, which also meant they were politically controlled by the FEG.[63] As the group became increasingly politicized through daily student life, many Vikings transformed into dynamic political actors in youth struggles at preparatory schools as well as the University of Guadalajara and "wished to study and continue participating in politics."⁶⁴ As a result of their political activism, Vikings came in direct contact with the group's methods of eliminating its opposition. Yet, apart from unorganized students at the University of Guadalajara, the Vikings were prepared to directly confront members of the FEG if necessary. A number of skirmishes between both sides transpired while the Vikings were establishing a foothold outside their barrio. Taking note of these confrontations, members of the FER decided to try to forge a relationship with the Vikings given that a number of its initial members had friends in the group.

Both groups united almost immediately after members of the FER contacted the leaders of the Vikings in 1970. Although initially Vikings and *feroces* were not united across ideological boundaries, they shared a common abhorrence towards authority, elitism, and particularly the FEG, and more importantly each side complemented what the other lacked. In the case of the FER, the Vikings supplied them with militants and a desperately needed foothold in the barrio, while *feroces* reciprocated with ideological indoctrination. While not every Viking joined the FER, the political program professed by *feroces* attracted the more politicized faction of the Vikings, who immediately joined the group in its struggle to control the University of Guadalajara.⁶⁵

With an established link with proletarian youth the FER underwent a radicalization process. The goals and aspirations of the FER expanded to wider social issues plaguing the city, particularly the communities where members and Vikings were residents. By late November 1970, the FER, with the assistance of the Vikings, commenced its program of radicalizing the barrios. The campaign in the barrios was meant not only to unite students against the FEG, but also to raise consciousness. Meetings and discussions with barrio youth were initially carried out by members of the FER, though a few prominent *Vikingos* also demonstrated their political astuteness by leading discussions on various topics related to the social and political issues facing the local community and country.⁶⁶ Vikings and *feroces* encouraged their comrades to take a more proactive role in their daily political lives and demonstrate to society that students could also be involved social actors. While indoctrination was lax during the student group phase, ideological instruction became more rigid when the FER went underground. In charge of supervising the radicalization of the barrio was Armando Rentería, a member of the FER, who during his tenure as the leader of this campaign, spearheaded the creation of more than 80 *comité de barrio* (barrio committees), some of them made up entirely of females.⁶⁷ The *feroces* presence in the San Andrés barrio was unquestionable. The group had succeeded in winning a large number of barrio youth in addition to other students at the University of Guadalajara and its affiliated schools. But besides networking with barrio youth, with the help of the Vikings, the FER expanded into other barrios around Guadalajara. Apart from providing the FER with members, Ramón Gil Olivio, a previous member of this organization, states "the Vikings' barrio origins was key" largely because they were able to obtain "paper and medicine on the black market."[68] In geopolitical terms, the barrio was also a "safe space" given it was unlikely the FEG would try to enter the it and risk being walloped by Vikings.

> I don't wanna be mistreated by no bourgeoisie.
> —Leadbelly, "Bourgeois Blues"

This student–proletariat identity embraced by the FER set the foundation for a controversial theory which developed after the group went underground. While the concept of the university as a factory was thrown around during the 1968 student movement, the idea failed to stick. The *feroces'* fight to democratize the University of Guadalajara and its elaboration of the student–proletarian moniker formed the basis of *la tesis de la universidad-fábrica* (the Thesis of the University Factory), a manifesto written by one of the leading revolutionary intellectuals of the guerrilla movement, Ignacio Torres Olivares, "El Sebas." Torres Olivares was originally from Guadalajara but was attending college in the northern city of Monterrey. There he participated in a student strike and meet Ramos Zavala, as well as other future revolutionaries of the urban guerrilla experience. In this assessment Torres Olivares urged students to fight authoritarianism and exploitation in the university, as well as the factories and countryside, and to think of themselves as agents of revolutionary change. The analogy between the university and the factory as places of exploitation added reinforcement to the student–proletarian identity conceptualized by the FER. The *tesis* argues "the university is part of a new industrial branch," that produces educated individuals who are expected to participate in the development of their nation. The "working force" is composed of teachers and students, thus making both groups into workers. Other than transforming students and teachers into workers, *la tesis de la universidad-fábrica* claims, "in capitalist society the massification of education transformed universities into producers of culture,[69] and in the Mexican case, the official propaganda of the PRI.

Because universities and schools were considered institutions created to endorse the ruling party's official propaganda, counter-hegemonic struggles had to be executed on two fronts: on the streets through direct action and through a war of ideas in the schools and universities.[70] While a branch of the FER was busy organizing barrio youth, the other faction continued to do political work at the University of Guadalajara. Apart from organizing proletariat youth, the FER still had as a primary objectives to re-appropriated institutions, namely the university, exploited by the national bourgeoisie and the PRI to safeguard their dominance.[71] While these strategies were not groundbreaking and vaguely entertained in preceding student movement, above all other urban-armed struggles the FER succeeded in applying these concepts and setting a precedent for other groups. With a workable political-line that united students across class boundaries and that embraced the struggle to regain control of universities, the FER garnered the attention of student groups across the country, but also the attention of the federal and local government. The ruling party agreed that allowing radical students to transform the university into a political space in which to advocate "foreign" ideas endangered the lives and minds of students, as well as the university's reputation.[72]

Apart from the militaristic component of their political agenda, revolutionaries also understood their struggle as an intellectual war against the ruling elite. Urban guerrillas represented the new wave of radical intelligentsia who sought to become an active voice and avenue for workers and peasants to channel their needs and build alongside students a strong revolutionary front against the state. While not all militants were on the same intellectual level, leaders were very clear in their manifestos and discourses that the battle to overthrow the State also needed to be a war of ideas.[73] Coined by Gramsci as the "war of the position," in order for a national liberation movement to succeed it was fundamental for revolutionary forces to re-appropriate spaces used by the ruling elite as strategic locations to project a false consciousness on the underclass. Once the dominated classes expropriated the university, the voice of the ruling elite would be replaced. In theory this would trigger the reclamation of other spaces and facilitate the complete eradication of ruling class culture. By regaining control of the university the FER sought to inculcate counter-hegemonic ideas into the minds of potential militants, and conscript students into to their struggle. It is not coincidental that frontal battles against police and secret service agents mushroomed in universities and preparatory schools around the country. Declassified police documents unveil a number of disturbances caused by the infiltration of the local police and counterinsurgency units on campuses and in student-related rallies.[74]

According to former *feroces,* the University of Guadalajara had transformed into a center of political power in the service of the state,[75] overrun by people loyal to the PRI. Vestiges of popular of education were loosely in place yet students received distorted narrations of Mexican history that glorified the ruling party as a pillar of national unity, while the actuality of marginalized groups and increasing political instability permeating across the country contradicted these interpretations. Revolutionaries posited that a collective revolutionary consciousness could only be accomplished once spaces taken over by the hegemonic culture were repossessed, and anti-capitalist forces regained the commanding voice in the universities. Members of the FER argued that in a culturally diverse society, the ruling class, besides possessing economic power, also practiced a form of domination over social groups under them that defined their elitist ideas and culture as the norm, and pretended to benefit all of society when in reality it functioned as a hegemonic tool to ensure the ruling class has control over culture, society, and politics.[76]

By taking back "the Bourgeoisie's University"⁷⁷ students would be able to counteract the dominant interpretation of Mexican history and class struggle used by the PRI to safeguard their control and power. While there were other social groups and cultural movements that challenged the norms of the ruling class, *feroces*' plan of action to challenge state power hit directly at the heart of the PRI's dominance, both politically and culturally. Student militants felt the ruling party with its distorted idealization of the peasantry and working-class created a false consciousness that made it seem these social groups were participating in the everyday decision-making, despite continuing to be marginalized by the ruling elite.⁷⁸

From the University to the Underground

One of the first major assaults planned by the FER occurred in the early hours of September 1970. The goal was to forcefully regain control of the student housing at the University of Guadalajara, which had been overrun by "free loaders."⁷⁹ At approximately 3 am residents were awakened by members of the FER, attacking the student-housing complex and taking control.⁸⁰ No one was killed or seriously injured during the strike, but several students residing in the housing complex were caught off guard and beaten. From within the complex Andrés Zuno, official spokesmen for the action and son of former Jalisco governor José Guadalupe Zuno, informed the press about the creation of the FER.⁸¹ As a representative he revealed "students decided to take over the student residency in order to drive out the gangsters and vandals who occupied the building" (meaning supporters of the FEG).⁸² During the operation the Vikings proved to be an indispensible asset by carrying out most of the dangerous actions. Still in control of the complex, the FER outlined their stipulations. They demanded the democratization of the university, the expulsion of the FEG, the prosecution of FEG members for crimes against students, and the guarantee of public education for all young people. University administrators responded to the takeover by sending an undisclosed number of police units to forcefully remove protesters from the complex. *Feroces* retreated without any major incident but students unaffiliated to the FER saw this action against the FEG as heroic and drew an unwavering amount of praise. From this ephemeral affair the FER rewoke a previous complacent student left, although also triggering political repression on the campus of the University of Guadalajara, high schools, and on the streets of Guadalajara.

Days after the takeover concluded with the intervention of the police, *feroces* coordinated rallies in departments throughout the University of Guadalajara to promote the newly founded student group and its intentions. The rallies amassed hundreds of curious students and created quite a commotion for administrators. Half way through the rally the situation turned violent when a contingent of *fegistas,* headed by their leader Fernando Medina Lúa, arrived at the demonstration and instigated a shootout with *feroces.* Medina Lúa was shot and later died from his wounds, sparking off an extensive witch-hunt against *feroces.*[83] News soon arrived about the bleak situation at the University of Guadalajara to ruling party officials in Guadalajara and Mexico City. While president Echeverría sought to resort to friendly relations between students and the PRI, the ensuing political violence in Guadalajara ran counter to his propositions. Jalisco's state government categorized the FER as a band of delinquents who only wanted to disturb the peace and create disorder in schools. The FER continued coordinated protests and propaganda campaigns decrying venality in university politics, demanding academic freedom, a voice in policy making, and denouncing the FEG. In response the FEG exploited the politics of fear and argued that radical student groups embodied the crisis in the Mexican education system and the consequences of allowing radicals to pervert the minds of defenseless and unworldly students with their idealist rhetoric and distorted interpretation of Mexican history.[84]

A serious blow to the group's structure occurred that same year when Arnuflo Prado Rosas, "El Compa," a charismatic rising leader and Viking, was assassinated in Guadalajara by the FEG.[85] Police reports concluded that a thuggish group aligned with the FEG called *Los Gordos* (the Fat Ones) orchestrated the murder of "El Compa."[86] His death drew national attention; hundreds of people from around the country attended the funeral. According to one former member of the FER, Benjamín Ramírez Castañeda, "Prado Rosas was a fundamental part of the organization who unified the San Andrés barrio and other student organizations within and outside the University of Guadalajara."[87] Politically, Prado Rosas' death did little to affect the FEG's dirty war tactics, but did engender a great number of Vikings to radicalize. In response to his sudden death, in a political maneuver, members of the FER took over a radio station in Guadalajara and announced their objectives to the people. In addition, they made a call to students to rise against the injustices of the FEG. The announcement was even translated into English for the American district of the city.[88]

In an act of vengeance, the FER killed Javier Agustín García Gariby, an FEG associate and Prado Rosas' assassin.[89] Because "El Compa" had been a venerated barrio hero and leader, his death took an enormous toll on the Vikings and *feroces'* morale. Realizing his death was a serious blow to the FER, Guillermo Gómez Reyes, a prominent figure in the FEG, guaranteed the almost if not complete elimination of the FER.[90] The assertion, despite being untrue, was enough to put the PRI and local government officials at ease. Provided the FEG admitted the actuality of student disturbances, leaders feared the PRI and local government would immediately lose confidence in the group and withdraw their support in exchange for another organization. With that in mind, it only made sense that political repression had to be even more severe. Widening repression appeared a logical step to curb the FER at the height of its power.

Contrary to previous anti-FEG movements, the FER was the first oppositional force capable of fighting back with the same intensity. Adding to this nuisance, government officials began abandoning their support for the FEG. Enraged by these actions, the FEG vocalized their discontent towards politicians and the lack of protection for its militants against the FER. One *fegista* even spoke directly with influential members of Jalisco's state government and provided the right officials with the names and addresses of those involved in the murders of their members. In an attempt to assure the crimes would be at the top of the investigators' priority list, the FEG threatened to "personally locate each and every Viking and kill them" if nothing was done immediately.[91]

Threatened by unremitting political persecution from both the state and the FEG, the FER was finally pushed underground in 1972. Police documents indicate that more than 100 revolutionaries were already imprisoned for participating in activities deemed a threat to national security.[92] Nonviolence became a policy of the past as it had proved ineffective in a number of circumstances. Besides evaluating their own situation, *feroces* followed the persecution of students in other parts of the country. They watched, read, and discussed how repressive forces aligned to the government were discriminately targeting people of their social category. Many felt it was time to "fight back" and demonstrate students were not going to allow state-sponsored violence against their peers or any other activists to continue without resistance.[93]

Going underground prompted leaders to re-shift their political goals. The nucleus headed by Alfredo Campaña Lopéz and other members of the JCM advocated that the group's political line required a comprehensive overhaul in which the primary change would be transforming into an urban guerrilla movement.[94] To assure the exponential radicalization of the youth, the FER formed more than 70 cells and dispersed them into sectors where the group had insufficient footing.[95] These cells immersed militants into student circles where they singled out specific persons they thought were likely to sympathize with their new political line. Revolutionaries continued drawing in militants with their student–proletariat premise as well as using to their benefit the growing discontent on campuses. Never losing site of the importance of radicalizing students, the FER created an armed revolutionary organization during a period in Latin American radical history where students were still considered improper agents of revolutionary change. Under a new political line, students in the FER brought militancy to a new level, and became the largest counter-hegemomic movement after the Cristero Rebellion in the 1920s.

As an urban guerrilla movement the FER continued maintaining its two fronts (in the streets and university) in order to "make the revolution" on different fronts and "drive the government crazy."[96] Members of the JCM continued to hold positions of power in the FER, especially after Zuno Jr. left the organization following the group's underground move. Strategically he was against taking up arms, but continued to offer his services to the FER as an indoctrination instructor. Militants engage in revolutionary actions, but these amounted to little. Most of their political maneuvers were executed in the university and other spaces where potential radical youth could be drawn into the movement.

The FER's strategies of student–proletariat organizing resonated in youth circles throughout the nation. Student groups like *Los Enfermos* (the Sick Ones) from Sinaloa sent a number of their militants to Guadalajara to learn from the FER's organizing tactics. Leaders of other urban guerrilla movements found the FER's form of political organization to be useful and summarily began sending brigades into *colonias populares*. When a number of urban guerrilla movements convened to form one single group in March 1973, they strategically chose Guadalajara as the site for the meeting, given the city's reputation as a major revolutionary bastion and for having a strong youth front supporting the FER. After a number of meetings between independent armed revolutionary organizations, the September 23rd Communist League was born in 1973, in which *feroces* comprised a major part of the initial membership, but not everyone agreed. Testifying to the confusion after the merge, former FER militant, Enrique Velázquez recalls, "many *feroces* didn't even know about the merge. Militants simply woke up one day and they were members of the *Liga*."[97]

The creation of the *Liga* precipitated a split in the FER spearheaded by the Campaña brothers. Refusing to join the newly formed coalition, ex-members of the FER created the *Fuerzas Revolucionarias Armadas del Pueblo* (Revolutionary Armed Forces of the People, FRAP). In essence, the FRAP garnered minor accolades for their contribution to insurgent politics, but were revered for having orchestrated two of the most acknowledged kidnappings of the urban guerrilla experience. On May 4, 1973, the FRAP kidnapped US Consulate, Terrance Leonhardy in Guadalajara. For the Mexican government the kidnapping was a serious international embarrassment and put into question the efficiency of its national security doctrine. In return for the consulate's safe release, urban guerrillas issued a statement demanding the release of 30 political prisoners and their safe passage to Cuba.[98] Pressured by the United States, the government agreed to the demands and released the guerrillas and Leonhardy was granted his freedom.[99] One year later the FRAP continued targeting high ranking officials and on this occasion kidnapped José Guadalupe Zuno, father of Andrés Zuno and Esther Zuno, the First Lady of Mexico, in Guadalajara. Because of Zuno's connection with the President, the FRAP expected their demands would be promptly met, however it proved the opposite. Attorney General Pedro Ojeda Paullada publicly announced Echeverría's stance on the situation by relay: "the nation and the government do not deal with criminals."[100] Instead, the president ordered large contingents of military police to Guadalajara and arrested more than 700 people.[101] As public outcry and government repression increased, 21 days after having been kidnapped Zuno Sr. was released.

Conclusion

The urban guerrilla struggles of the 1970s broke away from nonviolent tactics by embracing guerrilla warfare as the ideal method of changing Mexico's political system. This shift transformed the face of student radicalism, and opened a space for a youth hard-line to participate in struggles immune to co-option and the ruling party's rhetoric, given that urban guerrillas refused to negotiate with the government. Yet, because the armed revolutionary movements of the Dirty War eventually collapsed, post-1968 revolutionaries' contributions to insurgent politics have been underestimated. While student-led urban guerrilla movements *were* small in number and did not represent the goals and aspirations of the entire Mexican Left, their contributions to revolutionary praxis were substantial and have gone almost unnoticed.

Armed revolutionary movements in Mexico and throughout Latin America have gone through tremendous scrutiny, both by former participants reflecting back on their militancy, and by scholars who have ranged from those presenting a critical yet objective analysis to those who have strongly decried the guerrilla experience for disrupting democracy, and precipitated their country's respective Dirty War by using the "Two Devils Thesis." The purpose of this chapter is not to participate directly in this heated debate, but to understand the context in which these struggles emerged. The emergence of the FER was not founded on the basis of class resentment, but rather censorship, exclusion from openly participating in decision-making directly salient to their education, and the passivity of the traditional agents of revolution encouraged the leap to direct action. The FER demonstrated that despite students' privileges they could break down class barriers and be taken seriously as revolutionary agents of change. Despite an unsuccessful attempt at toppling the state and instituting a genuine version of popular history in the university curriculum, *feroces'* contributions to the ethos of revolutionary praxis and theory was noticeable in other revolutionary camps.

The case of student militancy in Guadalajara reveals two major dynamics of youth dissidence. First, the 1968 student movement meant different things to students. Second, this new wave of student militants sought to create a revolutionary movement that was genuinely popular by searching for new organizational strategies to facilitate cross-class alliances, beginning with proletarian youth. While their ideas did not go without criticisms, the legacy left by this underlying concept continues to find expression in contemporary student politics. During rallies and marches, political propaganda depicting students' alliance with workers and the peasantry manifests itself through chants and symbolism (e.g. the sickle and book). To this day former revolutionaries acknowledge the FER's fundamental contribution to the ethos and strategies of revolutionary politics and continue encouraging the democratization of Mexico through a student–proletariat mentality. Despite only being an independent urban guerrilla movement from 1972 to 1973, the FER defied pre-existing notions of students as credulous social actors.

Acknowledgments

I want to thank Eric Zolov, Elaine Carey, and Jecca Namakkal for offering constructive criticisms and suggestions in earlier versions. Shane Dillingham, Jennifer Boles, and Steven Allen also posed interesting questions that helped me construct this essay.

Notes

1. See Amerlia M. Kiddle and Marâ L.O. Muñoz, eds., *Populism in Twentieth Century Mexico: The Presidencies of Lázaro Cárdenas and Luis Echeverría* (Tucson: University of Arizona Press, 2010); Samuel Schmidt, *The Deterioration of the Mexican Presidency: The Years of Luis Echeverría* (Tucson: University of Arizona Press, 1991).
2. Besides not agreeing with the armed struggle, an overwhelming majority of Mexican society believed in the legacy and power of the 1910 Revolution and felt triggering a new revolution was superfluous.
3. Antonio Orozco Michel, interview with author, July 2008, tape recording, Guadalajara, Jalisco; Miguel Topete, interview with author, July 2008, tape recording and notes, Guadalajara, Jalisco. By 1971 the FEG had 70,000 affiliates. AGN, DFS, Exp. 100-12-1-71 L-19 H-80.
4. AGN, DFS, Exp. 100-12-1-71 L-3 H-34
5. AGN, DFS, Exp. 100-12-1-71 L-18 H-198.
6. AGN, DFS, Exp. 100-12-1-71 L-7 H-45.
7. Miguel Topete, interview with author, July 2008, tape recording and notes, Guadalajara, Jalisco.
8. This is not to say that student–worker/peasant alliances did not exist. In fact the first "modern" Mexican guerrilla movement, the *Grupo Popular Guerrillero* was a coalition of workers, peasants, teachers, professionals, and students. My point here is that these alliances regularly held prejudices against students.
9. José Luis Esparza, interview with author, March 2010, tape recording, Mexico City.
10. While Topete did not participate in the 1968 student movement, he mentions that after the massacre, students were taken in by a sense of revolutionary will to take extreme measures against the PRI. But in reality these groups were small and insignificant compared with the ones that emerged in the 1970s.
11. Elena Poniatowska, *Massacre in Mexico* (Columbia: University of Missouri Press, 1991), 7. Gilberto Guevara Niebla was one of the most outspoken activists against the armed struggle. The death of his cousin at the hands of urban guerrillas in Sinaloa only added to his hatred. See AGN, DFS, Exp. 100-4-73 L-226 H-2.
12. Fritz Glockner, *Memoria Roja: Historia de la guerrilla en México* (1943–1968) (México, DF: Ediciones B, 2007), 305.
13. Raúl Alvarez Garín, interview with author, July 2008, Mexico City, tape recording and notes, Comité 68.

14 See Arturo Acosta Chaparro, *Movimientos subversivos en México* (México, DF: n.p., 1990). Evidence suggesting the appearance of a guerrilla organization operating within the student movement is flimsy. I am more inclined to believe that instances of "direct action" during the 1968 student movement were isolated incidents. Independent groups agitated police and precipitated confrontations but these actions were disconnected to the student movement. 68ers generally accused the PRI of hiring *porros* (pro-government thugs) to provoke clashes with riot police. For an extensive overview of *porro* history see Hugo Sánchez Gudiño, *Génesis, desarollo y consolidación de los grupos estudiantiles de choque en la UNAM* (México, DF: Miguel Ángel Porrúa, 2006).
15 Guevara Niebla, *La democracia en la calle*, 52.
16 Alan Knight, "Cárdenas and Echeverría: Two 'Populist' Presidents Compared," in *Populism in 20th Century Mexico: The Presidencies of Lázaro Cárdenas and Luis Echeverría* (Tucson: University of Arizona Press, 2010), 22.
17 Eric Zolov, *Refried Elvis: The Rise of the Mexican Counterculture Movement* (Berkeley: University of California Press, 1999), 131.
18 Aguayo Quezada, *1968: Los archivos de la violencia*, 272.
19 Dios Corona, *La historia que no pudierón borrar*, 47.
20 See information in Galería 1 about the immediate post-massacre period.
21 "No hay detenidos en el Campo Militar No. 1: García Barragán," *Novedades*, October 16, 1968, 1.
22 See Rafael Santos Cenobio, *El movimiento estudiantil en la UAS (1966–1972)* (Sinaloa: Universidad Autónoma de Sinaloa, 2005).
23 For more information see Oscar Flores, "Del movimiento universitario a la guerrilla: El caso de Monterrey (1968–1973)," in *Movimiento armados en México, siglo XX*, vol. 2, ed., Verónica Oikión Solano and Marta Eugenia García Ugarte (Zamora: CIESA and Colegio de Michoacán, 2008).
24 Héctor Ibarra Chávez, *Juventud y rebelde e insurgencia estudiantil: Las otras voces del movimiento político y social en México en los años setenta* (México, DF: Centro de Estudios Antropológicos Ce-Acatl, 2010), 75.
25 Antonio Orozco Michel, interview with author, Guadalajara, July 2008.
26 Victor Pérez, interview by author, San Ángel, Mexico City, November 2009.
27 While not speaking from an urban guerrilla's perspective, Paco Ignacio Taibo II wryly, yet critically recounts his experience distributing propaganda in factories during the 1968 student movement. He states, "in the working-class neighborhoods we visited on occasion (after all, the manuals we had been reading and quoting until we bored ourselves stiff decreed that it was up to the working class to make a revolution) ... then took off after showering the factory with unreadable pamphlets that the employees of the Azcapotzalco refinery or the workers at the Vallejo or Xalostoc plants would later use for ass wipes." See Paco Ignacio Taibo II, *'68*, trans. Donald Nicholson-Smith (Seven Stories Press, New York, 2004), 21.
28 Barry Carr, "Mexican Communism 1968–1981: Eurocommunism in the Americas?" *Journal of Latin American Studies* 17, 1 (May, 1985): 201.
29 Gustavo Hirales Morán, *La Liga Comunista 23 de Septiembre: Orígenes y naufragio* (México: Ediciones de Cultura Popular, 1978), 12.
30 José Luis Chong, *Las guerrillas de México: Testimonios orales y artísticos* (México, DF: Universidad Autónoma de México, 2005), 30.
31 Alfredo Mendoza Cornejo, *Organizaciones y movimientos estudiantiles en Jalisco, 1963–1970* (Guadalajara: Universidad de Guadalajara, 1994).
32 Alfredo Tecla Jiménez, *Universidad, burguesía y proletariado* (México, DF: Ediciones de Cultural Popular, 1978), 10–11. See also Mary Kay Vaughan, *Cultural Politics and in*

Revolution: Teachers, Peasants, and Schools in Mexico, 1930–1940 (Tucson: University of Arizona Press, 1997).
33 Manuel Mora, "En la búsqueda por la democracia: La participación en la ciudad desde el protagonismo de los jóvenes," in *La democracia de los de abajo en Jalisco*, ed., Morge Alonso and Juan Manuel Ramírez (Guadalajara: Universidad de Guadalajara, 1996), 311–316.
34 Donald Hodges, *Mexican Anarchism after the Revolution* (Austin: University of Texas Press, 1992), 133.
35 Sergio Aguayo Quezada, *La Charola: Una historia de los servicios de inteligencia en México* (México, DF: Grijalbo, 2001), 51.
36 FER, "La política de la FEG contra el proletariado estudiantil en Guadalajara," Mandeville Special Collections Library, UC-San Diego, Reel 3 Folder 2, 2.
37 Besides the FEG, *Los Tecos* (The Owls), a group with fascist tendencies controlled the Autonomous University of Guadalajara, which was formed by conservatives against socialist education in 1937. For more information on the Owls see the public version at the AGN. A public version consists of all documents on a particular organization or person combined into a large booklet. This facilitates the investigator's research by not having to ask for single documents at a time. Though often times, the names and addresses have been blacked out on public versions. See also Alfredo Angulo, *La hora de los mártires: Apuntes para la historia del movimiento estudiantil y guerrillero en Guadalajara, 1970–1976* (México: Ediciones La casa de los cuentos del mago ciego tallador de vidrios, 1997), 12.
38 *Los Pinos* (The Pines) is the name given to the President's official residence. DFS, AGN, Exp. 100-18-29-966 L-15 H-168.
39 Laura Castellanos, *México Armado, 1943–1981* (México, DF: Ediciones Era), 197.
40 The Department of Philosophy and Letters was the only school in solidarity with the 1968 student movement. Sergio René de Dios Corona, *La historia que no pudierón borrar: La guerra sucia en Jalisco, 1970–85*, (Guadalajara: La Casa del Mago, 2004), 54.
41 See Renato Flores' testimony in Castellanos, *México Armado, 1943–1981*, 197; Gil Olivo, "Orígenes de la guerrilla en Guadalajara en la década de los setenta," 551; Carlos Sepúlveda Luna, Diez. no. 31 (Dec. 1989) cited in Angulo, *La hora de los mártires*, 19.
42 Donald Hodges, *Mexican Anarchism after the Revolution* (Austin: University of Texas Press, 1995), 128.
43 FEMOSPP, "La guerrilla se extiende por todo el país," (2001): 2.
44 Professors participated in the monitoring, often times reporting to administrators the presence of radical leftists in their classrooms. Instructors were also obliged to turn in their own colleagues.
45 AGN, DFS, Exp. 100-12-1-968 L-15 H-334.
46 Castellanos, *México Armado, 1943–1981*, 197. According to Palacios Rivera, a former member of the Mexican Communist Party, following his first incarceration in the wake of the massacre he was detained every week only because the police were curious. See Dios Corona, *La historia que no pudierón borrar*, 47.
47 Maricela Banderas Silva, interview with author, July 2008, notes and tape recording, Guadalarjara, Jalisco.
48 Raúl Alvarez Garín, interview with author, June 2008, tape recording, Mexico City, Comité '68; Sergio Zermeño, *México: Una democracia utópica del movimiento estudiantil del 68* (México: Siglo XXI Editores, 2003), 239–241, 256–269.
49 Jaime López, *10 años de guerrillas en México, 1964–1974* (México: Editorial Posada SA, DF, 1974), 95.
50 Topete, interview by author.

51 See Gilberto Guevara Niebla, *1968 largo camino a la democracia* (México, DF: Ediciones Cal y Arena, 2008), 69; Esteban Ascencio, ed., 1968: *Más allá del mito* (México, DF: Ediciones Milenio, 1998).
52 Topete, interview by author.
53 AGN, DFS, Exp. 100-2-1-70, L-3 H-304.
54 Michel Orozco, interview with author.
55 Dios Corona, *La historia que no pudierón borrar*, 57; Bertha Lilia Gutiérrez, interview with author.
56 Angulo, *La Hora de los Mártires*, 19.
57 See Antonio Orozco Michel, *La fuga de Oblatos: Una historia de la LC 23 de Septiembre* (Guadalajara: Casa del Mago, 2007); Aguayo Quezada, *La Charola*, 157–165.
58 Aguayo Quezada, *La Charola*, 157.
59 Orozco Michel, *La fuga de Oblatos*, 41.
60 AGN, DFS, Exp. 100-12-1-71 L-19 H-81.
61 Bertha Lila Gutiérrez, interview by author, Guadalajara, July 2008.
62 Lucio Rangel Hernández, *La Universidad Michoacana y el Movimiento Estudiantil 1966–1986* (Morelia: Universidad Michoacana de San Nicolás de Hidalgo, 2009), 65.
63 Aguayo Quezada, *La Charola*, 158.
64 Ibid., 158. Accurate numbers are hard to come by, and interviewees were unclear exactly how many were politically active. "Many" seemed to be the common response.
65 Topete, interview with author.
66 Michel Orozco, interview by author.
67 Laura Castellanos, "Cuando los Vikingos se hicieron feroces," *La Jornada* (online), http://www.jornada.unam.mx/2003/12/07/mas-laura.html (accessed March 18, 2009).
68 Ibid.
69 Castellanos, *México Armado*, 206; Tecla Jiménez, *Universidad, burguesía y proletariado*, 159; Ignacio Torres Olivares Torres and Pedro Orozco Guzmán, "La tesis de la universidad-fábrica," author's personal copy.
70 Topete, interview by author.
71 Gutiérrez, interview by author.
72 AGN, DFS, Exp. 100-14-1-70 L-5 H-247.
73 AGN, DFS, 11-239-73 L-6 H-1; *Madera* no. 3 (1974): 27, 74–76.
74 AGN, DFS, 100-23-1-73 L-23 H-237; AGN, DIPS, caja 2731, Estado de Sinaloa, Información de El Fuerte, 11 September de 1974, 39; AGN, DFS 100-231-73 L-23 H-277. A number of columns were published in the local newspaper *El Sol de Sinaloa* published by the Consejo Universitario Paritario of the Autonumus University of Sinaloa blaming *Los Enfermos,* which were going through a process of "lumpenization" for the "bloody deeds" that occurred a week earlier at the university.
75 Ramón Gil Olivo, "Orígenes de la guerrilla en Guadalajara en al década de los setenta," in *Movimientos Armados* en México, siglo XX, ed. Verónica Oikión Solano and Marta Eugenia García Ugarte (Michoacán: Colegio de Michoacán, 2006), 551.
76 AGN, DFS, Exp. 11-33-1-71 L-1 H-310.
77 Meaning the University of Guadalajara; FER, "La política de la FEG contra el proletariado estudiantil en Guadalajara," 1.
78 See *Madera* no. 3 (1974); Ignacio Arturo Salas Obregón, *Cuestiones fundamentales del movimiento revolucionario o manifiesto al proletariado* (México, DF: Editorial Tierra Roja, 2003).
79 Hodges, *Mexican Anarchism after the Revolution*, 133.
80 Aguayo Quezada, *La Charola*, 162.
81 AGN, DFS, 100-12-1-70 L-17 H-149.

82 Aguayo Quezada, *La Charola*, 161.
83 Orozco Michel, *La fuga de Oblatos*, 47.
84 AGN, DFS, Exp. 100-12-1-71 L-19 H-262.
85 AGN, DFS, 100-12-1-70 L-18 H-113 and AGN, DFS, 100-12-1-70 L-18 H-128.
86 AGN, DFS, 100-12-11 L-10 H-119-120, 124, and 128. The funeral was delayed as a result of a recommend autopsy. Also, the family was initially unable to pay for the funeral as well as the burial.
87 Dios Corona, *La historia que no pudierón borrar: La guerra sucia en Jalisco, 1970–85*, 68.
88 AGN, DFS, 100-12-11 L-10 H-119-120.
89 Angulo, *La hora de los mártires*, 18.
90 AGN, DFS, 100-12-1-71 L-19 H-213.
91 AGN, DFS, 100-12-1-70 L-18 H-137.
92 Aguayo Quezada, *La Charola*, 170.
93 Miguel Topete, interview with author.
94 Gil Olivo, "Orígenes de la guerrilla en Guadalajara en la década de los setenta," 558.
95 Ibid, 558.
96 Miguel Topete, interview with author.
97 Enrique Velázquez, informal conversation, March 2011, Mexico City.
98 AGN, DFS, Exp. 11-233-73 L-1 H-22. Among those released were Alfredo Campaña López and Carlos Campaña López.
99 For more information on the correspondences between the United States and the Mexican government regarding Leonhardy see AGN, DFS, Exp. 11-233-73 L-1 H-15.
100 Castellanos, *México armado*, 224.
101 Mario Rivera Ortíz and Mario Rivera Guzmán, *El secuestro de José Guadalupe Zuno Hernández* (México: Ediciones Medicina y Sociedad, 1992), 6; Castellaños, *México armado*, 223. See also Ramón Pimentel Aguilar, *El secuestro: ¿Lucha política o provocación?* (México: Editorial Posada, 1974).

6

A REVOLUTIONARY GROUP FIGHTING AGAINST A REVOLUTIONARY STATE

The September 23rd Communist League Against the PRI-State (1973–1975)

Romain Robinet

The *Liga Comunista 23 de Septiembre* (September 23rd Communist League), or *Liga*, was a Marxist–Leninist urban/rural guerrilla movement founded in Guadalajara on March 15, 1973, and active roughly until 1983. Like the *Partido de los Pobres* (Party of the Poor), the LC23S was in fact one of the two largest guerrilla groups in Mexico during the Cold War period. Founded by a coalition of independent armed revolutionary groups and composed predominately of students, the *Liga* advocated a communist-style revolution in Mexico. The ongoing political violence and the lack of a unifying revolutionary organization to combat the government was the motivating force behind the intellectual precursors of the *Liga*. The founding fathers of the *Liga* believed the 1910 Mexican Revolution was exhausted, had lost its capacity to transform society, and its legacy distorted to benefit a small, yet formidable political elite. Apart from directly threatening the legitimacy and power of the *Partido Revolucionario Institucional* (Institutional Revolutionary Party, PRI), acts of revolutionary violence against the ruling elite and prominent businessmen created a hostile relationship between them and the government. Businessmen chastised the government's inability to provide adequate security for the upper-class against kidnappings and murders. As revolutionary violence mushroomed in the mid-1970s, the PRI responded with an all-out counterinsurgency offensive specifically intended to eradicate the *Liga*. The manner in which the *Liga* and the PRI carried out their individual campaigns closely resembled a micro civil war through two opposing concepts of revolution. The PRI believed they had ownership over the legacy of the 1910 Revolution, which had to be perpetuated and safeguarded at any cost, whereas revolutionaries saw a communist revolution as the only felicitous avenue to topple the PRI and establish a revolutionary state.

The LC23S was created following the unification of seven independent guerrilla groups: the *Procesos*, the *Guajiros*, the *Enfermos*, the *Frente Estudiantil Revolucionario* (Student Revolutionary Front, FER), the *Movimiento Armado Revolucionario-23 de Septiembre* (September 23rd Armed Revolutionary Movement, MAR-23S), the *Lacandones*, and the *Macías*. By 1973, some of these movements were already in a process of extreme radicalization, therefore explaining why the *Liga* was, from its birth, one of the most radical Mexican guerrilla movements of the Cold War era. The group's actual size has been a topic of debate. For 1973 and 1974 documents from the *Dirección Federal de Seguridad* (DFS, Federal Security Directorate) reportedly put the number of militants at 445, of which 65 were female.[1] But this number is highly inaccurate since countless revolutionaries avoided being apprehended and thus never appeared in police records. Even the revolutionaries were unaware just how large the group was given their relationship with other comrades was strictly limited to their designated brigade and everyone was on a need-to-know basis, and even fewer personally knew the leadership.

In order to understand the *Liga*'s formation and its ideological blueprint, we have to take into account the influence it had on its sympathizers who wished to join the organization as devoted militants, but due to the group's obstinate security measures imposed by the leadership recruits found it increasingly strenuous to fully commit themselves to the cause. Also, a militant's voluntarism impressed their friends and families from which they built a strong solidarity network. Yet, even if they did not join or support the *Liga* they were labeled as conspirators by counterrevolutionary forces and, like the revolutionaries, became victims of the Dirty War. Thus, thousands of Mexican citizens were linked directly or indirectly with the micro civil war against the PRI. The questions that will guide this chapter are the following: How did this conflict emerge? Why did the revolutionaries think the 1910 Mexican Revolution was over, and why did they fail in their endeavor to foment a new revolution? To fully put into perspective and reconstruct the formation of the *Liga*, this chapter uses, in addition to simple police records, the group's underground monthly publication, *Madera,* and *Excélsior*, a mainstream newspaper edited by Julio Scherer García.[2]

The Genesis of the Liga Comunista 23 de Septiembre

The initiative to unite non-aligned armed struggles under the auspice of a single revolutionary organization can be traced back to the founding of the *Organización Partidaria* (Partisan Organization), in August 1971, by Diego Lucero and Leopoldo Angulo Luque from the *Guajiros* and Raul Ramos Zavala, the leading theoretician of the *Procesos*.[3] At the end of June 1971, two members of the *Procesos*, Raúl Ramos Zavala and Ignacio Arturo Salas Obregón, spoke to the *Guajiros* and agreed on spearheading the creation of one single guerrilla movement.[4] In January 1972, the first steps were taken to communicate with independent revolutionary movements across the country. Through Fernando Salinas Mora, a contact they had in Guadalajara, both Ramos Zavala and Salas Obregón met with members of the FER to outline their plan to unify independent guerrilla movements into one vanguard. For Ramos Zavala and Salas Obregón, choosing Guadalajara as one of the first cities to recruit militants was strategically decided largely because both leaders were impressed by the FER's ability to recruit proletariat youth from the surrounding barrios. When the *Liga* was ultimately created in 1973, the FER was among the leading contributors of militants to the newly founded revolutionary organization. But this initiative was almost thwarted after what has been commonly know as *invierno trágico* (the tragic winter of 1971–1972), in which Lucero and Ramos Zavala were killed in separate confrontations with the police. With both Lucero and Ramos Zavala dead, Salas Obregón, "Oseas," appeared as the only militant left with the intellectual capacity to be the leading theoretician.[5]

Students and Proletariats

Elaborating on the organizing strategies used by other revolutionary movements, namely the FER, guerrilla theorists did not confine the "proletariat" to the working class but broadened it to include peasants and students. To push this correlation between peasants, workers, and students, recruits were expected to read the *Tesis de la Universidad fábrica,* or Thesis on the University-Factory, a manifesto written by Ignacio Torres Olivares and Pedro Orozco Guzmán. Accordingly, higher education was integrated into the capitalist accumulation process.[6] To some extent, students, as part of the process, were proletariats. This theory provided a key to understanding the development of a massive higher education: capitalism had entered the university. Mexico was then a modern capitalist nation where revolution was possible and necessary. Moreover, the Thesis on the University-Factory solved habitual seminary Marxist contradictions. Could the proletariat be saved by a theory taught in bourgeois institutions? Universities had to pass from being the "superstructure" to the "infrastructure": if universities were factories, then dialectical materialism was more than ever the working class organic theory. Finally, students could temporarily leave their classes and join the guerrillas: it would sabotage the "university process of capitalist accumulation."[7] For the guerrilleros, the 1968 students' movement had been consequently "a revolutionary struggle of the proletariat" and "democrats" had prevented it from transforming itself into an "armed uprising to destroy bourgeois power."[8]

Students were recent proletarians (capitalist education was something new) and they could keep some bourgeois attitudes. Like students, peasants were impure proletarians. Peasants were often seen as reactionary elements or "petite bourgeoisie" members who refused collectivization: "Peasants who want us to struggle to keep small scale production do not have their place here."[9] The *Liga* theorists had indeed more difficulties to integrate them into the proletariat. As peasants were to disappear, the only option for them was to support the working class. On the whole, all these categories could be reduced in the revolutionary struggle led by the LC23S. The proletariat included workers, students and peasants but in a hierarchical order where authentic proletarians were superior to recent revolutionaries.

The Ideological War

Beyond kidnappings, murders, "expropriations," and confrontations with the police and secret service, the micro civil war between the Mexican state and the *Liga* was also fought through an ideological struggle. The *Liga* called for a different revolution than the one defended by the PRI. *Madera* helps us understand how the LC23S saw its actions. In order to prepare militants to carry out this ideological war, recruits were required to read the *Liga*'s monthly publication. Ideology and intellectual rigor were crucial to the LC23S's *guerrilleros*. Why did the Marxist–Leninist ideology have such a central role in the organization? The *Liga* was largely composed of students. The recruitment was linked with the students' own mastery of Marxism–Leninism. Students would gather to discuss Marxist authors and their theses in *círculos de estudios* (study circles), meetings of five or six students among whom a *guerrillero* was present under another identity. The more radical students were recruited that way. *Madera* was a Leninist newspaper, but Lenin was not the only source of inspiration for the *guerrilleros*: Frantz Fanon, Guy Debord and Mao were also important references for their ideological training. Even if all *guerrilleros* did not agree with every *Madera* article, they nonetheless risked their life to distribute it. The clandestine publication was then considered the gospel of the revolutionary movement and was required reading.

The 1973 economic crisis was interpreted as capitalism's final crisis: this apocalyptic Leninist interpretation justified their struggle. For the *guerrilleros*, the "capitalist world" was likely to "collapse because of the imminent sharpening of the economic and political crisis of imperialism."[10] Revolutionaries expected the intensification of speculation, growth of unemployment and the extension of a global "imperialist war."[11] Peasants and factory workers were the first victims of the economic crisis.

The *Liga* called then for a single anti-capitalist international movement. In Mexico, the "masses" had consolidated their "historic offensive" started "fifteen years before," that is to say starting from the railroad strike of 1958–1959. Two factors explained the revolutionary situation in Mexico: the "material conditions" (the economic crisis) and the subjective conditions (the political work of agitation since 1968).[12] For the LC23S, the "revolutionary proletariat" had to transform imperialist wars into "revolutionary civil wars."[13] The Leninist interpretation of imperialism was used to unify very different movements, causes or struggles, from Vietnam to Mexico. Even Augusto Pinochet's dictatorship was good news: it was becoming clearer that "bourgeois reformism and liberalism of the Allende" could not be "the revolutionary proletariat politics."[14] Why was Mexico so important in the organization of a world revolution? The Mexican proletariat battle was essential for the struggle against North American Imperialism and for the Central American and South American proletariat.

In this attempt to build a "revolutionary civil war," there was only one vanguard organization: the *Liga*. Because it had reached theoretical purity, the LC23S had to lead the revolution in Mexico. The search for theoretical purity started among the *Procesos* when this small group separated from the PCM. The LC23S chose to adopt dogmatically the Leninist interpretation, "Without revolutionary theory there cannot be revolutionary movement."[15] "Factory workers can only develop revolutionary politics when their struggle is guided by a vanguard theory."[16] The LC23S held the monopoly of legitimate Marxism and thus had the right to define what was revolutionary or not. To justify their "vanguard theory," *Madera* editors quoted Marx, Engels, and sometimes Mao. However, Lenin was the most cited of them: on March 27, 1974, in the editorial of the third *Madera*, of 13 citations, 12 referred to Lenin (the other referred to a *Madera* article of the same edition).[17] In another text written in May 1974, seven references out of ten invited the reading of the Russian revolutionary. The *Liga* was the only authorized exegete of Marx, Engels and Lenin. Consequently, *Madera* became as sacred as classical Marxists essays.

Why was their Marxism so reduced and dogmatic? Why did the LC23S seem to ignore Gramsci, Althusser or Ernesto Guevara? In fact, the LC23S guerilleros could not mention the Cuban Revolution: Castro's regime had good relations with Mexico and never helped any guerrilla in the Republic. As paradoxical as it may seem, all LC23S members had clear Guevarist influences, but their search for purity forced them to reject Cuba. If revolution was possible (and Cuba had proved it) they had to find a model other than Cuba. As communists, they logically sacralized the Russian Revolution, which they wanted to reproduce. They chose to avoid unorthodox theorists to maintain the purity of their warlike Marxism–Leninism.

For the *guerrilleros*, the organization was the embryo of the Revolutionary Party and Army.[18] It guided the proletariat whose "central task" could only be "the destruction of the bourgeois State and the consolidation of the dictatorship of the Proletariat."[19] The revolution would take from the "bourgeoisie" and "oligarchy" "its factories, its lands, its capital" and "suppress private property."[20] "Then wealth will grow quicker, as the workers will work for them and not for the capitalists, the working day will be shorter, workers will eat and dress better and their life will change completely."[21] How did the LC23S plan the communist revolution? First, the workers would go on strikes. The *Liga* would then encourage the formation of "clandestine committees" in charge of agitation and propaganda. These committees would afterwards provide the "revolutionary army" with soldiers.[22] After some revolutionary days of agitation and combat, the next step would have been a "political strike" leading to a "general uprising against the bourgeoisie."[23] Once again, the *guerrilleros* referred to "the revolutionary movement of 68" as a model.[24]

Expressions of Revolutionary Violence

The *Liga*'s revolutionary strategies supported the use of revolutionary violence against property and people. The justifications for taking such extreme measures were elucidated in communiqués, other types of propaganda, as well as in *Madera*. According to the group's political line the bourgeoisie had to be physically eliminated.[25] The *Liga* chose to "inferiorize" this social category in order to justify political violence. The "bourgeoisie" was consequently described as a "parasitic class" and as "decrepit, reactionary and rotten."[26] The guerrillas also underestimated the police and the army, which were only considered as the "rabid dogs" of the bourgeoisie.[27] This ideological blindness may have facilitated the organization to dismantle. Moreover, the *Liga* had other enemies: it denounced the democratic Left and other Mexican guerrillas as "opportunists" who only represented the "working-class aristocracy." It was indeed an insult for Lenin readers. Mexican leftist parties as well as trade unions, independent or linked to the ruling party, were considered "true counter-revolutionary organizations" that maintained "the domination of the bourgeois State" leading the *Liga* to call for the rapid "destruction of all types of trade-union."[28] Ostensible progressive newspapers like *Punto Crítico* and *Solidaridad* were also harshly criticized for being "opportunists."[29] Lucio Cabañas' *Partido de los Pobres* guerrilla movement or the *Fuerzas Revolucionarias Armadas del Pueblo* (FRAP, Revolutionary Armed Forces of the People) were nothing else than "militarists and petit bourgeois groups" that were about to fight against the proletariat.[30]

In August 1973, the members of the *Liga* leading committee agreed on the necessary "execution of the major number of police and army members (…) as a revenge and to take possession of their arms."[31] Violence was indeed an emotional response to the deep traumatism felt by the *guerrilleros*. Most of them, beyond the memory of the massacres of 1968 and 1971, were regularly confronted with the murder of their comrades at the hands of the police or the army. In fact, for these young people, friendships were very strong and strengthened by the activities' clandestine nature and their common political commitment. On both sides, in the *Liga* and among counterrevolutionary forces, the logics of vengeance can explain the global radicalization of the micro civil war. From an ideological perspective, the LC23S deeply thought that political violence (maybe more than propaganda) would convince the Mexican people of the necessity to achieve a new Mexican revolution.

The Organization's Structure

The *Liga* was a hierarchical organization, but at the same time its local structures had a large autonomy in order to be as efficient as possible. The *Liga* was an umbrella guerrilla movement made up of a variety of groups, and was indeed regionally very diverse. The *Liga* national leading committee coordinated the actions of the various zone committees, which themselves were divided into regional committees (each corresponding to a state of the Mexican Republic, see Table 6.1). In 1973, the leading committee was composed of the following *guerrilleros*: José Angel García Martínez (a member of the *Procesos*), Manuel Gámez, Rodolfo Gómez García (formally of the MAR-23S), "*Matus*" (Leopoldo Angulo Luque, from the *Guajiros*), José Ignacio Olivares Torres (ex-member of the *Movimiento Estudiantil Profesional*, MEP) and, of course, the charismatic theorist Salas Obregón, who had been appointed *Coordinador General de los Comités Coordinadores* (General Coordinator of the Coordinating Committees).[32]

Each regional committee was linked to the leaders of the different brigades operating in the area. For security reasons, *guerrilleros* used pseudonyms, did not always know the names of their comrades, the name of the brigade leader, nor the real identity of the *guerrillero* who belonged to a superior echelon.[33]

To sustain itself, the LC23S spent roughly between 600,000 and 700,000 pesos a month.[34] This helped to buy food, medicines, cars, printing equipment

TABLE 6.1 The geographical structure of the LC23S

Zone committee	Leaders of the zone committee	Regional committees
North-West	Manuel Gámez, Eleazar Gámez, Gustavo Hirales	Sinaloa, Sonora, Chihuahua, Durango
North-East	José Angel García Martínez, Héctor Torres González, Jesús Piedra Ibarra	Nuevo León, Tamaulipas
West	José Ignacio Olivares Torres, Pedro Orozco Guzmán, Alberto Ramírez Flores	Jalisco, Michoacán
South★	Wenceslao José García	Guerrero, Oaxaca
Mexico City	Ignacio Salas Obregón	Mexico City

★ There was later another committee in charge of the South, led by Juan Antonio Veloz Ramos, Ana Luisa Guerra Flores, José Manuel Baez Ávila, Francisco Márquez Guzmán, and by two other persons known as "Fernando" and "El Licenciado." AGN, DFS, Exp. 11-235-74 L-11 H-267.

and to pay the rent for the *casas de seguridad*, or safe houses which were ordinary houses or apartments where *guerrilleros* lived in hiding, as well as to purchase weapons and ammunition many of which were bought in the USA or on the black market.[35] Money generally came from *expropiaciones* (expropriations), bank robberies and ransoms. An expropriation was defined by the group as an appropriation of a part of the working-class past labor "anteriorly expropriated by the bourgeoisie from the workers." It was "carried out (...) by a part of the proletariat or by its revolutionary organizations."[36] It was not only a way to finance the LC23S but essentially a "struggle against capital."[37]

In Sinaloa, the *Enfermos* who were in control of the *Casa del Estudiante* (the Students House), expropriated money from the University of Sinaloa of which 10,000 pesos were transferred to the *Liga*.[38] During the first months, the leading committee collected the money and gave it to the zone committees depending on its priorities.[39] However, the leading committee members quickly realized that the organization would be less rigid if each zone committee managed its own budget financed by its own "expropriations."[40] In fact, the organization might have been even more decentralized; each brigade or commando may have been financially self-sufficient and therefore politically and militarily autonomous.

The LC23S was especially active in three cities: Guadalajara (with the FER), Mexico City (where the *Lacandones* gave birth to the *Brigada Roja,* Red Brigade or BR) and Monterrey (through the *Comité Estudiantil Revolucionario,* Student Revolutionary Committee or CER). It was also present in Ciudad Juárez (with the *Consejo Local de Lucha Estudiantil* or Local Student Struggle Council) and in urban areas in the Southeast of the country.[41]

The rural groups within the LC23S were significant, though it was largely urban. However, the LC23S failed to build an alliance with the *Partido de los Pobres*, preventing an even larger union of the Mexican armed struggles.[42] The *Liga*'s most salient rural guerrilla groups were then the *Brigada Revolucionaria Emiliano Zapata* (Emiliano Zapata Revolutionary Brigade or BREZ, Oaxaca), the *Brigada "Genaro Vázquez"* (Guerrero), the *Comité Político-Militar "Arturo Gámiz"* (Arturo-Gámiz Political Military Committee or CPMAG, Sonora, Chihuahua), and the *Comando "Oscar González Eguiarte"* (Sonora, Chihuahua).[43] Other groups affiliated to the *Liga*, like the *Enfermos* from Sinaloa, developed an insurrectional strategy linking rural and urban actions.

The Liga's First Failures

The first major action sponsored by the *Liga* was the kidnapping of Eugenio Garza Sada, an important businessman from Monterrey, on September 17, 1973. The aim was to publish a national manifesto in the press.[44] But the operation failed dramatically and Garza Sada was killed during the attempted kidnapping.[45] This development frightened Mexico's elite and as a consequence,

President Echeverría and his administration would no longer negotiate with the revolutionaries.

However, the LC23S had an alternative plan.[46] Ignacio Salas met with the West regional committee leaders, Olivares Torres, Orozco Guzmán, and Ramírez Flores, to organize two other kidnappings. The regional committee decided on abducting Anthony Duncan Williams, the Great Britain consul in Guadalajara, and a businessman named Fernando Aranguren Castiello. The goal of the operation was again to have access to mass media.[47] But this time, the LC23S decided ruthlessly they wouldn't take any war prisoners. If the revolutionary's demands were unsatisfied, the victims would be murdered, in revenge for the *guerrilleros* killed by the counterinsurgency forces: the double rapt was then called *Operación 29 de Agosto* (29th August Operation).[48] This was in memory of Fernando Salinas Mora, an FER member who was killed in August 1973 in Guadalajara.[49] On October 10, 1973, the LC23S commandos kidnapped both persons.[50] The *guerrilleros* wanted 2,500,000 pesos, diffusion of their communiqués, and asked the government to free 51 political prisoners.[51] Two days later, speaking for the Echeverría government, Pedro Ojeda Paullada surprised the nation by announcing on national radio and television that there would be no negotiations with the guerrillas.[52] The LC23S consequently should have killed its two prisoners after realizing their demands would not be met, but they resisted. Some of the *guerrilleros* did not believe the government would refuse to negotiate and they hesitated in murdering the victims, yet the revolutionaries in charge of the kidnappings agreed to a compromise.[53] They freed the Consul but kept Aranguren, and in exchange for his release demanded a large ransom and the publication of communiqués. However, for unexplained reasons, Aranguren was "executed" before any of the demands were met after Duncan Williams was freed on 14 October, two days earlier.[54] The plan failed: no political prisoners got out of jail, no money was given to the LC23S, no communiqués could convey to Mexican citizens the importance of their struggle and persuade them to rise up against the bourgeoisie.

Manufacturing Hostile Consent: the Media, Public Opinion and the LC23S

The kidnapping of salient businessmen would eventually backfire on militants and lead to the group's unpopularity. Aranguren's employees demanded his release and asserted he was not an enemy of the working class, but a fair boss. Employees were even prepared to pay his ransom with their wages.[55] When Aranguren was killed, *Excélsior* journalists condemned the "horrible and sterile crime."[56] The entire city of Guadalajara mourned the death. In the press, LC23S members appeared neither as real *guerrilleros* nor as true revolutionaries. For *Excélsior* journalists, they were not the representatives of the poor because they were neither earning an honorable living nor exploited.[57] "Leftist terrorism" was then only reinforcing suppression.[58] The PRI leaders reminded public opinion of the party's monopoly to define revolutions: two days after Aranguren's death, the PRI's president Jesús Reyes Heroles, on a trip to Guadalajara denounced the "insane minds" who were pretending to "take the country to psychosis."[59] For the PRI, revolutions could not be improvised.[60] Unlike the *guerrilleros*, Echeverría was underlining that the Mexican Revolution had not reached its end.[61]

Violent condemnation of the *guerrilleros* in the media manipulated citizens into believing it was justifiable to respond aggressively. Like other media, *Excélsior* entirely depended on the police and the army to obtain information on guerrilla activists and the state's counterinsurgency campaign. Mass media, particularly *Excélsior*, viewed the DFS more as a news source than a repressive institution. As a consequence, the counterrevolutionary forces easily imposed their own vision of the conflict in the public sphere. Miguel Nazar Haro, the DFS assistant director, could then announce a "hunt" throughout the country against groups that lay behind "a false ideology."[62] Nazar Haro and Florentino Ventura, who more or less understood the reasons why armed struggles emerged, impudently lied to discredit the *guerrilleros*, declaring that the authors of the double kidnapping were "all ordinary delinquents whose only aim [was] to get rich."[63] What did this new organization want? According to the journalist Victor Payán, "the pseudo-*guerrilleros* ... planned to spread terror in different parts of the country through violent activities, in order to change Mexico's political, social and economic system."[64] The *Liga* was not perceived as a proletarian revolutionary organization but as a "criminal association."[65] Calls for the violent destruction of the *Liga* were ubiquitous. Alberto Orozco Romero, Jalisco's Governor, was quoted saying that he would do his part to see the group eradicated by advocating to citizens the need for "a spirit of cooperation in order to exterminate these tyrannical minorities" and, like Nazar Haro, he called for a "general hunt."[66]

The 1974 Culiacán Uprising

On January 16, 1974, the *Liga* coordinated a historical uprising in Culiacán, Sinaloa when hundreds of militants from the *Enfermos* and the *Liga* with the help of farm workers, transformed the city and surrounding areas into a battlefield. In the imaginary of the 1970s guerrilla experience, the *Asalto al cielo* (literally, the assault on the sky) was a significant political manoeuvre intended to officially launch the communist revolution. Taking advantage of the *Enfermos'* strong connection with peasants and farm workers, the *Liga*'s leadership sought to exhibit their political and military capacities by executing a massive insurrection. Culiacán was strategically chosen as the site for the insurrection largely because of the *Enfermos'* success in becoming the leaders of "the proletariat movement in this region."⁶⁷ Given the cross-class alliance between students and peasants was incredibly solid and each side was prepared to carry out an operation of this calibre, leaders of the *Liga* set in motion the preparations for the insurrection. According to a passage in *Madera* it was estimated that the *Enfermos* were able to amalgamate around 50,000 farm workers, but today the number has been substantially reduced to 10,000.⁶⁸

According to *Excélsior*, approximately 300 student-revolutionaries participated in the insurrection. The *Enfermos* stole countless vehicles, guns, money, triggered armed confrontations with the local police, and vandalized the State capitol building with Molotov cocktails. Expressions of revolutionary violence also came in the form of symbolic attacks against "capitalism," namely the Cuauhtémoc Brewery and *Banco Agropecuario*, a farming bank. When it appeared that the insurrection had been quelled, the police summarily announced everything was under control. Despite its magnitude the total death toll on that day was only five and only 14 people were arrested.⁶⁹ While leaders were convinced the conditions in Sinaloa were ideal for an insurrection their prognosis proved incorrect. Although the insurrection fell short of the group's expectations, according to *Madera* the rebellion "triggered a day of agitation and struggle" in various parts of Mexico.⁷⁰ The *guerrilleros* were deeply enthusiastic: "REVOLUTION ADVANCES WITH A STRENGTH IMPOSSIBLE TO CONTAIN!"⁷¹ The LC23S then called for a national revolutionary day of action, which should have been larger than the 1958 workers' struggle and the 1968 students' movement.⁷² The *Liga* thought its actions provoked "an atmosphere of disorganization in the enemy lines."⁷³ Obsessed and traumatized by Tlatelolco (the massacre of 1968), the young *guerrilleros* thought the "bourgeoisie" was preparing to plan "one or various exemplary massacres" to suppress this revolutionary movement.⁷⁴ At this stage, they were unable to conceive a possible dismantling of their organization through arrests and torture. Nevertheless, around 40 *guerrilleros* fell "in the hands of the bourgeoisie" between the 16 January and the end of February 1974.⁷⁵

Decapitating the Liga

By 1974 the Dirty War was well under way as the counterinsurgency campaign against the *Liga* reached an unprecedented level. During the final years of the Echeverría administration the political prisoner population dropped considerably, leading one to believe that after guerrillas or sympathizers were apprehended they were summarily killed or "disappeared." While the *Liga* was believed to have a sophisticated security system in place, the arrest of prominent leaders illustrates the fissures in the program, as was the case for Orozco Guzmán, "Camilo," a leading intellectual who participated in Aranguren's murder.⁷⁶ Despite his murder at the hands of security forces, the militants remained hopeful in the current leadership and confident that "many more

Camilo's and many more working-class political leaders" would rise.⁷⁷ But the arrests continued. On January 31, 1974, Salvador Corral García (the architect of the Culiacán uprising) and José Ignacio Olivares Torres were caught by the DFS in Mazatlán.⁷⁸ According to former *Liga* revolutionary Gustavo Hirales, the two *guerrilleros* were caught on their way to Culiacán after a national meeting in Guadalajara.⁷⁹ The upshot of this double arrest proved to be exceptionally rewarding for the DFS. Olivares Torres' interrogation helped them identify five *guerrilleros* linked to the Duncan/Aranguren operation.⁸⁰ During the counterinsurgency campaign the DFS embraced an "eye for an eye" logic.⁸¹ According to *Excélsior*, the general public was made to believe Olivares Torres was killed by his own comrades, and that his death was a result of "serious divisions between subversive groups."⁸²

While Corral García and Olivares Torres' deaths were a major blow to the *Liga* the capture and "disappearance" of Obregón on April 25, 1974 proved to be even more severe. According to the FEMOSPP report, Salas Obregón was wounded in an armed confrontation in Tlalnepantla, a city in the state of Mexico. He was then transported to the Tlalnepantla hospital from where he was taken by DFS agents to the Military Camp Number 1.⁸³ DFS documents concerning his apprehension only mention the information he gave during his interrogation.⁸⁴ After he was transported to the clandestine military prison, Salas Obregón was never heard from again. But thanks to the information disclosed by Salas Obregón during his interrogation the DFS was able to identify 18 more revolutionaries and gained a deeper understanding of the guerrilla movement's structure.⁸⁵ While Salas Obregón's arrest was coincidental and not planned, his "disappearance" was surely premeditated. Given Salas Obregón's self-assigned messianic status and overall importance to the group, his "disappearance" spread chaos and confusion throughout the *Liga*. During the *Liga*'s Third National Meeting in 1974, a number of changes were made to the organization's structure. Salas consolidated his power in the group and the *Liga* was no longer controlled by the national committee, but rather by a triumvirate made up of Salas Obregón, Luis Miguel Corral García, and José Luis Martínez Pérez.⁸⁶ The National Commission sought to restructure and purify the movement. Consequently, when Salas Obregón fell to "the claws of the bourgeoisie" divisions became more explicit.⁸⁷ The leading nucleus then exploded but the very flexible structure of the guerrilla movement explained why political and military actions continued all around Mexico.

The "Revolutionary Civil War": Between Militarism and Propaganda

In 1974, in response to the growing repression, revolutionary violence on behalf of the *Liga* proliferated, marking the height of the micro civil war. In January of that same year two rural brigades associated with the *Liga* organized abductions to finance their struggle against landlords. The *Comité Político-Militar "Arturo Gámiz"* (CPMAG) led by Salvador Gaytán Aguirre, captured José Hermenegildo Sainz Cano, a local landlord, in order to "expropriate" one million pesos from his family.⁸⁸ For unexplained reasons he was still executed despite having paid the ransom.⁸⁹ Two days later another brigade, the *Brigada Revolucionaria Emiliano Zapata* (BREZ), kidnapped Raymundo Soberanis Otero, a 70-year-old landlord, and murdered him after his family failed to "precisely" respected the *guerrilleros* instructions.⁹⁰

In Mexico City, the *Brigada Roja* was becoming increasingly more and more professional. On March 12, 1974, at 10.30 am, the BR stole 958,598 pesos from a Banamex bank in Tlalnepantla, in only four minutes.⁹¹ At the beginning of June, the *guerrilleros* attacked a hospital reserved for PEMEX employees. Five LC23S members dressed as doctors stole the money which had been designated to pay the 700 hospital employees. They left the place throwing leaflets printed with the words: "Operation 10 June. Commando: Pedro Miguel Morón Chiclayo. Red Brigade of the September 23rd Communist League. Workers of the world unite!"⁹² The *Liga* was commemorating the *Halconazo* and the murder of the *Liga*'s Peruvian doctor, Pedro Morón, which had occurred only a few days before.⁹³ In memory of Pedro Orozco Guzmán, the LC23S organized the "Operation 24 December" which took place on December 10, 1974: within five minutes, the urban *guerrilleros* stole two millions pesos from two different banks and killed five policemen whose subsequent funeral drew thousands of mourners.⁹⁴ Was the entire nation against the *Liga Comunista*? Indeed, the LC23S name had become synonymous with organized crime. Even ordinary criminals tried to cover their action using the LC23S' dark reputation. On October 23, 1974, Alfredo Lopez Figueroa, a bank manager from Cananea (Sonora), received threats against his family from the "September 23rd Group" which sought "protection money" in exchange for not harming them. One of the DFS officials underlined in his report that the "style of redaction" showed that the authors must have been "ordinary delinquents."⁹⁵ However, LC23S propaganda was not efficient enough to contradict this image.

For the *guerrilleros*, distributing propaganda was a daily activity. They wanted to convince the working class, peasants and students to join the LC23S struggle. On the whole, factory workers rejected the *Liga*'s message. At the mere sight of the word "Communist," many of them threw away the leaflets.⁹⁶ Relations with peasants were also difficult. Gustavo Hirales emphasizes the incomprehension between them and the young *guerrilleros* preaching their gospel: during a meeting, the LC23S militants provided 50-page texts for "discussion." Under the *guerrilleros*' incredulous eyes, the peasants tore out a few pages in order to sit a bit more comfortably on the ground: "do not worry comrades; there are still so many pages to read."⁹⁷ As a matter of fact, only a modest section of the students were receptive to the *Liga*'s ideology. Thus, the reality seemed quite removed from *Madera* enthusiasm for which workers accepted revolutionary propaganda "in a very friendly way" and participated "actively" in the discussions.[98]

The violent reputation of the guerrilla does not entirely explain people's hostility to the *Liga*'s propaganda. To some extent, distributing propaganda can be incompatible with guerrilla warfare: trying to explain the reasons for a struggle takes time and political work implies a certain amount of stability. Guerrilla warfare requires the opposite: speed, mobility, and spontaneous acts. The balance between political and military actions is thus very hard to find. Some groups like the *Fuerzas de Liberación Nacional* (National Liberation Forces), preferred clandestine political work to the detriment of military actions. On the contrary, the *Liga* largely chose the military approach. Consequently, their numerous propaganda actions were shaped by a strict adherence to the essential rules of military operations. On April 18, 1974, three *guerrilleros* armed with guns distributed documents in a Mexico City high school and then ran away shooting in the air to draw attention to themselves.[99] Two days later, in Monterrey, six LC23S members distributed leaflets, carefully remaining in their car. They drove away due to an exchange of gunfire with the police.[100] On 6 May, five *guerrilleros* brought propaganda to workers in Huatabampo (Sonora): they invited them to rebel by conveniently providing Molotov cocktails and then moved on to another place to repeat the process.[101] Another strategy was to leave propaganda documents in empty classrooms or factory toilets, hoping someone would read them.

The Slow Collapse

What are the main reasons behind the *Liga*'s collapse? State-sponsored repression was instrumental to the *Liga*'s demise. But independent of the group's inability to weather the counterinsurgency campaign their disintegration can also be attributed to inner group feuds. Apart from the *Liga*'s lambasting the moderate left for being reactionary and opportunistic, the group also encountered serious internal factionalism. Mounting tension prompted leaders like Salas Obregón to hold a small minority of militants and leaders accountable for several of the *Liga*'s failures. Living up to his reputation as an obstinate and overtly paranoid person he executed "a general purge" resulting in the expulsion of numerous revolutionaries from different echelons.[102] Internal assassinations were also carried out against those who severely broke the *Liga*'s revolutionary code and many former revolutionaries have spoken out against these actions. Salas Obregón's capture and subsequent "disappearance" at the hands of the secret police in April 1974 set in motion the *Liga* disintegration. Within one year, factions such as the BREZ, the CPMAG, and ex-*Enfermos* chose to continue the struggle on their own while the Red Brigade and the FER remained with the *Liga*. Though the micro civil war between the State and the guerrillas did not come to an automatic halt, the project to unite guerrilla groups had come to a decisive end.

Active for a decade, the *Liga* failed to organize a national uprising to overthrow the bourgeoisie. To summarize the reasons for the *Liga*'s failure to overthrow the state we must look at a number of factors. First, without a mass base, toppling the government was bound to end tragically. The ideological dogmatism of the *Liga* prevented revolutionaries from building a strong student–worker alliance. Second, revolutionaries were confident that guerrilla warfare would paralyze the government, yet they totally underestimated its repressive capacity. Thirdly, the Left did not fully support the guerrillas. From the mid-1960s to 1973, a part of the Left, especially radical youth, viewed the guerrillas with "a blend of fascination, respect and fear."[103] However, as time went by, the Left clearly refused the illegal actions of the guerrillas, especially the 1973 operations of the *Liga*.

Finally, the *Liga* lost the ideological struggle because like other urban guerrilla movements, they lacked access to mass media, and on the ground its dogmatic interpretation of Marxism–Leninism was very difficult to understand for the average person. Militants were regularly sent into the cities and countryside to carry out the indoctrination process, but were immediately rejected by these communities. Fearing state-sponsored violence, communities resisted guerrillas' rhetoric about revolution and pushed them out of their areas. Also, many of these students had never been outside the city and new very little about rural life. Many experienced a cultural shock and were clearly unprepared to confront this challenge. Also, the *Liga*'s propaganda campaign had no chance against the PRI's control over mass media. The government hammered home a simple and understandable message in newspapers, radio and television: protect the 1910 Mexican Revolution from subversives. Newspapers reporting the outcomes of the counterinsurgency campaign venerated actions taken by the secret police to eliminate the guerrilla threat. Working alongside the ruling party, newspapers used a mixture of Cold War language against the *Liga*. Threatening labels like terrorist, uncultured, and subversives were habitually used in daily newspapers.

Conclusion

Did the *Liga* participate in the Mexican democratic transition? To some extent, the political violence of the entire guerrilla phenomenon can explain the opening up of the political system in 1977.[104] Nonetheless, at the time the *Liga* was evidently not fighting to establish a representative democracy respectful of human rights in Mexico, as ex-militants call for today. They were not fighting mainly against the PRI-state: according to their Marxist–Leninist ideology, their enemies were socio-economic forces, the national "bourgeoisie" and its so-called "servants" (the police and the army). On the other hand, the PRI executives and the repressive forces were fighting, from their own point of view, against the subversion and to preserve the legacy of the 1910 Mexican

Revolution. However, before choosing the guerrilla option, Left militants believed in a possible democratization of Mexico, but the violent repression of the 1968 student movement and the Corpus Christi Massacre of 1971 crushed their hope that Mexico could be democratized through nonviolent strategies. Indeed, the ex-*guerrilleros* returned to their first belief in democracy some years after. In prison, they abandoned the group's politico-military Marxism, and adopted for democratic procedures. On the whole, the *Liga* in itself had only a very reduced and indirect influence on the democratic transition. In fact, victims of the micro civil war between the state and guerrillas played a much greater role. A number of human rights associations formed by families, such as the Comité Eureka led by Rosario Ibarra de Piedra (whose son Jesús Piedra Ibarra, a LC23S member, disappeared in 1975), forced successive governments to face questions of human rights abuse.

Acknowledgments

I would like to thank the following people for the corrections made to this chapter: Naveen Kanalu, Gui-Xi Young, Gregory Hermann, Monica Antonescu and of course the editors of this book, Fernando Herrera Calderón and Adela Cedillo.

Notes

1 AGN, DFS, folders n°1 to n°4. The DFS (1947–1985), trained by the CIA, acted as a political police for the PRI-State. It regularly used torture to question *guerrilleros* and their relatives. Jorge Luis Sierra Guzmán, *El enemigo interno, Contrainsurgencia y fuerzas armadas en México* (México: Universidad Iberoamericana, 2003), 101–102.
2 The title *Madera* paid hommage to the first Guevarist guerrilla movement in Mexico, the *Grupo Popular Guerrillero* (Popular Guerrilla Group). More generally, this reference sheds light on the processes of heroisation inside guerrilla movements and the inscription of the *guerrilleros* in a larger history.
3 The *Guajiros* were founded in Mexico City in January 1971. Diego Lucero, had been part of the urban support network of the *Grupo Popular Guerrillero* and chose the armed struggle after the massacre of 1968. The *Procesos* was a faction from within the *Juventud Comunista Mexicana* (the Mexican Communist Youth). The group split from the JCM after its Third Congress in December 1970, during which Ramos Zavala and another comrade collectively wrote a document entitled the *Proceso revolucionario* (the Revolutionary Process), which became the group's primary manifesto. In 1971, a number of members of the Catholic group *Movimiento Estudiantil Profesional* (Professional Student Movement) merged with the *Procesos*, among Salas Obregón. According to the DFS documents, José Luis Sierra Villareal and Salas Obregón met Ramos Zavala in Netzahualcóyotl doing social work. AGN, DFS, Exp. 100-6-1-74 H-256 L-24; José Luis Alonso Vargas, "Los "Guajiros," orígenes y proyecto político," http://www.centrodeinvestigacioneshistoricas.com/los_guajiros.htm (accessed October 10, 2007); Gustavo Hirales Morán, *La Liga Comunista 23 de Septiembre: orígenes y naufragio* (México: Ediciones de Cultura Popular, 1977), 12–13.

4 José Luis Alonso Vargas, op. cit.
5 Salas took his *nom de guerre* from the biblical prophet Oseah, revealing his Liberation Theology background.
6 *Madera 1* (May 1972), http://www.centrodeinvestigacioneshistoricas.com/madera_no__1.htm (accessed 2007).
7 Ibid.
8 Gustavo Hirales Morán, *La Liga Comunista 23 de Septiembre: Orígenes y naufragio* (México: Ediciones de Cultura Popular, 1977), 18.
9 *Madera n°1*, 35.
10 *Madera n°2*, 16.
11 Ibid., 16–17. *Madera n°3*, 13.
12 *Madera n°2*, 3.
13 *Madera n°6*, 13.
14 *Madera n°2*, 18.
15 *Madera n°4*, 40.
16 *Madera n°2*, 6.
17 *Madera n°3*, 8.
18 *Madera n°2*, 29.
19 *Madera n°2*, 10.
20 *Madera n°5*, 65.
21 *Madera n°5*, 65.
22 *Madera n°1*, 34.
23 *Madera n°2*, 14. *Madera n°2*, 27.
24 *Madera n°2*, 27.
25 *Madera n°2*, 23.
26 *Madera n°3*, 62. *Madera n°7*, 31.
27 *Madera n°5*, 65.
28 *Madera n°3*, 63. *Madera n°3*, 65.
29 *Madera n°6*, 24.
30 *Madera n°5*, 3.
31 AGN, DFS, Exp. 100-6-1-74 L-24 H-256.
32 AGN, DFS, Exp. 100-6-1-74 L-24 H-256; AGN, DFS, Exp. 11-235-73 L-1 H-7.
33 This practice was theorized by the Uruguayan Tupamaros (*Movimiento de Liberación Nacional*). Tupamaros, *Nous les Tupamaros* (Paris: Maspero, 1971), 187.
34 AGN, DFS, Exp. 11-235-74 L-11 H-267.
35 AGN, DFS, Exp. 100-6-1-74 L-24 H-256.
36 *Madera 1* (May 1972), http://www.centrodeinvestigacioneshistoricas.com/madera_no__1.htm.
37 Ibid. A similar argument could have been found in the Tupamaros or Marighela's writings.
38 AGN, DFS, Exp. 11-235-73 L-1 H-7.
39 Ibid.
40 AGN, DFS, Exp. 100-6-1-74 L-24 H-256.
41 AGN, DFS, Exp. 100-12-1-73 L-24 H-357. The *Comité Obrero Revolucionario* of the LC23S was active in Minatitlán and Jáltipan (Veracruz).
42 A few months before the creation of the LC23S, during the negotiations led by the *Organización Partidaria*, Ignacio Salas and Lucio Cabañas (leader of the PDLP) agreed on a kind of coordination. A member of the LC23S then integrated the collective leadership of the *Brigada Campesina de Ajusticiamiento*, the armed organization of the PDLP. However, during the annual assembly of the PDLP, in May 1973, the LC23S *guerrilleros* criticized the unorthodox ideology and politics of the *Partido* and were consequently expelled from the meeting. For further information: Fernando

Pineda Ochoa, *En las profundidades del mar (El oro no llego de Moscú)* (México: Plaza y Valdés, 2003), 175; FEMOSPP, *Informe Oficial No censurado sobre la Guerra Sucia de Luis Echeverría,* http://www.criterios.com/modules.php?name=Noticias&file=article&sid=8177. AGN, DFS, Exp. 100-10-16-4-73 L-8 H-37; AGN, DFS, Exp. 11-235-73 L-1 H-10.
43 Fernando Pineda Ochoa, ibid, 161. AGN, DFS, Exp. 11-235-74 L-11 H-267; AGN, DFS, Exp. 11-235-74 L-2 H-351.
44 Gustavo Adolfo Hirales Morán, *Memoria de la guerra de los justos* (México: Cal y Arena, 1996), 276–277.
45 AGN, DFS, Exp. 80-57-73 L-1 H-109; AGN, DFS, Exp. 11-235-73 L-2 H-78; AGN, DFS, Exp. 11-235-74 L-11 H-23. Gustavo Adolfo Hirales Morán, ibid, 72, 297, 298, 299. "Un joven tomó el consulado francés," *Excélsior*, December 6, 1974. "Dice la policía que el 'Dr. Ulises' aceptó haber participado en el homicidio de Garza Sada," *Excélsior*, December 9, 1974. The FEMOSPP report mentions also Maximino Madrigal Quintanilla, Juan Corral and Hilario Juarez García.
46 According to DFS documents, the failure of the Garza Sada operation pushed the *guerrilleros* to plan two simultaneous actions in Guadalajara. AGN, DFS, Exp. 100-6-1-74 L-24 H-256.
47 Ignacio Salas had already written communiqués for press, radio and television.
48 AGN, DFS, Exp. 100-6-1-74 L-24 H-256.
49 AGN, DFS, Exp. 11-235-73 L-1 H-139; AGN, DFS, Exp. 11-235-73 L-4 H-110.
50 AGN, DFS, Exp. 11-235-74 L-6 H-35; AGN, DFS, Exp. 11-235-74 L-4 H-24.
51 Ibid.
52 AGN, DFS, Exp. 11-235-73 L-1 H-176.
53 AGN, DFS, Exp. 11-235-74 L-6 H-35.
54 Ibid.; AGN, DFS, Exp. 11-235-73 L-1 H-209; AGN, DFS, Exp. 100-6-1-74 L-24 H-256; AGN, DFS, Exp. 11-235-74 L-6 H-218.
55 Victor Payán and Emilio Viale, "Capturarón a tres sospechosos del secuestro de Aranguren; nada se sabe del industrial," *Excélsior*, October 17, 1973.
56 "Crimen vil y estéril," *Excélsior*, October 20, 1973.
57 Ramón de Ertze Garamendi, "Triple violencia?," *Excélsior*, October 19, 1973.
58 Abelardo Villegas, "Las tácticas de la izquierda," *Excélsior*, October 15, 1973.
59 Angel Trinidad Ferreira, "Frentes Políticos," *Excélsior*, October 19, 1973.
60 Ibid.
61 "*Ni terrorismo ni infecunda amargura detendrán al país: L.E.*," *Excélsior*, October 24, 1973.
62 Victor Payán, "Tres mujeres y cuatro hombres vinculados en el caso Aranguren, detenidos ayer en Guadalajara," *Excélsior*, October 21, 1973.
63 Victor Payán, "Hay seis detenidos, 2 hombres y 4 mujeres, por el secuestro de Williams y asesinato de Aranguren," *Excélsior*, October 24, 1973.
64 Victor Payán, "Se dicen guerrilleros los delincuentes detenidos en Satelite," *Excélsior*, December 2, 1973.
65 Angel Trinidad Ferreira, "La inquietud en Jalisco, obra de 20 individuos, puede cundir," *Excélsior*, November 22, 1973.
66 Ibid.
67 *Madera n°1*, 7.
68 *Madera n°2*, 47. Jesús Ramírez Cuevas, "Liga Comunista 23 de Septiembre. Historia del exterminio," *La Jornada*, March 28, 2004, http://www.jornada.unam.mx/2004/03/28/mas-historia.html (accessed 2007).
69 Angel Trinidad Ferreira, "En mítines en 9 campos intentarón agitar a campesinos," *Excélsior*, January 17, 1974.
70 *Madera n°2*, 1.
71 *Madera n°2*, 1.

72 *Madera n°2*, 8.
73 *Madera n°2*, 45.
74 *Madera n°2*, 48.
75 *Madera n°3*, 66.
76 *Madera n°1*, 42. FEMOSPP. Ibid.
77 *Madera n°1*, 43.
78 AGN, DFS, Exp. 11-235-74 L-6 H-35.
79 Gustavo Adolfo Hirales Morán, ibid., 259.
80 AGN, DFS, Exp. 11-235-74 L-6 H-35.
81 Gustavo Adolfo Hirales Morán, "La guerra secreta, 1970–1978," *Nexos*, June 1982. Corral García was found in Monterrey close to the Garza Sada house (though he did not participate in his murder), and Olivares Torres' body was discarded close to the Aranguren house in Guadalajara.
82 "Hallaron muerto al autor intelectual del asesinato de Aranguren," *Excélsior*, February 6, 1974.
83 FEMOSPP, ibid.
84 AGN, DFS, Exp. 11-235-74 L-11 H-238.
85 Ibid.; AGN, DFS, Exp. 100-6-1-74 L-24 H-256; AGN, DFS, Exp. 11-235-74 L-11 H-267. However, no militant was arrested as a result of Salas' confessions.
86 AGN, DFS, Exp. 11-235-74 L-11 H-267.
87 *Madera n°5*, 6.
88 AGN, DFS, Exp. 11-235-74 L-10 H-5.
89 AGN, DFS, Exp. 11-235-74 L-10 H-1.
90 Félix Velasco García, "Asesinaron sus secuestradores al septuagenario Raymundo Soberanis," *Excélsior*, February 26, 1974.
91 "6 hampones asaltaron la sucursal de Banamex en viveros de la Loma," *Excélsior*, March 13, 1974. Soberanis was related to the governor of Guerrero, Israel Nogueda Otero. Hence, the army raided the Costa Chica of Oaxaca and executed a devastating contrainsurgency campaign. Laura Castellanos, *México armado (1943–1981)* (México, DF: Era, 2007), 234.
92 Luis Segura and Emilio Viale, "Atraco a la pagaduría del hospital de Pemex en Azcapotzalco," *Excélsior*, June 6 1974.
93 "Gilberto Vargas, creo que mató a dos de sus compañeros, dice que obró en su defensa," *Excélsior*, May 29, 1974.
94 Luis Segura and Emilio Viale, "Más de dos millones de botín," *Excélsior*, December 11, 1974.
95 AGN, DFS, Exp. 11-235-74 L-23 H-93.
96 Isael Petronio Nájera Cantú, interview with author, 2005.
97 Gustavo Hirales Morán, 243.
98 *Madera n°5*, 39.
99 AGN, DFS, Exp. 11-235-74 L-10 H-254.
100 AGN, DFS, Exp. 11-235-74 L-11 H-68.
101 AGN, DFS, Exp. 11-235-74 L-19 H-64.
102 *Madera n°3*, 8.
103 José Woldenberg. *Memoria de la izquierda* (México: Cal y Arena, 1998), 35.
104 Ilán Bizberg, "La transformation politique du Mexique: fin de l'ancien régime et apparition du nouveau?," *Critique Internationale*, April 2003, 123.

7

ARMED STRUGGLE WITHOUT REVOLUTION

The Organizing Process of the National Liberation Forces (FLN) and the Genesis of Neo-Zapatism (1969–1983)

Adela Cedillo

Marxism and its various currents once dominated interpretations of armed revolutionary movements in Latin America. One of its central tenets was that capitalism's contradictions and crises engendered recurring political struggles by the exploited classes until they achieve total revolution. However, in the past two decades, new interpretations on collective insurgent action and its outcomes have brought into question the Marxist structural determinism and its idea of the revolutionary class subject.[1] This chapter looks at revolutionary attempts not from a teleological metanarrative but as phenomena that led to complex historical processes.[2]

The case study focuses on the *Fuerzas de Liberación Nacional* (National Liberation Forces, FLN), a politico-military organization that for 24 years (1969–1993) prepared for a people's war that never took place. What happened instead was that one of its armed branches, the Zapatista Army of National Liberation (*Ejército Zapatista de Liberación Nacional*, EZLN), carried out an indigenous uprising on January 1, 1994 in Chiapas, became independent of the FLN and its socialist objectives, and since then has had a global resonance.[3] This essay looks at the period since the FLN's appearance in 1969 to the founding of the EZLN in 1983, which coincides with the so-called Dirty War. It is important to emphasize that, at least until 1993, the EZLN was subordinate to the FLN both politically and militarily, hence the genesis of neo-Zapatism should not be traced to Chiapas, but rather to the city of Monterrey, Nuevo León, where a small group of professionals and students originally conceived this insurgent project.

This chapter argues that in order to understand the emergence of the FLN and its singularity within the spectrum of armed organizations in Latin America, one must analyze the structural factors (global, national and local), the formation of collective identities expressed in organizations, and the political subjectivity. It is not my intention to go into a detailed discussion of all the variables mentioned, but to provide a general sketch that highlights the ways in which determination, contingency, and agency coexist.

This study also offers a succinct account of two fundamental stages in the organization's life: the first evaluates the formation of its politico-military structure and its extermination within the context of a national counterinsurgent policy (1969–1974), and the second focuses on its reconstruction, as well as how the group forged an alliance with indigenous agrarian activists, which ultimately became the nucleus of a *campesino* army in Chiapas (1974–1983).

Armed Rationality

In the context of the Cold War, between 1960 and the late 1980s, armed struggles were more or less a permanent factor on the Latin American stage given that various left-wing political forces considered conditions ripe for a continental revolution.[4] The Cuban (1959) and later the Sandinista (1979) Revolutions contributed to the growth of a specific guerrilla imaginary within the region and encouraged the circulation of ideologies that supported the armed struggle, such as Castro–Guevarism, Maoism, and Vietnamese Marxism. In each country guerrilla culture took different shapes according to structural conditions (the economic system, the type of political regime, historical traditions of political violence, and/or dependence on a foreign government) and conjunctural situations (level of confrontation between the government and the opposition, divisions within elites, the power of social movements, the intensity of repression, and the degree of left-wing radicalization). As of 1960, dozens of armed revolutionary groups surfaced throughout Latin American with a range of ideologies, backgrounds, strategies, tactics, military power, organizational capacity, and social bases.[5]

In Mexico, under the authoritarian political system maintained by the Institutional Revolutionary Party (PRI), some left wing groups entertained the option of armed struggle in the early 1960s, motivated by the Cuban experience. The dearth of democracy, the systematic repression of social movements and the lack of channels of negotiation between the governing class and the opposition, triggered an awakening in youth searching for other forms of political participation. Concurrently, some progressive intellectuals began teaching Marxism in the universities where a number of semi-legal communist groups were active. Institutions of higher education gradually became epicenters for politicization and recruitment, although this never reached massive proportions.

State violence against social movements manifested itself in a series of massacres between 1962 and 1971 in Xochicalco, Morelos; Chilpancingo, Iguala, Atoyac, and Acapulco, Guerrero; Villahermosa, Tabasco; and Tlatelolco and San Cosme in Mexico City.[6] Other forms of repression included military assaults on union offices and universities, strike-breaking, attacks on demonstrations and meetings, imprisonment and torture of social activists. All this caused a triple alignment, involving the faults inherent in the system's political structure, a threat to the collective identity of certain social agents, namely students and *campesinos*, and their adoption of a guerrilla culture, originally conceived of as a form of self-defense. Their radicalization engendered an armed challenge against the state, yet this process was not widespread since individuals do not react mechanically and are divided by their framing processes.[7] The so-called ultra-leftists were convinced that there was a historical necessity, a political pertinence, and a moral obligation for the armed struggle, while the democrats defended the semi-legal struggle, arguing that subjective conditions were not ripe for an armed uprising.[8]

Even within the so-called ultra-left, the participation of individuals and collectives was diverse, due to differences in the diagnostics and prognostics of the national situation, as well as different politico-military strategies. Each group felt the need to forge its own identity, to differentiate itself not only from democrats, but also other armed revolutionary organizations, which in turn triggered a war of ideas between them. Contrary to the dominant narratives that identify *guerrilleros* as delirious extremists, adventurers, and provocateurs,[9] leaders were organic intellectuals who deeply discussed the different currents of revolutionary thought and sought to raise the political and ideological level of militants.[10] Thus, the main battle revolutionaries fought was to define the collective meaning of the political environment, which is the kernel of hegemonic competition.[11]

The fragmentation of the armed left can also be explained through political subjectivity, involving not only ideology but also the imaginary and the domains of valuation and emotional-affectivity. Dissimilar utopias, regionalism, leadership rivals, incompatible worldviews between urban and rural groups, and even personal differences in everyday militancy had strong bearing in what might have caused the multiplication of guerrilla groups.[12]

Another key factor for understanding the formation of politico-military organizations is their mobilizing structures.[13] Subversive ideas and their corresponding cultural expressions in music, literature, film, painting, design, and radio, circulated through certain social networks. Activist circles discussed the armed option, collectively agreed to go underground, and began to recruit among family and friends. In that way, networks of belonging increased the chances of someone passing from an individual dissatisfaction to active participation in the revolutionary struggle. The FLN shared these constitutive elements with other armed groups, yet they were unique in certain characteristics that will be discussed below.

The Configuration of a "Peaceful" Guerrilla

> Vivir por la patria o morir por la libertad.[14]
> —Vicente Guerrero (FLN-EZLN slogan)

The city of Monterrey, capital of the state of Nuevo León, is considered the cradle of Mexican industry. The upshots of industrialization during the post-revolutionary period were accelerated capital accumulation, urban development, demographic growth, the exacerbation of inequality among social classes and the emergence of labor and communist movements.[15] From the times of Lázaro Cárdenas (1936–1940), the polarization between conservatives (high clergy, industrialists, and members of the PAN, among others), liberals (grouped around the PRI and the masonic lodges), and socialists (in unions, associations, and parties like the PCM) marked local society.[16] In this context of deep political discord, some of the most important guerrillas emerged during the 1960s.

Such is the case of César Germán Yáñez. Around 1958, this young middle-class law student and some of his colleagues became members of the Vicente Guerrero Lodge, part of the *Asociación de Jóvenes Esperanza de la Fraternidad* (Association of Youth Hope of the Fraternity, AJEF, a type of youth school preceding freemasonry), which was the only lodge that taught Marxist-Leninism. This resulted in the formation of a group called *Vanguardia Socialista* (Socialist Vanguard, VS), which under Yáñez's direction participated in student, labor, *campesino*, urban, and anti-imperialist movements.[17] The VS also helped to establish the state committee of the *Movimiento de Liberación Nacional* (National Liberation Movement, MLN), an experiment to unify the Mexican left, founded in 1962, but dissolved only two years later.[18]

In 1965 the VS changed its name to the *Unión Revolucionaria Socialista* (Socialist Revolutionary Union, URS), and its members made several trips to Cuba. Inspired by their experience on the island, they set out to build a platform for the dissemination of Castro–Guevarism by establishing the Monterrey section of the *Instituto Mexicano-Cubano de Relaciones Culturales "José Martí"* ("José Martí" Mexican–Cuban Institute for Cultural Relations, IMCRC) in 1967.[19] The center only organized cultural activities, it was not illegal; however, the URS used it to recruit sympathizers for the armed struggle. After almost a decade of open activism curtailed by repression, Yáñez and his comrades were convinced that the only option was to take up arms.

The URS established contact with Mario Menéndez, the editor of a left wing, slightly sensationalist magazine called *Por qué?* (Why?) from Mexico City.[20]

Even before the 1968 student movement, Menéndez had secretly organized the *Ejército Insurgente Mexicano* (Mexican Insurgent Army, EIM), a guevarist guerrilla movement. After the Tlatelolco massacre, he managed to bring together some 20 members to start a guerrilla *foco* in the Lacandon jungle in the southern state of Chiapas, one of the poorest in Mexico.[21] Students and professionals from Mexico City, Veracruz, Yucatán, and Nuevo León established the first EIM encampment in January 1969. Their experience in the jungle became an example of what not to do in terms of *foquismo*. Ideological disagreements, lack of structure and strategic planning, and makeshift approaches to even the most basic survival needs brought on the dissolution of the group.[22] However, the Monterrey collective continued on with their objectives and on August 6, 1969, Alfredo Zárate and Raúl Pérez Gasque joined Yáñez, Carlos Vives, Mario Sáenz, Graciano Sánchez Aguilar, Mario Sánchez Acosta, and Raúl Morales and founded the FLN.[23] The militants elected Yáñez and Zárate as first and second national leaders and agreed the organization would have a vertical and centralist structure. The top leader adopted the *nom de guerre* "Pedro," leading the press to label the collective as "Brother Pedro's Group," in reference to his Masonic background.[24]

In their discourse the FLN adhered to Castro–Guevarism, but their ideology was eclectic, incorporating tenets from Leninism, Maoism, Vietnamese Marxism, and the leftist revolutionary nationalism embraced by the MLN.[25] As any armed group, the FLN aspired to be the vanguard of a new revolution that would topple the government, establish socialism, and liberate the country from US imperialism. They chose guerrilla warfare as their military strategy, with the aim of forming an insurrectional *foco* in a rural setting that would later become the nucleus for a future people's army. What was quite unique about the FLN was that they did not seek to begin the revolution, but rather to prepare for its imminent coming according to the historical laws propounded by Marxism.[26] Another distinguishing feature was that they did not believe the revolutionary subject belonged to a single social class, instead it would emerge from an alliance between workers, *campesinos*, students and/or progressive petty bourgeoisie.

The FLN also rejected militarism in their everyday methods of struggle; they prohibited robberies, kidnappings, and other expropriations as sources of financing, given the negative image they might have on the population. The alternative was to build, with infinite patience, collaborative networks that could expand and guarantee the guerrilla's survival.[27] The networks were made up of cells called *Estudiantes y Obreros en Lucha* (Students and Workers in Struggle, EYOL) whose duty was to provide resources (financial, material, informational, etc.) to the organization. The first networks were formed in the states of Nuevo León, Puebla, Veracruz, Tabasco, and Mexico City, taking advantage of relationships established when the IMCRC and the EIM were still active.

Between 1969 and 1973 the organization established several safe houses, bought cars and weapons, and launched the guerrilla *foco*.

In terms of recruitment, the FLN were selective, dividing potential members into three levels of militancy: professionals, contributors, and sympathizers. On the first level, there was only room for elements with outstanding preparation, capable of shaping the vanguard. The other two levels were made up of family members, friends, and old comrades close to the founders, mostly middle- and upper-middle-class students and professionals, along with a smaller group of workers. The FLN were successful in converting some of their pre-political networks into political networks and by January 1974, they had incorporated approximately 120 members.[28]

The FLN chose the Cañadas region in the Lancandon jungle as the site to set up their armed branch and acquired a plot of land near the El Diamante ranch, an area that bordered Carib and Tzeltal communities. They named their ranch *El chilar* (the Chile Field) because they passed themselves off as chile dealers (*chileros*).[29] The goal was the foundation of the *Núcleo Guerrillero Emiliano Zapata* (Emiliano Zapata Guerrilla Nucleus, NGEZ), named for the leader who best represented the agrarian demands of the 1910 Revolution. Reclaiming Zapata's legacy was a way to establish symbolic continuity among the different generations of revolutionary movements.

"Pedro" and three militants founded the NGEZ on March 27, 1972, a few days after the publication of the Lacandon Community Decree in the Official Gazette of the Federation, which allocated the fabulous amount of 614,321 hectares of land to 66 Carib families (also called *Lacandones*), an act whose true aim was a government monopoly over the region's timber and other natural resources.[30] Unaware of this situation and assuming that the marginalized poor held more revolutionary potential than other sectors, the eight members of the NGEZ attempted to recruit some Carib youths through exchanging products and offering Spanish language instruction, literacy, and healthcare advice. However, militants were unable to raise the Carib youths' political consciousness after security forces detected their presence in Chiapas and forced them out of the area.

On February 13, 1974, in a reconnaissance mission to find those responsible for the murder of businessman Eugenio Garza Sada, executed by the September 23 Communist League a few months earlier, police discovered an FLN safehouse in Monterrey, inhabited by Napoleón Glockner and Nora Rivera. During the interrogation and torture, both confessed that the location of the general headquarters of the FLN was in the town of Nepantla in the State of Mexico.[31] On the night of February 14, the Military Police carried out Operation Nepantla, a surprise attack meant to eliminate the guerrillas living in that safe house. The soldiers killed five revolutionaries, among them Alfredo Zárate, and arrested two others.[32]

Concurrently, the DFS broke down the Monterrey front with the arrest of 12 of the group's collaborators.[33] Documents found in Nepantla provided the location of El Chilar, leading the Military Police to mobilize forces into the Cañadas on February 16 in Operation Diamante. But the guerrillas, who had heard the news on the radio, were able to leave the camp with the help of their Carib contacts.[34] The 46th Infantry Battalion of the 31st Military Zone, located in the state capital of Tuxtla Gutiérrez, took command of the operation. Between February and March 1974, militants and the army were involved in two separate confrontations that resulted in the death of two soldiers. The guerrillas managed to find shelter in the jungle but the Tzeltal communities betrayed them. Once in their hands, the army disappeared three militants, as well as executed and buried in unmarked graves three others, among them "Brother Pedro."[35] *Campesinos* handed over the chileros not only because they did not know where they came from, but also because they were unsympathetic to the armed struggle.[36] In this manner, the first counter-insurgent operation in the Lacandon jungle came to an end.

The FLN were the only armed revolutionary organization to be practically exterminated without having committed any assaults against the state or the oligarchy. Of the founders, only Mario Sáenz and Fernando Yáñez survived and went on to lead a tactical withdrawal and rebuild the organization. One of their priorities was to settle scores: in November 1976 an FLN commando executed Glockner and Rivera for having provided compromising information to security forces.[37] Also, after 1974 the FLN searched for their disappeared comrades in the Cañadas until 1979, when they realized they were never going locate them.[38]

In spite of its repression and isolation, and the Electoral Reform of 1977, which legalized the democratic left in Mexico, and the Amnesty Law of 1978, which freed the majority of political prisoners, the FLN held on to its armed project and, between 1975 and 1980, made several attempts to re-establish a camp in the mountains of the Lacandon jungle. During this period, the tragic death of several leaders hindered the organization's development: in 1975 the army accidentally found and killed Julieta Glockner and Graciano Sánchez in Cárdenas, Tabasco; Mario Sáenz died from a hunting accident in 1977, while searching the jungle for a site for the new guerrilla *foco*; and a FLN deserter treacherously killed Jorge Velasco in a safe house in Macuspana, Tabasco in 1980.[39] After the leadership was replaced with new militants the FLN once again sought out their objectives.

The Re-encounter Between the Mestizo Vanguard and the Indigenous World

The crux of the agrarian issue in Chiapas came from the conversion of farmland into livestock ranches to meet the demands of international markets. This process started in the 1950s and meant the release of tens of thousands of peons. Eager to reassure the big landowners who owned 60 percent of the state of Chiapas, the government responded to the demand for land by opening the Lacandon jungle to settlement, although its terrain was unsuitable for farming.[40] Indigenous people stripped of their land by *caciques*, *campesinos* who failed to benefit from agrarian reform, former peons, and other unemployed labourers, spread freely throughout the jungle until the Lacandon Community Decree abruptly outlawed the possibility of establishing new *ejidos* in the area. From 1974 onwards, Tzeltal, Tzotzil, Chol, and Tojolabal communities began to fight for their right to populate the jungle. This struggle has gone through many stages and has not yet been resolved.[41]

Enticed by the misfortunes of these disenfranchised people, a number of churches and left-wing organizations approached them with the offer of new religious and political identities. North American evangelical churches were among the first to support the settlers. In response, the Catholic Church, represented by the Diocese of San Cristóbal, engineered an ambitious evangelical program beginning in the 1960s and directed at all the indigenous groups in their jurisdiction, which included the Lacandon jungle. Bishop Samuel Ruiz, influenced by liberation theology, promoted a catechesis against the structures of domination and idealized the indigenous community as a model for the kingdom of heaven on earth.[42]

The Diocese performed a significant amount of community building and became a de facto power in Chiapas. One of its achievements was the First Indigenous Congress of Chiapas, which took place from October 13 to 15, 1974 in San Cristóbal de las Casas, with the support of the state government. The event commemorated the 500th anniversary of Fray Bartolomé de las Casas's birth and brought together 1,230 delegates from the Tzotzil, Tzeltal, Chol, and Tojolabal ethnic communities who, contrary to what the state authorities expected, touched on topics such as health, housing, education, and land.[43]

The Congress helped to identify the common issues faced by the indigenous peoples, yet the Diocese did not have the capacity to organize the communities politically and instead promoted links between them and left-wing groups such as the *Unión del Pueblo* (People's Unity, UP) and *Línea Proletaria* (Proletarian Line, LP), which arrived in Chiapas in 1974 and 1977.[44] These groups adopted a particular kind of Maoism that prioritized work with the masses through democratic assemblies. Their aim was to create a social base ready to fight, not for revolution, but for basic economic demands such as public services, infrastructure, and everything else the state had not provided to its invisible citizens. The Maoists reoriented the *campesino* movements from the struggle for land to the creation of cooperatives and credit unions. In the Lacandon jungle, two important organizations emerged under the UP and the LP's guidance: the *Unión Ejidal Quiptic Ta Lecubtesel* (1975) and the *Unión de Uniones Ejidales y*

Grupos Campesinos Solidarios de Chiapas in 1980, which presided over a group of as many as 12,000 *campesinos*.[45]

Initially, the FLN refused to get involved in land struggles because their main interest laid in the jungle's geostrategic conditions. No other region combined the features of isolation, mountainous terrain, threatening fauna, and vast vegetation, an ideal setting for a people's army. On the other hand, aside from the *ejido* commissariat and some popular stores (branches of the National Company for Popular Subsistance, CONASUPO), federal institutions and the PRI had no presence in the jungle, and even the police and the army were unfamiliar with the region. In addition, the proximity of the Tehuantepec Isthmus favored the country's potential division with the consolidation of a liberated zone connected to Central America, and the Guatemala border as a rearguard for tactical withdrawal.[46]

Contrary to traditional Marxism, which underestimated peasants agents of change and subordinate to the proletariat, the FLN considered them to be the only revolutionary class in Mexican history. That being the case, the group did not hesitate to incorporate them into their cross-class alliance project. According to one militant, *campesinos* in Chiapas:

> … lived in a state of exploitation and misery, bad health and ignorance, which were ideal elements need to help construct a support base for the guerrilla group and political-military activities. Their long tradition of struggling against domination, formidable community spirit—forged as a defense mechanism against capitalist penetration—and repression, identified campesinos as a sector that has much to gain from a socialist revolution, and that has nothing to lose but their misery.[47]

For the FLN these conditions should have facilitated the recruitment of *campesinos* and the development of their political consciousness. In a failing shared with other attempts to form guerrilla focos in indigenous zones, such as Che's efforts in Bolivia, the FLN ignored the culture, history, identity, and worldview of these communities who had only a minimal connection to capitalism. The guerrillas valued the indigenous people as a teleological subject and not as an ethnic subject with their own aims. One of the NGEZ's errors was to ignore the fact that as long as the government kept alive the promise of agrarian distribution, *campesinos* had no motive for participating in armed struggle, particularly the Caribs who were the only ethnic group to directly benefit from the Lacandon Decree. Because the guerrillas focused on organizing depoliticized indigenous people who owned their land, their revolutionary objectives were doomed to fail. Yet the upper ranks of the FLN did not consider the NGEZ as a failure. On the contrary, they believed it had been an excellent lesson in how to survive in the jungle without assistance from the locals.[48]

It was not until the Sandinista victory in Nicaragua that the FLN proposed to abandon *foquismo* and adopt the strategy of a people's war of national liberation inspired by the Maoist and Vietnamese experiences.[49] In contrast with *foquismo*, which advocated the formation of a vanguard of exemplary combatants, the strategy of people's war prioritized the preparation of the popular army's bases. Beginning in 1978, the FLN's approach to indigenous groups became more tactical. A group of militants was established in San Cristóbal de las Casas, to create a platform for community work in the region of Los Altos (the Highlands). Through literacy instruction, first aid and vaccination brigades, the organization began to establish itself in marginalized Tzeltal and Tzotzil communities, hoping to identify elements susceptible to recruitment.[50]

According to "Renee," a former militant, by sheer luck the FLN met indigenous students from Chiapas at the National Autonomous University of Mexico (Universidad Nacional Autónoma de México).[51] These students happened to have family links that reached all the way to Sabanilla and Huitiupán, two northern municipalities known for their poverty and agrarian conflicts.[52] By 1978, the agrarian movement was in decline due to military repression and the arrival of communist, Maoist, and socialist organizations. It is worth noting that various communities that found themselves in the same conditions adopted different political analyses and selected different allies, ranging from the economist left to the ultra-left, producing intra- and inter-community divisions.

In 1978, in the *ejido* of Lázaro Cárdenas in northern Huitiupán, which had been struggling for four decades over land issues, the FLN managed to recruit *Paco*, a Tzotzil youth who had headed land occupations and other direct actions against regional *caciques*. Gradually *Paco* incorporated family members into the organization and provided information on others who were living in the Emiliano Zapata and Tierra y Libertad *ejidos* in the valley of San Quintín.[53] The new FLN recruitment model involved removing indigenous people from their communities in order to train them in urban safe houses. What characterized the first group of indigenous recruits was not only that they were all poor, but that they had been politicized and radicalized through an internal process, and were open to armed struggle given that they believed legal and peaceful channels had been exhausted. Nonetheless, the *campesino* recruits had a local vision of the struggle, which meant they focused on regional *caciques* and landowners as their main enemies. FLN addressed this issue from a revolutionary pedagogy standpoint: they convinced recruits to believe the struggle was against imperialism, the bourgeoisie, the state and its armed branches, and it had to occur on a national level. Therefore, they trained them politically, militarily, and technically to transform them into the support bases for the people's army.

The Consolidation of the FLN and Their Outside Links

In 1978, five of the group's main cadres composed the first Political Bureau. They agreed to publish an underground magazine named *Nepantla. Órgano de agitación y comunicación interna de las FLN*, to aid the political formation of their members. The magazine started to circulate among professional militants on February 14, 1979 with limited printing, and was published at irregular intervals until 1993.[54] It is the most important source for understanding the organization's ideology and development.

In 1979, the revolutionary upsurge in Nicaragua made a positive impact on the FLN's university recruitment as it revived expectations about the armed struggle.[55] Also, the group grew substantially following the arrival of a number of indigenous recruits, which led to the formulation of the *FLN Statutes* in 1980. In this document the FLN outlined its socialist project, structure, and politico-military line, as well as regulations for each and every aspect of internal discipline.[56] This was the first document to reveal a blueprint of the future EZLN, as a rural people's army with a regular structure and adherence to the Geneva Convention.[57]

Around this period, the FLN sent a solidarity brigade to Managua, Nicaragua and established links with the *Frente Sandinista de Liberación Nacional* (Sandinista National Liberation Front, FSLN). Due to President José López Portillo's official support for FSLN, the Nicaraguan government paid little attention to the armed struggles in Mexico. In fact, there is no evidence to suggest that any armed organization from abroad collaborated with the FLN, but this did not prevent them from providing support to other revolutionary movements. For instance, beginning in 1982, the FLN gave protection to William Morales, a militant of the *Fuerzas Armadas de Liberación Nacional de Puerto Rico* (Armed Forces of National Liberation of Puerto Rico, FALN), a man wanted by the FBI for his participation in terrorist acts on US soil.[58] The FLN helped Morales hide and in exchange he taught them how to manufacture explosives; however, a security mistake led the FBI to detect his presence in Puebla. On May 26, 1983, security forces supported by FBI agents arrested Morales and killed two members of the FLN Political Bureau, "Mario Marcos" and "Ruth." Among those captured was a young Tzeltal man who was injured and summarily tortured until he revealed where the FLN was located in Chiapas. The DFS did nothing to eliminate the organization, although two years later the young man was thrown from a helicopter over a jungle community to spread terror among campesinos.[59]

The Origin of Two Zapatista Armies

The FLN concluded that the communities of the San Quintín valley had a combative character and would be an ideal place to establish a guerrilla epicenter. This was largely because a 1978 presidential decree established the Montes Azules Biosphere Reserve, which originally included the San Quintín valley. Both the first Lacandon decree and the new one threaten the region's *ejidatarios* who feared a repetition of the eviction of 21 *ejidos* who were relocated to unusable land in 1974. The failure to award land due to the state and federal governments' lack of political will, coupled with ongoing repression, gradually radicalized the communities.

The FLN returned to the Cañadas with indigenous members who had received top-level training and were related by blood to *campesinos* from the area chosen as the scenario for operations, thus facilitating initial recruitment.[60] Mestizo militants could also rely on their 13 years of experience in the jungle (1969–1983), and learning from their mistakes while adapting to their surroundings. On November 17, 1983, two of the three national leaders of the FLN, Fernando Yáñez ("Pedro's" brother) and Gloria Benavides (survivor of Nepantla), "Rodolfo" and three of the most senior indigenous recruits, "Frank," "Jorge" and "Javier," established the first neo-Zapatista camp.[61] Thus, the EZLN was born one year after the end of the last Dirty War administration. Its persistence was a sign that armed revolutionary movements had not been entirely defeated.

Anti-Zapatista academic literature and journalism written by Carlos Tello, María del Carmen Legorreta, Maité Rico, and Bertrand De la Grange, attribute the founding of the EZLN to the Diocese's support for the guerrillas and to the use of Maoist political networks. Ex-militants point out that the Dioceses allowed the guerrillas to penetrate the region under its jurisdiction, but never provided sustained support to the FLN-EZLN.[62] With regard to the Maoists (the UP merged with the LP from 1978), they provided a degree of politicization and organizational work without precedent in the Lacandon jungle, yet until 1983 none of the FLN indigenous militants had been formed by the LP; moreover, following the split within the Unión de Uniones in 1983, the communities expelled the Maoists from the region.[63]

What these authors fail to discuss is the constitution of the ethnic political subject. Indigenous activists, who combined political, religious, and community leadership, and represented large social bases, were mustered into the EZLN beginning in 1984. Both the Diocese, as well as the Maoists (but to a lesser extent) trained a number of these leaders, but in the end they underwent a process of empowerment that placed them beyond external influences and gave them absolute control over their communities' destinies.[64]

One can speak of two EZLNs: the first, founded in 1983 thanks to the tenacity of the FLN and the conviction of small indigenous group in the North that pacific struggle had been exhausted; the other, born in the second half of the 1980s out of the decision of communities who analyzed their local context and realized the relevance of armed militancy. This second EZLN, nurtured by the indigenous peoples of the Lacandon jungle and, on a smaller scale, from the Highlands and the North, is the movement that became independent of its founders and questioned the neoliberal end of history in 1994.

Conclusions

This chapter has sketched out a little known, non-linear path that goes from the Vicente Guerrero Lodge to the EZLN. It has addressed the organization of the FLN and its outcome. I conclude that structural contradictions, by themselves, did not radicalize the militants who founded the FLN. Nor was the founding of the EZLN determined by the clash of pre-capitalist conditions in Chiapas with national and international capitalism. On the other hand, not everything can be attributed to the volition of the militants and the guerrilla fever of the 1970s. One must look instead at complex interactions between macrostructures and agents.

In this study, it has been observed that the actors perceived the lack of political opportunities and the repression that threatened certain collective identities in relation to a specific ideological-imaginary climate and to the spaces and networks through which these ideas circulated. Even in 1978, when the context changed, the FLN rejected the regime's attempts at political overture because they considered them insufficient and opted instead for dogmatic long-term interpretative frames that ultimately determined the organization and their armed branch's longevity. Hence, within an objective context of structural contradictions, the determining factors that generated this revolutionary attempt were framing processes, political subjectivity, and mobilizing structures, all of which resulted in the formation of a solid collective identity.

Acknowledgments

I would like to thank Elizabeth Henson, Alexander Aviña, and Christopher Gunderson for commenting on earlier versions of this essay. Also, I would like to thank Nasheli Jiménez and Fernando Herrera Calderón for their help with the translation.

Notes

1 See Timothy Wickham-Crowley, *Guerrillas and Revolution in Latin America: A Comparative Study of Insurgents and Regimes since 1956* (Princeton: Princeton University Press, 1992); Donatella della Porta, *Social Movements, Political Violence and the State: A Comparative Analysis of Italy and Germany* (Cambridge: Cambridge University Press, 1995); Elizabeth Jean Wood, *Insurgent Collective Action and Civil War in El Salvador* (New York: Cambridge University Press, 2003).
2 There is still no theoretical model for understanding Latin American guerrilla movements. I believe that Wickham-Crowely's empirical backing in his work is

insufficient and his model cannot be generalized. To analyze collective action, I have opted to use some categories from the political process model, but not extensively, because it lacks a political subject and collective identity theory, and underestimates the role of economic factors.

3 In part, the EZLN owes its fame to the fact that it has been the only guerrilla movement to use digital media successfully, as well as advocate an attractive postmodern leftist discourse. Because neo-Zapatista strategy adheres to principles of non-violence and self-defense, this has prevented the organization from being characterized as terrorist in contrast with other revolutionary groups. The EZLN's independence from its founding organization is reflected in the fact that while there is a lot of worldwide research on indigenous rebellion, little has been done on the FLN. The works by Carlos Tello, *La rebelión de Las Cañadas* (México, DF: Cal y Arena, 2000) and Maité Rico y Bertrand de la Grange, *Marcos, la genial impostura* (México, DF: Aguilar, 1998); and this author's thesis, "El fuego y el silencio: Historia de las Fuerzas de Liberación Nacional Mexicanas (1969–1974)," BA Thesis, Universidad Nacional Autónoma de México, 2008, and "El suspiro del silencio. De la reconstrucción de las Fuerzas de Liberación Nacional a la fundación del Ejército Zapatista de Liberación Nacional (1974–1983)," MA Thesis, Universidad Nacional Autónoma de México, 2010, are the only pieces that deal with the history of the FLN in detail.

4 Jorge Castañeda, in *Utopia Unarmed: The Latin American Left after the Cold War* (New York: Vintage Books, 1994), considers these groups a sort of counter-elite that incited violence and precluded Latin America's progress towards democracy, an argument that Gilbert Joseph discusses in "What We Know and Should Know. Bringing Latin America More Meaningfully into Cold War Studies," in *In from the Cold: Latin America's New Encounter with the Cold War,* ed., Gilbert M. Joseph and Daniela Spenser (Durham: Duke University Press, 2008). To assume that democracy was Latin America's destiny is also a metanarrative, and to characterize the armed left as a volitional collective, lacking in social legitimacy and alien to the population, undermines the role that each politico-military organization played in its local context, a role which cannot be generalized.

5 For an account of the armed groups that surfaced, see Daniel Pereyra, *De Moncada a Chiapas. Historia de la lucha armada en América Latina* (Madrid: Los libros de la Catarata, 1997) and Castañeda, op. cit

6 Most of the massacres were against *campesino* and student movements. For a detailed description, see Laura Castellanos, *México armado (1943–1981)*, (México, DF: Era, 2007); Enrique Condés, *Represión y rebelión en México (1959–1985)*, vol. I–III (México, DF: Porrúa, 2007–2009); Fritz Glockner, *Memoria roja* (México, DF: Ediciones B, 2007).

7 "Framing processes" are defined as the "conscious strategic efforts by groups of people to fashion shared understandings of the world and of themselves that legitimate and motivate collective action," Doug McAdam, John D. McCarthy and Mayer N. Zald ed., *Comparative Perspectives on Social Movements: Political Opportunities, Mobilizing Structures, and Cultural Framings* (Cambridge: Cambridge University Press, 1996), 6.

8 For more on the debates between the moderate left and the ultraleft, see Cedillo, op. cit. (2008), 186–189.

9 On the construction of guerrillas as public enemies, see Jorge Mendoza García, "Otra ofensiva gubernamental: la ideologización hacia la guerrilla," *Memoria,* 149, 18–27.

10 It is important to note that in the case of urban guerrillas, all the leaders came from the universities. In the countryside, they belonged to the rural teacher training schools. Castellanos, op. cit.

11 See Ernesto Laclau and Chantal Mouffe, *Hegemony and Socialist Strategy* (London: Verso, 1989). Both authors define hegemony as the discursive articulation of various ideological elements surrounding a "central empty signifier" that allows for the consolidation of dislocated and dispersed social groups. This argument surpasses the essentialist formulation of subjects pre-constituted by their class identity and poses instead the fragmentation of subject positions.
12 The relevance of subjectivity is palpable in the numerous testimonies of ex-militants and in historical novels such as Carlos Montemayor, *Guerra en el paraíso* (México, DF: Seix Barral, 1997); Gustavo Hirales, *Memoria de la guerra de los justos* (México, DF: Cal y Arena, 1996); Arturo Ulloa Bornemann, *Surviving Mexico's Dirty War. A Political Prisoner's Memory* (Philadelphia: Temple University, 2007).
13 Mobilizing structures imply "those collective vehicles, informal as well as formal, through which people mobilize and engage in collective action," McAdam *et al.*, op. cit, 3. In the case of guerrillas, the emphasis is on informal channels (networks of family, friends, neighbors, colleagues) because most of those who became involved, while having some experience in social activism, were not militants in established parties or organizations; thus, these organizations were not a means of recruitment.
14 "To live for the motherland or to die for freedom."
15 For more on these events, see Alex Saragoza, *The Monterrey Elite and the Mexican State, 1880–1940*, (Austin, University of Texas Press, 1988); Israel Cavazos Garza, *Breve historia de Nuevo León,* (México, DF: COLMEX/FCE, 1994).
16 Cedillo, op. cit (2008), p. 147.
17 The local government regularly would call in security forces to repress mobilizations. Yáñez and his comrades went to prison on a number of occasions, but public pressure helped to free them quickly. AGN, DFS, Estado de Nuevo León, 1-V-66, 100-17-3/4-66, L-1, H-157.
18 Ibid. p. 77 and AGN, DFS, "Situación que prevalece en los distintos sectores sociales del estado de Nuevo León, 6 de noviembre de 1964," Exp. 100-17-3-264, L-1, H-101-106.
19 AGN, DFS, Exp. 100-17-3-69, L-6, H-98-101. It is important to note that while the Cuban Embassy provided assistance in the promotion of cultural activities, it refused to finance or militarily train the URS. Contrary to what Rico and De la Grange (op. cit. p. 127) have maintained, Yañez's group never received help from Cuba, as can be confirmed through several documents in the secret service archive. Fidel Castro maintained good relations with PRI governments and opted for non-interference in Mexico's internal affairs.
20 On this magazine and other leftist independent publications, see Jacinto Rodríguez Munguía, *La otra guerra secreta. Los archivos prohibidos de la prensa y el poder* (México, DF: Océano, 2007). Menéndez was an enthusiastic advocate of the Cuban Revolution, participated in the Organization of Latin American Solidarity (OLAS) Conference, and reported on armed experiences in Guatemala, Venezuela, and Colombia.
21 AGN, DFS, Exp. 11-4-70, L-106, H-181. The *foco* was not fixed in a particular territory, rather it moved around the jungle. Classic texts on *foquismo* include Ernesto Guevara, "La guerra de guerrillas" (1960) and Régis Debray, "Révolution dans la révolution?" (1967).
22 The members from Mexico City formed a second group, the Comité de Lucha Revolucionaria (Committee for Revolutionary Struggle, CLR), which was the first to place bombs in government buildings and business offices. In 1971, the police arrested the entire membership of the CLR, who revealed Menéndez was the leader of the dissolved EIM, even though he no longer participated in any underground movement. Menéndez, however, not once betrayed an FLN militant.

23 AGN, DFS, Exp. 11-212-74 L-14 H-114. Fernando Yáñez, César's brother, participated in the founding meeting as an observer. Soon after, Mario's sister, Elisa Irina Sáenz, became the first female member.
24 In June 1971, authorities discovered an FLN safe house in Monterrey for the first time after neighbors reported it to be occupied by drug dealers. After the police found information on the group and several militants, the press reported the findings. They also detained family members and people indirectly related to militants, though revolutionaries were able to dodge security forces. "El bautizo de fuego," *Nepantla, órgano de agitación y comunicación interna de las FLN*, 6, July 22, 1979, 2.
25 The group's documents did not reflect rich theoretical discussions, but afforded a pragmatic and empiricist view of the revolutionary process. The numerous communiqués of the FLN are available at AGN, DFS, Exp. 009-011-005 L-1, 9/oct./ 80, H-1-92.
26 Yvon Le Bot, *El sueño zapatista. Entrevistas con el Subcomandante Marcos, el mayor Moisés y el comandante Tacho, del Ejército Zapatista de Liberación Nacional* (Barcelona: Plaza y Janés, 1997), 124.
27 AGN, DFS, Exp. 009-011-005 L-1, 9/oct./ 80, H-1 and ss. Self-sustainability projects included everything from agriculture and livestock to the manufacture of footwear and clothing, mechanics, and printing workshops.
28 "Nuestra Historia," *Nepantla, órgano de agitación y comunicación interna de las FLN*, 6, July 22, 1979, 2. It is important to clarify that for security reasons, those closest to militants, such as parents, wives, and children, could not be recruited.
29 AGN, DFS, [Primera declaración de Carlos Arturo Vives Chapa, 21 de marzo de 1974], Exp. 11-212-74, L-14, H-40.
30 The resolution ignored both *ejido* endowments to other colonizers and those in administrative process, which caused a good deal of agrarian conflict known as the problem of the Lacandon decree. For more particulars, see Jan de Vos, *Una tierra para sembrar sueños. Historia reciente de la Selva Lacandona, 1950–2000* (México, DF: Fondo de Cultura Económica, 2002); Neil Harvey, *The Chiapas Rebellion: The Struggle for Land and Democracy* (Durham: Duke University Press, 1998); Sara Washbrook, ed., *Rural Chiapas Ten Years after the Zapatista Uprising* (New York: Routledge, 2007).
31 AGN, DFS, Exp. 11-212-74, L-2, H-53.
32 The others who died were Mario Sánchez, Carmen Ponce, Anselmo Ríos and Dení Prieto Stock, whose death particularly affected a sector of the intellectual community given that she was the daughter of playwright Carlos Prieto Argüelles. The detainees were Gloria Benavides and Raúl Morales. During the operation the military's strength was overtly disproportionate to the guerrillas; they used teargas, triple action grenades, as well as 618 M-2 cartridges, and no soldiers died. AGN, SEDENA, [Fuerzas Armadas de Liberación Nacional, Operación Nepantla, 16 de febrero de 1974], Vol. 70, Exp. 215, F. 40.
33 "Hallan las madrigueras del 'hermano Pedro,'" *La Prensa*, México, February 21, 1974, pp. 12–13. The only collaborator from the Mexico City network to be caught was Alberto Híjar, a famous art critic and university professor. Besides being tortured by police forces, detainees spent months or even years in the infamous Lecumberri Penitentiary, well-known for its cruel, inhumane, and degrading conditions.
34 In interviews conducted by the author with the Carib in Nahá and Metzabok in 2003, they expressed their incomprehension of the military persecution of the "chileros" because they did not seem like "criminal men." Clearly, some of the Carib supported them not because they understood their struggle, but in solidarity.
35 The detainees-disappeared were Carlos Vives, Elisa Sáenz, and Raúl Pérez, who were taken to Military Camp Num. 1 in México, DF. Federico Carballo and Juan

Guichard were among the dead. For a reconstruction of the events, see Cedillo, op. cit. (2008), 318.
36 Manuel Méndez, interview with author, March 23, 2005, municipality of Ocosingo, Chiapas.
37 Cedillo, op. cit. (2010), 87–91. Internal executions of those considered informants or traitors were part of the organization's military code. However, the cruelty shown in these executions made the family members of the dead assume that the police or military had been behind them; hence, the episode became the most controversial in the history of the FLN.
38 AGN, DFS, Exp. 009-011-005, H-94 & 95.
39 Cedillo, op. cit. (2010), *passim*.
40 Antonio García de León, *Fronteras interiores. Chiapas: una modernidad particular* (México, DF: Océano, 2002), 106.
41 An interesting anthropological take on this process is examined by Xóchitl Leyva Solano and Gabriel Ascencio Franco, *Lacandonia al filo del agua* (México, DF: CIESAS/UNAM/FCE, 2002).
42 De Vos, op. cit. p. 228. On the bishop's background, see Carlos Fazio, *Samuel Ruiz, El caminante* (México, DF: Espasa Calpe, 1994); Jean Meyer, *Samuel Ruiz en San Cristóbal, 1960–2000* (México, DF: Tusquets Editores, 2000), and on Ruiz's conversion from liberation theology to a millenarian indigenous theology, see Julio Ríos, *Siglo XX: muerte y resurrección de la Iglesia Católica en Chiapas: dos estudios históricos* (San Cristóbal de las Casas: UNAM, 2000).
43 Antonio García de León, "La vuelta del Katún. Chiapas: a veinte años del Primer Congreso Indígena," *Chiapas*, 1, 1995, http://www.ezln.org/revistachiapas/No1/ch1leon.html, (accessed November 6, 2010).
44 In the early 1970s, the UP divided into a semi-legal faction and an underground one. Both projects were politically and organically different. The most complete history of the semi-legal UP can be found in María del Carmen Legorreta. *Religión, política y guerrilla en Las Cañadas de la Selva Lacandona* (México, Cal y Arena, 1998).
45 Jorge Torres, "Unión de Uniones Ejidales y Grupos Campesinos Solidarios de Chiapas," in *Poder popular. Construcción de ciudadanía y comunidad,* ed., Adolfo Orive, (México, DF: Juan Pablos Editor, 2010), 53–200.
46 "Nuestra Historia," *Nepantla, órgano de agitación y comunicación interna de las FLN*, 9, March 15, 1980, 11. There was also discussion surrounding the possibility of establishing politico-operative contact with Guatemalan armed organizations. However, the extent of the armed conflict made it impossible for the FLN to stretch their presence beyond the border zone.
47 Ibid., 10. The FLN embraced the Leninist interpretation that posited the revolution would initially take place not in countries where capitalism was fully developed, but rather in "the weakest link of imperialism," much like Russia, which had an agrarian semi-feudal system. Militants used this analogy to identify *campesinos* as the weakest link in the system.
48 "Renee," ex FLN militant, interview with author, June 12, 2009, Mexico City.
49 The texts that list these strategies systematically are Mao Zedong, *Selected Military Writings of Mao Tse-tung*. (Peking: Foreign Languages Press, 1966) and Vo Nguyen Giap, *People's War, People's Army: the Viet Công Insurrection Manual for Underdeveloped Countries* (New York: Praeger, 1962).
50 María Gloria Benavides, interview with author, February 12, 2004, Mexico City.
51 "Renee," interview with author, June 17, 2009. True identity of militant will remain undisclosed.
52 On these agrarian struggles and their outcomes, see Ana Bella Pérez Castro, *Entre montañas y cafetales* (México, DF: UNAM/IIA, 1989); Sonia Toledo, *Fincas, poder y*

cultura en Simojovel, Chiapas (San Cristóbal: UNAM/UNACH, 2007) and María Cristina Renard, "Movimiento *campesino* y organizaciones políticas. Simojovel-Huitiupán (1974–1990)," *Revista Chiapas,* 4, http://membres.multimania.fr/revistachiapas/No4/ch4renard.html (accessed December 2, 2010).
53 Ibid. Indigenous groups from Lázaro Cárdenas, Huitiupán and El Calvario, Sabanilla founded Emiliano Zapata and Tierra y Libertad in 1968 and 1971.
54 *Nepantla. Agitation and internal communication bulletin of the FLN*. Approximately one hundred or so issues were published. A few issues are held in the DFS reserve at the Archivo General de la Nación, AGN. The only complete collection is probably in the possession of the EZLN.
55 Rafael Sebastián Guillén Vicente, a professor of Design for Graphic Communication at the Universidad Autónoma Metropolitana (Metropolitan Autonomous University) was recruited during this period. Though, he would later come to be known as Subcomandante Insurgente Marcos of the EZLN. Tello, op. cit. 112.
56 AGN, DFS, "Estatutos de las FLN," Exp. 009-011-005, L-1, H-115. A fragment of the *Statutes* is published in John Womack, Jr.'s documentary anthology, *Rebellion in Chiapas: An Historical Reader* (New York: The New Press: 1999), 192–197. For a full analysis of this document, see Cedillo, op. cit. (2010), 124.
57 It is important to note that when the police found the safe house in Macuspana, in 1980, there were confidential FLN documents, including the *Statutes*. This means the DFS had knowledge about the plans to form the EZLN, as recorded in the report produced: AGN, DFS, "Fuerzas de Liberación Nacional," November 21, 1980, Exp. 009-011-005, L-1. It is unknown why there was no further surveillance and persecution of the FLN.
58 In 1979 Morales escaped from Bellevue Hospital in New York, where he was being treated for wounds inflicted when a bomb detonated in his hands. Alberto Ponce de León, "El FBI en México: Un secuestro frustrado en la frontera," http://erickfalcon.wordpress.com/about/el-fbi-en-mexico-un-secuestro-frustrado-en-la-frontera, (accessed September 25, 2010).
59 "Renee," interview with author, June 17, 2009. The press focused on Morales and nobody mentioned the FLN during the five years he was imprisoned. This episode caused a diplomatic rift, given that the Mexican government denied Morales' extradition to the United States and instead permitted his political asylum in Cuba in 1988.
60 De Vos was right in assuming that the FLN's penetration route into the jungle was identical to that opened by the founders of the Emiliano Zapata and Tierra y Libertad *ejidos*. De Vos, op. cit. 335.
61 Rico and De la Grange, op. cit. 167; Tello, op. cit. 110, *"Mensaje enviado por el Subcomandante Insurgente Marcos al arranque de la campaña EZLN: 20 y 10, el fuego y la palabra,"* November 10, 2003, in: http://palabra.ezln.org.mx/comunicados/2003/2003_11_10.htm, (accessed December 10, 2010).
62 Even an important member of the FLN-EZLN, who after 1995 was singled out as a traitor, denied any such support. Maité Rico and Bertrand de la Grange, "Entrevista con Salvador Morales Garibay," *Letras libres*, February 1999, http://www.letraslibres.com/index.php?art=5673, (accessed December 3, 2010).
According to "Renee," the bishop stated that the Diocese would respect the decisions of the indigenous people regarding armed struggle, as long as the guerrillas refrained from involving the Basic Ecclesial Communities in the war. The catechesis of liberation, promulgated by Samuel Ruiz, probably contributed to increased political consciousness among the indigenous, but this did not lead them directly to the guerrillas.

63 Le Bot, op. cit. 170. The break with the Maoists convinced some *campesinos* that the legal route was futile. Some Maoists returned later on to work with the Unión de Uniones in the jungle, but they did not have the same power as before.
64 There are a number of publications on the formation of the EZLN, but few include the testimonies of indigenous leaders and former militants. See Marco Estrada Saavedra, *La comunidad armada rebelde y el EZLN: un estudio histórico y sociológico sobre las bases de apoyo zapatistas en las cañadas tojolabales de la Selva Lacandona (1930–2005)*, (México, COLMEX, 2007).

8

SUBJUGATING THE NATION

Women and the Guerrilla Experience

Lucía Rayas

It was not until 2000 that historians and other researchers could explore the period in Mexican history between 1965 and 1982 with relative ease, especially if their questions pertained to issues of repression (forced "disappearance," torture, executions, and illegal captivity). Indeed, the *Partido Revolucionario Institucional* (PRI) had to step down before the public was granted admittance to state archival sources, albeit major barriers continued in place that prevented complete access to these documents. The state, as one of its working tactics, protected and hid what it considered sensitive information. This period can be characterized as the beginning of the end of the PRI's legitimacy.

The outburst of social unrest that the country saw included around 30 guerrilla groups throughout the country, which the state finally crushed through direct repression. Whatever modes of suffocating social unrest were undertaken, they were, for the most part, illegal. In this chapter I will review the repression carried out by the state during this period, which used Cold War arguments to support its national security doctrine. In combating the "enemy within," the state discovered it also encompassed women. This work focuses on the gender dimensions of state repression, particularly during a terrible time when people "disappeared" never to be heard from again.

Women and Mexican Guerrilla Movements

During the mid to late 1960s and early 1970s, more than 30 guerrilla groups were created throughout Mexico. They emerged in several states and cities (Chihuahua, Sinaloa, Nuevo León, Michoacán, Guerrero, Jalisco, Distrito Federal, among others), around the same time. Their creators and participants were, for the most part, young people disenchanted with a state of affairs that allowed no dissidence or even mild critical political expression. Even when analyses today may point to "bad timing" or a lack of sensibility on behalf of Mexican guerrilla groups to have arrived at the idea—and action—of armed struggle, protagonists of those movements claim there were little avenues left after having witnessed—often as activists themselves—the 1968 massacre or the 1971 student repression. On the other hand, the Cuban revolution was still quite new and kept its brilliance and shine as a Latin American promise.[1]

Most figures regarding Mexican armed revolutionary groups—number of guerrillas involved, their ages, the male/female ratio, the duration of their struggle, and how many were "disappeared" or were killed—are largely unknown. The clandestine nature of their organizations and activities compounds the darkness of the tracks left by the state repressive institutions. So, when faced with the issue of numbers of women, their ages and socio-economic backgrounds, motivations and experience, we can at best rely on the recent efforts to safeguard the social memory of these groups. The testimonies, whether written or spoken, upon which my work is based, cannot compensate for the absence of "hard facts" (impossible to obtain in this field and period) that some social scientists would be intent on having. Instead, they offer a polyphony of versions, standpoints, choice of words, perspectives, criticism and self-reflection that grows into a coherent whole against the context's backdrop.

Interestingly and appropriately, the most solid efforts towards bringing forth women's experience in these "socialist armed movements"[2] have come from women ex-participants themselves. There have been four public events from 2002 to 2010 organized especially by former guerrilla women to speak up or to remember women who died. The first of these, held in Mexico City in 2002, was called "Women and the 'Dirty War'"; the second, in 2003, was held in a conference room in the Mexican Senate, and was titled "National Meeting of Female Ex-Guerrillas"; the third, "II National Meeting of Female Ex-Guerrillas," took place in Mazatlan, Sinaloa, in 2008; and finally, in 2010, "From Girls to Guerrilla Fighters" also took place in Mexico City. With the exception of the last session, many men participated in the gatherings to commemorate former female combatants.

The only one of these events of which there is a written record is the second meeting.[3] Based on the testimonials offered, as well as on field research of my own, the gender dynamics of the guerrilla groups can be said to correspond to those of the larger Mexican society: traditional gender roles of masculine superiority and female subordination were largely untouched. Questioning the political *status quo* of the country was unrelated, in these young rebels' eyes, to a critique of women's place in society and to the feminist assertion that the "personal is political," already present in many women's agenda, both in the US and Europe, roughly around the same time.

Narrations describing women in guerrilla groups by both men and women tend to stress the feminine characteristics of the "compañeras." Qualities such as "being warm care-takers," providing love, both nurturing and romantic, having discipline, and sometimes even fortitude, were ways to describe female revolutionaries. This is unsurprising, as mentioned above, if one considers these movements as part of the larger society, but also because classical socialist literature, a likely source of reading and inspiration for members of these groups, clearly state that women's subordinate status is a "secondary contradiction" (perhaps with the exception of Alexandra Kollontai and Clara Zetkin) that needs no further thought (or action). These writings sustain traditional values regarding women's roles and family life; the struggle for women's rights was deemed a "bourgeois concern" and not a socialist one. In this way, Mexican guerrilla women, clearly being social transgressors who entered a male dominated world (that of the armed struggle), also played roles of care and reproduction within their organizations.

Based on the memoirs of the Second National Meeting of Guerrilla Women, together with interviews, the film called *Mujer Guerrilla*[4] about four former Mexican armed combatants of the 1960s and 70s, and Cristina Tamariz's work on the Liga Comunista 23 de Septiembre,[5] we can understand some of the experiences of Mexican women participating in the urban armed groups[6] of those days.

Most of the women[7] who became combatants in these armed socialist groups were in their late teens or early twenties when they joined their respective organizations. Even though tens of women joined the different organizations, there is a vague estimate that ponders there were around seven to eight men per woman in these organizations.[8] They were high school or university students, or young professionals (secretaries, school teachers, store attendants, etc.). Their socio-economic backgrounds are somewhat varied, but many claim to have grown up in the lower middle-class or middle class of Mexico, in different cities—Mexico City, Monterrey, Guadalajara, etc.; several speak of their family homes as places in which they lived comfortably or "had everything they needed" (these women are in their early or mid-sixties today, thus, their childhood years may well have been those of the so-called "Mexican [economic] miracle"— mid-1940s to mid-1960s—a time of great economic growth in the country, largely due to the state's economic policies; for a while, the trickle-down effect of this growth was felt by most).

Common to their narratives about motivations to become activists are the state repression during 1968 and/or 1971, noting the living conditions of some poorer sectors of Mexican society, and the influence of (usually male) friends or romantic partners who were already involved in an organization, whether armed or soon to become armed.

> ... during my teen years, in my neighborhood, I met Arnulfo Prado Rosas, "el compa" [who later became one of the most prominent activists of the left, in Guadalajara], who showed me an aspect of life completely unknown to me: politics. Imperceptibly, a politicization process began to take place in me ... [9]

Notably, as in the case of other women involved in formal politics, the testimony of Martha Maldonado, one of the militants of the MAR (Movimiento de Acción Revolucionaria) first, and then of the Liga Comunista 23 de Septiembre (from now on LC23S), highlights her father's political relations and acquaintances (he was governor of the state of Baja California for the ruling party) as crucial to her future involvement. As many PRI members of the day, his stance was a politically progressive one, brandishing the ideas of "revolutionary nationalism."[10] In her own house, Martha, who studied in Moscow, met several relevant men of the Mexican left, including General Lázaro Cárdenas and rural guerrilla fighters Rubén Jaramillo and Genaro Vázquez; she was also aware of unjust political persecution and assassinations of politically committed peasants.

> When I left for studies in Moscow, they had just killed Rubén Jaramillo, he had been in my home one day before his death. I also met Genaro Vázquez; during the days of his persecution, he took refuge in my house. I saw the death of peasants, I heard of and experienced the unfair treatment inflicted upon them thanks to the people who surrounded my father.[11]

Radicalization by the women who decided to bear arms, then, was usually a process they underwent under the guidance or company of others, enmeshed in an era in which revolutionary ideals and struggles were visible. Ché and Tania, the icon of a guerrilla woman, were prominent actors not only in socialist Latin American literature, but also in the poetry—whether recited or sung—of the times.

As in most political organizations, there were levels to one's participation. Many women went through a moment of "collaboration," to later become militants which, in due time, led to a "full-time militancy," often stepping into clandestinity with all its implications. Edna, in the documentary *Mujer Guerrilla* is eloquent about it: "Clandestinity is like being born again. You become another person, with another name. You must fabricate an alibi; you create a new life-history." Becoming an underground activist was often a thing of necessity. Tita narrates how, after the death of Arnulfo, her romantic partner, she was forced into leading a secret life.[12] She broke up all family and social ties; "I felt repression was on my heels ... I had two choices: running away or getting more deeply involved. We knew it was a journey with no return ..." As an idea, it may have been a very romantic one: "a full-time revolutionary." In practice, living conditions were not necessarily the best: "… we lived in small tenement houses rooms. There were no luxuries or expensive meals. Our dress was also austere. Besides, we were always accountable for the money assigned to us."[13] Together with revolution and clandestinity come self-sacrifice and denial of personal needs. At these, women were exemplary, as they are, also, feminine characteristics in the traditional gender imaginary.[14]

The daily lives of these women implied discipline both physical and otherwise. Basic to their survival was bodily fitness. A few women of the organization called MAR (*Movimiento de Acción Revolucionaria*) were trained in Korea. The organization's commitment was to train a few of their cadres, who would return to Mexico to train more people. The Mexican women who came back from this training underwent serious military education.

> The compañeros greatly admired my capacity for military practices, and their recognition encouraged me to go on. Training in Korea was hard because I had to do the same as men: long hikes, different types of exercises, judo, karate and shooting practice. The only concession I enjoyed was carrying 5 kilos less in my backpack.[15]

Guerrilla women from other organizations also received at least basic military training and were able to use some weapons. Many participated in "expropriations," which were armed attacks on different-sized businesses, ranging from smaller shops to bank offices and large industries. The rationale behind these actions, as well as the abduction of prominent people, was to build-up means for survival as an organization, acquisition of weaponry, and the publication of their media (this is the case of *Madera*, the periodical edited by the LC23S). A different kind of discipline came from following orders without question. Belonging to an armed organization meant submission—by choice— to the groups' leadership. Militants must move constantly, keep anonymity, be always watchful and, above all, be in constant communication with one another.[16] Not hearing from one another, as established, probably meant someone had been captured and the group was running risks.

Remarkably, whereas during the first years of existence of these guerrilla groups leadership was commonly male, the last leadership formations, by the mid-1970s, included women. Strikingly, the majority of armed actions narrated by survivors of these groups included women.[17] Thus, it is not unusual to hear explanations about how sexism was not prominent amongst militants.

Yolanda Casas, a petite woman, former member of the Lacandones armed group, retold the story of her participation in an "expropriation" of a sports-gun shop in Mexico City, emphasizing how her innocent looks and size (she was 17 years old) allowed her to keep watch on the shop so as to determine the best *modus operandi* for her group. While the actual action was taking place, she comments: "here I go, small and skinny, but I bet I must have looked like a giant while pointing a gun at the store keepers ...."[18]

The Cold War and the National Security Doctrine: Finding the "Enemy Within"

Historically, but particularly after 1945, Mexico's main aim vis-à-vis the United States had been to be able to maintain its national sovereignty despite sharing a 3,000-kilometer border with one of the world's superpowers. Mexico's "special relationship" with the USA entailed a delicate balance between showing independence in its foreign policy, while maintaining stability within its borders. Mexico was allowed to follow its own course on many fronts, not only politically, but also in terms of economic policies.[19] Being able to show the international community independence from the United States awarded the government a degree of legitimacy at a national level. Mexico's long-term, supportive relationship with the "unsavory" government of Cuba is a prime example of this international behavior, autonomous from US dictates, but there are others.

Particularly during the period this essay covers, from the late 1960s to the early 80s, Presidents Luis Echeverría Álvarez and José López Portillo who worked extensively to give Mexico an image and presence of international leadership and solidarity; these actions were often contrary to US preferences. For instance, Mexico's stance towards the Allende government in Chile, and the welcoming and even invitation of political exiles from Chile and other countries in the Southern Cone during military dictatorships. Other examples include Echeverría organizing the Charter of Economic Rights and Duties of States at the UN (passed by the UN Assembly on December 1974) and playing a visible role in the grouping of Third World countries, as well as López Portillo's leadership in the Central American revolutionary situation of the late 1970s and early 80s. The list could go on.

What was Mexico expected to give in return? Stability. The exchange rate of Mexico's external independence and autonomy was domestic order. This was tantamount to a guarantee that there would be no turmoil south of the border. This independence in the global arena helped do just that for the country. It provided Mexico, among other things, with a façade that made it at least hard to imagine it was not democratic[20] inside its borders. Achieving this internal control, however, was a completely different matter. At a time when no human rights discourse was readily available, and with a regime accustomed to not having to open-up dialogue or negotiation with those frankly opposing or criticizing it, or to comply with legal methods to face dissidence, internal stability, from time to time, came at a hard price for some.

The fact that the rhetoric of the Cold War, the heavy-handed anti-communist discourse, was not current speech in Mexico—revolutionary nationalism's lingo was progressive, exultant of revolutionary qualities—did not mean Mexico did not, on occasion, adhere to these sentiments. For example, "foreign agitators" were sometimes signaled as the source of rebelliousness during the 1968 student movement.[21] One other element of the Cold War that took root was the national security doctrine, which, in Mexico's struggle against the "communist threat," created an "ideological frontier" within the country.[22] The enemy within was to be found on the other side of this ideological divide. Mexican intelligence, fed by "reasons of state," undertook close vigilance of its own citizens as it identified "the enemy" as certain leftist organizations, which of course included guerrilla groups.[23] Carlos Montemayor claims the state has always characterized guerrilla movements within a "combat strategy," never once stopping to consider their reasons for being, let alone developing a vision of them as social processes.[24] If this holds true today,[25] the 1970s were certainly a blinder time for social concerns by the state. Thus, its covert operations acted on intelligence information carrying out repressive tactics beyond the first circle of targets. Typically it was neighbors, family—immediate and extended—friends, schoolmates, and professors, or supposed militants, that were under the secret services' radar. Typically, too, the state acted with severe counter-insurgency measures, including collective apprehensions, torture, extrajudicial executions, and forced "disappearances."

According to Alberto G. López Limón, in a report on Mexicans who were "detained-disappeared,"[26] between 1971 and 1983 there are 43 women in that category, linked to guerrilla groups. It is worth keeping in mind the illegal nature of these acts, in those days perpetrated by the state. That is, one or another state repressive institution would illicitly "detain" these women—in their homes or in any public place—for them never to be heard from again. It is a form of abduction. Almost every activist detained under these circumstances spent some time "disappeared." If they did not "disappear" for good, this was usually the moment during which they underwent severe torture sessions. Figures that detail dates of apprehension and dates of "formal imprisonment,"[27] show a period of one to two weeks in between. A considerable lapse to inflict grave damage on detainees.

Woman/Nation: Torture/Woman: Torture/Nation

Woman/Nation

The nation is usually represented as a female figure. The metaphor of woman as nation is contrasted by the idea of the state as a masculine entity. Put succinctly, from a gender perspective, "the state" in modernity was constructed around the rights of man—understood as such and not as a metonymy for humanity—totally fitting with a social contract founded upon "the masculine fraternity."[28] Women were excluded from this contract and from the citizenship inherent to it, while men were included both as members of the polity and as representatives of their families. This is how the state was formed. The nation, on the other hand, is linked to biological, cultural and symbolic reproduction and continuity—women's tasks[29]—the woman/nation dyad evokes genealogical unity. The woman/nation is watched over by the state. In the case of Mexico (as of any country), this woman represents national culture; her gender characteristics match the nationalism upon which the nation-state was founded.

Besides several other features, such as having a specific physique—the idea of "national beauty" relies on this woman/nation—this woman would be a good mother that safeguards tradition, that educates and raises individuals useful to society. Whereas this idea of woman has changed over the years, its essence remains, together with expectations of female behavior. As woman/nation and as "mother of the nation," the body of this imaginary woman becomes the body of the nation. This is a desexualized and regulated body. Its limits must be protected as metaphors of national borders. Real women symbolically represent that imaginary woman.

Torture/Woman[30]

In their introduction to the book *Contra la tortura* (Against Torture), Subirats, Calveiro, and other authors define torture as "an instrument of violence aimed at destroying the moral and physical integrity of human beings, at reducing their existence to the most degraded vital expression, at nullifying their will power and at fully taking their personhoods and lives under the will of their torturer and the state institutions that encourage and organize it."[31] Torture aims then at destroying a person's subjectivity, at alienating her/him from their own will. It is a system that uses "aggressive interrogation techniques and physical and moral pressure methods through electrical, chemical, physical and psychological means."[32] Torture's purpose is to extract confessions and obtain information, provoke terror in people, break people's will power, punish them and show them the power of the perpetrators. In sum, to achieve someone's subjection. Torturing someone also serves the purpose of setting a precedent: what is practiced on a body–person becomes a message for all.[33]

Torture occurs outside the legal realm—this is why it usually takes place during periods of "forced disappearance"—and submits people to social isolation as well as stripping them of their rights. In exchange for promises to stop torture, people are asked for information. This web of illegality leaves marks on the detainee's body, the territory upon which the executioner performs his unlimited power. Domination over the most intimate places of the body and of the human spirit is thus exercised.[34] Torturing extends to those people or groups that may have information the executioner deems valuable, in an attempt to terrorize and exterminate the collective will of the group, a group whose limits are blurry;

a collectivity drawn by intelligence information which often holds together only through the machinations of the system. By torturing the collectivity, the executioner seeks to destroy all links among them, to extinguish trust in one another. For this purpose and with the aim of "teaching a lesson" as well as to torture vicariously, torture often takes place in front of family members or other members of the collectivity.

For torture to achieve its terrifying object (destroying the self, the subjectivity of the person), there is a need to mark the one who will be subjected to torture as an "other"; someone dehumanized who arrives at that category by means of ideological mechanisms and hierarchical orders to deem this "other" an "enemy," a "traitor," a "terrorist." This ideological alienation is compounded by other means that differentiate and deride such as covering the faces of those being tortured (not seeing so as to amplify the isolation), being unable to clean-up or change clothes, forcing nudity, being underfed. All contributes to a sense of abjection. Elaine Scarry in *The Body in Pain* states that torture unmakes the world of those tortured.[35] She says torture reverts people into a pre-linguistic stage, in which the person who suffers loses articulation to be left only with visceral sounds and screams. Pain is inexpressible and humiliation unutterable.

In this regard, it is very stirring to note that, while being interviewed, the majority of women choose silence when their narration arrives at the point of detention and prior to incarceration or exile. Only it is not "plain silence," but a productive one. In this, I have found, men do not react that differently. It is the quality of having suffered unutterable pain which takes over. Today, some 40 years later, this period passes fast in their stories, in only a few words. Tita, during a long interview, only mentioned having heard her partner's screams—while she herself was being "interrogated"—and knowing she had to struggle to maintain the alibi they both had agreed upon. Yolanda, the petite woman who robbed the sports-gun shop, spent more time in jail (6 years and 9 months) than as an activist in a guerrilla group. Of her detention, she recalls:

> ... they humiliated us, they trampled on us ... hurt us in every possible way: physically, mentally ... I was in the hands of Nazar Haro [the terrifying head of the Dirección Federal de Seguridad]. I was small in size; I used my dimension, my presence, to play innocent and give time for my compañeros to run away in case "I spoke." I tried to avoid speaking in case the madness of the atmosphere forced me to. I did not know for how long I would be able to stand [the torture] in the hands of these assassins.[36]

Usually, when a militant "fell" into the hands of the state, a series of other people followed. Some of the organizations had a time rule regarding for how long it was expected "the fallen" would not give away names, addresses, phone numbers, etc. This makes it clear that, like Yolanda, they did not know how even revolutionaries reacted to torture. This undoing of the world was a feared and well-acknowledged possibility. To make things worse, if the militant's legal personality was known, family members were in jeopardy. Edna recounts how, while in the hospital (she was shot by accident by another woman guerrilla-in-training and required immediate medical attention), police tortured her and her father. "To this day, I do not know what they did to him,"[37] and she does not tell us what she endured (her gestures are eloquent, however). Some things are better left in stillness.

Torture/Nation

The reification of women's bodies common in most societies with traditional gender roles, acquires a renewed potency under conditions of torture. In the case of Mexican militant and guerrilla women of the period under study (as I am certain happens with women from other countries and times), this new potency stems from at least two sources: on the one hand, women are punished for having dared challenge the system or having broken the dictates their identification with the nation demands of them. In other words, for having challenged the state that, in theory, protects them. The other source of their punishment comes from having left their traditional domestic gender roles aside to act in the public sphere. The idealized body of the mother-land—from which we all come, of the nation, is thus tormented and with it, at a symbolic level, the bodies of the mother, the wife, the daughter, the sister are tormented at once. This symbolic operation makes it even more relevant to dehumanize the woman being tortured.

The jargon utilized during the years of the Cold War was effective in creating a credible and distant other: communism was construed as an epidemic (an illness) to eradicate, and its "agents" were sources of infection; a subhuman condition that validates their extermination. Yet, sometimes this extermination was not immediate. During the years of the Dirty War,[38] people were often left alive (even if barely) if their existence was determined useful to the secret services, either because it was thought they (still) had information the state needed, or because they could be used to inflict agony on yet someone else. Indeed, some testimonies also emphasize that the worst hardship was to witness others being tortured. Powerlessness often matched, at later times, when a sound, a color, a smell, some texture, brings back, in a rush of memories, the traumatic experience.

All means used to inflict pain on men were (and are) used on women as well: beating, electric shocks, mock executions, death threats, water-boarding, suffocating, isolation, being left suspended by hands or feet, sleep and sensory deprivation. Acts of sexual violence such as rape—on a regular basis, individually and collectively—and other forms of sexual abuse, touching and the use of sexually offensive language, have been all too common forms of torture and ill-treatment of women by state agents.[39] Rape represents putting patriarchal power in place; it is an affront with a multiplicity of echoes, since it confirms the possession of the submitted one, and the affirmation of the possessor. Rape damages women in their innermost intimacy. When it takes place in front of partners or family members, it holds a particular relevance because it implies those present could not protect the woman, while blatantly tarnishing the family honor, which, at an imaginary level, the woman bears.

Alejandra Cárdenas, a former participant in the Partido de los Pobres (the rural guerrilla group of Lucio Cabañas) says:

> ... we all went through similar ordeals; the punishment on women still has a very heavy sexual connotation, right? ... besides the beatings and waterboarding and all else, one has to endure very severe sexual aggression which leaves indelible marks. I want to say that even when I've been to therapies and all those treatments, I still have nightmares when there are certain kinds of news. I still wake up screaming ... so, the experience is fixed never to leave again. One must accept it; it has to be acknowledged that we will live with it ... [40]

Women are also tortured by threats to act—and/or actual acts—against their children or parents, as a means to attack filial relationships and the family structure women are supposed to support. Several cases have been documented, such as the abduction of the family of Margarita Andrade Vallejo in 1975. Margarita was part of the leadership of the *Brigada Roja* (the last armed group to operate in Mexico City, a remnant of the LC23S) during 1974–1976. After the fall of one *compañera* from this group, the DFS seized Margarita's parents and three siblings during 10 to 12 days. They were taken to an underground jail, passing for a warehouse. They were released thanks to the connections of Margarita's father. We don't know much of their captivity time, but after their liberation, they were watched 24 hours a day for two years.[41] Having learned of her family's ordeal, Margarita promised it would never happen again. Upon her imminent capture, she took her own life.

Episodes involving family members are potentially maddening situations, as are torture sessions inflicted on pregnant women, which include psychological manipulations about the future of the child. A well-documented effect of torture on pregnant women is frequently irreversible emotional damage on the child, in the medium or long term, sometimes ending in suicide.[42] Amnesty International recognizes emotional disturbance in those who suffered abuse before being born, and found several cases among people born in the 1970s in Latin America whose mothers were held captive. Some of the testimonies about the years of the Dirty War in Mexico mention having been kidnapped and tortured in the women's own homes.[43] This intrusion into the private home exerts unimaginable violence on intimacy and causes tremendous insecurity. Torture inherently reinforces the imaginary passivity of women. This forced passivity, the impotence and complete dependence on the torturer, also feminizes[44] men subjected to torture. The exercise of torture on the bodies of people—male and female—affirms the masculinity of the perpetrator in the production of pain and suffering. They hold the power to reduce the other to a passive victim.[45]

Closing Remarks

The Mexican secret police of the 1960s and 70s, the DFS (Federal Security Directorate) was known to be implacable and very powerful.[46] Since the inception of Mexican secret services (1918), the logic of what was a matter of their attention (or defining national security) lay in circles close to the executive, far from social scrutiny and lacking a juridical framework. Their activities also remained within a sphere of laxness, which included little analysis of the information they gathered. This openly existing institution, by this time dreaded by many, operated in the dark, without checks and balances. The national security doctrine during the Cold War established the idea of an "internal enemy" which, combined with the methods of the DFS, found enemies not only in the young guerrilla rebels, but also in others who opposed the idea of national society as defined by the regime. Women immersed in politics, particularly those who defy the state, altered gender relations. They become distant from the mythical unity of imaginary national communities. Their participation in social movements harshly questions underlying presumptions about the nation-state in which the latter, patriarchal, protects and guards the former, who is supposed to guarantee the continuity of a national "us" defined by limits that demand prescribed behaviors. The castigation imposed by the state on dissident women, I contend, also aims at re-establishing a gender order, and torture and disappearance as an exemplary punishment for having rebelled.

With the exception of the case of Rosendo Radilla, in which the Inter-American Court of Human Rights determined the Mexican state is responsible for his forced disappearance in 1974,[47] impunity floats rampant regarding all cases of illegal acts against Mexican women and men abducted during the episode known as the Dirty War. Stories like the ones in Spain or Argentina, where real commissions to investigate past crimes by the state were established, where civil society was an active interlocutor and actor, could be examples to follow. It does not matter that the Mexicans lost in these decades were many fewer or "sparse" by comparison, it is about establishing a social memory (history is, perhaps, ambitious still) that incorporates the presence and absences of these dreamers of the past whose actions and sheer existence may be seen as an element that, together with many others, pushed for the transition of ruling parties in the year 2000.

Acknowledgments

I would like to thank Andrés Besserer and Iván Besserer, for accompanying me throughout this writing process with loving care.

Notes

1. Bertha Lilia Gutiérrez and Rosa María González, interviews with author, Summer, 2008, Guadalajara, Jalisco.
2. "Socialist armed movement" is the generic name former militants generally use, to avoid having to refer to one particular group or the other.
3. María de la Luz Aguilar Terrés (comp.), *Memoria del Primer Encuentro Nacional de Mujeres Exguerrilleras*. México, n.e. 2007.
4. Becerril Bulos, Claudia, Arizbeth Becerril Bulos (Colectivo Patito), *et al.*, *Mujer Guerrilla. El puño de la mujer ¡atentando contra el poder!*, México, 2007 (documentary film).
5. Cristina Tamariz, *Operación 23 de septiembre. Auge y exterminio de la guerrilla urbana en la Ciudad de México (reportaje)*, BA thesis, UNAM, 2007.
6. Mexican rural armed groups seem to have had fewer women in their ranks. Consistent with the idea of tighter social constraints for peasant women in rural Mexico during those years, some of the women known to have been in arms in rural guerrillas in the state of Guerrero, came from urban environments (testimonies of Catarino Cortés on Aurora de la Paz—Second Meeting of Mexican Guerrilla Women—and of Alejandra Cárdenas in the memoirs of the First Meeting of Mexican Guerrilla Women).
7. When writing about the women who participated in the socialist armed movement of Mexico's 1960s and 70s, I don't claim to be able to pinpoint everyone's experience.
8. Yolanda Casas (former "Lacandones"—one of the groups that formed the LC23S—activist), in the documentary *Mujer Guerrilla*.
9. Bertha Lilia Gutiérrez (Tita), presentation in conference "De niñas a guerrilleras," ENAH, March 2010.
10. See Tamariz, 44–46.
11. Quoted in Tamariz, 45.
12. Gutiérrez, "De niñas a guerrilleras."
13. Quoted in Tamariz, p. 47.
14. See "Introducción. Reflexiones teóricas," in Rayas, *Armadas*, (México, DF: El Colegio de México, 2007).
15. Tamariz, p. 46.
16. Edna's testimony in documentary *Mujer Guerrilla*.
17. Tamariz, chapters 3 and 4.
18. Casa's presentation at the UNAM's PUEG (Programa Universitario de Estudios de Género) Conference "Güeras y prietas," celebrated on October 2008.
19. It is relevant, for example, to remember that Mexico kept a "closed" economy until 1985, when it finally entered GATT.
20. A word of caution: "democratic" is used, in this context, as encompassing more than "fair elections." It implies the existence of and compliance with a rule of law and fairness in treatment to all.

21 Several examples could be seen in the catalogue of the exhibit "Memoria y representación. La fotografía y el movimiento estudiantil de 1968 en México," curated by Alberto del Castillo and shown in the Mexican museum "Centro Cultural Universitario Tlatelolco" from October 2010 to January 2011.
22 Meneghini, Mario, "Doctrina de seguridad nacional y guerra antisubversiva," lecture presented on October 2006, at the III Jornadas "La hispanidad hoy" at the University of Córdoba, Argentina, http://bitacorapi.blogia.com/2006/103101-doctrina-de-seguridad-nacional-y-guerra-antisubversiva.php (accessed March 18, 2011).
23 While it is obvious that resorting to armed struggle—opposing the regime in the most extreme possible way—may and often will entail illegal actions, the state should, in theory, always act within the rule of law.
24 Montemayor, Carlos. "Los movimientos guerrilleros y los servicios de inteligencia. Notas reiteradas y nuevas conclusiones," in *Los grandes problemas de México. Seguridad nacional y seguridad interior*, Arturo Alvarado and Mónica Serrano eds. (México, DF: El Colegio de México, 2010), 54.
25 Interestingly, in the material quoted here, Montemayor, who died February 2010, narrates a scene with a high Mexican security officer in which Montemayor asks "Why do you think the guerrillas in Mexico keep recurring?" to which the officer replies, "Because we have not ended with the last one of them." Carlos Montemayor continues, "Isn't it more relevant [to their continued existence] that the social conditions under which the guerrillas emerged persist?" The reply: "Hadn't thought of that," p. 50.
26 López Limón, Alberto, "Combatientes revolucionarias detenidas-desaparecidas," in Aguilar Terrés, op. cit., 197–202. This author's report is based on figures prepared by the "Comité pro-defensa de presos, perseguidos, desaparecidos y exiliados políticos" (Eureka) and on informational reports by the DFS (Dirección Federal de Seguridad/ secret political police, now extinct).
27 See Chapter 3 in Tamariz.
28 Carole Pateman, *The Sexual Contract* (Stanford: Stanford University Press, 1988), *passim*.
29 Nira Yuval-Davis, "Género y nación," in *Mujeres y nacionalismos en América Latina*, ed., Natividad Gutiérrez Chong (México: UNAM IIS, 2004), *passim*.
30 This section covers some theoretical general ground regarding torture in itself, to move further into analyzing the peculiar gender effects of torture.
31 Eduardo Subirats, Pilar Calveiro, *et al.*, "Contra la tortura," in *Contra la tortura* (Monterrey, México: Fineo editorial, 2006) 9. Translation by the author.
32 Subirats, Calveiro, *et al., ídem*.
33 Pilar Calveiro, "La decisión política de torturar," in *Contra la tortura*, Eduardo Subirats, Pilar Calveiro, *et al.*, (Monterrey, México: Fineo editorial, 2006) 23.
34 Ibid., 9–10.
35 Elaine Scarry, *The Body in Pain. The Making and Unmaking of the World* (New York: Oxford University Press, 1985) *passim*.
36 Casas in "Güeras y prietas."
37 Ovalle in documentary *Mujer Guerrilla*.
38 In the introduction to this article, it was stated that figures remain obscure given the opacity that surrounds the Dirty War in Mexico. The sheer lack of institutional official recognition of the atrocities inflicted in this period attests to the futility of suggesting a comprehensive version of things. However, historian Adela Cedillo, who has researched the topic for years, presented the following information after intense archival investigation: during the years of the Dirty War, approximately 43 women were detained-disappeared; over 20 were assassinated; 89 more were

incarcerated; and 7 exiled. Of these women, at least two were detained-disappeared with their husbands and children; 4 gave birth while in captivity; and more than 8 were detained-disappeared while being pregnant. They and their children were victims of the infamous practice of torture. Adela Cedillo, "Mujeres, guerrilla y terror estatal en la época de la *revoltura* en México," unpublished article.
39 Amnesty International, *Broken bodies, shattered minds. Torture and Ill-treatment of women* (London: Amnesty International Publications, 2001), 42.
40 Cárdenas in Aguilar Terrés, p. 148.
41 Tamariz, pp. 111–112.
42 Minerva Armendariz, *Morir de sed junto a la fuente, 30 años después* (México: unedited manuscript provided by author), 124. Amnesty International, *Vencer el miedo. Violaciones de los derechos humanos contra la mujer en México* (http://asiapacific.amnesty.org/library/Index/ESLAMR410091996?open&of=ESL-315)
43 See some of the testimonies in the memoirs of the First National Meeting of Female Ex-Guerrilla, Aguilar Terrés, and op. cit. Some instances are also found in the testimonies offered during the Second National Meeting (still unpublished).
44 Feminizes in as much as "the feminine" is the subordinate part in the traditional gender system.
45 Franco quoted in Elizabeth Jelin, "Engendered Memories," in *State Repression and the Labors of Memory* (US: SSRC and the University of Minnesota Press, 2003), 80.
46 My source for most information about Mexican secret services is Sergio Aguayo, *La charola. Una historia de los servicios de inteligencia en México* (México, DF: Grijalbo, 2001).
47 See sentence at http://www.corteidh.or.cr/docs/casos/articulos/seriec_209_esp.pdf (accessed March 20, 2011).

9

ARMED FORCES AND COUNTERINSURGENCY

Origins of the Dirty War (1965–1982)

Jorge Luis Sierra Guzmán

From 1963 and 1982, the Mexican government experienced the proliferation of armed revolutionary movements of various sizes and strengths, originating not only in the poorest and most unstable regions, but also in major cities throughout the country. Before 1965, Mexico lacked a modern counterinsurgency doctrine to prepare it against guerrilla-style insurrections. Even though the military was able to defeat the guerrilla assault on the Madera barracks in Chihuahua that same year, they also realized a number of fissures and problems in the armed forces. In the absence of a professional intelligence service, the Mexican government failed to contain the subsequent proliferation of more than 30 guerrilla organizations that orchestrated a number of revolutionary actions, "expropriations," kidnappings, assassinations, and transformed the cities and countryside into battlefields.[1]

The Mexican government in conjunction with the armed forces executed a comprehensive and violent Dirty War against "subversive" groups. Thousands of students, leftists, unionist, peasants, and professionals aligned to armed revolutionary organizations were killed, disappeared, tortured, and illegally incarcerated. While the majority of those who faced state-sponsored violence were connected to guerrilla movements, ordinary people were also repressed. The strategies employed by the Mexican armed forces to wipe-up rural and urban guerrilla movements closely resemble the counterinsurgency tactics exercised during the military dictatorships in the Southern Cone and Guatemala.[2] During this enigmatic period in Mexico's history, the government never expressed its desire to negotiate or hold peace talks with guerrillas; instead, the military together with paramilitary groups, intelligence and police agencies, virtually destroyed all armed revolutionary movements, leaving just small cells incapable of orchestrating new revolutionary actions.[3]

During the administrations of Gustavo Díaz Ordaz (1964–1970), Luis Echeverría (1970–1976), and José López Portillo (1976–1982), each president called on the armed forces and other counterinsurgency units to see that guerrilla outbreaks were completely exterminated, while turning a blind eye to an unprecedented amount of human rights abuses. The consequences of this massive counterinsurgency campaign were monumental. This chapter analyzes the counterinsurgency strategy instituted by the government to combat urban and rural guerrillas in the 1960s and 70s. To contain and destroy guerrilla *focos* in jungle or mountains, the armed forces underwent a serious modernization process involving a large improvement in their arsenal, strategies, and capabilities. The strategy of containment and suppression required the paramilitarization of security forces, namely the Olympia Battalion, the *halcones* (the Hawks) and the White Brigade or *Brigada Blanca*.[4] This process also included granting counterinsurgency groups impunity and protection for having broken the law and violated people's human rights.

The 1970s was a period marked by unprecedented violence unseen since the 1910 Mexican Revolution. The manner in which the government intended to precipitate the destruction of armed movements plunged the country into a war that lasted more than 15 years and covered almost the entire national territory. At the end of the Dirty War in 1982, the government was more than certain guerrillas had been fully suppressed.[5] Lacking revolutionaries to fight against, counterinsurgency units underwent a period of decomposition and rampant corruption. Many former agents and soldiers sought to continue using their expertise and developed links with drug traffickers and organized crime.[6] But the guerrilla threat never entirely vanished. More than two decades after the Dirty War a new wave of post-Cold War armed resistance movements inherently connected with the guerrilla movements of the 1970s and probably more powerful and better organized, emerged and declared war on the Mexican government. The emergence of insurgent movements in Chiapas, Guerrero, and Oaxaca in the mid-1990s reveals that the strategies employed to annihilate the guerrilla groups of the 1970s had only temporary effects.[7]

Forging a Counterinsurgency Doctrine

A network of security branches, namely the Federal Security Directorate (DFS), the General Directorate of Political and Social Investigations (DGIPS), the Research Division for the Prevention of Crime (DIPD), and the Second Section of Military Intelligence (S-2) were the architects of the counterinsurgency campaign against both rural and urban guerrilla movements. Created in 1947, the DFS was composed of elite military officers initially responsible for President Miguel Alemán Valdés' (1946–1952) safety. During its first 30 years, military officers, namely Leancho Castillo Venegas, Manuel Rangel Escamilla, Fernando

Gutiérrez Barrios, and Luis de la Barreda, became the primary leaders of the DFS.[8] During their tenure as directors each individual sought to improve the groups' function as a security force, as well as upgrade its structure and training according to the social and political environment in the world and Mexico.

Before the first modern uprising in the mid-1960s, the Mexican armed forces lacked a counterinsurgency doctrine. According to José Luis Piñeyro, from 1959 to 1964 military manuals and strategies on anti-guerrilla strategies were nonexistent, largely because guerrilla warfare was not a common practice used by resistance movements in the early 1960s.[9] Apart from Rubén Jaramillo's rebellion, the government was never genuinely confronted with a major threat to its power, much less with the strength to militarily challenge the armed forces.[10] During the administration of Adolfo López Mateos (1958–1964) the military was incessantly called in to contain widespread social struggles proliferating in the cities at the beginning of his administration. Yet, despite the military's success in quelling civil disobedience, the López Mateo administration was well aware that Mexico's domestic security doctrine required major modernization. The triumph of the 1959 Cuban Revolution and Cold War policies exported by the United States functioned as a pretext for the Mexican government to update their national security system in order to prevent a communist uprising in their country. Because of the need to improve the armed forces, the administration sanctioned the spending of millions of pesos assuring the military and other security forces received the best training possible.

The proliferation of labor strikes and student movements prompted the Mexican government to increase the military's level of training and arsenal, mainly for its infantry. According to José Luis Piñeyro, "labor strikes and student conflicts played a salient role in accelerating the modernization of a 'repressive apparatus.'"[11] During the 1950s, the armed forces monitored the labor movements that threatened to begin a nationwide strike, and were less concerned with uprisings in the countryside given that the epicenter of political instability remained concentrated in urban areas where worker militancy was on the rise. Large military contingents were sent to break up the Railroad Worker's Strike in 1959 and strikes at Teléfonos de México and Mexicana Airlines in 1960. Troops also broke up rallies and arrested student leaders in Mexico City and Acapulco in 1961. That same year, roughly 3,000 troops occupied the capital of San Luis Potosí to control riots and the post-election unrest.[12]

At the end of López Mateos' administration, after increasing signals of unrest in rural areas, the Army began developing the first military counterinsurgency exercises. In a text entitled *Memoria, Diciembre 1960 a Noviembre 1961*, the Secretary of Defense commented on the political and social climate prevailing at the beginning of the decade by saying: "Political conflicts, student upheavals, and subversive outbreaks have surfaced mainly in Guerrero and San Luis Potosí, but also in Chihuahua, San Luis Potosí, Veracruz, Oaxaca, Chiapas, Michoacán,

TABLE 9.1 Arms purchases by Mexico from the USA in 1960

Material	Quantity
0.30 cal Browning machine guns	350
0.30 cal machine guns	2,600
0.30 cal M2 carbines	10,000
105 mm cal explosive and smoke grenades	2,000
0.75 mm cal explosive and smoke grenades	2,000
0.50 and 0.30 cal cartridges	1,269,911
0.30 cal M1 cartridges	1,999,800

Source: Memoria. Secretaría de la Defensa Nacional. December 1959—November 1960. APR. México, 1960, 40. Quoted in Piñeyro.

Coahuila, Tamaulipas, Zacatecas, Jalisco, Hidalgo, Querétaro, and Yucatan."[13] Besides improving soldiers' military training in the early 1960s, Mexico purchased an array of weapons from the United States. Among the items purchased were Browning machine guns, M2 rifles, grenades, ammunition, and 60 different types of vehicles to enhance the military's power (see Table 9.1).

Because of the proliferation of urban social movements López Mateos foresaw an imminent wave of rural unrest. In order to move large contingents to conflict areas in 1962, the Army purchased 2,113 vehicles from the USA and bought transportation vehicles for infantry and artillery equipment. The purchases also added 60 Swiss-Spaniard 20 mm cannons to be installed in fighter aircraft MK-III Vampire Jets.

Within this context the armed forces developed a "social action" program meant to deter peasants from attempting to solve their social problems through armed conflicts. In August 1964, Carlos Munguía, a lieutenant colonel in the infantry, described the "social action" campaign as "a new kind of civil–military relationship" that used health care and community meetings to convince peasants to not resort to violence. Munguia's analysis inaugurated a new military doctrine to prevent guerrilla outbreak in states where large sectors of the rural population were on the brink of rebellion.[14]

A Dirty War Foretold: Madera 1965

Despite the military's "hospitable" intentions, civil discontent failed to dissipate. In the early hours of September 23, 1965, a dozen teachers, *campesino* leaders and students assaulted the Madera military barracks, in the southwestern region of the Sierra Tarahumara, in the state of Chihuahua. The assault was executed by a nascent and undertrained revolutionary organization called *Grupo Popular*

Guerrillero,[15] which in the social imaginary is considered Mexico's first modern armed struggle, and the first to profess a socialist political program calling for the overthrow of the government. During the assault the majority of the insurgents were killed in the very first minutes. Among those who perished in the attack was the group's leader Arturo Gámiz, a journalist[16] and elementary school teacher; doctor Pablo Gómez Ramírez, a *campesino* leader and former member of the Popular Socialist Party; Salomón Gaytán, the group's military commander; and Antonio Scobell Gaytán, one of the leaders of the Workers General Union of Peasants of Mexico (UGOCEM).

Sergeant Lorenzo Cárdenas Barajas, an alleged deserter from the armed forces, provided the revolutionaries with military training prior to the assault on the Madera barracks. Although, according to survivors of the GPG, Barajas was still following military orders and belonged to an intelligence network that infiltrated the rebel group, after it had ambushed a military patrol and killed several *caciques* in the region. On the contrary, Professor Francisco Ornelas, one of the survivors of the assault on the Madera barracks doubts that Cárdenas Barajas was a government spy.[17] However, Oscar González Eguiarte, a rising revolutionary figure in the wake of the group's disintegration argued that the sergeant was a "traitor."[18] Finding out about the attack beforehand, military leaders at the Madera barracks took precautionary measures by doubling the amount of troops and supplies. While the attack was summarily put down by the well-equipped military, a number of rebels were able to escape the onslaught by retreating into a wooded area adjacent to the barracks. Two C-54 airplanes dropped 60 paratroopers into the surrounding communities to chase those who managed to reach the forest. In addition, the Mexican Air Force dispatched four aircrafts fully equipped with rocket launchers and machine guns to fly over the mountains and hunt for the rebels.

Meanwhile, in the capital Chihuahua, the authorities announced the possible visit of Secretary of National Defense, General Marcelino García Barragán, though he failed to arrive in Madera to make a first-hand evaluation of the situation. Instead, Governor Práxedes Giner Durán arrived at the site of the assault accompanied by General Tiburcio Garza Zamora, Commander of the 5th Military Zone, and General Flavio Gijón Melgar, the person in charge at the barracks. Soldiers were ordered to clean and put into coffins the bodies of five soldiers killed in action. After having evaluated the situation with the governor and his colleagues, Garza Zamora commented to a number of reporters "the Governor and I think this incident has no importance. I believe these gentlemen were wrong, and because they fired bullets, people were wounded and killed." Governor Giner went further in his assessment, saying, "Nothing has happened, absolutely nothing. It comes down to a bunch of misguided fools." However, Governor Giner's statement proved to be false. The failed assault on the Madera barracks marked the beginning of contemporary guerrilla movements in Mexico.

During the administration of Díaz Ordaz, the president contributed to the military's professionalization and reinforced the country's national security doctrine. In the first part of his tenure Díaz Ordaz sent 306 officers to US military academies, demanding that the military officially incorporate guerrilla warfare as part of soldiers' training. This led to the creation of special Army units specifically prepared to deal with unconventional warfare in rural environments. The new military doctrine instructed each of the 34 military zones existing at the time to become familiarized with the area and existing civil strife through Regional Tactical Exercises (ETR).[19] In the early months of 1965, the Mexican Army increased the number of ground forces, creating eight new infantry battalions, and deploying 12,000 soldiers and 700 Navy troops in the first joint military exercises on the Isthmus of Tehuantepec.[20] These exercises covered the entire country with the exception of Mexico City. The exercises included training troops to protect the country's vital installations, as well as combat subversion, sabotage, civil disturbance, peasant and trade union movements, prevent arms smuggling, quell armed uprisings, monitor borders, and fight drug trafficking.[21] In his analysis, general Castillo described the partnership between paramilitary groups called Rural Defense Corps (CDR) and the Army as cohesive. Initially, the CDR assisted the Army in repairing power lines and telegraph lines, as well as restoring and building bridges and roads in rural areas. However, Piñeyro highlights that by 1966, the new role of the CDR was cooperating with the Army to maintain order in rural areas through espionage, the exchange of intelligence, and fighting rural guerrillas.

But guerrilla movements were not a phenomenon exclusive to rural areas. Before the 1970s small urban guerrilla groups surfaced in the cities, inspired by the Cuban Revolution and anti-imperialist sentiments. In order to combat nascent groups, Díaz Ordaz ordered paramilitary security units to help control radical manifestations and discontent. One of these contingents was the Olympia Battalion, an elite unit comprised of military officers. Besides the Battalion, student groups loyal to the government called *porros* worked in conjunction with local law enforcement and riot police to repress student dissent.[22] When students organized a meeting at the Plaza of the Three Cultures on October 2, 1968, the Olympia Battalion arrived and surrounded the area as students were leaving the rally. Suddenly the military began shooting into the crowd, killing a number of students and innocent bystanders in the process. The massacre in Tlaltelolco marked the end of the 1968 student movement, but also exhibited the ruling party's willingness to use excessive force to quell movements that brought into question its power.

The paramilitarization of pro-government organizations continued into the 1970s. One group was born following a proposal put forward by General Luis Gutiérrez Oropeza, then Presidential Chief of Staff. Gutiérrez Oropeza believed it was necessary to create a counterterrorism security group to protect the capital's public transport system, electricity lines, and sewage system. Close to 2,000 young people and delinquents were recruited from around the city to form the *Halcones*.[23]

Oropeza's proposal was immediately approved by President Díaz Ordaz, and acknowledged by the Secretary of Defense, Marcelino García Barragán, then Interior Minister, Echeverría, and director of DFS, Fernando Gutiérrez Barrios. In a famous photograph, Oropeza appears at the Cuchillo del Campo military camp shaking hands with one of the instructors assigned to train the Hawks. Also included in the picture was General Jesús Gutiérrez Castañeda, who later became Chief of Staff during President Echeverría's administration, Gutiérrez Barrios, and Colonel Manuel Díaz Escobar, the commander of the Hawks. The photograph has been used to exhibit the bond between these individuals and their loyalty to one another. Lieutenants and captains in the armed forces used what they learned from taking courses on counterinsurgency techniques in the United States, Japan, and France to train the Hawks.[24]

The group was divided up into four subgroups: the *Charros*, an armed group; the *halcones*, a team of hit men; the *Aquarius*, a faction made up of members with student-like characteristics meant to infiltrate universities and student organizations; and the *Pancho Villa* faction, which also terrorized university campuses.[25] Each faction proved to be effective in carrying out violent acts against students on and off campus. By infiltrating student groups, the *halcones* were able to target specific people they believed were student leaders, but also learn ahead of time about rallies and demonstrations. The group's most recognized action occurred on June 10, 1971, when the government ordered them to suppress a student demonstration in Mexico City. The *halcones* arrived at the march armed with large sticks and semi-automatic guns. The demonstrators, unarmed and ill prepared to confront the *halcones,* continued their march until a violent clash ensued on the streets. Photographs and testimonies reveal that the *halcones* were working alongside the police in suppressing the demonstration. While students accused the government of causing the clash, the PRI and the armed forces denied the *halcones* existed and blamed the assault on criminals unaligned to the government.[26]

Containing the Guerrillas' Expansion

While the assault on the Madera barracks failed in its attempt to acquire arms for a larger armed insurrection against the government, the PRI was forced to reconsider their national security doctrine and revamp the military's training. Consequently, the armed forces adopted a "Low Intensity War" strategy, as taught at the School of the Americas since 1961.[27] According to the Pentagon, this counterinsurgency strategy was defined as "paramilitary, political, psychological, economic measures needed to be taken in order to defeat 'subversion.'"[28] The

Mexican government appropriated this strategy and immediately began to prepare their soldiers and agents.

Following the disastrous assault on the Madera barracks, a number of survivors of GPG tried, unsuccessfully, to reorganize guerrillas in Chihuahua under a new organization called the September 23rd Movement. At the forefront of this new project was Oscar González Eguiarte, a student who did not participate in the attack on the barracks as he did not arrive on time, yet was able to amalgamate survivors into his new organization. On April 3, 1966, the group performed its first action when members sabotaged a railway approximately 70 kilometers from the Madera barracks.[29] Two years later, after killing a policeman, González Eguiarte fled into the mountains of Chihuahua and Sonora. When he was finally detained by the military, in an act of pure vendetta he was tortured, had the bottom of his feet peeled off, and was forced to walk on them before being executed.[30] Despite having been a short-lived armed struggle, the GPG and its advocacy of radical change and armed insurrection precipitated the ruling party to take a number of anti-subversive measures, against not only insurgents and their movements, but also people unassociated to these struggles but who adhered to radical tenets.

However, the apparent disintegration of the armed movement in Chihuahua did not mean the end of the guerrilla movements in Mexico. Between 1965 and 1974, the Mexican armed forces were faced with the emergence of two separate guerrilla organizations based in the state of Guerrero, with a solid *campesino* base and led by two schoolteachers-turned-revolutionaries. Influenced by the 1959 Cuban Revolution and the proliferation of *foquista* movements in Latin America, these guerrillas represented the radicalization of sectors of the peasantry in Mexico and the governments' failure to resolve injustice and inequalities in the countryside.[31] Before becoming armed organizations, the National Revolutionary Civic Association (ACNR, 1968–1972) and the Party of the Poor (PDLP, 1967–1974) participated in popular movements, as well as in *campesino* struggles. Before taking their movements into the mountains and initiating an armed struggle against the state, both leaders had had a number of violent experiences that drew them to armed resistance. For instance, Cabañas retreated into the mountains and took up arms after the state police massacred *campesinos* at a rally in Atoyac de Alvarez, on May 18, 1967.

During the counterinsurgency campaign in the countryside the federal government used Guerrero as the ideal location to put into practice their new anti-subversive doctrine. In May 1971, newspapers reported the mobilization of troops into two areas of the Sierra Madre Occidental: Xochipala and Atoyac de Alvarez. The campaign was spearheaded by the commanders of the 27 and 35 military zones, and organized after the visit of Secretary of Defense Hermenegildo Cuenca Díaz.[32] The first maneuver was to saturate the state with troops, leading to the immediate establishment of 10,000 soldiers in the surrounding mountains where the armed struggles were presumed to be operating. By 1974, the Army had fully occupied the state.[33] Hermenegildo Cuenca Díaz[34] often visited the state to personally supervise the military operations and evaluate its progress. In the meantime, the Army reinforced its presence in the foothills of the Sierra Madre Occidental.[35]

The presence of military convoys, helicopters, airplanes, and armored vehicles became more prevalent as the Army fully established itself in the region.[36] In response to the militarization of the state, armed groups responded with a wave of attacks on military convoys. From June 1972 to September 1974, PDLP brigades orchestrated a number of ambushes causing 150 military casualties while experiencing no guerrilla losses.[37] In Santo Domingo, a guerrilla attack resulted in the deaths of 14 soldiers, 39 wounded, and 100 prisoners. In Puerto Gallo, 11 soldiers were killed by guerrilla fire and many were taken as prisoners. However, it was quite typical of Cabañas to release prisoners after attempting to indoctrinate them in the mountains.[38] Besides trying to physically eliminate guerrillas through armed confrontations, "disappearances," and executions, the government devised a psychological counterinsurgency campaign. Thousands of leaflets were distributed with photographs of Vázquez Rojas and Cabañas that read: "These are criminals, bandits, who steal women and your property, report them to watch your home, as these men put your family in danger."[39] Newspapers also ran stories explaining military operations and the tracking down of guerrillas. Using vernacular language, articles were written to justify the military's presence in the region in order to capture "criminals and thugs."[40]

Besides exploiting mass media and using it as a mechanism to discredit guerrillas, the military introduced a social work campaign intended to win over the support of local communities. While military contingents were prowling the mountains in search of revolutionaries they distributed clothes, food, and medicine to villages in the area. This sort of campaign produced dubious results, yet the presence of the armed forces in the region was enough to spread a sense of fear throughout communities. The first campaigns by the Army and the federal government led to the isolation of guerrilla groups. The PDLP, which initially benefited from the Army's obsession with fighting the ACNR, lost some contact with peasant groups who supported them with money, food, or combatants.

From the beginning of the conflict, the Army took both armed groups seriously and immediately organized a number of contingency plans. The first military operation named "Operation Friendship" was executed between July 25 and August 13, 1970, in Ilatenco, Tlaxcalitlahuaca, Tierra Colorada, Pazcala, Colombia, Atenco, and Colon communities.[41] According to military documents, the soldiers severely tortured, raped, killed, and "disappeared" peasants from these communities.[42] According to a historian and former guerrilla, in response to the repression a guerrilla brigade began to kidnap moneylenders, prominent businessmen, and *caciques* throughout Guerrero.[43] Encouraged by the successful kidnapping of Donaciano Radilla Luna, a representative of the Bank of the South, from which they received 1.5 million pesos for his ransom in 1970, the ACNR increased its revolutionary activities committed hijackings and bank robberies in Mexico City. Because of the upward surge of guerrilla activities, on May 13, 1971 the armed forces commenced a counterinsurgency campaign under the name "Operation Spiderweb," in which the Air Force was ordered to bomb villages considered bastions for Vázquez Rojas, and also areas where guerrillas were presumably hiding.[44] Also, the government began to pursue ACNR cells in Mexico City.

The Beginning of the End

On November 19, 1971 the abduction of Jaime Castrejón Diez, rector of the Autonomous University of Guerrero, provoked an immediate response by the military. Police forces in collaboration with the 49 Infantry Battalion combed the mountains in search of revolutionaries. A week later, the Armed Liberation Commando Vicente Guerrero from the ACNR took responsibility for the kidnapping and demanded the release of nine imprisoned guerrillas and 2.5 million pesos. The demands were quickly met, and Castrejón was released in early December, though the Army had already launched an anti-guerrilla campaign with the supported of troops sent from Mexico City and the judicial police in the region. The plan appeared to have worked because a commando aligned to the ACNR was forced to leave their main camp and remained in the mountains of Guerrero and Michoacán, far from their areas of influence and logistical support.

A major blow to the ACNR occurred when Vázquez Rojas was arrested by an Army patrol on February 2, 1972, after having suffered a car accident. According to survivors he was killed in a military hospital in Chilpancingo, while the military argues he perished in the accident. The soldiers seized photographs, audiotapes, and a diary with names and addresses of the group's members.[45] Vázquez's death signaled the end of the ACNR, which enabled the Army to then concentrate its efforts on eliminating Cabañas and the PDLP. By 1972, the Army had improved its combat abilities and counterinsurgency tactics as part of National Defense Plan #2, designed to address national security threats. Military campaigns began to use more and more aircrafts and helicopters in order to move troops, weapons, and equipment quickly into the mountains. In every confrontation with guerrillas, the Army gained ground in the mountains and left little space for the guerrillas to retreat. Nearly 24,000 soldiers, a third of the entire Army had been deployed to Guerrero.[46]

The abduction of Guerrero's Governor Rubén Figueroa in May 1974 by Cabañas' forces proved to be a major mistake and marked the guerrillas' end.

Throughout the five months the governor was held, the federal government launched a military offensive with the support of state and federal judicial officers under the banner of rescuing Figueroa. Between August and November 1974 fighting intensified and Cabañas forces had to be divided into three groups. The first was in charge of guarding Rubén Figueroa, the second monitored the Army's maneuvers, while the third unit, led by Cabañas, orchestrated confrontations. While during this period the PDLP caused dozens of casualties to the Army and police forces, the Army was able to replenish its manpower. Figueroa managed to escape in early September 1974 and caused a great deal of confusion within the PDLP. Meanwhile, the morale of the counterinsurgency forces tremendously increased after having succeeded in a number of operations. Among these successes the military wiped out 24 guerrillas in November and less than a month later Cabañas was killed in a confrontation in the mountains in a place called El Otatal, a municipality of Tecpan de Galeana.

Urban Counterinsurgency

The destruction of armed movements in Guerrero was followed by the challenge of now eliminating urban guerrilla movements in the cities. Many of these organizations grew at the same time as rural guerrilla movements were active in the mountains. However, urban guerrilla movements operated without a strong mass base, and with only a few exceptions lacked comprehensive military training.[47] More than 30 armed organizations emerged in major cities, namely Mexico City, Guadalajara, and Monterrey, and were possibly more militaristic than rural guerrillas because of their strong advocacy of revolutionary violence.[48] Working in different regions of the country, urban guerrillas divided up the territory into small independent cells for a number of security reasons, but more importantly, to prevent their leaders from getting apprehended. Yet, while the number of urban guerrilla movements exceeded the number operating in rural areas, only a few, namely the September 23rd Communist League or *Liga*, and the National Liberation Forces or FLN, were considered viable threats by the ruling party and leaders of the counterinsurgency campaign.

To eradicate urban guerrillas, the government initially used the police and DFS agents, but both branches lacked adequate training. Moreover, it made little sense if the military was brought into the city, because it was specifically trained to combat guerrilla movements in the mountains.[49] Because the city was an entirely different domain, specialized counterinsurgency units had to be created in order to effectively challenge urban subversion. National security personnel met daily to evaluate the political situation and devise a comprehensive line of attack. While the DFS was partially successful in capturing guerrillas and thwarting revolutionary activities, high-ranking security officers continued to deliberate how to eradicate guerrilla movements rather than contain them.

After the *Liga* was created in early 1973, the newly formed coalition of previously independent armed revolutionary organizations immediately orchestrated a number of operations. During its first year the *Liga* executed kidnappings and elaborate operations against "symbols of capitalism." On September 17, 1974, a *Liga* commando killed Eugenio Garza Sada, one of Mexico's most revered business tycoons from Monterrey. The death of Garza Sada was a tremendous blow for the business community, but also Echeverría's administration, which faced harsh criticisms from elites who criticized the government's inability to defeat the guerrillas, and more importantly, to defend them from revolutionary violence.[50] Echeverría was personally affected by the death as the president also thought highly of Garza Sada as a person, and respected his business skills as well as philanthropy. Just a month later another brigade aligned to the group kidnapped industrial magnate Fernando Aranguren and Duncan Williams, the British consul in Guadalajara. The conditions for the safe return of both individuals required the government to free a number of political prisoners, though it refused to negotiate their release. Failing to coerce the government to comply with their demands, the *Liga,* in an act that continues to be a topic of discussion, released Duncan, but killed Aranguren.

Echeverría's presidency ended in shame because he was unable to wipe out guerrilla movements. When newly elected president López Portillo took power he vowed to continue the fight against armed revolutionary organizations and bring back political stability to Mexico. While López Portillo's counterinsurgency campaign initially did not differ much from his predecessor, that all changed following the attempted kidnapping of his sister by the *Liga*. Even though his sister escaped unharmed, López Portillo took the attempted kidnapping personally, prompting him to intensify the counterinsurgency campaign against guerrillas into a total war. His personal grudge against the *Liga* quickly transformed into an obsession. While a number of urban guerrilla movements were concurrently active, the president made it his primary goal to eradicate the *Liga*.

Secretary of Defense Felix Galván Lopez characterized the *Liga* as a group of common criminals, adding he was waiting for the new administration to take steps to finally eliminate the group.[51] While a number of agencies and groups were involved in the counterinsurgency campaign against urban guerrilla movements, the White Brigade was specifically created to eradicate urban subversion, namely the *Liga*. The military was occupied with removing vestiges of guerrilla activities in the countryside, so it made sense that a unit specializing in urban guerrilla warfare had to be created. Founded in 1976, the White Brigade was composed of selected agents from an array of police, military, and secret service branches, under the thumb of DFS director Miguel Nazar Haro, who in the social imaginary of the Mexican Dirty War has been compared with some of the most vicious torturers of the Argentine and Chilean Dirty War.

The White Brigade carried out a vicious counterinsurgency campaign against urban guerrillas, but in doing so violated the law and citizen's human rights. Recruitment for the White Brigade was often done forcefully and those selected by high-ranking military personal were expected to join without any complaints. If they refused or deserted their unit, officers risked being sentenced to death for their insubordination. Once an agent was integrated into the White Brigade, as a part of their initial training they were sent to countries and regions where guerrilla movements were already taking place, namely, Ireland, Lebanon, and South America.[52] The size of the White Brigade is debated, but an article published in 2001 by *Bajo Palabra* reports that despite the group's effectiveness, it amounted to no more than 162 agents.

As part of their training, each agent was given the *Plan de Operaciones No. Uno Rastreo*, a document that outlined the counterinsurgency campaign. Within this document a section was specifically designated to the *Liga* entitled *Campaña de Orientación al Público en Contra de la Liga Comunista 23 de Septiembre*,[53] which provided agents with pertinent information about the group.[54] Over the years, the document was updated as more information about the *Liga*'s structure, leaders, and militants became available. Besides providing agents with information on their adversary the document also outlined the White Brigade's structure. Officials were required to operate in small units in civilian clothes, carry a wide range of weapons, use any means necessary to identified "subversives," and extract information from detainees.[55] Following revolutionaries' detention they were immediately interrogated and tortured, and it was only after these procedures took place that it was decided whether or not the individual was to be officially prosecuted. While secret detention centers were established throughout cities (not large concentration camps), Military Camp No. 1 served as the White Brigade's headquarters and also a common location where revolutionaries were tortured and imprisoned. If agents decided not to send revolutionaries to a regular prison, typically prisoners were killed and their bodies were thrown into the streets as a message to other guerrillas, or "disappeared" using the same methods employed by military regimes.[56] Similar to in Argentina, "death flights" were a regular form of "disappearing" revolutionaries. Militants were generally taken to a military base on the coast, put on military planes, and thrown into the ocean.

During its seven-year period the White Brigade succeeded in eliminating the *Liga*, but the cost of the counterinsurgency campaign amounted to more than 1,000 deaths and disappearances. Although the White Brigade was dismantled during the presidency of Miguel de la Madrid, former members were given high-ranking positions in the government. By 1982, the Mexican government succeeded in eliminated the armed struggles. However, the cost of the counterinsurgency effort resulted in a number of human rights abuses and violations. So far, no single member of the White Brigade or other paramilitary groups has been arrested or processed for their participation in what we know as the Dirty War.

The government won the internal war, but failed to set up the conditions for peace. Enjoying impunity, some former members of the White Brigade and the DFS formed criminal organizations and entered the drug trafficking and car theft businesses. Finding solutions to poverty and social disparities in the countryside, namely the states of Guerrero, Oaxaca, Chiapas and the Huasteca region was never part of an integrated and strategic governmental plan to reduce political violence. While revolutionary groups remained intact in Guerrero, Oaxaca and Chiapas, they eventually receded only to re-emerge in the 1980s and 90s signaling that insurgency conditions remained prevalent. In the end, the Dirty War opened the door to a much more violent Mexico, where organized crime and new high-powered guerrilla organizations took the place of the old-style, idealistic armed movements of the 1960s and 70s.

Notes

1 Jorge Luis Sierra Guzmán, *El enemigo interno: Contrainsurgencia y fuerzas armadas en México* (México: Plaza y Valdés, 2003).
2 See Greg Grandin, *The Last Colonial Massacre: Latin America in the Cold War* (Chicago: University of Chicago Press, 2004).
3 The disintegration of urban guerrilla movements can also be attributed to issues unrelated to state-sponsored terrorism. Groups fell apart due to internal issues, the lack of a mass base, and political polarization.
4 See Gustavo Castillo García, "El gobierno creó en 1976 brigada especial para 'aplastar' a guerrilleros en el valle de México," *La Jornada*, 7 de julio de 2008; Sergio Aguayo Quezada, *La Charola: Una historia de los servicios de inteligencia en México* (México: Grijalbo, 2001); Jorge Torres, *Nazar Haro: La historia secreta* (México: Debate, 2008).
5 Mario Arturo Acosta Chaparro, *Movimiento subversivo en México* (México: n.p., 1990).
6 See Luis Astorga, *El siglo de las drogas. El narcotráfico, del Porfiriato al nuevo milenio* (México, Plaza y Janés, 2005).
7 Here I am particularly talking about the Zapatista National Liberation Army (EZLN) and the People's Revolutionary Army (EPR).
8 Granados Chapa, Miguel Angel, "Plaza Pública," Diario Unomásuno, 21 de enero de 1982. Archivo CIHMA.
9 José Luis Piñeyro, "El profesional Ejército Mexicano y la asistencia militar de Estados Unidos (1965–1975)," BA Tesis, Colegio de México, 1976, 72.
10 Tanalís Padilla, *Rural Resistance in the Land of Zapata: The Jaramillista Movement and the Myth of Pax-Priísta, 1940–1962* (Durham: Duke University Press, 2008).
11 Ibid.
12 Piñeyro, "El profesional Ejército mexicano…," 74.
13 Ibid. 75.
14 Ibid, 76.
15 See Fritz Glockner, *Memoria Roja: Historia de la guerrilla en México de 1943 a 1968* (México, DF: Ediciones B, 2008).
16 Gámiz was a journalist writing articles for *La Voz de Chihuahua* newspaper about local social and political events in 1963.
17 Francisco Ornelas, interview by author, 24 September, 2001, notes, Mexico City.

18 Oscar González Eguiarte, "Sobre los acontecimientos en Madera," in *Morir de sed junto a la fuente*, ed., Minerva Armendáriz Ponce (México: Universidad Obrera de México, 2001), 71–72.
19 Piñeyro, "El profesional Ejército Mexicano…" 83.
20 Ibid, 81.
21 Ibid.
22 For a study of right-wing student groups at the National Autonomous University of Mexico see Hugo Sanchez Gudiño, *Génesis, desarrollo y consolidación de los grupos estudiantiles de choque en la UNAM* (México: Miguel Ángel Porrúa, 2006).
23 Tirado, Erubiel, "La seguridad nacional en México," BA Thesis, UNAM, 1997, 104.
24 Ibid.
25 Ibid., 105.
26 Álvaro Delgado, "'El Fish' se confiesa," *Proceso*, 5 October 2003, 22.
27 See Lesley Gil, *The School of the Americas: Military Training and Political Violence in Latin America* (Durham: Duke University Press, 2004).
28 Juan Fernando Reyes Peláez, "El largo brazo del estado: La estrategia contrainsurgente del gobierno mexicano," in *Movimientos armados en México, Siglo XX*, ed. Verónica Oikión Solano and Marta Eugenia García Ugarte (Zamora: CIESAS and Colegio de Michoacán, 2008), 405–413.
29 Acosta Chaparro, *Movimiento subversivo*, 27.
30 Glockner, *Memoria Roja*, 221–225.
31 For more information see the essay in this volume by Alexander Aviña and Armando Bartra, *Guerrero bronco: Campesinos, ciudadanos y guerrilleros en la Costa Grande* (México, DF: Era, 2000) and Claudia E. G. Rangel Lozano and Evangelina Sánchez Serrano, "La Guerra sucia en los setenta y las guerrillas de Genaro Vázquez y Lucio Cabañas en Guerrero," in *Movimientos armados en México, Siglo XX*, 495–525.
32 "25 batallones contra bandas en Guerrero," *Últimas Noticias*, May 21, 1971.
33 General José Francisco Gallardo, *Always Near, Always Far: The Armed Forces in Mexico* (San Francisco: Global Exchange, 2001), 7.
34 "Cuenca Díaz is considered the symbol of the Army's complete modernization, since he was the first soldier completely formed in a post-revolutionary professional system to occupy the highest military command in the Republic." Ibid.
35 Mayo Baloy, *La guerrilla de Genaro y Lucio: análisis y resultados* (México, DF: Editorial Diógenes, 1984), 88.
36 Ibid.
37 Armando Bartra, *Guerrero Bronco…*, 140.
38 To prevent the ongoing demoralization of soldiers who refused to go into in the mountains or fled their units during guerrilla attacks, the Secretary of Defense redistributed troops stationed in the military zones of Acapulco and Chilpancingo with those located in Nayarit and Durango. Also, as an added incentive, soldiers' salaries were doubled.
39 Baloy, 88–89.
40 Héctor Ibarra Chávez, *Pensar la guerrilla en México* (México, DF: Ediciones Expediente Abierto, 2006), 98.
41 National Security Archive, Draft Report by the Special Prosecutor for past Political and Social Movements, Chapter 6, "La Guerra sucia en Guerrero," http://www.gwu.edu/~nsarchiv/NSAEBB/NSAEBB180/060_Guerra%20Sucia.pdf (accessed April 30, 2011).
42 Ibid, 37.
43 Juan Fernando Reyes Peláez, *Los Movimientos Armados en México, (1940–1985)* (Mexico–San Diego, California: University of California-San Diego, 2000), unpublished manuscript, 33.

44 "La Guerra sucia en Guerrero," 39.
45 Ibid.
46 Ibid, 61.
47 The *Movimiento de Acción Revolucionaria* (MAR) is the only organization that received proper military and guerrilla training. The organization was founded by students on scholarship at the Patrice Lumumba University in Moscow. Before returning to Mexico revolutionaries were trained in North Korea.
48 Hugo Esteve Díaz, *Las armas de la utopía: la tercera ola de los movimientos guerrilleros en México* (México: Instituto de Proposiciones Estratégicas, 1996), 72.
49 Oscar Loza, *Tiempo de espera* (Culiacán: Universidad Autónoma de Sinaloa-Comisión de Derechos Humanos, 2004), 18.
50 For a comprehensive evaluation on the murder of Garza Sada see Jorge Fernández Menéndez, *Nadie supo nada: La verdadera historia del asesinato de Eugenio Garza Sada* (México, DF: Grijalbo, 2006).
51 "El ejército contra la Liga," *La Prensa,* 23 April 1977.
52 Former White Brigade member, interview with the author, Mexico City, 1983.
53 Orientation Campaign for the Public Against the September 23rd Communist League.
54 Antonio Jáquez, "Nazar Haro deja de ser intocable," *Proceso,* 5 de enero 2003, 9.
55 Ibid.
56 Carlos Marín, "La Brigada Blanca existe, *Proceso,* 7 de enero 1980, 8.

10

TRANSCENDING VIOLENCE

A Crisis of Memory and Documentation[1]

Elaine Carey

In the 1991 film *El bulto*, the protagonist Lauro awakens from a 20-year coma induced by an injury he sustained on June 10, 1971 during the Corpus Christi massacre. That summer, activists marched from *Instituto Politécnico Nacional* (National Polytechnic Institute) Casco de Santo Tomás campus in Mexico City only to be met by young men armed with clubs who attacked demonstrators and onlookers on the streets of San Cosme. A paramilitary group trained at the *Escuela de Policía* (Police Academy), the *Halcones* served under the direction of the government of the Federal District.[2] Skilled in Japanese martial arts, the *halcones* existed to quell riots.[3] After 20 years, Lauro's awakening brings him to a changed Mexico where his ex-radical friends have joined the establishment, his children are young adults, and his wife is remarried. The heart-warming ending of the film leads viewers to believe that Mexico and its rulers in 1991, the *Partido Revolucionario Institucional* (Institutional Revolution Party, PRI), have rectified the problems of the past. So much so that the embrace of the revolutionary family extended even to ex-radicals of the 1960s who too enjoyed a comfortable bourgeois life within its revolutionary ideals.[4]

In *El bulto*, the reality and memory of the past seemed fraught only with the personal odyssey of acceptance rather than a crisis of civil society. Young people like Lauro opted for armed confrontation when their attempts to bring forth reform through the political process were thwarted by the government. In turn, fictional Lauro's real comrades endured countless years of harassment, repression, torture, disappearance, and death. The political corruption of the PRI and its ability to craft messages bled into the media outlets that portrayed the guerrillas as monsters who blighted the glory of revolutionary ideals. These myths further undermined the ability of civil society to respond to a crisis in government but also to decry the sustained use of state-sponsored terrorism. Retrospectively, the 1970s appears more as a dress rehearsal for the continuing crisis that afflicts the nation, and *El bulto* more a nostalgic dream rather than the reality.

As with the ever-expanding drug war in Mexico, a crisis of civil society plagues Mexico today as it did in the 1970s. *Pax priísta* may have come to a superficial end in 2000, but that federal and limited conclusion does not erase the ongoing struggles to sustain a cohesive and profound opposition. The chapters in this collection demonstrate the multiple apparitions of civil discontent, and the means by which ordinary Mexicans organized to undermine an authoritarian one-party system masquerading as a legitimate democracy.

In the 1970s, young men and women sought to create a new government or a new society. As discussed here, Mexican attempts at organizing organic civil opposition movements continually encountered violence in various forms: violent attacks against union leaders and strikers, teachers' and students' organizations, or the public condemnation and imprisonment of ideological artists and intellectuals.[5] Many met unspeakable brutality despite a federal recognition of their freedoms. The scholars of the present and past collected in this edition document the mobilization of civil society to resist the Mexican government. Their struggles led to the crafting of a Dirty War that pre-dated those in Chile and Argentina that have drawn greater scrutiny. My comments seek to enhance the rationale for such an edited collection: Why was Mexico's violent past able to reside in the shadows for so long? Moreover, I problematize a hierarchical human rights investigation that underscores old political rivalries and entrenchment that ultimately destroyed Mexico's attempt to address the past and to chart a new course of human rights.

In the Shadow of the Revolution

To consider this disjuncture between the past and the construct of memory in the present, we must consider the PRI's historical ability to craft a mythical state of the revolutionary family to which all the chapters allude. Echeverría's term in office may be described as quixotic. He was progressive and conciliatory, but also authoritarian and confrontational; ultimately, he was Machiavellian. On the one hand, his innovative socialist-style programs outraged certain Mexican elites since he questioned the nationalist morals of certain entrepreneurs and industrialists. On the surface, he positioned Mexico in a more adversarial stance in its relations with the United States.[6] On the other hand, his reforms offered certain ex-activists a road back into the revolutionary family. He co-opted 1968 ex-student activists and their demands into the governmental infrastructure by creating positions for them and offering them fellowships for study abroad or post-graduate study. Over time, these scholars and bureaucrats echoed much of the state rhetoric, or they simply have remained silent regarding the violence.[7] Those activists that resisted his patronage however, were hunted down, kidnapped, disappeared, and murdered by government forces.

With Echeverría becoming president in 1970, the nation's political pendulum swung to the left. Echeverría was a man with a vision. He hoped to recapture President Lázaro Cárdenas' (1934–1940) stature and to place Mexico as a prominent defender of the developing world.[8] To achieve his goals, though, he had a serious liability issue: the Tlatelolco massacre. Because of the summer of 1968, the illusion of democracy that had previously played out quite well in Mexico's historical electoral façade began to crumble. Voter absenteeism reached an all-time high of 58 percent in the 1970 election. However, Echeverría easily "won" with 85 percent of the vote, but he took office in a time of continued political strife with students and a rapidly declining economy.[9]

Even in 1968, Echeverría played a key role in the violations of autonomy at *Universidad Nacional Autonóma de México* (National Autonomous University of Mexico, UNAM) and the massacre despite the highly publicized fact that he, as a university student, had written legal briefs defending UNAM's right to autonomy.[10] As Secretary of Interior from 1964 to 1970, Echeverría held the power to issue orders to the army, the police, and the *granaderos* (riot police). Throughout the summer of 1968, President Díaz Ordaz continually referred the students to Echeverría because domestic issues were under his jurisdiction.[11] Once president, however, Echeverría publicly distanced himself from Díaz Ordaz and the events of the summer of 1968. That was facilitated by the fact that Díaz Ordaz publicly took responsibility for what had transpired during his administration, thus providing Echeverría with a convenient way out.

In the 1970s, the PRI employed extreme force against insurgent forces whose mobilizations and actions were portrayed as leading to an apocalyptic end of the revered Revolution. While Echeverría reached one hand to the activists of 1968, his fist came down upon the guerrillas, whether campesinos, obreros, or discontented youth. The secrecy of the brutality ensured a lack of uniform resistance from civil society. As Fernando Herrera Calderón addresses, elites financed right-wing student organizations to maintain order while the government long employed strategic assassinations of opposition leaders. Echeverría postured as a friend of the counterculture while deploying paramilitary forces throughout the country. He appealed to certain sectors of his party that wanted him to control the student problem, but his public courting of Salvador Allende while criticizing the USA led to political rifts within his own party. These overtures and criticisms received publicity in the state-funded media outlets. Of course, these acts did not endear Echeverría to more conservative factions in the PRI. These growing schisms became particularly evident and became more politicized throughout his presidency leading to a growing split within the ruling party.

In November 1971, the CIA reported:
> Luis Echeverría began his six-year term of office on 1 December 1970. Since then, he has set a frantic pace and has shown determination to give his administration a more popular and activist image than that of his predecessor, Gustavo Díaz Ordaz. Echeverría has contended with several political crises early in his term and his forceful style in dealing with them has gained him popularity with the liberal elements but at a very high cost. There is reason for concern that Echeverría will stimulate demands and expectations that his administration cannot meet and that disillusion may become more serious than the apathy Echeverría tried to dispel.
>
> Intensified strains within the ruling party, bitter relationships between politicians that have developed since Echeverría took office as well as the proliferation of small extremists groups—both political and criminal—and rumors of military discontent are potential threats to the Echeverría government.[12]

Only a year into his presidency, even the CIA and the US government were voicing their concern about the Mexican president. Within six months of his presidency, Echeverría confronted one of his greatest challenges and contributed to the strains within the PRI. This incident foreshadowed the problems that plagued his presidency, highlighted his personal inadequacies, and haunted his term of office into the present.

In March 1971, problems stemming from the 1968 student movement and its activists and sympathizers became a growing problem for Echeverría and his administration's relations with the Soviet Union and the United States. As discussed by Oikión Solano, in March 1971, Attorney General Julio Sánchez Vargas announced the arrests of key leaders of the *Movimiento de Acción Revolucionaria* (Mexican Revolutionary Action, MAR). Several guerrillas had allegedly received sponsorship and training by North Korea.[13] They had made contacts with the North Korean government while students at the Patrice Lumumba Friendship University in Moscow. Sánchez Vargas stated, "They have received military and political training at different times since 1968 in a military base near Pyongyang (N. Korea) sponsored by the government of that country ... Their purpose was to establish a Marxist–Leninist regime. They were trained in the use of all types of weapons, explosives, rural and guerrillas tactics and they received political indoctrination."[14]

As activists flashed the "Venceremos" signs to photographers gathered in the court room, Fabricio Gómez Souza admitted in court that the MAR planned to overthrow the government through armed warfare.[15] The arrests of MAR members and the alleged connection to the Soviet Union led to the expulsion of five Soviet diplomats in Mexico. Moreover, Mexico called its envoy from Moscow for consultation; however, the majority of the Mexican diplomatic staff remained on assignment.[16] Mexico had long served as a "soft" battleground of the Cold War, now it appeared that the PRI had lost control. That loss of control circulated in the international press. While Echeverría's government tried to mend its relations with the Soviet Union, conservative factions in the United States viewed this as proof that the Soviets were using Mexico as a base of operation against the United States by using college scholarships as tools of indoctrination to foster revolution abroad.[17] In April 1971, the Central Intelligence Bulletin concluded:

> This case is but another in the annals of Soviet diplomatic history illustrating the duplicity of that country's diplomacy as one hand is outstretched in pursuit of friendly economic and cultural links throughout the Western Hemisphere while the other nurtures indigenous subversion. Although the young revolutionaries had received training in North Korea, Mexico was not deluded about who had masterminded the entire effort and the government's actions taken against the Soviet diplomats was meant to serve warning that Mexico will not tolerate interference either through the Soviet Embassy or the embassies of Poland, Czechoslovakia, or Cuba.[18]

The authors in this collection recognize the transnational ideological influences that flowed from Cuba, the Soviet Union, France, Germany, China, and Vietnam. As Alan Eladio Gómez discusses, Mexican concepts of revolutionary acts also flowed north, influencing Chicanos. Despite these global and transnational influences, the authors more specifically note the internal problems that fueled those who joined the Mexican armed forces. Activists who attempted to promote political change through peaceful methods and met violence came to the conclusion that armed confrontation might create the opportunity to construct a new society. As discussed by Adela Cedillo and Romain Robinet, other militants came to these conclusions through a careful analysis of Mexican society, laying the groundwork for a long revolution. In turn, teachers, normal schools, students, workers, and campesinos and their civil organizations became the targets of suspicion. These same sectors of society had few resources to challenge the PRI crafted messages and media control.

In Mexico, the threat of revolution fueled a Cold War swagger that contributed to a build-up of the security system under both Díaz Ordaz and Echeverría that remained fluid to the demands and the desires of those in power. When journalists and opposition leaders exposed corruption or illegality, those forces could easily be disbanded and rebuilt under new agencies with distinct missions.[19] Hence, Echeverría's administration fell under attack from diverse sectors of the society, yet he engaged in secret negotiations to further support funding of paramilitary organizations. In their analysis of contemporary struggles, scholars, such as Josiah Heyman and Peter Andreas, have argued that a dynamic occurs when covert actors' attempts to defeat government control actually lead to a further build-up of the government apparatus that uses force to demonstrate the value and seriousness of its response.[20] This is exactly what happened in the 1970s just as today. Michael Kenney has further elaborated on these concepts by demonstrating that bureaucracies have difficulty in responding to organizations that have more fluid structures.[21] What remains striking between the 1970s guerrillas and the present ones was that they never yielded tremendous technological or financial advantage as those groups confronting the government today. Significantly, the guerrillas did not have governmental patronage, which remains a facet of Mexican drug trafficking.[22]

The existence of *halcones* and the escalation of the Dirty War undermined Echeverría's reformist posturing with the creation of the *Apertura Democrática* (the democratic opening). Echeverría stated that the reforms were to create a more independent, developed, and just society. He argued that his three fundamental goals were to strengthen the popular classes that had been forgotten since Cárdenas, to create a national business class with a social vision, and to diversify Mexico's foreign relations to challenge, and to undermine, the influence of the United States on its borders.[23] Of course, his rhetoric did not hide his corruption or his ability to enrich himself at the expense of the people. More importantly, members of the popular classes, as described in the articles in this volume, joined by educated young people bore the brunt of Echeverría's Dirty War.

Echeverría's posturing as a global democratic citizen came as the country descended into economic, political, and social crisis. Yet, this chaos too, as the authors present, had a long history. The diverse organizations evolved from the past attempts to rectify the goals of the Revolution. As presidential policies following the Cárdenas administration shifted from campesinos and workers to the emerging middle class and elite, conflict emerged. Alex Aviña positions Lucio Cabañas as an heir to Emiliano Zapata and the ideals of the Revolution. His struggle did not emerge in the 1960s, but it was a continued struggle within the state.[24] Moreover, all the authors demonstrate that the revolutionary heritage of the PRI had been tarnished in Chihuahua, Guerrero, Jalisco, Mexico DF, and countless other states.

Human Rights, Globalization, and Activists in Business Suits

Despite the concerns of some Mexican conservatives, Echeverría did leave the presidency. In spite of his attempt to be a spokesperson for the developing world, he was not given an international platform at the United Nations. Instead, the legacy of Echeverría seemed to disappear from the political landscape as he left for retirement in 1976. In the following years, his successor José López Portillo, the last of the nationalist presidents, issued a general amnesty to ex-activists from 1968 and 1971, yet many activists involved in the Dirty War remained underground.[25] The amnesty coincided with further devaluations followed by a banking crisis that financially devastated the nation.

Since the late 1970s, ex-activists have demanded answers to the massacre of October 2, 1968, the attack on peaceful protesters on June 10, 1971, and the Dirty War. With pressure from the ex-activists, it was during the administration of President Vicente Fox—an ex-Coca Cola executive and member of the right-of-center *Partido Acción Nacional* (National Action Party, PAN)—that the investigation ensued. Among his many campaign promises, he pledged to form a more open government and to address the past. He appointed Dr Ignacio Carrillo Prieto as Mexico's Special Prosecutor for Social and Political Movements in 2001, who has pursued cases against certain public officials who have been accused of human rights violations during the 1960s and 1970s. The investigations increasingly focused on Luis Echeverría. Initially, proponents hailed that the case against him revealed an important and dramatic shift in contemporary Mexican politics away from a time when ex-presidents, governors, and high-ranking military officers were granted immunity from any type of legal action. It also showed the influence that the generation of '68 has had on Mexican society by redefining itself as a central proponent of human rights in a highly volatile political time.[26]

Yet, Mexico's "Pinochet moment" is rife with problems revealing on-going historical tensions within the Mexican government and its stance on human rights, whether international or national.[27] From the beginning of his presidential term, Echeverría adopted a more populist stance than his predecessor Díaz Ordaz.[28] For the elite and powerful, the legacy of 1968 played out in the struggle over responsibility for the violence which created strained relationships between powerful men within the PRI and the PAN.

How was Echeverría able to orchestrate and commit such human rights violations while the at same time position himself as a defender of the developing world? The Díaz Ordaz and Echeverría administrations violated the Universal Declaration of Human Rights (UDHR) during the 1968 student movement, the Corpus Christi demonstration, and the Dirty War even though Mexico had been a member of the United Nations when the UDHR was approved in 1948. Even with its approval, there was not a specific universal language of human rights in Mexico, as in much of the world at that time, during the 1960s and 1970s. The United States under Richard Nixon and Henry Kissinger never criticized the human rights records of Latin American nations and contributed to such violations by supporting dictatorships in Brazil, Chile, and Argentina. Mexico's own constitution has one of the strongest guarantees of human rights in the world.[29] The Mexican constitution provides for freedom of expression, of the press, of association, and of movement, but it also guarantees adequate pay and working conditions for workers and access to land for peasants. While Secretary of the Interior, Echeverría proclaimed that the Díaz Ordaz administration was committed to the goals of the constitution as well as to creating a political space for all forms of expressions and ideologies.[30] As president, Echeverría further committed to these promises by releasing some political prisoners and allowing some activists and opposition party members to return from exile. Despite the existence of such written and communicated guarantees, Mexico, like many other countries, violated its own laws.

Of course, once a candidate is elected, he routinely ignores his campaign promises. Thirty-six years after those promises of Echeverría, Fox too argued that he would stand for a more open government. His appointment of Carrillo Prieto served to institutionalize that transparency. That openness led to the accessibility of the archives that all the scholars employed in this text; moreover, scholars and activists in Mexico employed those same papers and archives to assist the Special Prosecutor in his investigation. Activists from 1968 and 1971 and militants from the Dirty War found validation in their suspicions when they too accessed their own security files.

Prior to Fox's election, Mexico had established its own *Comisión Nacional de los Derechos Humanos* (National Commission on Human rights, CNDH) in 1990, almost 22 years after the massacre in Tlatelolco and the subsequent years of the Dirty War.[31] The CNDH emerged from groups such as Comité Eureka and provincial and community groups that promoted the rights of, for example, ex-activists, consumers, students, community residents, and other groups.[32] Ironically, in 1989, the immediate predecessor to the CNDH, the *Dirección General de Derechos Humanos*, was formed under the Secretary of Interior, the very agency that oversaw and committed some of the most horrific crimes.

In 1998, the Comité '68 Pro Libertades Democráticas and other human rights organizations were successful in the release of government documents pertaining to the 1968 student movement and the Dirty War. Many of these scholars, journalists, and activists worked closely with Carillo Prieto, yet the procedures of documentation remained opaque. Mexican journalists worked closely with their US counterparts to uncover further evidence, sharing information across borders to create new histories. The release of documents showed a grisly past of human rights violations from the 1960s and 1970s.

With this evidence, human rights organizations pressured the government. In turn, Mexico entered into several treaties that prohibit international human rights violations such as torture, arbitrary detention, extrajudicial execution, and forced disappearance.[33] Many of these are guarantees that are also found in the Mexican constitution.[34] With Mexico's own guarantees as well as its ratification of international human rights conventions, it seemed that officials would proceed to address the past in a legal manner; however, even the ratification of such treaties became entrenched in the political culture of Mexico. David Wilkinson of Human Rights Watch reported that when Mexico ratified the 2002 Inter-American Convention on Forced Disappearances of Persons, "it included an interpretative declaration stating that 'it shall be understood that the provisions of said Convention shall apply to acts constituting the forced disappearance of persons ordered, executed, or committed after the entry into force of the Convention.'"[35] Thus, not only was Echeverría protected from legal actions, but so was every president to Fox.[36] The question in the human rights community remained to what extent does the Fox administration plan to prosecute human rights violators in Mexico?

Evidence mounted against members of the *Dirección Federal de Seguridad* (Federal Security Directorate, DFS) such as Miguel Nazar Haro and Luis de la Barreda Moreno along with their ex-boss, the Secretary of Interior Mario Moya Palencia.[37] In 2003, Carrillo Prieto issued the arrest warrants for Nazar Haro and De la Barreda. Both were charged in the disappearance of Jesús Piedra Ibarra and other members of the LC23S.[38] In 2004, he sought an arrest warrant for Echeverría for genocide. Carrillo Prieto argued that he used the term genocide to side-step statues of limitations placed upon him by the international conventions as well as Mexican legal codes.[39] The following day, a judge threw out the arrest warrant as more photos of the Corpus Christi massacre were published in Mexico City newspapers.[40]

In response to the growing evidence that supported the veracity of such claims against Echeverría, the *New York Times* published an editorial that questioned the sincerity of Fox to investigate the crimes of the past and the existence of Mexican democracy.[41] The editorial in the *New York Times* led to a rebuttal by Carrillo Prieto and Mexican intellectual Enrique Krauze.[42] Carrillo Prieto, who appealed the decision, insisted that it was under Mexico's new system that action has finally been taken, arguing that one of Fox's main objectives was to fight against the impunity of previous Mexican leaders. Recognizing that the old ruling party still exists and yields tremendous power, Krauze argued that the transparency of the judiciary process and ability of the press to report on the case reflects a very recent, and more democratic, shift in Mexico.

Krauze's statements reflected the historical evolution toward a more transparent government, but it also underscored the continuing political nature of the investigation into Echeverría. As 1968 activist Ignacia Ana Rodríguez asked me in 2007, "Why should Echeverría be able to live out his life on house arrest in his mansion?"[43] She recalled that when she was captured the police beat her, thus she entered prison bruised and with a broken nose. Other survivors of the Dirty War wear the evidence of Echeverría's crimes: missing digits, limbs, mental anguish, and post-traumatic stress. The loss of their comrades to state-sponsored repression and murder received greater attention as the cases progressed. Prior to 2006, people remained hopeful.

In 2006, Carillo Prieto released a final report at the end of Fox's term of office.[44] It documented 12 massacres, 120 extrajudicial killings, 800 forced disappearances and 2,000 acts of torture against detainees. The release of the report remains rife with controversy including censorship. Notwithstanding recognition of crimes and the work to produce the report that brought together scholars, activists, and bureaucrats, the office of the Special Prosecutor was abandoned further shortly after the end of Fox's term of office. The cases against De la Barreda and Nazar Haro were halted in 2006, and they were released from house arrest. Of all the three presidents responsible for the Dirty War the only living survivor was Echeverría, but his case was thrown out on March 26, 2009. As Rosario Ibarra de la Piedra, the mother of Jesús Piedra Ibarra declared, it was business as usual in Mexico.

Mexico's "Pinochet moment" never materialized. While the truth emerged in the final report issued by Carrillo Prieto, a wide-spread truth commission and forum for public reconciliation never took place, leaving an open wound that civil society continues to organize to address.[45] The inability of the state to address the crimes of the past adds to the nation's duress during this period of heightened violence and increased militarization under President Felipe Calderón Hinojosa further exacerbates a growing crisis within the human rights community and those who report the truth. In turn, the numbers of walking victims and survivors continues to grow alongside those who are too afraid to grieve for their lost loved ones. The failure of the state to properly address the past compounds citizens' distrust in the government, the police, and armed forces. Returning to our fictional Lauro, the melodramatic twists of his acceptance and redemption are a myth within the nation's collective memory. An unanswered, anguished past ensures that that memories will only intensify to showcase Mexico's lack of transparency, democracy, and human rights.

Notes

1 This initially began as a paper during the NEH seminar Human Rights in the Age of Globalization, June–July 2005 at Columbia University directed by Andrew Nathan.
2 "Tarjeta enviada al secretario de Gobernación sobre las actividades del grupo Halcones," September 25, 1969, Archivo de Bucareli, Informes de la Dirección Federal de Seguridad, 1964–1972, reprinted in *Nexos* (June 1998).
3 Declaración a la DFS de Leopoldo Muñiz Rojas, alias "El Guilligan," ex-miembro del grupo del Halcones, January 14, 1972, report compiled by Luis de la Barreda Moreno, Director of Federal Security, Archivo Bucareli, Informes de la Dirección Federal de Seguridad, 1964–1972, reprinted in *Nexos* (June 1998).
4 For an example see Albert Ulloa Bornemann, *Surviving Mexico's Dirty War: A Political Prisoner's Memoir* (Philadelphia: Temple University Press, 2007).
5 Judith Adler Hellman, *Mexico in Crisis* (New York, Holmes & Meier, 1979). Students were influenced by the strikes of teachers and railroad workers in the late 1950s as

well as the medical student strikes of the early 1960s. Memoirs of working class leaders include: Valetín Campa, Valetín. *Mi testimonio: Experiencias de un comunista mexicano* (México, DF: Ediciones de Cultura Popular, 1978); Demetrio Vallejo, *Yo acuso*. (México, DF: Editorial Hombre Nuevo, 1973); José Revueltas, *México 68: Juventud y revolución* (México, DF: Ediciones Era, 1978).

6 Central Intelligence Agency, "Update of Mexico Handbook," No. 0570, November 1971, CIA Database, National Archives II, College Park, MA (hereafter NACP).

7 Many former activists expressed feelings of betrayal in interviews with the author. Carmen Landa, interview with author, October 21, 1997, Mexico City; Aída González, interview with author, November 30, 1997, San Mateo Tlatenango, Mexico; Lillian Lieberman, interview with author, April 4, 1997, Mexico City; Marcelino Perelló, interview with author, June 6, 1997, Mexico City.

8 During his presidency, Echeverría sought to organize developing countries to demand higher prices for the raw materials. He proposed this theme at the United Nations in 1974 and went on a tour of 14 developing countries to gain support for his initiative. See Yoram Shapira, *Mexican Foreign Policy Under Echeverría* (Beverly Hills, CA: Sage Publications, 1978); James Reston, "The Coming Class War," *The New York Times*, (August 27, 1975). In 1976, at the time of his retirement, Alan Riding reported that aides to the in-coming president hoped that Echeverría would be chosen to succeed Kurt Waldheim at UN Secretary General; Alan Riding, "Retiring is not so retiring," *The New York Times*, May 16, 1976.

9 Samuel Schmidt, *The Deterioration of the Mexican Presidency: The Years Luis Echeverría*, translated by Dan A. Cothran (Tucson: University of Arizona Press, 1991), 32. See also Sergio Tamayo, "The 20 Mexican Octobers: A Study of Citizenship and Social Movements" (PhD diss., University of Texas at Austin, 1994); Daniel Cosío Villegas, *La sucesión: Desenlace y perspectivas* (México, DF: Cuadernos de Joaquín Mortiz, 1976). For a discussion about the declining economy see Jorge Martínez Ríos, *El perfil de México en 1980* (México, DF: Editores Siglo XXI 1972). Díaz Ordaz and his finance minister Antonio Ortiz Mena left a balanced budget at the end of their terms in office. Ortiz Mena had also been a presidential consideration. Upon Echeverría's election, he resigned his post as finance minister and became the president of the Inter-American Development Bank.

10 Luis Echeverría, "La revolución mexicana y la universidad," *El Nacional*, January 11, 1946, reprinted in Carlos J. Sierra, *Luis Echeverría: Raíz y dinámica de su pensamiento* (México, DF: Testimonio de Atlacomulco, 1969): 79–81.

11 For a discussion of the students' relationship with Díaz Ordaz see Herbert Braun, "Protests of Engagement: Dignity, False Love, and Self Love in Mexico During 1968," *Comparative Studies in Society and History* (July 1997), 511–549; Elaine Carey, *Plaza of Sacrifices: Gender, Power, and Terror in 1968 Mexico* (Albuquerque: University of New Mexico Press, 2005), 107–109.

12 Update on Mexican Handbook.

13 "Police Hunt Mexican Guerrillas," *Daily Telegraph*, March 17, 1971; "Mexican Guerrillas Trained by N. Korea," *Japan Times*, March 17, 1971. CIA Database, NACP.

14 "Mexican Guerrillas Trained by N. Korea."

15 "Mexico Guerrilla Admits to Armed Plot," *Japan Times*, March 18, 1971.

16 "Mexico Expels 5 Russians," *Washington Post*, March 19, 1971.

17 Rowland Evans and Robert Novak, "Soviet Backfire in Mexico," *Washington Post*, March 24, 1971.

18 *Central Intelligence Bulletin*, April 1971.

19 For a discussion of the Mexican press, see Chappell Lawson, *Building the Fourth Estate: Democratization and the Rise of the Free Press in Mexico* (Berkeley: University of

California Press, 2002); Jacinto Rodríguez Munguía, *La otra guerra secreta: Los archivos prohibidos de la prensa y el poder* (México, DF: Random House, Mondadori, 2007).
20 Josiah McC. Heyman, "State Escalation of Force: A Vietnam/US–Mexico Border Analogy," in Heyman, ed., *States and Illegal Practices*, 285–314; Peter Andreas, *Border Games: Policing the U.S.–Mexico Divide* (Ithaca: Cornell University Press, 2000).
21 Michael Kenney, *From Pablo to Osama: Trafficking and Terrorist Networks, Government Bureaucracies, and Competitive Adaptation* (University Park: Pennsylvania State University Press, 2007).
22 Stanley A. Pimental, "The Nexus of Organized Crime and Politics in Mexico," in *Organized Crime and Governability: Mexico and the U.S.–Mexico Borderlands*, ed., John Bailey and Roy Godson (Pittsburgh: University of Pittsburgh Press, 2000), 33–57.
23 For a glowing review of Echeverría and his attempts to bring change see Gabriel A. Uribari, *Tiempo de Echeverría* (México, DF: Martin Casillas Editores, 1985).
24 Similar to Rubén Jaramillo. See also Tanalís Padilla, *Rural Resistance in the Land of Zapata: The Jaramillista Movement and the Myth of the Pax-Priísta, 1940–1962* (Durham: Duke University Press, 2008).
25 After López Portillo, Mexican presidents, many US educated, embraced free market policies. Many guerillas remained underground into the 1990s for fear of retribution.
26 Andrew Reding, "Democracy and Human Rights in Mexico," A Special Report by the North American Project of the World Policy Institute (New York: World Policy Institute, 1995).
27 Marshall Beck, "Echeverría and Impunity," *NACLA Report on the Americas* (September/October 2004), 3
28 For a biography of Díaz Ordaz and Echeverría, Enrique Krauze, *Mexico Biography of Power: A History of Modern Mexico, 1810–1996*, translated by Hank Heifetz (New York: Harper Perennial, 1997); Schmidt, *The Deterioration of the Mexican Presidency: The Years Luis Echeverría*; Tamayo, "The 20 Mexican Octobers: A Study of Citizenship and Social Movements."
29 Reding, "Democracy and Human Rights," 13–20.
30 "La política del régimen: Echeverría interpreta el pensamiento del señor Presidente," *Novedades*, December 15, 1964 reprinted in Sierra, *Echeverría*, 41.
31 See La Comisión Nacional de los Derechos Humanos de México, February 12, 2008. http://www.hrw.org/es/node/62435/section/3
32 Jorge Carpizo, *Derechos humanos y ombudsman* (México, DF: Comisión Nacional de Derechos Humanos, 1993). For a brief discussion of Comité 68, see Elaine Carey and José Agustín Román Gaspar "Carrying on the Struggle: El Comité 68," *NACLA Report on the Americas* special issue "Against Impunity: The Decline of the Mexican Social Pact," May/June 2008. See also http://www.comiteeureka.org.mx/.
33 For a discussion of Mexico's human rights see, David Wilkinson, *Justice in Jeopardy: Why Mexico's first real effort to address past abuses risks becoming its latest failure* (New York: Human Rights Watch, 2003). The treaties include International Covenant on Civil and Political Rights, ratified by Mexico on March 23, 1981; Convention Against Torture and Other Cruel, Inhuman, or Degrading Treatment or Punishment, ratified by Mexico on January 23, 1986; Inter-American Convention to Prevent and Punish Torture, ratified by Mexico on June 27, 1987; and Inter-American Convention on Forced Disappearance of Persons, ratified by Mexico on April 9, 2002.
34 *Constitución Política de los Estados Unidos Mexicanos*.
35 Wilkinson, *Justice in Jeopardy*, 20.
36 It is interesting to note that with the election of Vicente Fox, Carlos Salinas returned from exile and his brother Raúl was released from prison. Salinas has returned to being a political broker in Mexico.

37 De la Barreda died in 2008. See "Murió Luis de la Barreda, ex titular de la disuelta Dirección Federal de Seguridad," *La Jornada*, (June 10, 2008).
38 For more information and documents, see *Archival Evidence of Mexico's Human Rights Crimes: The Case of Aleida Gallangos,* National Security Archive Electronic Briefing Book No. 307, by Kate Doyle and Jesse Franzblau, posted March 9, 2010, http://www.gwu.edu/~nsarchiv/NSAEBB/NSAEBB307/index.htm, accessed March 15, 2011.
39 Enrique Krauze, "Past Wrongs, Future Rights," *The New York Times* (August 10, 2004).
40 *La Jornada*, (July 29 and July 30, 2004).
41 Editorial: "Justice for Mexico's Dirty War," *The New York Times* (July 29, 2004).
42 Krauze, "Past Wrongs, Future Right"; Ignacio Carrillo Prieto, letter to the editor, *The New York Times* (August 6, 2004).
43 Ana Ignacia Rodríguez, discussion with Elaine Carey and José Agustín Román Gaspar, November 7, 2007, Mexico City.
44 See Official Report Released on Mexico's "Dirty War": *Government Acknowledges Responsibility for Massacres, Torture, Disappearances and Genocide, National Security Archive,* accessed on April 5, 2011, http://www.gwu.edu/~nsarchiv/NSAEBB/NSAEBB209/index.htm.
45 In Mexico, as in other countries, writing and speaking serve as the only tools to address and confront the trauma. See Cathy Caruth, ed., *Trauma. Explorations in Memory.* (Baltimore: Johns Hopkins University Press, 1995) and Dominick LaCapra, *Writing History, Writing Trauma.* (Baltimore: Johns Hopkins University Press, 2000).

CONTRIBUTORS

Alexander Aviña received his BA in History at Saint Mary's College of California (2002) and his PhD in Latin American History at the University of Southern California (2009). He has conducted field research in Mexico, primarily in Mexico City and the state of Guerrero, funded by the University of Southern California and a Fulbright–García Robles Fellowship. His specialization is Modern Mexico with an emphasis on rural social movements and politics, post-1940 Mexico and the Cold War, and peasant politics. He has also published essays that focus on Guerrero's peasant guerrillas of the 1960s and 70s and state terrorism in Guerrero. He is currently revising his dissertation, "Insurgent Guerrero: Genaro Vázquez, Lucio Cabañas and the Guerrilla Challenge to the Postrevolutionary Mexican State, 1960–1996," into book manuscript form. He is currently an Assistant Professor in the Department of History at Florida State University.

Fernando Herrera Calderón received his PhD at the University of Minnesota, Twin Cities and is currently Visiting Assistant Professor at Beloit College. He received a BA in Latin American Studies and Spanish from Humboldt State University (2004), and an MA in History from the University of Oregon (2006). He specializes in student radicalism, the Cold War in Mexico, and guerrilla culture.

Elaine Carey is an Associate Professor at St. John's University in Queens, New York and the Lloyd Sealy Research Fellow at John Jay College of Criminal Justice. Her research and teaching interests include Latin American social movements, international human rights, globalization and crime, history of narcotics, and gender studies. Elaine has received numerous grants, including

Fulbright–García Robles fellowships 1996–97 and 2007–08 and funding from the National Endowment for the Humanities. She is the author of *Plaza of Sacrifices: Gender, Power, and Terror in 1968 Mexico* (2005) and co-editor with Andrae Marak of the forthcoming *Transnational Flows of Contraband and Vice in North America*. Her work has also appeared in *Américas: The Magazine of the OAS, History Compass, Journal of Women's History, NACLA Report on the Americas, Post-Identity*, and *Radical Teacher*. From 1998 to 2002, she taught Latin American and women's history at the University of Detroit Mercy. While at UDM, Elaine co-founded the James Guadalupe Carney Latin American Solidarity Archive (CLASA; http://libarts.udmercy.edu/clasa/), an activist and teaching archive on Latin American solidarity and human rights movements. Continuing her work on human rights, she serves as an expert witness for gender-based violence asylum claims from Mexico and Central America. Currently, she is completing a book entitled *Selling is More of a Habit: Women and Drug Trafficking in North America, 1900–1970*.

Adela Cedillo is a graduate student in Latin American Studies at the National Autonomous University of Mexico. Her specialization is in armed revolutionary movements, human rights, and the Cold War in Mexico. Her book, *El fuego y el silencio: Historia de las Fuerzas de Liberación Nacional de México (1969–1974)*, is the first comprehensive history on the organization that gave birth to the Zapatista National Liberation Army, or EZLN, and was published by the Comité '68 Pro Libertades Democráticas as part of a collection to commemorate the 40th anniversary of the 1968 massacre. She has also published a litany of essays and articles in books and Mexican journals. Currently she is in the process of preparing a two-volume book on the history of the FLN. In addition to her academic work, she is also an advisor for "Nacidos en la Tempestad," a human rights organization composed of the sons and daughters of former guerrillas active during the Dirty War.

Héctor Guillermo Robles Garnica is a survivor of the Mexican Dirty War and a former member of two guerrilla movements: the Frente Estudiantil Revolucionario (Student Revolutionary Front, or FER), and subsequently the Fuerzas Revolucionarias Armadas del Pueblo (People's Revolutionary Armed Forces, or FRAP). He is the author of *Guadalajara: la guerrilla olvidada, presos en la isla de la libertad* (1996), and recently finished writing an update to his memoir.

Alan Eladio Gómez is a historian and Assistant Professor in the School of Justice and Social Inquiry at Arizona State University. Organized around the over-arching theme of cultures of resistance, his research and teaching topics include: history of social movements in Mexico, the USA and the US–Mexico borderlands; the political cultures of US/Third World Left radicalism; the relational logics of white supremacy, violence, law and state formation; prison rebellions and incarceration logics; situated knowledge, radical pedagogies and neo-liberal education; and the intersections of gender, revolution and international solidarity. Dr Gómez' research has been published in Radical History Review and Latino Studies. Prior to coming to ASU, he taught at Ithaca College and Cornell University. Dr Gómez received his PhD in History (2006) and his MA in Latin American Studies (2002)—both at the University of Texas at Austin. He is currently writing two book-length manuscripts: *Armed with my Dignity Intact: Prison Rebellions, Masculinity and Third World Solidarity* and *Decolonizing the Américas: Latinos/as, Latin America, and the U.S. Third World Left in the 1970s*.

Jorge Luis Sierra Guzmán studied psychology at the National Autonomous University of Mexico (UNAM), and international journalism at the University of Southern California. He specializes on topics of military and national security. He also has a long history of involvment in the human rights movement, has collaborated with numerous NGOs, and has received fellowships to institutions and universities in Washington DC, Mexico, and Argentina. He is the author of numerous articles and the book *El enemigo interno: Contrainsurgencia y fuerzas armadas en México* (2003).

Elizabeth Henson is a doctoral candidate in Latin American History at the University of Arizona and a veteran of social movements of the 1960s and 70s in the United States. Her research has been funded by the Tinker Foundation and the Fulbright–Hayes Doctoral Dissertation grant.

Lucía Rayas is a sociologist and a historian. She has done postgraduate work in translation first and gender later at El Colegio de México. Currently she teaches contemporary history of Mexico at the Mexico Study Centre of the University of California, and at the Master's Program of the Escuela Nacional de Antropología e Historia (ENAH). She is finishing her doctorate in history, on gender and state repression from the 1960s to the 80s, at the ENAH. Her articles and translations have appeared in numerous national and international publications. She is the author of *Armadas: Un análisis de género desde el cuerpo de las mujeres combatientes*, Colegio de México (2009).

Romain Robinet specializes in twentieth-century Mexican history and is a graduate of the Institut d'Études Politiques de Rennes (2006), the Institut d'Études Politiques de Paris (2007), and Paris I Sorbonne (2008). In 2009 he joined the Department of History of the Institut d'Études Politiques de Paris and is currently a PhD candidate. His PhD dissertation, *Le Monde étudiant et la société mexicaine (1910–1940)*, is about student movements during the interwar period in Mexico. His theses include: *Le Club de l'Horloge (1974–1989): déplacements, idéologies, stratégies*, under the supervision of Gilles Richard at the Institut d'Etudes Politiques de Rennes; and *La victoire du prolétariat ou la mort. Les* *débuts de Ligue Communist du 23 Septembre (1973–1974) et lecher du mouvement socialiste armé mexicain*, under the supervision of David Redondo at the Institut d'Études Politiques de Paris.

Verónica Oikión Solano received her Doctorate from the National Autonomous University of Mexico, and is a Professor and Researcher at the Centro de Estudios Históricos at El Colegio de Michoacán. Her publications include: *El Constitucionalismo en Michoacán. El período de los gobiernos militares, 1914–1917* (1992); *Michoacán en la vía de la unidad nacional, 1940–1944* (1995); *Los hombres del poder en Michoacán, 1924–1962* (2004); and co-editor of *Movimientos armados en México, siglo XX* (2006). Apart from her publications Prof. Oikión Solano has also received awards and recognitions in Mexico, for example the Premio Marcos y Celia Maus and Honorable Mention for the Premio Francisco Javier Clavijero de Historia y Etnohistoria.

BIBLIOGRAPHY

Archival Sources

Archivo General de la Nación (AGN)
DFS: Dirección Federal de Seguridad
DGIPS: Dirección General de Investigaciones Políticas y Sociales
SEDENA: Secretaria de la Defensa Nacional
National Security Archives
Mandeville Special Collections Library, UC San Diego

Newspapers and Magazines

Excélsior, October 1973
Madera, January 1974
Nepantla
Proceso
El Día

Theses and Unpublished Manuscripts

Alvarado Lecuona, Luis Antonio. *El Movimiento de Acción Revolucionaria y su influencia en la Reforma Política mexicana en 1977*. BA Thesis, UNAM, 2008.
Aréstegui Ruiz, Rafael. *Campesinado y lucha política en la Costa Grande de Guerrero*. Tesis, Universidad Autónoma de Guerrero, 1984.
Armendáriz, Minerva. *Morir de sed junto a la fuente, 30 años después*. Undated manuscript.
Cedillo, Adela. *El fuego y el silencio. Historia de las Fuerzas de Liberación Nacional Mexicanas (1969–1974)*. BA Tesis, Universidad Nacional Autónoma de México, 2008.
Cedillo, Adela. *El suspiro del silencio. De la reconstrucción de las Fuerzas de Liberación Nacional a la fundación del Ejército Zapatista de Liberación Nacional (1974–1983)*. MA Tesis, Universidad Nacional Autónoma de México, 2010.

Cedillo, Adela. "Mujeres, guerrilla y terror estatal en la época de la *revoltura* en México." Unpublished article, 2010.
Meneghini, Mario. "Doctrina de seguridad nacional y guerra antisubversiva," lecture presented on October 2006, at the III Jornadas "La hispanidad hoy" at the University of Córdoba, Argentina, http://bitacorapi.blogia.com/2006/103101-doctrina-de-seguridad-nacional-y-guerra-antisubversiva.php
Muñoz Cortes, Alicia. *The Struggle of the Mujeres to Liberate Olga Talamante, A Political Prisoner.* Master's Thesis: San José State University, 1999.
Oikión Solano, Verónica, "Juventud y Revolución. La Central Nacional de Estudiantes Democráticos," paper presented in the *XIII Reunión de Historiadores de México, Estados Unidos y Canadá*, Santiago de Querétaro, 26–30 October 2010, at http://13mexeuacan.colmex.mx/
Oikión Solano, Verónica, "*Diario Bastardo.* Un testimonio carcelario para la memoria histórica del Movimiento de Acción Revolucionaria," paper presented at the *Seminario Internacional Políticas de la Memoria en regímenes democráticos. Las experiencias española y mexicana en contraste*, Zamora, El Colegio de Michoacán, 12–13 May 2005.
Peñaloza Torres, Alejandro. *La Lucha de la Esperanza: Historia del MAR (1965-1971)*, BA Thesis, ENAH, 2004.
Reyes Peláez, Juan Fernando. *Los movimientos armados en México (1943-1985)*, unpublished manuscript.
Tamayo, Sergio. *The 20 Mexican Octobers: A Study of Citizenship and Social Movements.* PhD dissertation, University of Texas at Austin, 1994.

Articles

Bizberg, Ilán. "*La transformation politique du Mexique : fin de l'ancien régime et apparition du nouveau ?*" in *Critique Internationale*. Paris: n°19, April 2003.
Braun, Herbert. "Protests of Engagement: Dignity, False Love, and Self Love in Mexico During 1968," *Comparative Studies in Society and History* (July 1997): 511–549.
Carr, Barr. "Mexican Communism 1968–1981: Eurocommunism in the Americas?" *Journal of Latin American Studies* 17, 1 (May 1985): 201–228.
Doyle, Kate. "After the Revolution: Lázaro Cárdenas and the Movimiento de Liberación Nacional" [electronic briefing book]. *The National Security Archive*, 2004.
Gómez Caballero, Alma. "Una breve cronología que enmarca: Madera 1965: las causas." September 21, 2005. http://www.jornada.unam.mx/2005/11/07/informacion/87_madera.html (accessed May 31, 2006).
Gómezjara, Francisco. "La experiencia cooperativa coprera de Costa Grande, Guerrero." *Revista del México Agrario* 9:4 (1976): 131–140.
Gómezjara, Francisco. "El proceso político de Jenaro Vázquez Rojas hacia la guerrilla campesina." *Revista Mexicana de Ciencias Políticas y Sociales,* 88, April–June (1977): 87–127.
Guzmán Macario, Pável Uliánov. "Guerrilleros michoacanos," in *Cuarto Poder de Michoacán*, Morelia, 10 January 2011.
Hirales Morán, Gustavo Adolfo. "*La guerra secreta, 1970-1978,*" in *Nexos*. México: n°54, June 1982.
"Madera '65: Cronología: ¿Cómo se fue Fraguando el Ataque?," *El Heraldo de Chihuahua*, September 23, 1995.

Martinez, Alma. "Un Continente, Una Cultura?: The Political Dialectic for a United Chicana/o and Pan American Popular Political Theater Front, Mexico City, 1974," Dissertation, Stanford University, 2006.

Martinez, Elizabeth. "A View from Nuevo Mexico: Recollections of the *Movimiento* Left." *Monthly Review* 54: 3 (July–August 2002), 79–86.

Mateos-Vega, Mónica. "Existe otro México clandestino más peligroso que la guerrilla: Entrevista con Carlos Montemayor." *La Jornada*, February 28, 2007, online (accessed May 29, 2008).

Mendoza García, Jorge. "Otra ofensiva gubernamental: la ideologización hacia la guerrilla." *Memoria*, 149, 18–27.

Meyer, Lorenzo. "El presidencialismo: Del populismo al neoliberalismo," *Revista Mexicana de Sociología*, 55, 2 (April–June 1993).

Ordorika, Imanol. "The Limits of University Autonomy: Power and Politics at the Universidad Autónoma de México." *Higher Education* 46, 3 (October 2003): 361–388.

Pimentel, Julio and Abdallán Guzmán Cruz. "Sobre la guerra sucia en Michoacán," in *Cambio de Michoacán*. Morelia, 25 June 2005.

Ponce, Samuel. "Fabricio Apolo Gómez Souza: 'Todas las formas de lucha son válidas si cambian la realidad," in *Cambio de Michoacán*. Morelia, 26 January 2002, 5.

Ponce de León, Alberto, "El FBI en México: Un secuestro frustrado en la frontera," http://erickfalcon.wordpress.com/about/el-fbi-en-mexico-un-secuestro-frustrado-en-la-frontera (accessed 2010).

Renard, María Cristina. "Movimiento campesino y organizaciones políticas. Simojovel-Huitiupán (1974–1990)." *Revista Chiapas*, 4, http://membres.multimania.fr/revistachiapas/No4/ch4renard.html (accessed 2010).

Rico, Maité and Bertrand de la Grange. "Entrevista con Salvador Morales Garibay." *Letras libres*, (February 1999), http://www.letraslibres.com/index.php?art=5673.

Rico Galán, Víctor. "Chihuahua: de la desesperación a la muerte." *Sucesos para todos*, October 15, 1965.

Sánchez, Consuelo. "El significado actual de la rebelión estudiantil de 1968. Más allá del liberalismo y la izquierda liberal." *Memoria, Revista de Política y Cultura*, 247, October 2010, 55–62.

Sherman, John W. "Comparing Failed Revolutions: Recent Studies on Colombia, El Salvador, and Chiapas," *Latin American Research Review* 41:2 (2006), 260–268.

Vargas Valdez, Jesús. "Los Olvidados." *La Fragua de los Tiempos*. March 18, 2001. http://www.madera1965.com.mx/buscadocs.html (accessed April 10, 2011).

Zolov, Eric. "Expanding our Conceptual Horizons: The Shift from an Old to a New Left in Latin America," *A Contracorriente: A Journal of Social History and Literature in Latin America* 5: 2 (Winter 2008): 47–73.

Internet Primary Sources

Alonso Vargas, José Luis. "*Los "Guajiros," orígenes y proyecto político.*" http://www.centrodeinvestigacioneshistoricas.com/los_guajiros.htm (accessed 2007).

Centro de Investigaciones Históricas de los Movimientos Sociales *"Rubén Jaramillo Ménez.»* "*Testimonio acerca de un compañero: Fernando Salinas Mora 'el Richard'*.» http://www.centrodeinvestigacioneshistoricas.com/fernando_salinas.htm (accessed 2007).

Inter American Court of Human Rights. *Caso Radilla Pacheco vs Estados Unidos Mexicanos:* http://www.corteidh.or.cr/docs/casos/articulos/seriec_209_esp.pdf (accessed 2010).
Salcedo García, Carlos. "*Testimonios sobre la vida de Olivia Ledesma Flores.*" http://www.centrodeinvestigacioneshistoricas.com/olivia_ledezma.htm (accessed 2007).

Websites

http://cihmsac.blogspot.com/ (accessed 2011).
http://investigacionesrubenjaramillomenez.blogspot.com/ (accessed 2011).
http://guerrasuciamexicana.blogspot.com/ (accessed 2011).
http://palabra.ezln.org.mx/comunicados/ (accessed 2011).
http://www.gwu.edu/~nsarchiv/mexico/ (accessed 2011).

Records and Films

Un hombre llamado Lucio: Comandante: Lucio Cabañas Barrientos, Vol. I–II. Discos Pueblo Rebelde.
Tort, Gerardo, director. *The Guerrilla and the Hope: Lucio Cabañas.* México, DF: La Rabia Films, 2005.
Retes, Gabriel, Director. *El bulto.* 1992, 105 mins. DVD.

Interviews

José Bracho, interview by Alexander Aviña, March 9 and May 15, 2007, Acapulco, Gro.
Hilario Mesino, interview by Alexander Aviña, May 17, 2007, Atoyac de Alvarez, Gro.
Tita Radilla, interview by Alexander Aviña, May 16, 2007, Atoyac de Alvarez, Gro.
Consuelo Solís Morales, interview by Alexander Aviña, May 30, 2007, Mexico City.
Antonio Orozco Michel, interview by Fernando Herrera Calderón, July 2008, tape recording, Guadalajara, Jalisco.
Miguel Topete, interview by Fernando Herrera Calderón, July 2008, tape recording and notes, Guadalajara, Jalisco.
José Luis Esparza, interview by Fernando Herrera Calderón, March 2010, tape recording, Mexico City.
Raúl Alvarez Garín, interview by Fernando Herrera Calderón, July 2008, Mexico City, tape recording and notes, Comité 68.
Maricela Balderas Silva, interview by Fernando Herrera Calderón, July 2008, notes and tape recording, Guadalajara, Jalisco.
Bertha Lilia Gutiérrez, interview by Fernando Herrera Calderón, July 2008, tape recording, Guadalajara, Jalisco.
Carmen Landa, interview by Elaine Carey, October 21, 1997, Mexico City.
Aída González, interview by Elaine Carey, November 30, 1997, San Mateo Tlatenango, Mexico.
Lillian Lieberman, interview by Elaine Carey, April 4, 1997, Mexico City.
Marcelino Perelló, interview by Elaine Carey, June 6, 1997, Mexico City.
"Renee," ex FLN militant, interview by Adela Cedillo, June 12, 2009, Mexico City.

María Gloria Benavides, interview by Adela Cedillo, February 12, 2004, Mexico City.
Collective interview with Carib people by Adela Cedillo, December 2003, municipality of Ocosingo, Chiapas.
Manuel Méndez, interview by Adela Cedillo, March 23, 2005, municipality of Ocosingo, Chiapas.
Ernesto Reyes, interview by Alan Gómez, tape recording, July 27, 1999, Mexico City.
Raúl Salinas, interview by Alan Gómez, audio recording, June 16, 2004, Austin, Texas.
Isael Petronio Nájera Cantú, interview by Romain Robinet, 2005.

Secondary Works

Aboites, Luis. *Breve historia de Chihuahua*. México, DF: El Colegio de México, 1994.
Acosta Chaparro. Arturo. *Movimiento subversivo en México*. México, DF: s.n., 1990.
Agamben, Giorgio. *Homo Sacer: Sovereign Power and Bare Life*. Stanford: Stanford University Press, 1995.
Aguayo, Sergio. *La charola. Una historia de los servicios de inteligencia en México*. México, DF: Grijalbo, 2001.
Aguilar Camín, Héctor and Lorenzo Meyer. *A la sombra de la Revolución Mexicana*. México, DF: Cal y Arena, 1989.
Aguilar Terrés, María de la Luz, ed. *Memoria del Primer Encuentro Nacional de Mujeres Exguerrilleras*. México, DF: n.e. 2007.
Agustín, José. *Tragicomedia mexicana 2: La vida en México de 1970 a 1988*. México, DF: Planeta, 1990.
Agustín, José. *Tragicomedia Mexicana 1: La vida en México de 1940 a 1970*. México, DF: Planeta, 1998.
Alonso, Ana M. *Thread of Blood: Colonialism, Revolution, and Gender on Mexico's Northern Frontier*. Tucson: University of Arizona Press, 1995.
Andreas, Peter. *Border Games: Policing the U.S.–Mexico Divide*. Ithaca: Cornell University Press, 2000.
Angulo, Alfredo. *La hora de los mártires: Apuntes para la historia del movimiento estudiantil y guerrillero en Guadalajara, 1970–1976*. México: Ediciones La casa de los cuentos del mago ciego, 1997.
Aranda Flores, Antonio. *Los cívicos guerrerenses*. México, DF: Luysil, 1979.
Arias, Enrique Desmond and Daniel M. Goldstein, eds. *Violent Democracies in Latin America*. Durham: Duke University Press, 2010.
Armendáriz, Minerva. *Morir de sed junto a la fuente*. México: Universidad Obrera de México, 2001.
Ascencio, Esteban, ed. 1968: *Más alla del mito*. México, DF: Ediciones Milenio, 1998.
Aviña, Alexander. "'We have returned to Porfirian Times:' Neopopulism, Counterinsurgency, and the Dirty War in Guerrero, Mexico, 1969–1976," in *Populism in 20th Century Mexico: The Presidencies of Lázaro Cárdenas and Luis Echeverría*, eds. Amelia M. Kiddle and María L.O. Muñoz, 106–121. Tucson: University of Arizona Press, 2010.
Bailey, John and Roy Godson, eds. *Organized Crime and Governability: Mexico and the U.S.–Mexico Borderlands*. Pittsburgh: University of Pittsburgh Press, 2000.
Bartra, Armando. *Los herederos de Zapata: movimientos campesinos posrevolucionarios en México, 1920–1980*. México, DF: Era, 1985.

Bartra, Armando. *Guerrero bronco: campesinos, ciudadanos y guerrilleros en la Costa Grande*. México, DF: Era, 2000.
Bartra, Roger ed. *Caciquismo y poder político en el México rural*. México, DF: Siglo XXI, 1975.
Basurto, Jorge. "Populism in Mexico: From Cárdenas to Cuauhtémoc," in *Populism in Latin America*, ed. Michael L. Connifff. Tuscaloosa: University of Alabama Press, 1999.
Becker, Marjorie. *Setting the Virgin on Fire: Lázaro Cárdenas, Michoacán Peasants and the Redemption of the Mexican Revolution*. Berkeley: University of California Press, 1995.
Bellingeri, Marco. *Del agrarismo armado a la guerra de los pobres: Ensayos de guerrilla rural en el México contemporáneo, 1940–1974*. México, DF: Ediciones Casa Juan Pablos/Secretaría de Cultura de la Ciudad de México, 2003.
Benjamin, Walter. "On the Theory of Knowledge, Theory of Progress," in *The Arcades Project*, trans. Howard Eiland and Kevin McLaughlin. Harvard: Harvard University Press, 1999.
Benjamin, Walter. "On the Concept of History," in *Selected Writings: Volume 4, 1938–1940*, eds. Howard Eiland and Michael W. Jennings. Cambridge, MA: The Belknap Press of Harvard University Press, 2003.
Bensussan, Gérard and Labica, Georges. *Dictionnaire critique du marxisme*. Paris: PUF, 1999.
Berger, Dan, ed. *The Hidden 1970s: Histories of Radicalism*. New Jersey: Rutgers Press, 2010.
Blackwell, Maylei. *¡Chicana Power! Contested Histories of Feminism in the Chicano Movement*. Austin: University of Texas Press, 2011.
Brands, Hal. *Latin America's Cold War*. Cambridge: Harvard University Press, 2010.
Buffie, Edward and Allen Sangines Krause. "Mexico 1958–86: From Stabilizing Development to the Debt Crisis," in *Developing Country Debt and the World Economy*, ed. Jeffrey D. Sachs. Chicago: University of Chicago Press, 1989.
Campa, Valetín. *Mi testimonio: Experiencias de un comunista mexicano*. México, DF: Ediciones de Cultura Popular, 1978.
Cansino, César and Israel Covarrubias. *Sobre el populismo. En el nombre del pueblo. Muerte y resurrección del populismo en México*. Ciudad Juárez: Universidad Autónoma de Ciudad Juárez & Centro de Estudios de Política comparada, Xalapa, 2006.
Careaga, Gabriel. *Mitos y fantasías de la clase media en México*. México, DF: Cal y Arena, 2005.
Carey, Elaine. *Plaza of Sacrifices: Gender, Power, and Terror in 1968 Mexico*. Albuquerque: University of New Mexico Press, 2005.
Carpizo, Jorge. *Derechos humanos y ombudsman*. México, DF: Comisión Nacional de Derechos Humanos, 1993.
Carr, Barry. *Marxism and Communism in Twentieth-Century Mexico*. Lincoln and London: University of Nebraska Press, 1992.
Carr, Barry. "The Fate of the Vanguard under a Revolutionary State: Marxism's Contribution to the Construction of the Great Arch," in *Everyday Forms of State Formation: Revolution and the Negotiation of Rule in Modern Mexico*, eds. Gilbert Joseph and Daniel Nugent, 326–352. Durham: Duke University Press, 1994.
Caruth, Cathy, ed. *Trauma. Explorations in Memory*. Baltimore: Johns Hopkins University Press, 1995.
Castañeda, Jorge. *Utopia Unarmed: The Latin American Left after the Cold War*. New York: Vintage Books, 1994.

Castañeda, Salvador. *La patria celestial*. México, DF: Ediciones Cal y Arena, 1992.
Castañeda, Salvador. *Diario bastardo (Diario desde la cárcel)*. Torreón, Instituto Coahuilense de Cultura-Gobierno del Estado de Coahuila, 2004.
Castañeda, Salvador. *La negación del número. (La guerrilla en México, 1965–1996: una aproximación crítica)*. México, DF: Consejo Nacional para la Cultura y las Artes & Ediciones Sin Nombre, 2006.
Castellanos, Laura. *México armado: 1943–1981*. México, DF: Era, 2007.
Cavazos Garza, Israel. *Breve historia de Nuevo León*. México, DF: COLMEX/FCE, 1994.
Cedillo, Adela. *El fuego y el silencio. Historia de las Fuerzas de Liberación Nacional*. México, DF: Edición del Comité del 68 Pro Libertades Democráticas, A.C., 2008.
Chavez, Ernesto. *"¡Mi Raza Primero!" (My People First!): Nationalism, Identity, and Insurgency in the Chicano Movement in Los Angeles, 1966–1978*. Berkeley: University of California Press, 2002.
Chong, José Luis. *Las guerrillas de México: Testimonios orales y artísticos*. México DF: Universidad Autónoma de México, 2005.
Churchill Ward and Jim Vanderwall. *The COINTELPRO Papers: Documents from the FBI's Secret Wars Against Dissent in the United States*. Boston: South End Press, 2001.
Cleaver, Harry. "The Inversion of Class Perspective in Marxian Theory: From Valorization to Self-Valorization," in *Open Marxism: Theory and Practice* vol. II, eds. Werner Bonefeld, Richard Gunn and Kosmas Psychopedis. London: Pluto Press, 1992. 106–144.
Condés Lara, Enrique. *Represión y rebelión en México (1959–1985)*, vol. I–III. México, DF: Benemérita Universidad Autónoma de Puebla & Miguel Ángel Porrúa Editor, 2007–2009.
Cook, Maria Lorena. *Organizing Dissent: Unions, the State and the Democratic Teachers' Movement in Mexico*. University Park: Pennsylvania State University Press, 1996.
Córdova, Arnaldo. *La revolución en crisis: la aventura del maximato*. México, DF: Era, 1974.
Cornejo, Alfredo Mendoza. *Organizaciones y movimientos estudiantiles en Jalisco, 1963–1970*. Guadalajara: Universidad de Guadalajara, 1994.
Cosío Villegas, Daniel. *La sucesión: Desenlace y perspectivas*. México, DF: Cuadernos de Joaquín Mortiz, 1976.
Cruz, José G. *Traición a la Patria*. México, Ediciones José G. Cruz, 1971.
Davis, Diana E. *Mexico City in the Twentieth Century*. Philadelphia: Temple University Press, 1994.
Debray, Régis. *Revolution in the Revolution? Armed Struggle and Political Struggle in Latin America*. New York: Grove, 1967.
Delgado, Álvaro. *El Ejército de Dios: Nuevas revelaciones sobre la extrema derecha en México*. México, DF: Plaza y Janés, 2004.
Della Porta, Donatella. *Social Movements, Political Violence, and the State. A Comparative Analysis of Italy and Germany*. New York: Cambridge University Press, 1995.
Della Rocca, Salvador Martínez. *Estado y universidad en México, 1920–1968: Historia de los movimientos estudiantiles en la UNAM*. México: J. Boldó i Climent, 1986.
Dios Corona, Sergio René. *La historia que no pudieron borrar: La guerra sucia en Jalisco, 1970–85*. Guadalajara: La Casa del Mago, 2004.
Encarnación Ursúa, Florencio. *Las luchas de los copreros guerrerenses*. México, DF: Editora y Distribuidora Nacional de Publicaciones, 1977.
Engels, Frederick. *Anti-Dühring*. Progress Publishers, 1947.

Estandía, Rogelio Cárdenas. *Luis Echeverría Álvarez: Entre lo personal y lo político.* México, DF: Editorial Planeta, 2008.
Estrada Castañón, Alba Teresa. *El movimiento anticaballerista: Guerrero 1960, Crónica de un conflicto.* Chilpancingo: Universidad Autónoma de Guerrero, 2001.
Estrada Saavedra, Marco. *La comunidad armada rebelde y el EZLN: un estudio histórico y sociológico sobre las bases de apoyo zapatistas en las cañadas tojolabales de la Selva Lacandona (1930–2005).* México, DF: COLMEX, 2007.
Farber, Peter and Jeff Roche. *The Conservative Sixties.* New York: Peter Lang Publishing 2003.
Fazio, Carlos. *Samuel Ruiz. El caminante.* México, DF: Espasa Calpe, 1994.
Flamm, Michael. *Law and Order: Street Crime, Civil Unrest, and the Crisis of Liberalism in the 1960s.* Columbia University Press, 2007.
Foran, John. *Taking Power: On the Origins of Third World Revolutions.* Cambridge: Cambridge University Press, 2005.
García de León, Antonio. *Fronteras interiores. Chiapas: una modernidad particular.* México, DF: Océano, 2002.
Garín, Raúl Álvarez. *La Estela de Tlatelolco: Una Reconstrucción histórica del Movimiento estudiantil del 68.* México, DF: Ítaca, 2002.
Glick, Brian. *Covert Action Against U.S. Activists and What We Can Do About It.* Boston: South End Press, 1989.
Glockner, Fritz. *Memoria Roja: Historia de la Guerrilla en México de 1943 a 1968.* México DF: Ediciones B, 2007.
Gómezjara, Francisco. *Bonapartismo y lucha campesina en la Costa Grande de Guerrero.* México: Editorial Posada, 1979.
Grandin, Greg. *The Last Colonial Massacre: Latin America and the Cold War.* Chicago: University of Chicago Press, 2004.
Grandin, Greg and Gilbert Joseph, eds. *A Century of Revolution: Insurgent and Counterinsurgent Violence during Latin America's Long Cold War.* Durham: Duke University Press, 2010.
Grange, Bertrand de la y Maité Rico. *Marcos, la genial impostura.* México, DF: Aguilar, 1998.
Gudiño, Hugo Sánchez. *Génesis, desarrollo y consolidación de los grupos estudiantiles de choque en la UNAM.* México, DF: Miguel Ángel Porrúa, 2006.
Haber, Paul Lawrence. *Power from Experience: Urban Popular Movements in Late Twentieth-Century Mexico.* University Park: Penn State University Press, 2006.
Harvey, Neil. *The Chiapas Rebellion. The Struggle for Land and Democracy.* Durham: Duke University Press, 1998.
Hegel, G.W.F. *Science of Logic.* Cambridge: Cambridge University Press, 2010.
Hellman, Judith Adler. *Mexico in Crisis.* New York, Holmes & Meier Publishers. 1979.
Hernández, Lucio Rangel. *La Universidad Michoacana y el Movimiento Estudiantil 1966–1986.* Morelia: Universidad Michoacana de San Nicolás de Hidalgo, 2009.
Heyman, Josiah, ed. *States and Illegal Practices.* London: Berg Publishers, 1999.
Hipólito, Simón. *Guerrero, amnistía y represión.* México, DF: Editorial Grijalbo, 1982.
Hirales Morán, Gustavo Adolfo. *La Liga Comunista 23 de Septiembre: orígenes y naufragio.* México, DF: Ediciones de Cultura Popular, 1977.
Hirales Morán, *Memoria de la guerra de los justos.* México, DF: Cal y Arena, 1996.
Hobsbawm, Eric. *The Age of Extremes: The Short Twentieth Century 1914–1991.* London: Joseph, 1994.

Hodges, Donald. *Mexican Anarchism after the Revolution.* Austin: University of Texas Press, 1992.
Jacobs, Ian. *Ranchero Revolt: The Mexican Revolution in Guerrero.* Austin: University of Texas Press, 1983.
James, Joy, ed. *Imprisoned Intellectuals: America's Political Prisoners Write on Life, Liberation and Rebellion.* Lanham, MD: Rowman and Littlefield, 2003.
Jardón, Raúl. *El Espionaje contra el Movimiento Estudiantil: Los documentos de la Dirección Federal de Seguridad y las agencias de inteligencia estadounidense en 1968.* México, DF: Ítaca, 2003.
Jelin, Elizabeth. *State Repression and the Labors of Memory.* Minneapolis: SSRC and University of Minnesota Press, 2003.
Jiménez, Alfredo Tecla. *Universidad, burguesía y proletariado.* México DF: Ediciones de Cultural Popular, 1978.
Joseph, Gilbert M. and Daniela Spenser, eds. *In from the Cold. Latin America's New Encounter with the Cold War.* Durham: Duke University Press, 2008.
Katsiaficas, George. *The Imagination of the New Left: A Global Analysis of 1968.* Boston: South End Press, 1987.
Katz, Friedrich. *The Life and Times of Pancho Villa.* Stanford: Stanford University Press, 1998.
Kearns, Gerry. "Bare Life, Political Violence, and the Territorial Structure of Britain and Ireland," in *Violent Geographies: Fear, Terror, and Political Violence*, eds. Derek Gregory and Allan Pred, 7–36. London: Routledge, 2007.
Kenney, Michael. *From Pablo to Osama: Trafficking and Terrorist Networks, Government Bureaucracies, and Competitive Adaptation.* University Park: Pennsylvania State University Press, 2007.
Kiddle, Amelia M. and María L.O. Muñoz, eds. *Populism in 20th Century Mexico: The Presidencies of Lázaro Cárdenas and Luis Echeverría.* Tucson: University of Arizona Press, 2010.
Kilcullen, David. *The Accidental Guerrilla: Fighting Small Wars in the Midst of a Big One.* Oxford: Oxford University Press, 2009.
Kilcullen, David. *Counterinsurgency.* Oxford: Oxford University Press, 2010.
Knight, Alan. "Caciquismo in Twentieth-Century Mexico," in *Caciquismo in Twentieth-Century Mexico*, eds. Alan Knight and Wil Pansters. London: Institute for the Study of the Americas, 2005.
Krauze, Enrique. *Mexico Biography of Power: A History of Modern Mexico, 1810–1996*, translated by Hank Heifetz. New York: Harper Perennial, 1997.
LaCapra, Dominick. *Writing History, Writing Trauma.* Baltimore: Johns Hopkins University Press, 2000.
Laclau, Ernesto and Chantal Mouffe. *Hegemony and Socialist Strategy.* London: Verso, 1989.
Lara, Enrique Condés. *Represión y rebelión en México (1959–1985)*, vol. I–III. México, DF: Porrúa, 2007–2009.
Lawson, Chappell. *Building the Fourth Estate: Democratization and the Rise of the Free Press in Mexico.* Berkeley: University of California Press, 2002.
Le Bot, Yvon. *El sueño zapatista. Entrevistas con el Subcomandante Marcos, el mayor Moisés y el comandante Tacho, del Ejército Zapatista de Liberación Nacional.* Barcelona: Plaza y Janés, 1997.
Legorreta Díaz, María del Carmen. *Religión, política y guerrilla en Las Cañadas de la Selva Lacandona.* México, DF: Cal y Arena, 1998.

Lewis, Paul. *Generals and Guerrillas: The Dirty War in Argentina*. Westport, CT: Praeger, 2002.
Leyva Solano, Xóchitl y Gabriel Ascencio Franco. *Lacandonia al filo del agua*. México, DF: CIESAS/UNAM/FCE, 2002.
López, Jaime. *10 años de guerrillas en México, 1964–1974*. México, DF: Editorial Posada S.A., 1974.
Loza Ochoa, Oscar. *Tiempo de espera*. Culiacán: Universidad Autónoma de Sinaloa-Comisión de Derechos Humanos, 2004.
Mabry, Donald. *The Mexican University and the State: Student Conflicts, 1910–1971*. College Station: Texas A&M University Press, 1982.
Mao Zedong. *Selected Military Writings of Mao Tse-tung*. Peking: Foreign Languages Press, 1966.
Mariscal, Jorge. *Brown-Eyed Children of the Sun: Lessons from the Chicano Movement, 1965–1975*. Alburquerque: University of New Mexico Press, 2005.
Marx, Karl. "Speech at the anniversary of the *People's Paper*," in *Marx and Engels Selected Works, Volume 1*. Moscow: Progress Publishers, 1969.
Marx, Karl. *Capital: A Critique of Political Economy, Volume 1*. New York: Penguin Classics, 1990.
Mayo, Baloy. *La guerrilla de Genaro y Lucio. Análisis y resultados*. México, DF: Diógenes, 1980.
McAdam, Doug, John D. McCarthy and Mayer N. Zald, eds. *Comparative Perspectives on Social Movements: Political Opportunities, Mobilizing Structures, and Cultural Framings*. Cambridge: Cambridge University Press, 1996.
Medina, Luis. *Hacia el nuevo Estado: México, 1920–1994*. México, DF: FCE, 1995.
Meyer, Jean, *Samuel Ruiz en San Cristóbal, 1960–2000*. México, DF: Tusquets Editores, 2000.
Michel, Antonio Orozco. *La fuga de Oblatos: Una historia de la LC23 de Septiembre*. Guadalajara: Casa del Mago, 2007.
Montemayor, Carlos. *Guerra en el paraíso*. México, DF: SeixBarral, 1997.
Montemayor, Carlos. *Las armas del alba: Novela*. México, DF: Joaquín Mortiz, 2003.
Montemayor, Carlos. *La fuga*. México, DF: Fondo de Cultura Económica, 2007.
Montemayor, Carlos. *La guerrilla recurrente*. México, DF: Debate, 2007.
Montemayor, Carlos. *Violencia de estado en México: Antes y después de 1968*. México DF: Grijalbo, 2010.
Montemayor, Carlos. *Las mujeres del alba*. México, DF: Grijalbo, 2010.
Montemayor, Carlos. "Los movimientos guerrilleros y los servicios de inteligencia. Notas reiteradas y nuevas conclusiones," in *Los grandes problemas de México. Seguridad nacional y seguridad interior*, eds. Arturo Alvarado and Mónica Serrano. México, DF: El Colegio de México, 2010, 41–59.
Mora, Manuel. "En la búsqueda por la democracia: La participación en la ciudad desde el protagonismo de los jóvenes," in *La democracia de los de abajo en Jalisco*, eds. Morge Alonso and Juan Manuel Ramírez. Guadalajara: Universidad de Guadalajara, 1996.
Niebla, Gilberto Guevara. *1968 largo camino a la democracia*. México DF: Ediciones Cal y Arena, 2008.
Oikión Solano, Verónica and Marta Eugenia García Ugarte, eds. "El Movimiento de Acción Revolucionaria. Una historia de radicalización política," in *Movimientos armados en México, siglo XX*, eds. Verónica Oikión Solano and Marta Eugenia García Ugarte. Zamora: El Colegio de Michoacán/ CIESAS, 2006, vol. II, 417–459.

Oikión Solano, Verónica and Marta Eugenia García Ugarte, eds. *Movimientos armados en México, siglo XX*. Zamora, Michoacán: El Colegio de Michoacán/CIESAS, 2007.
Oikión Solano, Verónica and Marta Eugenia García Ugarte, eds. "El movimiento universitario de 1966 en Michoacán: una historia de confrontación política," in *154 años de movimientos estudiantiles en Iberoamérica*, eds. Silvia González Marín and Ana María Sánchez Sáenz. México, DF: Instituto de Investigaciones Bibliográficas, UNAM, 2011, 387–402.
Oikión Solano, Verónica and Marta Eugenia García Ugarte, eds. "El impacto de la oposición armada en la Reforma Política del Estado. Las decisiones de 1977," in *Formas de gobierno en México. Poder político y actores sociales a través del tiempo*, ed. Víctor Gayol. Zamora, El Colegio de Michoacán, 2011 (in press).
Olivo, Ramón Gil. "Orígenes de la guerrilla en Guadalajara en la década de los setenta," in *Movimientos Armados en México, siglo XX*, eds. Verónica Oikión Solano and Marta Eugenia García Ugarte. Zamora: El Colegio de Michoacán/CIESAS, 2006, 549–566.
Olmos, David Cilia and Enrique González Ruíz, eds. *Testimonios de la guerra sucia*. México: Editorial Tierra Roja, 2006.
Orive, Adolfo, ed. *Poder popular. Construcción de ciudadanía y comunidad*. México, DF: Juan Pablos Editor, 2010.
Ornelas Gómez, Francisco. *Sueños de libertad*. Chihuahua: [no publisher], 2005.
Orozco Orozco, Víctor. *Diez ensayos sobre Chihuahua*. Chihuahua: Doble Hélice, 2003.
Ortiz, Orlando. *Genaro Vázquez*. México, DF: Diógenes, 1972.
Orwell, George. *The Road to Wigan Pier*. London: Victor Gollancz, 1937.
Padilla, Tanalís. *Rural Resistance in the Land of Zapata: The Jaramillista Movement and the Myth of the Pax-Priísta, 1940–1962*. Durham: Duke University Press, 2008.
Palomares Peña, Noé G. *Propietarios Norteamericanos y Reforma Agraria en Chihuahua, 1917–1942*. Juárez: Universidad Autónoma de Ciudad Juárez, 1991.
Parra Orozco, Miguel Ángel. *Oro Verde: Madera, Vida de una Región Chihuahuense*. Chihuahua: [no publisher], 1998.
Paz Paredes, Lorena and Rosario Cabo. "Café caliente," in *Crónicas del sur: Utopías campesinas en Guerrero*, ed. Armando Bartra, México: Era, 2000, 129–274.
Pereyra, Daniel. *De Moncada a Chiapas: historia de la lucha armada en América Latina*. Madrid: Libros de la Catarata, 1994.
Pérez Castro, Ana Bella. *Entre montañas y cafetales: luchas agrarias en el Norte de Chiapas*. México, DF: UNAM/IIA, 1989.
Pineda Ochoa, Fernando. *En las profundidades del mar (El oro no llego de Moscú)*. México: Plaza y Valdés, 2003.
Poniatowska, Elena. *Massacre in Mexico*. Columbia: University of Missouri Press, 1991.
Pulido, Laura. *Brown, Black, Yellow and Left: The Making of the Third World Left in Los Angeles, 1968–1974*. Berkeley: University of California Press, 2006.
Quezada, Sergio Aguayo. *La Charola: Una historia de los servicios de inteligencia en México*. México DF: Grijalbo, 2001.
Radilla Martínez, Andrea. *Poderes, saberes y sabores: una historia de resistencia de los cafeticultores, Atoyac, 1940–1974*. Chilpancingo: self-published, 1998.
Revueltas, José. *México 68: Juventud y revolución* México, DF: Ediciones Era, 1978.
Ríos Figueroa, Julio. *Siglo XX: muerte y resurrección de la Iglesia Católica en Chiapas: dos estudios históricos*. San Cristóbal de las Casas: UNAM, 2000.
Rivas Ontiveros, José René. *La izquierda estudiantil en la UNAM: Organizaciones, movilizaciones y liderazgos (1958–1972)*. México, DF: Porrúa, 2007.

Rodríguez Munguía, Jacinto. *La otra guerra secreta: Los archivos prohibidos de la prensa y el poder.* México, DF: Random House Mondadori, 2007.

Román Román, Salvador. *Revuelta cívica en Guerrero (1957–1960): La democracia imposible.* México, DF: Instituto Nacional de Estudios Históricos de la Revolución Mexicana, 2003.

Salas Obregón, Ignacio Arturo. *Cuestiones fundamentales del movimiento revolucionario o manifiesto al proletariado.* México, DF: Editorial Tierra Roja, 2003.

Sandoval Cruz, Pablo. *El movimiento social de 1960.* Chilpancingo: Universidad Autónoma de Guerrero, 1999.

Santos Valdés, José. *Madera: Razón de un Martirologio.* México, DF: [no publisher], 1968.

Saragoza, Alex. *The Monterrey Elite and the Mexican State, 1880–1940.* Austin: University of Texas Press, 1988.

Scarry, Elaine. *The Body in Pain. The Making and Unmaking of the World.* New York: Oxford University Press, 1985.

Scherer, Julio and Carlos Monsiváis. *Los patriotas: de Tlatelolco a la guerra sucia.* México, DF: Aguilar, 2004.

Schiavon, Jorge A. "México-Estados Unidos. Estabilidad y seguridad a cambio de autonomía," in *En busca de una nación soberana. Relaciones internacionales de México, siglos XIX y XX*, eds. Jorge A. Schiavon, Daniela Spenser and Mario Vázquez Olivera. México, DF: CIDE/SRE, 2006, 423–462.

Schmidt, Samuel. *The Deterioration of the Mexican Presidency: The Years of Luis Echeverría.* Tucson: University of Arizona Press, 1991.

Semo, Ilán ed. *La transición interrumpida, México 1968–1988.* México: Universidad Iberoamericana, 1993.

Shapira, Yoram. *Mexican Foreign Policy Under Echeverría.* Beverly Hills, CA: Sage Publications, 1978.

Sherman, John W. "The 'Mexican Miracle' and Its Collapse," in *The Oxford History of Mexico*, ed. Michael C. Meyer and William H. Beezley. Oxford: Oxford University Press, 2000.

Sierra, Carlos J. *Luis Echeverría: Raíz y dinámica de su pensamiento.* México, DF: Testimonio de Atlacomulco, 1969.

Sierra Guzmán, Jorge Luis. *El Enemigo Interno: Contrainsurgencia y Fuerzas Armadas en México.* México, DF: Plaza y Janés/Universidad Iberoamericana, 2003.

Spenser, Daniela ed. *Espejos de la guerra fría: México, América Central y el Caribe.* México, DF: CIESAS/Porrúa, 2004.

Stern, Steve J. "New Approaches to the Study of Peasant Rebellion and Consciousness: Implications of the Andean Experience," in *Resistance, Rebellion, and Consciousness in the Andean Peasant World: 18th to 20th Centuries*, ed. Steve J. Stern, 3–28. Madison: University of Wisconsin Press, 1987.

Stoll, David. *Between Two Armies in the Ixil Towns of Guatemala.* New York: Columbia University Press, 1993.

Stoll, David. *Rigoberta Menchú and the Story of all Poor Guatemalans.* Boulder: Westview Press, 2008.

Suárez, Luis. *Lucio Cabañas: el guerrillero sin esperanza.* México: Grijalbo, 1985.

Subirats, Eduardo, Pilar Calveiro, et al. *Contra la tortura.* Monterrey: Fineo editorial, 2006.

Taibo II, Paco Ignacio. *'68.* Trans. Donald Nicholson-Smith. Seven Stories Press, New York, 2004.

Tello, Carlos. *La Política Económica en México, 1970–1976.* México, DF: Siglo XXI, 1979.

Tello, Carlos. *La rebelión de las Cañadas*. México, DF: Cal y Arena, 2000.
Toledo, Sonia. *Fincas, poder y cultura en Simojovel, Chiapas*. San Cristóbal: UNAM/UNACH, 2007.
Trouillot, Michel-Rolph. *Silencing the Past: Power and the Production of History*. Boston: Beacon Press, 1995.
Tupamaros. *Nous les Tupamaros*. Paris: Maspero, 1971.
Ulloa Bornemann, Alberto. *Surviving Mexico's Dirty War. A Political Prisoner's Memory*. Translated by Arthur Schmidt and Aurora Camacho de Schmidt. Philadelphia: Temple University, 2007. (In Spanish *Sendero en tinieblas*. México, DF: Ediciones Cal y Arena, 2004.)
Uribari, Gabriel A. *Tiempo de Echeverría*. México, DF: Martin Casillas Editores, 1985.
Vallejo, Demetrio. *Yo acuso*. México, DF: Editorial Hombre Nuevo, 1973.
Vaughan, Mary Kay. *Cultural Politics and in Revolution: Teachers, Peasants, and Schools in Mexico, 1930–1940*. Tucson: University of Arizona Press, 1997.
Vayssière, Pierre. *Les révolutions d'Amérique Latine*. Paris: Seuil, 2001.
Verdugo Arnoldo Martínez, ed. *Historia del comunismo en México*. México, DF: Grijalbo, 1985.
Vo Nguyen Giap. *People's War, People's Army: the Viet Công Insurrection Manual for Underdeveloped Countries*. New York: Praeger, 1962.
Vos, Jean de. *Una tierra para sembrar sueños. Historia reciente de la Selva Lacandona, 1950–2000*. México, DF: FCE, 2002.
Washbrook, Sara, ed. *Rural Chiapas Ten Years after the Zapatista Uprising*. New York: Routledge, 2007.
Wasserman, Mark. *Capitalists, Caciques, and Revolution: The Native Elite and Foreign Enterprise in Chihuahua, Mexico, 1854–1911*. Chapel Hill: University of North Carolina Press, 1984.
White, Christopher. *Creating a Third World: Mexico, Cuba, and the United States during the Castro Era*. Albuquerque: University of New Mexico Press, 2007.
Wickham-Crowley, Timothy P. *Guerrillas and Revolution in Latin America. A Comparative Study of Insurgents and Regimes since 1956*. Princeton, Princeton University Press, 1992.
Woldenberg, José. *Memoria de la izquierda*. México, DF: Cal y Arena, 1998.
Womack Jr., John. *Rebellion in Chiapas: An Historical Reader*. New York: The New Press, 1999.
Wood, Elizabeth Jean. *Insurgent Collective Action and Civil War in El Salvador*. New York: Cambridge University Press, 2003.
Wright, Thomas. *Latin America in the Era of the Cuban Revolution*. Westport: Praeger, 2001.
Yankelevich, Pablo. ed. *México, país refugio. La experiencia de los exilios en el siglo XX*. México, DF: Plaza y Valdés/CONACULTA, 2002.
Young, Cynthia. *Soul Power: Culture, Radicalism, and the Making of a U.S. Third World Left*. Durham: Duke University Press, 2006.
Yuval-Davis, Nira. "Género y nación," in *Mujeres y nacionalismos en América Latina*, ed. Natividad Gutiérrez Chong. México, DF: UNAM/IIS, 2004, 67–82.
Zamora, Emilio. *The World of the Mexican Worker in Texas*. College Station: Texas A&M University, 1993.
Zermeño, Sergio. *México: Una democracia utópica del movimiento estudiantil del 68*. México, DF: Siglo XXI Editores, 2003.
Zizek Slavoj. *In Defense of Lost Causes*. London: Verso, 2008.
Zolov, Eric. *Refried Elvis: The Rise of the Mexican Counterculture Movement*. Berkeley: University of California Press, 1999.

INDEX

agrarian movements (in Chihuahua) 11
Alemán, M. 3, 44, 183–4
Amnesty Law (1978) 71, 154
anarchists 3
anti-subversive campaign 7, 73, 172–3; archive materials 10; in Guerrero 54–5; methods of interrogation 8; "social program" 185; state terrorism 11, 12, 167; in the university 105, 109; urban repression 192–4; *see also* death flights
Aranguren Castiello, F. 137
Arizona Rangers 25
armed struggles (Mexico): peasant and worker response 7; differences between other revolutionary movements 7; Old and New Left 51; post-1968 62, 109–10, 149–50
Asociación Nacional Obrero Campesina Estudiantil (ANOCE) 90
Association of Youth Hope of the Fraternity (AJEF) 151
Atoyac 43, 44, 52–3
Autonomous University of Nuevo León (UANL) 5
Autonomous University of Sinaloa (UAS) 109
Avila Camacho, M. 3, 44

Bolshevik Revolution 61
Bracero Program 30
Brown Berets 87

Caballero Aburto, R. 47, 49
Cabañas Barrientes, L. 35, 48, 49–50, 190, 203; caciques (political bosses) 2; organizing in Durango 51; politicalización 41–2
Campa, V. 3
Campesino Brigade of Executions (BCA) 54; *see also* Party of the Poor
Cananea, Sonora 24–5
Cantú, Mario 81, 87, 89–90, 92, 96–8
Cárdenas Barajas L.: training the GPG 33
Cárdenas, L. 3, 25, 44, 48, 91, 110, 151, 157, 170;
exiles from Latin America 5
Carrillo Prieto, I. 204–6
Castro, F. 33
Catholic Church 110; in Chiapas 155
Centro Acción Social Autónomo (CASA) 88
Centro Cultural Rubén Salazar (CCRS) 90
Centro para la Libre Expresión Teatraly Artística (CLETA) 85, 92
Chacón, Ramón Raúl 81–2, 89–90, 92–3, 96, 98
charrismo 3
Charter of Economic Rights and Duties of States (United Nations) 172
Chiapas: agrarian reforms 155
Chicano (Movement) 12, 96–8; connection with struggles in Mexico 81–2; Echeverria 85–6; in San Antonio 87–8
Chicanos Organizados Revolucionarios de Aztlán (CORA) 89

Index

Chihuahua 3, 10
Coalition of Popular Forces (COP) 48
Cold War 1–2, 12, 149; Guerrero 55
Colegio Jacinto Treviño 81, 90, 93, 96
Colonia Rubén Jaramillo 81, 91–3, 97
Comité 68 205
Comité Eureka 144
Communist Youth (JC) 109, 113; Third Congress 110, 82
Constitution of 1917, 2
Corpus Christi Massacre 5, 85, 144
Counter Intelligence Program (COINTELPRO) 83, 86
counterculture 9
Cuatro Amigos 25
Cuba 3; Cold War policies and Mexico 5; Mexican guerrillas 5, 7
Cuban Revolution 20, 21, 60, 149, 184 187
Cuenca Díaz, H. 189–90

de la Barreda, L. 184
de la Madrid, M. 9, 194; *see also* DIPD, DISEN
de la O, P. 81–2
Debray, R. 21
"death flights" 8; drug transportation 9
Department of Agrarian Affairs and Colonization (DAAC) 28; occupation 30
Díaz Ordaz, G. 3, 4, 29, 30, 47, 111, 183, 187, 200, 202; on Madera assault 19; national security doctrine 7; post-Tlatelolco 108; violation of human rights 204
dictatorship of the proletariat 5
Directorate for Investigation and National Security (DISEN) 9, *see also* de la Madrid, M.
Dirty War in Mexico: compared to Chile and Argentina 8, 47, 108, 182–3, 199; in Argentina and Chile 82; published materials 10; in the social imaginary of society 9–10
Duncan Williams, A. 137, 193

Echeverría, L. 5, 19, 84–6, 90, 105, 172, 183, 188, 200, 202–3; aperture democrática 5, 105; exiles 5; national security doctrine 7; Tlatelolco Massacre 5
Ejidos 22
Electoral Reform (1977) 71, 154
Emiliano Zapata Guerrilla Nucleus (NGEZ): indigenous organizing 153, 156

Enfermos (Sick Ones) 109, 138

Federal Security Directorate 6, 31, 47, 81, 95–6, 98, 178, 183, 206
Female Ex-Guerrillas Conferences 168, 169
female revolutionaries: radicalization 170–1; experience with torture 175–8; Women and Nation 173–4;
First Encounter of the Sierra Heraclio Bernal 28; Second Encounter 32
Foquismo 21
French Intervention 23
Frente Armado del Pueblo (FAP) 97

Galván López, F. 193
Gámiz, A. 20, 26, 27–8, 34, 186; taking up arms 31–3
García Barragán, M. 4, 108, 186
Garza Sada, E. 137–8, 153, 193
Gaytán family 27; Salvador Gaytán 27, 31
General Directorate of Political and Social Investigations (DGIPS) 183
General Union of Mexican Workers and Campesinos (UGOCM) 20, 26–9, 31, 35, 97
Giner Dúran, P. 19, 25
Gómez Ramírez, P. 27, 28, 30, 186; burial 35; reassignment 33
Gómez Sousa, F. 61–2, 63
González Eguiarte, O. 186, 188
granaderos (riot police) 4, 200
Guadalajara 2; student radicalism 12
Guerrerense Civic Association (ACG) 48–9
Guerrero 3, 10, 189–90; Chilpancingo massacre 49–50; counterinsurgency and the state 46; "Operation Friendship" 190
Guevara Niebla, Gustavo 107
Guevara, Ernesto "Che": Guerra de guerrillas 21
Guevaristas 3; in Chihuahua 20
Gutiérrez Barrios, F. 183–4
Gutiérrez Oropeza, L. 4, 187

Hawks (halcones) 5, 183, 188, 198
Historical Report to Mexican Society 10
human rights 2; Attorney General's Office 7; and post-dirty war society 10, 12

imperialism 1
Independent Peasant's Union (CCI) 91–2
Indian wars (Chihuahua) 24
Industrial Workers of the World 88

Institutional Revolutionary Party (PRI) 1–2, 42, 111, 129, 149, 167, 198; revolutionary nationalism 4
Instituto de Intercambio Cultural México-URSS 61
Internal National Conference 72; *see also* MAR 9 de abril
International Terrorist Alliance (AIT) 81

Jalisco 10
Jaramillo R. 6, 170 , 184
"José Martí" Mexican-Cuban Institute for Cultural Relations (IMCRC) 151

Lacandones 107
Ladwig Ramírez, Carlos 111–12
Latifundio 22
Law Enforcement Administration Assistance (LEAA) 83
League of United Latin American Citizens (LULAC) 87
Leninists 3
Liberal Mexican Party 88
Liga Comunista Espartaco (LCE) 70
Lombardo Toledano, Vicente 29, 32
López Mateos, A. 3, 27, 184
López Portillo, J. 6, 85, 172, 183, 193; economic reform 9; electoral reform and amnesty 8; national security doctrine 7; political reform 71
Luján Adame, F. 26

Madera (document), 132–4, 142, 171; *see also* September 23rd Communist League
Madera assault 6, 19; town 24–5; workers 25; *see also* Popular Guerrilla Group (GPG)
Maldonado, M. 170
Maoism 155–6, 159
Maoists 3, 182, 185–6, 188–9; formulation of assault 33–4
MAR-9 de Abril 72, 135
Mascarones, Los 82, 87–8, 89, 92
Medrano, Florencio "El Güero" 91–2, 94, 96, 98
Menéndez, M. 151–2; Mexican Insurgent Army (EIM) 152
Mexican Communist Party (PCM) 3, 21, 35, 49, 50–1, 110, 133, 151
Mexican Miracle 2, 20, 36, 47, 55

Mexican Revolution 2; Cabañas 42, 54; Chihuahua 20, 36; and the Cold War 4; the ultra left 5
Mexican student movement (1968) 1, 50, 85, 107, 108, 199; post-student radicalism 108–9, 113; *see also* Plaza de las Tres Culturas
Mexican-American Youth Organization 87
Mexico City 2, 3, 10
Michoacán 3, 10
Military Camp Number One 108
Montemayor, C. 35
Monterrey 2
Movement of National Liberation (MLN) 51, 52, 151
Movimiento de Acción Revolucionaria-23 (MAR-23) 69–70
Movimiento Estudiantil Chicano/a de Aztlán 85

National Action Party (PAN) 2, 151
National Archive (AGN) 10; "archive of terror" 11
National Autonomous University of Mexico (UNAM) 85, 92, 157, 200
National bourgeoisie 1
National Center of Democratic Students (CNED) 63
National Commission on Human Rights (CNDH) 205
National Liberation Forces (FLN) 12, 82, 148, 192; ideology and Students and Workers in Struggle (EYOL) 151–3; indigenous groups and FLN 156–7; Operation Diamante 154; Operation Nepantla 153–4; restructure 158–9
National Polytechnic Institute (IPN) 20, 26, 92, 107, 198
National Revolutionary Civic Association (ACNR) 6, 11, 42, 53; repression 190–1; *see also* Genaro Vázquez Rojas
National Security Archive 10–11
National Strike Committee (CNH) 4, 108
National Synarchist Union (UNS) 3
National Teacher Training School 48
Nazar Haro, M. 193, 206
Nicaraguan Revolution 157
normal school 27, 48, 70; students and the armed struggle 32
North Korea 12, 63, 64 *see also* Revolutionary Action Movement
Nuevo León 3, 10, 151

Organization of American States (OAS) 5, 22
Organized Revolutionary Artistic Front (FARO) 85

Party of the Democratic Revolution (PRD) 73
Party of the Poor (PDLP) 6, 11, 42, 54–5, 93, 97, 129, 134; issues with PDLP 70; local–regional traditions of rebellion 55; repression 191–2; *see also* Lucio Cabañas Barrientes
Pax priísta 9, 199
People's Electoral Front (FEP) 29
Peoples' Friendship University Patrice Lumumba 61
Pinochet, A. 8
Plaza of the Three Cultures 4; massacre 84, 87, 105, 112, 187, 200
Popular Guerrilla Group (GPG) 6, 11, 19, 21, 26–9, 3169, 189; beginning of the dirty war 6; legacy 35; outline of objectives 32
Popular Revolutionary Army (EPR) 7
Popular Socialist Party (PPS) 20, 35, 186; Pablo Gómez 27; youth groups 26, 28
Procesos, Los 69
Professional Student Movement (MEP) 135
Proletarian Line (LP) 155
Puebla 3
Puerto Rican Independentistas 81, 90

Radilla, R. 44 178
railroad worker's strike (1959) 184
Ramos Zavala, Raúl 117, 130–1; issues with PCM 110;
Raza Unida Party 82
Research Division for the Prevention of Crime (DIPD) 9, 183; *see also* de la Madrid, M.
Revolutionary Action Movement (MAR) 12, 60–6, 97, 170, 201; 2 de Octubre and Ejército Popular 63; Commission 66; demise 71–3; factionalism 69; internal struggles 61; revolutionary "schools" 65; structure 62, 64–5; student support 68
Revolutionary Armed Forces of the People (FRAP) 122, 134
Revolutionary Family 2
Revolutionary Teacher's Movement 48
revolutionary volunteerism 105
Reyes, J. 29

Rico Galán, V. 35
Ruiz Corintas, A. 3
Rural Teacher Training School of Ayotzinapa 49

Salas Obregón, A. 130–1, 135, 137, 140, 142–3
Salazar, Rubén 87
San Cosme (July 10, 1971) 5
Scherer, J. 8
Secretary of Interior 10
Secretary of National Defense 10, 108
September 23rd Communist League (LC23S) 12, 70, 90, 129–31, 153, 170, 192, 194; brigades 136; demise 139–40; ideology 132–3; Partisan Organization 130; revolutionary violence 134–5, 137
September 23rd Movement (M-23) 21, 27
Sierra Madre Occidental 23; mining lumber company 24
Sierra Tarahumara 34
Sinaloa 3, 10
Socialist education 110; popular education 118
Socialist Revolutionary Union (URS) 151
Socialist Vanguard (VS) 151
Solis, R. 81
Sonora 3
Spartacists 3
Special Prosecutor for Social and Political Movements of the Past (FEMOSPP) 10, 204
Student Federation of Guadalajara (FEG), 111, 106, 111–12, 114, 116
Student Revolutionary Front (FER) 12, 106, 110, 113–14, 130; proletarian youth and identity 114–16
student-proletariat 107, 131–2
Symbonese Liberation Army 81–2

Tabasco 3
Talamante, O. 82
Teatro Nacional de Aztlán (TENAZ) 85
Terraza family 25
Thesis of the University Factory 117, 131
Torres Olivares, I. 117
trade unions 3
Trotskyists 3

Union del Pueblo (UP) 97, 155, 159
United Farm Workers 87

United Proletariat Party of America (PPUA) 12, 81, 83, 93–4; Ejército Popular de Liberación Unido de América and Frente Amplio Nacional Democrático Antiimperialista (FANDA) 94–7
Universidad Michoacana de San Nicolás de Hidalgo 70
University of Guadalajara (UdeG) 106, 115–16; 1968 student movement 112; educational reform 113; pre-1970 student activism 110–11
university: autonomy 4; LC23S 131; promoting the official propaganda of the PRI 117–18

Vallejo, D. 3

Vázquez Rojas, G. 35, 41–2, 48, 49–50, 52, 91–2, 170, 190
Vietnamese Marxism 62, 149
Vikings 114–17

Wars of Reform 23
White Brigade (Brigada Blanca) 183, 194; *see also* Miguel Nazar Haro
Worker-student alliances 107

Yañez, César G. 151

Zapata, E. 43
Zapatista Army of National Liberation (EZLN) 7, 148; creation 158–60; the topic of armed struggle 9